GENDER

IDEAS, INTERACTIONS, INSTITUTIONS

RECENT SOCIOLOGY TITLES
from
W. W. NORTON

To learn more about Norton Sociology, please visit wwnorton.com/soc.

GENDER

IDEAS, INTERACTIONS, INSTITUTIONS

LISA WADE

Occidental College

MYRA MARX FERREE

University of Wisconsin–Madison

W. W. NORTON & COMPANY, INC.

New York · London

W. W. Norton & Company has been independent since its founding in 1923, when William Warder Norton and Mary D. Herter Norton first published lectures delivered at the People's Institute, the adult education division of New York City's Cooper Union. The firm soon expanded its program beyond the Institute, publishing books by celebrated academics from America and abroad. By midcentury, the two major pillars of Norton's publishing program—trade books and college texts—were firmly established. In the 1950s, the Norton family transferred control of the company to its employees, and today—with a staff of four hundred and a comparable number of trade, college, and professional titles published each year—W. W. Norton & Company stands as the largest and oldest publishing house owned wholly by its employees.

Editor: Sasha Levitt
Assistant Editor: Thea Goodrich
Project Editor: Diane Cipollone
Manuscript Editor: Katharine Ings
Managing Editor, College: Marian Johnson
Managing Editor, College Digital Media: Kim Yi
Senior Production Manager: Ashley Horna
Media Editor: Eileen Connell
Associate Media Editor: Laura Musich
Marketing Manager: Julia Hall
Design Director: Jillian Burr
Photo Editor: Stephanie Romeo
Permissions Manager: Megan Jackson
College Permissions Associate: Bethany Salminen
Composition: Achorn International
Manufacturing: Maple-Vail Book Group

Library of Congress Cataloging-in-Publication Data

Wade, Lisa (Professor)
    Gender : ideas, interactions, institutions / Lisa Wade, Myra Marx Ferree. —
First edition.
        pages cm
    Includes bibliographical references and index.
    ISBN: 978-0-393-93107-5 (pbk.)
1. Sex role. 2. Sex differences. 3. Feminist theory.   I. Ferree, Myra Marx.   II. Title.
    HQ1075.W33 2015
    305.3—dc23

                                                                        2014032092

Permission to use copyrighted material is included in the Credits section of this book, which begins on page 401.

W. W. Norton & Company, Inc., 500 Fifth Avenue, New York, NY 10110-0017
wwnorton.com

W. W. Norton & Company Ltd., Castle House, 75/76 Wells Street, London W1T 3QT

2 3 4 5 6 7 8 9 0

ABOUT THE AUTHORS

LISA WADE is an associate professor of sociology at Occidental College in Los Angeles. She earned an MA in human sexuality from New York University and an MS and PhD in sociology from the University of Wisconsin-Madison. She is the author of over two dozen research papers, book chapters, and educational essays. Aiming to reach audiences outside of academia, Dr. Wade founded the popular blog *Sociological Images* and appears frequently in print, radio, and television news and opinion outlets. You can learn more about her at lisa-wade.com or follow her on Twitter (@lisawade) or Facebook (/lisawadephd).

MYRA MARX FERREE is the Alice H. Cook Professor of Sociology at the University of Wisconsin-Madison. She is the author of *Varieties of Feminism: German Gender Politics in Global Perspective* (2012), co-author of *Shaping Abortion Discourse* (2002), and *Controversy and Coalition* (2000), and co-editor of *Gender, Violence and Human Security* (2013), *Global Feminism* (2006), and *Revisioning Gender* (1998) as well as numerous articles and book chapters. Dr. Ferree is the recipient of various prizes for contributions to gender studies, including the Jessie Bernard Award and Victoria Schuck Award. She continues to do research on global gender politics.

CONTENTS

PREFACE

Writing a textbook is a challenge even for folks with lots of teaching experience in the subject matter. We would never have dared take on this project without Karl Bakeman's steady encouragement. His confidence in our vision was inspiring and his patience and unshakeable faith in the project kept us going. With his help, and the hard work invested in us by Sasha Levitt, to whose care he entrusted our project, this book has taken form. Sasha's meticulous reading, thoughtful suggestions, and words of encouragement have been invaluable. We have become fast friends in the process of bringing this book to life.

Of course, Karl and Sasha are but the top of the mountain of support that Norton has offered from beginning to end. The many hands behind the scenes include project editor Diane Cipollone for keeping us on schedule and collating our changes, production manager Ashley Horna for turning a manuscript into the pages you hold now, assistant editor Thea Goodrich for her logistical help in preparing that manuscript, designer Jillian Burr for her keen graphic eye, and our copyeditor, Katharine Ings, for crossing our t's and dotting our i's. The many images that enrich this book are thanks to photo editor Stephanie Romeo and photo researcher Elyse Rieder. We are also grateful to have discovered Leland Bobbé, the artist whose half-drag portraits fascinated us. Selecting just one was a collaborative process aided by the further creative work of Jillian Burr and Debra Morton Hoyt. We're grateful for the result: a striking cover that we hope will catch the eye and spark conversation.

We would also like to thank the reviewers who commented on drafts of the text in its early stages—especially and always the extraordinary Gwen Sharp—but also Shayna Asher-Shapiro, Kristen Barber, Shira Barlas, Sarah Becker, Emily Birnbaum, Valerie Chepp, Nancy Dess, Lisa Dilks, Mischa DiBattiste, Mary Donaghy, Julia Eriksen, Angela Frederick, Jessica Greenebaum, Nona Gronert, Lee Harrington, Sarah Hayford, Penelope Herideen, Rachel Kaplan, Madeline Kiefer, Caitlin Maher, Janice McCabe, Karyn McKinney, Carly Mee, Beth

Mintz, Stephanie Nawyn, Megan Reid, Jaita Talukdar, Kristen Williams, and Kersti Alice Yllo. Our gratitude goes also to the friends who took preliminary versions out for test-drives—Dianne Mahany, Naama Nagar, Gwen Sharp—and the students at Babson College, Occidental College, Nevada State College, and the University of Wisconsin-Madison who agreed to be test subjects.

Most of all, we are happy to discover that we could collaborate in being creative over the long term of this project, contributing different talents at different times, and jumping the inevitable hurdles without tripping each other up. In fact, we were each other's toughest critic and warmest supporter. Once upon a time, Lisa was Myra's student, but in finding ways to communicate our interest and enthusiasm to students, our roles were reversed. Today, we appreciate each other's strengths more than ever and rejoice in the collegial relationship we developed in the process of doing this book. We hope you enjoy reading it as much as we enjoyed making it.

Lisa Wade
Myra Marx Ferree

GENDER

IDEAS, INTERACTIONS, INSTITUTIONS

A MAN IN HEELS IS RIDICULOUS.

—CHRISTIAN LOUBOUTIN

Introduction

In the late 1500s, under the reign of Abbas I, the Persian army defeated the Uzbeks and the Ottomans and re-conquered provinces lost to India and Portugal. These soldiers were widely admired throughout Europe as some of the most vicious and effective killers who had ever lived.[1]

And they wore high heels.[1] They fought on horseback; heels kept their feet in the stirrups when they rose up to shoot their muskets.

Enthralled by the military men's prowess, European male aristocrats began wearing high heels as a testament to their own virility. The aristocrats adopted high-heeled shoes in order to associate themselves with the Persian army's masculine mystique. In a way, they were like today's basketball fans wearing Air Jordans. They weren't necessarily any better at horseback warfare than your average Bulls fan is on the court, but the shoes symbolically linked them to the soldiers' extraordinary achievements. As symbols, the high heels invoked not just power, but a distinctly *manly* power related to victory on the battlefield, just as the basketball shoes link the contemporary wearer to Michael Jordan's amazing athleticism in a male-dominated sport.

Shah Abbas the I, who ruled Persia between 1588 and 1629, shows off not only his scimitar, but also his high heels.

As with most fashions, there was trickle down. Soon men of all classes were donning high heels, stumbling around the cobblestone streets of Europe feeling pretty suave. Women decided they wanted a piece of the action, too. In the 1630s, masculine fashions were "in" for ladies. They cut their hair, added military decorations to the shoulders of their dresses, and smoked pipes. High heels were the height of masculine mimicry.

These early fashionistas irked the aristocrats who first borrowed the style. The whole point of nobility, after all, was to be *above* everyone else. In response, the elites started wearing higher and higher heels. France's King Louis XIV even decreed that no one could wear heels higher than his.[2] In the New World, the Massachusetts colony passed a law saying that any woman caught wearing heels would incur the same penalty as witches.[3] The masses persisted, however, so the aristocrats tried a different tactic: They dropped high heels altogether. It was the Enlightenment now and there was an accompanying shift toward logic and reason. Adopting the new philosophy, aristocrats began mocking people who wore high heels, suggesting that wearing such impractical shoes was, well, stupid.

On and off since the mid-1700s, the footwear that aristocrats once used to prove that they were superior—and later laughed at with derision—has continued tweaking the toes of women in every possible situation, from weddings to the workplace. Meanwhile, the shoe has remained mostly out of fashion for men.

The attempts by the aristocrats to keep high heels to themselves are part of a phenomenon that sociologists call **distinction**: efforts to distinguish one's own group from others. In this historical example, we see elite men working hard to make both class- and gender-based distinctions. Today high heels are still a marker of gender distinction. With few exceptions, only women (and people impersonating women) wear high heels. Some of us love them, and some of us still think they're pretty stupid, and there remains the sense that the right pair brings a touch of class.

Distinction is a main theme of this book. The word *gender* exists only because we distinguish between people in this particular way. If we didn't care about distinguishing men from women, then the whole concept would be utterly unnecessary. We don't, after all, tend to have words for physical differences that don't have meaning to us. For example, we don't make a big deal out of the fact that some people have the gene that allows them to curl their tongue and some people don't. There's no concept of *tongue aptitude* that refers to the separation of people into the curly tongued and the flat tongued. Why would we need such a thing? The vast majority of us just don't care.

Gender, then, is about distinction. Like tongue aptitude, it is a biological reality. Because we are a species that reproduces sexually, we come, roughly, in two body types: one built to gestate new life and one to mix up the genes of the species. The word **sex** is used to refer to these physical differences in primary sexual characteristics (the presence of organs directly involved in reproduction) and secondary sexual characteristics (such as patterns of hair growth, the amount of breast tissue, and distribution of body fat). We usually use the words **male** and **female** to refer to sex, but we can also use **male-bodied** and **female-bodied** to specify that sex refers to the body and may not extend to how a person feels or acts.

Louis XIV, King of France from 1643 to 1715, gives himself a boost with high hair and high heels.

We all know, though, that there is more to gender than this. There's all the other stuff that comes to mind when we talk about men and women. It's the dividing of the world into pink baby blankets and blue, suits and dresses, *Maxim* and *Cosmopolitan* magazines, and action movies and chick flicks. These are all examples of the world divided up into the **masculine** and the **feminine**, into things we associate with men and women. The word **gender**, then, refers to the symbolism of masculinity and femininity that we connect to being male-bodied or female-bodied.

This is where distinction comes in. Much of what we believe about men and women is not naturally occurring difference that emerges from our male and female bodies. Instead, it is an outcome of active efforts to produce and maintain difference: a sea of people working together every day to make men masculine and women feminine. To a surprising extent, the idea that there are two types of people—male-bodied masculine ones and female-bodied feminine ones—is, in fact, quite fantastical.

One of these people is not like the others. We perform gendered distinctions like the one shown here every day, often simply out of habit.

So why would we work so hard to maintain such a fantasy?

Imagine those aristocrats stomping their high-heeled feet in frustration with the lowly copycats. It might seem funny now, but the need to be different from everyone else was a very serious matter. Successful efforts at distinction ensured that these elite men really *seemed* different and, more importantly, better than women and other types of men. This is at the very core of aristocracy: the idea that some people truly are superior and, by virtue of their superiority, entitled to hoard wealth and monopolize power.

What the aristocrats understood is that difference is necessary for hierarchy. If one wants to argue that Group A is superior to Group B, there must be a Group B. We can't think more highly of one type of person than another unless we have at least two types. Distinction, then, must be maintained if we are going to value certain types of people more than others.

Wealth and power continue to be hoarded and monopolized. These inequalities are justified—made to seem normal and natural—by producing differences that make group membership seem meaningful and inequality inevitable or right. This impulse to distinguish oneself from others is motivated, also, by understandable impulses to feel connected to our in-group, know who we are, and give our lives meaning. We all, then, engage in actions designed to align ourselves with some people and differentiate ourselves from others. Thus we see the persistence of social classes, racial and ethnic categories, the urban-rural divide, gay and straight identities, liberal and conservative parties, and various Christian and Muslim sects, among other distinctions. These categories aren't all bad; they give us a sense of belonging and bring joy and pleasure into our lives. But they also serve as classifications by which we can unevenly distribute power and privilege.

Gender is no different in this regard. There is a story to tell about both difference and hierarchy and it involves both pleasure and pain. We'll wait a bit before we seriously tackle the problem of gender inequality, spending several chapters learning just how enjoyable studying gender can be. There'll be funny parts and fascinating parts. You'll meet figure skaters and football players, fish and flight attendants and, yes, feminists, too. Eventually we'll get to the part that makes you want to throw the book across the room. We won't take it personally. For now, let's pick up right where we started, with distinction.

> **THE ONES WITH EYELASHES
> ARE GIRLS; BOYS DON'T HAVE
> EYELASHES.**
>
> —FOUR-YEAR-OLD ERIN DESCRIBES HER DRAWING[1]

2

Ideas

It is worth meditating on the fact that most of us use the word *opposite* when describing the relationship between men and women. There are other ways to express this relationship. It was once common to use the phrase "the fairer sex" or "the second sex" to describe women. We could simply say "the other sex." Today, though, we usually use the word *opposite*.

Seventeenth-century Europeans—the same ones fighting over high heels—didn't believe in "opposite" sexes; they didn't even believe in *two* sexes.[2] They just believed in a superior and an inferior version of a person. They also thought that men and women had identical reproductive organs, just arranged differently: Men's were pushed out of the body when exposed to "heat" during fetal development, while women's genitals remained inside. As the drawings on the next page show, they saw the vagina as simply a penis that hadn't emerged from the body; the womb no different than a scrotum; the ovaries just internal testes. As the lyrics to one early song put it: "Women are but men turned outside in."[3]

Seventeenth-century anatomists were wrong about the internal genitalia, of course. We're not the same sex. The uterus and fallopian tubes of the female body are not formed from the same fetal tissue that builds the penis and scrotum in males. But neither is it correct to say that male and female bodies are opposite.

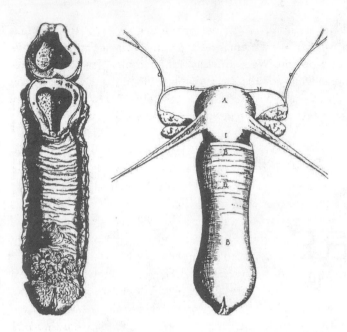

This anatomical illustration from 1611 of the interior of a vagina (left) and the exterior of a vagina and uterus (right) shows the Renaissance idea of female genitalia—an internal phallus.

In fact, the penis and scrotum *do* have something in common with female anatomy. The same tissue that becomes the scrotum and penis in males becomes the outer labia and clitoris in females, and both testes and ovaries come from the same fetal tissue. So while it's not perfectly correct to say that there's only one sex, it's also not perfectly correct to say that we're opposites.

Nevertheless, *opposite* is the word we use, and it has strong implications: that whatever one sex is, the other simply is not. Today most people in most Western countries are familiar with the general idea that men and women have contrasting strengths and weaknesses. In sociology, this is referred to as the gender binary. The word **binary** refers to a system with two—and only two—separate and distinct parts, like binary code (the 1s and 0s used in computing) or a binary star system (in which two stars orbit around each other). So the phrase **gender binary** refers to the idea that there are only two types of people—male-bodied people who are masculine and female-bodied people who are feminine—and those types are as the word *opposite* suggests: fundamentally different and contrasting.

Because we tend to think in terms of a gender binary, we routinely speak about men as if they're all the same and likewise for women. The nervous parent warns his thirteen-year-old daughter that "boys only want one thing," while the Valentine's Day commercial insists that women love dark chocolate. In fact, most of us embrace gender categories in daily life and talk about "men" and "women" *as if* membership in one of these categories says a great deal about a person. We might say, for example, "I'm such a girl!" when we confess that we're addicted to strawberry lip balm, or repeat the refrain "boys will be boys" when observing the antics of a young male cousin. If we're feeling hurt, we might even comfort ourselves by saying "all men suck" or "women are crazy."

Still, you may not feel like *you* fit neatly into the gender binary as a stereotypical man or woman. In fact, many people will say that they sort of are . . . and sort of aren't . . . the stereotype. Maybe you're a woman who adores romantic comedies but is also first in line for the next superhero movie. Or maybe you're a man who enjoys a bubble bath after a rugby game. This sort of mixing and matching of interests is typical. Accordingly, a large number of us don't believe that we, *personally*, conform to a stereotype.

To make sense of the tendency to talk as if the stereotypes about men and women are true, even though we don't all think they apply to us, some of us imagine that we must be unusual. Most other people, we surmise, are better described by the gender binary than we are. Let's call this **the personal exception theory of gender**: There are men, there are women, and there's me. This theory allows those of us who don't fit into the binary to reconcile our own complex identity with what we think we know about men and women by assuming that we're unusually unique.

The personal exception theory, however, doesn't stand up to the evidence. First of all, it is a bit too self-congratulatory. And, second, when we stop and look at our best friends, our family members, and our boyfriends and girlfriends, we actually know many people who don't fit into the stereotypes. So maybe we *think* we see stereotypical men and women on reality TV shows, when we walk down the street, or even in class or at work, but many people we know *well* are exceptions to the rule. This leads us to the first of many probing questions we will attempt to answer throughout this book:

 If the gender binary doesn't describe a large number of the people we know, where does the idea come from?

In this chapter, we explain that people who grow up in most contemporary Western societies learn to use a set of beliefs about gender as a scaffold for understanding the world. If we are well socialized, we will, out of habit and largely without thinking, put people and things into masculine and feminine categories and subcategories. We apply the binary to human bodies, imagining men and women to have different and non-overlapping anatomies and physiologies. We also apply it to objects, places, activities, talents, and ideas.

We become so skilled at layering ideas about gender onto the world that we have a hard time seeing it for what it really is. We don't notice when gender stereotypes don't make sense. Even more, we tend to see and remember things consistent with gender stereotypes, while missing or misremembering things inconsistent with those stereotypes. In other words, gender is a logic that we are talented at manipulating, but it is manipulating us, too.

Don't feel bad or weird about it. Essentially all societies notice and interpret sex-related differences in our bodies, so we are no different in that sense. Yet, many of the ideas about gender found in other societies would seem pretty unusual to us. We begin this chapter, then, with a quick tour through a few examples of other gender ideologies, revealing that gender may be universal, but how we think about it is far from it.

GENDER IDEOLOGIES

The gender binary is a specific type of idea. It is an **ideology**, or a set of ideas widely shared by members of a society that guides identities, behaviors, and institutions. When we look around the world and backward through history, we discover a dizzying array of different gender ideologies, ones that reveal the gender binary as just one of many ways of thinking about gender.

Some societies acknowledge three, four, or even five genders. More than one hundred American Indian tribes recognized or recognize people who are simultaneously masculine and feminine.[4] These individuals act, dress, and talk like and do the work of the other sex, but they aren't considered male or female. They are something else—*two-spirit*. Male-bodied two-spirits and female-bodied two-spirits are considered a third and fourth gender. They live with and raise families with members of the same sex but are still considered a different gender than their partner. In Polynesia, similar members of the community are called *māhū* (Hawaii), *akava'ine* (Cook Islands), *fakaleiti* (Tonga), or *fa'afafine* (Samoa), which translates to "in the manner of a woman."[5] Like biologically male two-spirits, these individuals adopt feminine roles, but they are not expected to be sexually interested in members of the same sex. The Navajo also have a fifth category for a person whose gender is unstable and constantly changing, a *nádleehé*: one day a man, another day a woman, and a third day a two-spirit. If a person is a nádleehé, no one is surprised by these changes.

In India and Bangladesh, feminine men identify as *hijra* and, in Oaxaca, Mexico, they identify as *muxe*.[6] Unlike two-spirits and the third genders of Polynesia, who adopt the everyday behaviors and typical appearance of the other sex, hijras and muxes perform an *exaggerated* femininity, more like a burlesque. Both hijras and muxes represent a third gender distinct from gay

Two hijras prepare to dance in a transgender conference in New Delhi.

men, who don't identify as feminine at all or in the same way. In translation, the term *hijra*, for example, is more like the English word *eunuch* than the word *homosexual*. In 2013, the prime minister of Bangladesh affirmed the hijra as a third gender recognized by the state.

In Brazil, *travestis* are men who use hormones and injections to feminize their bodies.[7] Travestis don't think that they actually are women, though; they simply believe that they are feminine men. And they have no desire to have *female* bodies, just feminine ones.

In still other instances, it is not genitals that determine one's gender at all. Anthropologist Christine Helliwell describes how, despite her female body, her gender was uncertain for the duration of her time among the Dayak, subsistence farmers in the community of Gerai in West Borneo:

> *Gerai people remained very uncertain about my gender for some time after I arrived in the community.... This was despite the fact that people in the community knew from my first few days with them both that I had breasts (this was obvious when the sarong that I wore clung to my body while I bathed in the river) and that I had a vulva rather than a penis and testicles (this was obvious from my trips to defecate or urinate in the small stream used for that purpose, when literally dozens of people would line the banks to observe whether I performed these functions differently from them). As someone said to me at a later point, "Yes, I saw that you had a vulva, but I thought that Western men might be different."[8]*

For the Dayak, being a man or woman is not tied to genitals. It is tied to expertise. A "woman" is a person who knows how to distinguish types of rice, store them correctly, and choose among them for different uses. Helliwell explained that as she learned more about rice and gained practice in preparing and cooking it, she became "more and more of a woman" in their eyes. Still, for many, her gender remained at least a little bit ambiguous because she "never achieved anything approaching the level of knowledge concerning rice-seed selection held by even a girl child in Gerai."

The Dayak are not unique in divorcing gender from genitals. The Hau in New Guinea see masculinity and femininity as parts of the character that grow and fade with age and experience. For the Hau, children are not male or female until puberty; then, over the life course, men lose masculinity with every son they father and women gain masculinity with each son they bear, until elders are again genderless. In Zambia, the Lovedu assign gender by social status rather than genitals.[9] A high-ranking woman "counts" as a man. She might marry a young woman and be the socially recognized "father" to their children (who are biologically fathered by the young women's socially endorsed lovers). A similar system has been documented among the Nnobi in Nigeria.[10]

In the Netherlands, children are taught that men and women are different but overlapping categories.[11] The Dutch do not teach children that men have "male" hormones and women have "female" hormones, as we typically do in the United States; instead, they teach them that all people have a mix of so-called male and female hormones, just in different proportions.[12] Further, they also teach children that hormone levels vary among men and among women (not just between them) and that these levels rise and fall in response to different situations and as people of both sexes age. Like the Hau, they believe age and gender are intertwined.

Sometimes the biological quirks of a community shape its gender ideology. In an isolated village in the Dominican Republic, a rare genetic condition called 5-alpha-reductase deficiency became so concentrated that its presence in the community became routine. The condition made genetically male children appear to be female until puberty, at which time what had been thought to be a clitoris grew into a penis and their testes suddenly descended from their abdomen. These children would then simply adopt male identities and live as men the rest of their lives. The villagers experienced this as a completely routine event, calling such boys *guevedoces* or "eggs at twelve" (with "eggs" a euphemism for testicles). A similar phenomenon happens among the Simbari in Papua New Guinea. They name the girls who grow up to be men *kwolu-aatmwol*, or "female thing transforming into male thing."

In some places, strict social rules lead to the acceptance of temporary or permanent sex-switching. In Afghanistan, girls are not allowed to obtain an extensive education, appear in public without a male chaperone, or work outside

Mehran Rafaat, a six-year-old bacha posh in Afghanistan, poses cheekily with her twin sisters. After puberty, she will stop playing the part of a boy and be considered a girl again.

the home.[13] These restrictions are typically discussed as a burden for girls and women, but they can also be a burden on their families. Daughters can go out in public if they are chaperoned by a brother. This is useful for the whole family. The girls get more freedom and the parents can send their children on errands, to school, or on social visits without their supervision. Since boys can also work outside the home, sons can be a source of extra income. Families without sons can't do any of these things, so some simply pick a daughter to be a boy. They cut her hair, change her name, and put her in boy's clothes. This type of child is called a *bacha posh*, or "dressed up as a boy." One father of a bacha posh explains:

> *It's a privilege for me, that she is in boys' clothing. . . . It's a help for me, with the shopping. And she can go in and out of the house without a problem.*

Sex-switched children are accepted in Afghanistan. In fact, the phenomenon is common enough that most people are unsurprised when a biological girl suddenly becomes a social boy. Relatives, friends, and acquaintances accept and participate in the illusion. Later, when the child reaches puberty, she typically becomes a girl again. Meanwhile, the family might choose a younger sibling to take over her role. This flexibility of gender for children echoes the Hua idea that sex isn't relevant until puberty.

Haki is one of the remaining "sworn virgins" of Albania. Born female, Haki has
lived her entire adult life as a man.

Unlike a bacha posh in Afghanistan, girls in Albania can live as boys *and* grow up to be socially recognized men.[14] To do so, girls have to publicly promise that they will remain virgins. The role of the *virgjinesha*, or "sworn virgins," emerged in the early 1400s when intergroup warfare left a dearth of men in many communities. Since only men had certain rights—to buy land, for example, or pass down wealth—all families needed either a man or a "man." Many girls would take the oath after their father died. There are only about forty sworn virgins left in Albania today. As women are granted more and more rights, fewer and fewer girls feel the need to adopt a male identity for themselves or their families.[15] We saw a similar identity emerge in the African Dahomey Kingdom in the 1700s; when the male population was decimated by war, women were allowed to become warriors, but only if they promised to remain childless.[16]

These examples show us that gender ideologies can vary considerably. In other words, it is possible to interpret the meaning and significance of our sexed bodies in many different ways. Our own ideology—the gender binary—is somewhat unusual in requiring all bodies to fit into two—and only two—categories. The gender binary, unlike the other ideologies we explored, demands that certain traits and talents align with our bodies throughout our entire lifetime, to the exclusion of aspects of one's personality or other factors such as age, status, or expertise. In the next section, we will explore our tendency to rigidly apply the binary to our bodies.

THE BINARY AND OUR BODIES

Eden Atwood is a successful jazz singer, actress, and activist. She founded the Interface Project, an organization that collects the stories of people with **intersex** bodies, people who are born with a reproductive or sexual anatomy that doesn't seem to fit the typical definitions of female or male. Atwood herself has an intersex condition, androgen insensitivity syndrome (AIS).[17] At fertilization, a Y sperm combined with an X egg, putting her on the biological path to becoming male. But the cells of her body lacked the ability to detect the hormones that typically masculinize a body. So, even though she had XY chromosomes and developed testicles that produced testosterone and other androgens, her testes remained in her abdomen, and the development of her external genitalia followed the female body plan.

Born with androgen insensitivity syndrome, Eden Atwood is an acclaimed performer and activist on behalf of people with intersex bodies.

Atwood's story suggests that while we tend to take for granted that everyone is unambiguously male or female, the path to such a straightforward body involves many steps. Step one is conception. If a sperm with an X chromosome meets an egg, the fertilization kicks off the development of a female; if the sperm contains a Y chromosome, it kicks off the development of a male. Since all eggs have an X chromosome, men typically have an XY chromosomal profile and women have an XX. This, however, is just the beginning of a complex process.

If the fertilized egg is XY, we should expect to see the development of testes that make a particular cocktail of androgens and estrogens. These hormones instruct the fetal cells to follow a male body plan, building a penis and scrotum as well as seminal vesicles and a prostate, and connecting each testicle to the urethra with an epididymis and vas deferens. At puberty, the boy will grow pubic hair in a different pattern than his female counterparts and experience a deepening of the voice. He will probably not have much breast tissue. If asked, he will probably say he is a man and feel good about that. This is his **gender identity**, a sense of oneself as male or female.

Without the intervention of a Y chromosome, a fertilized egg will follow a female development path. The fetus will develop ovaries and internal and external genitalia (e.g., labia, a clitoris, vagina, and uterus, and fallopian tubes). At puberty, the brain will instruct the ovaries to produce a different cocktail of androgens and estrogens that stimulate feminine patterns of body fat, an upside-down triangle of pubic hair, breasts, and a menstrual cycle. The adult will usually comfortably identify as female.

These paths toward male-bodied/male-identified and female-bodied/female-identified individuals involve at least seven steps, shown in Table 2.1. Most of us assume that these criteria all line up, but that's not always the case. As with Atwood, these traits don't always co-occur. Dozens of conditions can

TABLE 2.1 | STEPS TOWARD A MALE OR FEMALE BODY TYPE AND
                 IDENTITY

Step	Male Path	Female Path
Chromosomes	XY	XX
Gonads	testes	ovaries
Hormones	androgens/estrogens	estrogens/androgens
External genitalia	penis, scrotum	clitoris, labia
Internal genitalia	seminal vesicles, prostate, epididymis, vas deferens	vagina, uterus, fallopian tubes
Secondary sex characteristics	pubic hair, deep voice, Adam's apple	pubic hair, breasts, menstruation
Gender identity	male-identified	female-identified

result in an intersexed body, one that is not clearly male or female, or a body that doesn't match the identity of the person who inhabits it. In fact, it is estimated that one out of every 100 people isn't 100 percent female- or male-bodied or feels like he or she is trapped in the body of the wrong sex.[18]

The 1 Percent

People with intersexed bodies are living proof that not everyone fits into a gender binary that allows only for opposite sexes. We'll review just a few examples. As you read, remember that you probably know at least one intersex person— and you likely don't know who they are—so make sure you approach the issue as if we're talking about someone you care about. In fact, while some people are diagnosed as intersexed at birth, other times it's discovered later in life; sometimes a person never learns of it at all.

A chromosomally male person has XY sex chromosomes and a chromosomally female person has XX chromosomes. So what is someone who has three sex chromosomes? An X, another X, *and* a Y? Chromosomal mix-ups occur in various ways. In addition to being XXY, a person can be XXXY, XXX, XYY, or even just have one sex chromosome, an X. These conditions are caused by a mistake in the cell division with which our bodies make egg and sperm. Sometimes sex chromosomes "stick" to each other and resist dividing with the rest of our chromosomes. Through this process, a person can make a sperm or egg with no chromosomes or two chromosomes instead of just one.

A person born XXY may be the result of an XY sperm merging with an X egg. This condition is called Klinefelter syndrome.[19] A person with Klinefelter syndrome appears and typically identifies as a man but tends to have physical characteristics caused, in part, by low testosterone: Compared to other men, Klinefelter men tend to be especially tall and have broader hips, less body hair, and less muscle control and coordination. Most Klinefelter men are infertile. A person born with three X chromosomes (after an XX egg merges with an X sperm) has what is called triple X syndrome.[20] Most XXX women will never be diagnosed because they typically don't exhibit any symptoms (other than being slightly tall), and they usually have no problem getting pregnant. Women with Turner syndrome are born with only one chromosome, which occurs when an X egg or sperm merges with an egg or sperm without a sex chromosome.[21] These women tend to be short with distinctive features: a webbed neck, low-set ears, and a higher likelihood of obesity. Most Turner women are infertile, and they are at a higher risk for certain health problems.

Congenital adrenal hyperplasia (CAH) is an example of an intersex condition caused by hormones. As the phrase suggests, the condition occurs when a fetus has a hyperactive adrenal gland that produces masculinizing hormones. If the fetus is XX, then the baby will be born with masculinized genitals, most notably an enlarged clitoris that resembles a small- to medium-sized penis. Most babies born with CAH identify as female when they grow older. Atwood's condition, AIS, is also a hormone-based departure from the path to unambiguous male and female bodies; it is caused by an inability of cells to recognize androgens released by the testes both before and after birth.

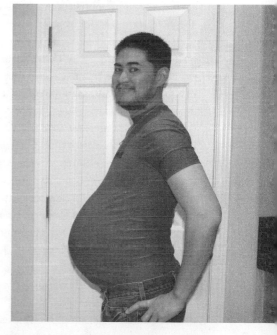

Transsexual people are another example of a group whose gender markers don't all line up. A **transsexual** is a person who experiences **gender dysphoria**, the sense of being a man in a woman's body, or vice versa. They may have routine chromosomal and hormonal development, but their gender identity doesn't match their bodies. Some transsexual people take hormones to masculinize or feminize their bodies, have sex-reassignment surgery to re make their bodies into ones with which they feel more comfortable, and live as the other sex. The child of recording artists Sonny and Cher is a transgender adult. Born Chastity, he now goes by the name Chaz.

Some transsexual people want nothing more than to be as male or female as possible. Others don't transition completely. They may take hormones to approximate the hormonal balance of the

Thomas Beatie was female-bodied at birth but chose to live his adult life as a man. Because he opted not to undergo a hysterectomy, he was able to give birth to three children.

other sex but not get surgery, or they might get "top surgery" (breast implants or breast removal) but not "bottom." Thomas Beatie became famous for becoming pregnant. Beatie is a female-to-male transsexual, or transman. Identifying as a man in a woman's body, Beatie had his breasts removed and took testosterone that masculinized his body, but he never had his uterus removed. When he and his wife decided to have a baby, Beatie carried it. The media was flooded with images of a "pregnant man" with a beard and a swelling stomach. Beatie, like others who refuse to embody only male or female characteristics, fails to fit into the gender binary.

While people with gender dysphoria sometimes choose to undergo surgery to change their sex, intersex children, until recently, were given no choice at all. Most were operated on in their first years of life; doctors often convinced confused parents to intervene with surgery in order to ensure that their children's bodies conformed to the gender binary, even when surgery was medically unnecessary. Upon adulthood, many of these children have questioned the necessity of these procedures, noting the pain and suffering that accompanies any surgery; the frequent loss of sexual, reproductive, or urogenital function; the inability of infants or small children to give consent; and the mis-assignment of children to the wrong gender. Their work has influenced many doctors to delay surgery until people with intersexed bodies can make informed decisions, but surgeries on infants have not ended. Discomfort with bodies that deviate from the gender binary continues to motivate some physicians and parents to choose unnecessary surgery for infants and children.

Eden, Chaz, Thomas, and the other estimated 1 percent of the human population who are intersex or transsexual don't fit into the gender binary. So how do we resolve these cases? What sex *are* they? To qualify as male or female, does a person's body have to match *every* gender criterion, from chromosomes to genitals to identity? If so, what do we call the estimated 68 million people on earth who can't claim a "perfectly" male or "perfectly" female body? Would it be better to pick just one criterion as *the* determinant of sex? Which one? Should genitals trump chromosomes? Or are chromosomes more "fundamental"? Should it be up to the individual, regardless of his or her body type? How do we figure it out? Moreover, who cares? If bodies function but don't fit into the gender binary, is that a problem? Who gets to decide? And where do we draw the line? How many millimeters should separate a child with a small penis at birth and a child diagnosed as intersex?

Questions abound. And the truth is, we can't answer them satisfactorily. We can't because we're trying to impose a false binary on reality. Human bodies just don't come in the neat packages that a gender binary assumes. Still, you might object that a small percentage of the population doesn't detract much from the *overall* applicability of the gender binary. The rest of us fit in rather naturally, right?

The Other 99 Percent

Remember that the gender binary doesn't just specify that there are two sexes, it also makes the much stronger claim that we are "opposite sexes": that what is true about one sex will be inversely true in the other. In reality, our bodies are far more alike than different. Even for physical characteristics on which there is a clear gender difference, we see a great deal of overlap. Height is a great example. The average man is five and a half inches taller than the average woman.[22] So men are taller than women, right? Well, not really. The *average* man is taller than the *average* woman, but because both men and women come in a range of heights, some women are taller than men (25 percent of women are as tall as or taller than 10 percent of men). This is not a *binary* difference, one that posits that all men are taller than all women; it's an *average* difference, a measure of tendency, not absolutes (Figure 2.1).

We see this type of overlap in all sex-related traits. There are hairy women and men who can't grow a mustache; men with breasts and women with flat chests; women with strong bodies and broad shoulders and slender men who lift weights with little result. Even our reproductive abilities aren't perfectly binary. There are women who can't bear children, including all women who live

FIGURE 2.1 | THE RANGE AND OVERLAP IN HEIGHT AMONG AMERICAN MEN AND WOMEN

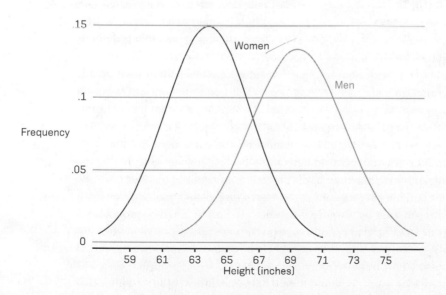

Source: National Center for Health Statistics. 2012. *Anthropometric Reference Data for Children and Adults: United States, 2007–2010*, cdc.gov/nchs/data/series/sr_11/sr11_252.pdf

Victoria's Secret model Adriana Lima struts her stuff on the runway, displaying a body bestowed to her by nature and painstakingly sculpted by personal trainers and dieticians.

past menopause. The truth is that our physical traits—height, hairiness, shape, strength, agility, flexibility, and bone structure—overlap far more than they diverge and vary widely over the course of our lives.

We *believe* in a gender binary, though, so the vast majority of us work hard to try to minimize this overlap, pressing our bodies into ideal male or female shapes. This is true even of the people we consider to be the most naturally perfect. Supermodel Adriana Lima, for example, once revealed the incredible routine she uses to prepare her body for the Victoria's Secret catwalk.[23] For months before the show, she explained, she works out every day with a personal trainer. For the three weeks before, she works out twice a day. A nutritionist gives her protein shakes, vitamins, and supplements to help her body cope with the workout schedule. She drinks a gallon of water a day. For the final nine days before the show, she consumes only protein shakes. Two days before the show, she begins drinking water at a normal rate; for the final twelve hours, she drinks no water at all.

While this is an extreme example, consider how much time, energy, and money non-supermodels spend trying to get their bodies to conform to our beliefs about gender. Women choose to eat salad when they'd rather have a burger and fries, while men are encouraged to make a spectacle of overeating. Gyms are effectively gender segregated, with most men at the weight machines trying to build muscles and most women on the aerobic machines trying to lose weight. Women try to tone their bodies by building lean but not overly noticeable muscles and may even smoke cigarettes to lose weight; men drink protein shakes and try to bulk up. Gender differences in size aren't very pronounced, but we sure do work hard to make it appear that way.

Similarly, women take pains to keep their faces, legs, arms, armpits, and bikini lines free of hair if there is any chance of gender-inappropriate body hair being spotted. Men's leg, body, and armpit hair, in contrast, is seen as naturally masculine; shaving it would seem bizarre. By shaving, women preserve the binary idea that women do not have body hair and men do (though men do have their own hair taboos, like back hair, and there is increasing pressure on men to have hairless chests).

People also tend to choose clothes that preserve the illusion of the gender binary. Many women wear padded or push-up bras to lift and enhance their breasts and wear low-cut tops that emphasize and display cleavage (which men aren't supposed to have). High heels create an artificially arched spine that pushes out the breasts and buttocks. Form-fitting clothes reveal women's curves, while less form-fitting or even baggy clothes on men make their bodies appear more linear and squared off. Fitted clothes also help women appear small, while baggier clothes make men seem larger. Come to think of it, it's interesting to put on the clothes of the other sex and see how much they contribute to our masculine and feminine appearances. We highly recommend it.

When diet, exercise, and dress don't shape their bodies into so-called opposite ideal forms, some men and women resort to chemicals and cosmetic surgeries. Men are more likely than women to take steroids to increase their muscle mass or get bicep, tricep, chin, and calf implants that make their bodies appear more muscular and formidable. Women are more likely to take diet pills. Some undergo liposuction. If they don't think they're curvy enough, some women choose to get buttock implants or have a breast augmentation. Conversely, breast *reduction* surgeries are one of the most common plastic surgeries performed on boys and men, who are often horrified by the slightest suggestion of a "breast." The surgery is now the second most common cosmetic procedure for boys under eighteen (exceeding breast augmentation for girls of the same age) and the fifth most common procedure for men of all ages.[24]

In addition to working on the shape of their bodies, people learn different ways of moving their bodies that help tell a story of big, muscular men and small, delicate women. Masculine movements tend to take up space, whereas feminine movements minimize the space women inhabit. A masculine walk is wide, with the arms held slightly away from the body and the elbows pointed slightly out. A feminine walk, in contrast, involves placing one foot in front of the other, swinging the arms in front of the body, and tucking the elbows for a narrower stride. A masculine seated position is spread out. A man might open his shoulders and put his arms out to either side and spread his legs or rest an ankle on a knee, creating a wide lap. Women, in contrast, are taught to contain their bodies when seated. Women often sit with their legs crossed at the knees or the ankles, with their hands in their lap, and their shoulders turned gently in.

The sheer power we have over our bodies is illustrated by **drag queens** and **kings**, conventionally gendered and often heterosexual men and women who dress up and behave like members of the other sex, usually for fun or pay. Some

W A R P A I N T

BY COCO LAYNE

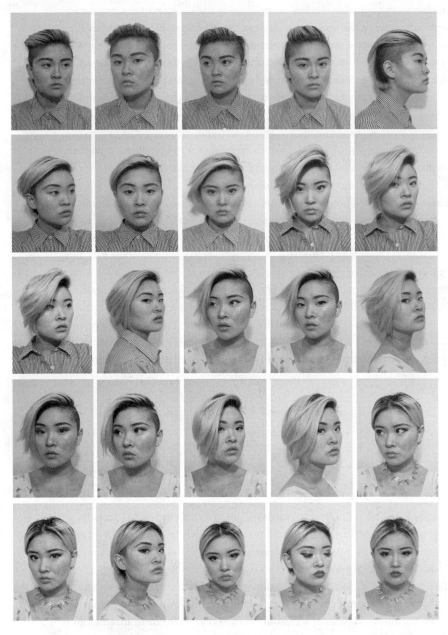

In her "Warpaint" project, artist Coco Layne shows how she transitions from appearing male to appearing female by way of her hairstyle, makeup, and clothes.

make a hobby, or even a career, of perfecting gender display, manipulating their bodies to signify either masculinity or femininity at will.

Drag kings and queens are excellent examples of how physical characteristics can be manipulated, but we all do drag in the sense that we use our bodies to display gender. None of the tools used by drag queens to make their bodies look feminine is unfamiliar to a culturally competent woman. Makeup, fitted clothes, high heels, jewelry, and carefully styled hair are everyday tools of femininity. The queen may wear heavier makeup, higher heels, and more ostentatious jewelry than the average woman, but it's a quantitative instead of a qualitative difference.

If male and female bodies *were* naturally "opposite," as the binary suggests, we wouldn't feel compelled to work so hard to make them appear that way. Instead, much of the difference we see is a result of how we adorn, manipulate, use, and alter our bodies, not our bodies themselves. Surgery to correct the "ambiguous" genitals of intersex children and sex-reassignment surgery are both ways that people respond to a gender binary that makes their bodies problematic; working out, dieting, and wearing push-up bras are other ways. The cumulative effect of this collective everyday drag show is a set of people who act and look like "women" and a set who act and look like "men."

In sum, the logic behind the gender binary—that people come in two strongly distinct types—doesn't account for the 1 percent whose biological markers aren't clearly in the male or female category. Nor does it accurately describe the other 99 percent who are actively working—to a greater or lesser degree—to force their bodies into a binary that doesn't exist in nature. Without all of this intervention, some people would still appear very masculine or feminine since some of our bodies do naturally conform to those types. Still, if we didn't work so hard at it, men and women wouldn't look *as different* as they do.

THE BINARY AND EVERYTHING ELSE

In addition to imposing a binary on ourselves, we disembody gender, using it as a guiding logic with which to understand not just people, but the world around us. We do this through **social construction**, a process by which we make reality meaningful through shared interpretation.[25] The metaphor of "construction" draws attention to the fact that we are *making* something. We are *layering* objects with ideas, *folding* concepts into one another, and *building* connections between them. This construction is "social" because, to be influential in society, the meaning ascribed to something must be shared.

Some examples of social construction might help. Consider the word *hippo*. The word doesn't look or sound anything like an actual hippopotamus, but

English speakers have agreed that this particular assortment of lines and curves—*hippo*—means a giant, gregarious, aquatic artiodactyl with stumpy legs and thick skin. And, likewise, when I say "hip" plus "oh," you know what I mean because we've given that order of those sounds that meaning. Money is also a social construction. The dollar bill has little inherent value. In fact, whether it has a "10" on it or a "100" makes it no more or less valuable in itself; the paper isn't worth more or less. But we've all agreed that bills *represent* money and the 10s and 100s represent *amounts* of money. People take those zeros very, very seriously. Almost everything in our lives is socially constructed.

In the process of social construction, we often layer objects, characteristics, behaviors, activities, and ideas with masculinity or femininity. Sociologists use the noun *gender* as a verb when talking about the *process* by which something becomes coded as masculine or feminine. So we will sometimes say that something is gendered or that we "gender" or are "gendering" things. In fact, we "gender" just about *everything*:

Who, stereotypically, is a sports fan? Who do we expect to play rugby? Soccer? How much opportunity do women have to play American football? Men are allowed to figure skate, but are male figure skaters "masculine"? Are women basketball players feminine? Who cheers for whom?

Who, stereotypically, drinks Diet Coke? Coke Zero? Monster energy drinks? At dinner, who do we expect will order a steak? A salad? Who do we think is more likely to become a vegetarian? At a bar who, stereotypically, orders beer? A cosmopolitan? Whiskey? White wine?

Who, stereotypically, listens to pop music? Hard rock? Who loves to sing? Who plays the drums? The flute? Who DJs? Who dances? Who writes for *Rolling Stone*?

Which teenagers, typically, babysit? And which mow lawns? Who, stereotypically, majors in computer science, engineering, physics? How about sociology? After college, who, stereotypically, becomes a therapist? A CEO? For those who do not go to college, who do we expect will become a construction worker? A receptionist?

Even animals are divided by gender! What kind of person owns a snake? Who, stereotypically, loves cats? Dogs? Are men allowed to love unicorns?

Because we've grown up learning to see gender in the world, we see it whether we like it or not. Metaphorically, this is because we wear **gender binary glasses**, a pair of lenses that separate everything we see into masculine and feminine categories. We acquire prescriptions for our gender binary glasses as we learn the ways of our culture. We may even have several different pairs of glasses. And we've probably had our prescription tweaked as ideas about gen-

der have changed around us. Some of us may even have a weaker prescriptio
than others. We all, however, own a pair of those glasses.

And it's a good thing. Our gender binary glasses give us **cultural competence**, a familiarity and facility with how the members of a society typically
think and behave. It's how we know that *most people* think unicorns really appeal only to girls, even if you personally insist that the love of unicorns should
know no bounds. This knowledge is important. In order to interact with others
in a meaningful way, we need a shared understanding of the world. Sometimes
we'll disagree, of course. A guy who grew up in Taos, New Mexico, with a father
who sells healing crystals and reads tourists' auras may have a different idea
about what counts as masculine than his college roommate, whose dad is the
football coach. But when they argue, they will likely still argue about what is
and isn't masculine. In other words, they may have different prescriptions, but
they are both wearing glasses.

We all wear glasses, but we aren't passive victims of a fixed gender binary.
We can also actively wield it in sophisticated ways.

Dividing and Subdividing the Binary

While reading the list of questions on the previous page, you might have come
across an example that you disagreed with. Toy poodles, you might have pro-
tested, aren't usually thought of as masculine, even though they're dogs. Indeed. A savvy application of the gender binary to the world doesn't simply mean
dividing everything into feminine and masculine categories; it also means
*sub*dividing all these things to add *degrees* of masculinity and femininity to
the world. Things aren't just masculine or feminine; they are also more or less
masculine or feminine. We understand that a toy poodle is a feminine subcategory of dog while a pit bull is a masculine subcategory. Likewise, most people
agree that cooking dinner is considered a feminine task, unless dinner involves
grilling steak in the backyard or is done for pay at a restaurant. Similarly, housework is feminized and yard work is masculinized (whether done as a job or a
chore), unless we're talking about flower gardening, a subcategory of yard work
associated with women. The process of subdivision makes gender a complex
cultural system rather than a single, rigid division of the world into masculine
and feminine.

Subdivision also has a way of protecting the binary by allowing us to explain
away all deviations from the binary with reference back to the binary itself. If
the guitar is a masculine instrument, how do we explain the pretty girl singing a
love song while gently strumming a guitar cradled in her lap? We subdivide the
guitar into electric (more masculine) and acoustic (more feminine) and further

subdivide playing styles such that gentle strumming is feminized and louder, more aggressive playing is seen as more appropriate for a man.

Likewise, if emotion is coded female, then what is anger? The masculinization of anger is a result of subdividing emotions in order to preserve the idea that women are more sensitive than men. Somehow our belief that men are prone to anger coexists with our belief that they rationally control their emotions. We don't resolve the contradiction by admitting that the stereotype is false (men are emotional after all). Instead, we resolve it by subdividing emotions into masculine and feminine types. Because of the gender binary, men can be angry without being labeled "emotional."

Subdivision allows us to dismiss the toy poodle, pretty strummer, and emotional man as exceptions that prove the rule. In this way, the binary functions to preserve the illusion that the gender binary is real. Divisions of gender also make the gender binary appear to be timeless, even as cultures are constantly changing. When women began wearing pants in the first half of the 1900s, for example, their choice of attire threatened to upset the gender binary: Men wear pants and women wear skirts. The invention of tight jeans and hip-hugging slacks feminized the pant, subdividing it to reaffirm the binary: Men wear men's pants and women wear women's pants. Subdivision, then, makes the gender binary endlessly flexible, able to accommodate whatever challenges and changes it encounters.

Whether out of conviction, mere habit, or the desire to see the world in the same way as people around us, we routinely apply a gender binary to characteristics, activities, objects, and people. This isn't reality because things like pants don't have either genitals or a personality; it's ideology. We just so happen to have an ideology that posits a gender binary, and we apply that binary to our world by peering at it through gender binary glasses. The trouble is the lenses bring the world into false focus.

BLURRED VISION AND BLIND SPOTS

Having a prescription for gender binary glasses doesn't necessarily mean we can put them on and take them off at will, though we get better at it as we become more conscious that they're there. To a greater or lesser degree, all of us misperceive the world because of the lenses through which we look at it.

False Connections and Unnoticed Contradictions

Gender ideologies aren't just ideas that are "out there"; they also have a way of lodging themselves firmly in our subconscious. Cells in our brains that process and transmit information make literal connections between and among concepts, such that some ideas are associated with other ideas. This phenomenon, called **associative memory**, is a very useful human adaptation. It's how we learned to think "big mouth, sharp teeth" and then "danger!" It's why we couldn't separate the idea "red" from "stop" even if we tried. (Both associations can save our lives.) Associative memory latches onto gender, too, so when we grow up with a gender binary, our brain forms clusters of ideas revolving around the concepts of masculinity and femininity.

Researchers can tap into our subconscious brain organization with the Implicit Association Test (IAT).[26] The IAT measures subconscious beliefs by comparing how quickly we can make connections between items. We are faster to connect two associated items than nonassociated items. In one study, gender-stereotyped words like *mechanic* and *secretary* were flashed on a computer screen, followed by a male or female name.[27] The viewer's task was to identify that name as male or female as quickly as possible. Results showed that, on average, it takes longer for a person to identify a name as male if it was preceded by a word like *secretary* than with a masculinized word like *mechanic*. Viewers have to cognitively "shift gears" in order to identify a name as male if they were shown a word they implicitly associated with women. Many studies have confirmed this experiment, showing that we unconsciously associate feminine things with one another and masculine things with one another (you can take the IAT yourself online at http://implicit.harvard.edu/).

We all have a part of our brain dedicated to encoding the gender binary. People who explicitly endorse gender stereotypes tend to show the strongest unconscious associations, but even those of us who refute stereotypes test "positive" for them on the IAT. And when our ability to think about resisting gender stereotypes is inhibited (when we are distracted or asked to respond quickly), essentially all of us revert to stereotypical thinking.[28] For instance, when asked to perform the challenging task of recalling a series of random words, study respondents often use the gender binary as a scaffold on which to structure their recollections. In one such study, people were offered a set of masculine, feminine, and neutral words like *wrestling, yogurt, bubble bath, ant, pickup truck, shirt, water, steak,* and *flower*. When asked to recall the words later, respondents would cluster the words by gender, saying *wrestling, pickup truck,* and *steak* in a row, then *yogurt, bubble bath,* and *flower.*[29] Sometimes they would even add gendered words that weren't on the original list.[30] Somehow, they just seemed to fit.

When we do this, we aren't relying on any logical connections between and among these things. The contents of the categories "masculine" and "feminine" are, in fact, a bizarre jumble of unrelated, sometimes even contradictory, ideas. Wrestling, pickup trucks, and T-bones share nothing in common, except that we associate them with men. Likewise, nothing connects yogurt, bubble bath, and

flowers besides the cultural prescriptions that tie them all to women and femininity (and perhaps because, for the same reason, we sometimes make bubble
bath smell like flowers).

Gender categories are not only incoherent; they're often contradictory. Consider how women are believed to be naturally inclined to do the most selfless job
in the world (raising children) at the same time that they are stereotyped as vain
and overly concerned with trivial, superficial things (like fashion and makeup).
If the latter is true, do women really make good parents? Likewise, men are
believed to be especially capable of running a company, but they are also stereotyped as dopes who can't be counted on to remember to run the dishwasher.
Are they focused and competent or not?

Associative memory also falsely *dis*connects masculine ideas from feminine ones, making it harder to form connections between these ideas. For example, even though we are taught that women have small hands and good coordination, making them ideal for needlework and sewing, we rarely notice that
it might also make them excellent surgeons. The ways in which sewing and
surgery are alike tends to escape our notice because they've been cognitively
connected to femininity and masculinity, respectively, which our brains have
already learned are opposites.

Gender ideologies, then, shape our cognitions as they're happening. They
also mold our memories such that our recall frequently betrays us.

False Memories and Forgetfulness

In a classic study, five- and six-year-olds were shown both stereotype-consistent
pictures (e.g., a boy playing with a train) and stereotype-inconsistent pictures
(e.g., a boy cooking on a stove).[31] Asked to recall what they had seen one week
later, children had more difficulty remembering the stereotype-inconsistent
pictures and sometimes reversed the sex of the person in the picture (e.g., they
remembered a *girl* cooking) or changed the activity (e.g., they remembered a
boy *fixing* a stove). Many later studies have confirmed that children are more
likely to forget an experience that deviates from stereotypes—skateboarding
girls or belly-dancing boys—than one that fits in.[32]

Adults also have a better memory for stereotype-consistent experiences than
stereotype-inconsistent ones. Stereotype-inconsistent experiences are more
likely to be forgotten or misremembered compared to stereotype-consistent
ones.[33] Many participants will claim to recall (false) memories vividly. In one
study, people were asked to watch a dramatized account of a bicycle theft.[34] The
actors playing the thieves varied. In some videos, the criminal was a masculine man, in others a feminine man, a feminine woman, or a masculine woman.
Study subjects could remember more about the theft if the criminal conformed

to gender stereotypes. This is because, just as with the words *yogurt*, *bubble bath*, and *flower*, it is easier to remember a set of ideas if they conform to a pre-existing schema (in this case, criminal behavior = masculine = men). The authors write, "When eyewitnesses are exposed to a theft, gender schemas will enhance recall," but only if the criminal followed gender expectations and conventions.[35]

This phenomenon applies even to memories that we would think would be impervious to such effects. In one surprising study, French high school students were asked to fill out a quick survey about whether men or women were better at math and art.[36] Reminded of the gender stereotypes, they were then asked to report their own scores on a national standardized test that they'd taken two years prior. Amazingly, women underestimated their own performance on the math portion of the test and overestimated their performance on the art portion. Men misremembered in the opposite direction.

In these ways, and in many others, our gender binary glasses distort what we see. They often bring things into false focus and affect our cognition and memory. When we see counterevidence, it tends not to enter into our daily in-terpretation of the world. We may soon misremember it as having confirmed our pre-existing beliefs. And our brain has been trained to direct us to make gender-stereotypical associations even if we are consciously prepared to say that those stereotypes are nonexistent or wrong.

Without this distortion, the gender binary would appear patently false. Pre-serving it requires constant *in*attention to evidence that falsifies it. These cog-nitive processes that we all share help us dismiss, forget, or misremember "ex-ceptions to the rule." So the wide range of bodies we see in real life doesn't cause us to abandon the idea that male and female bodies are dramatically different. Most men don't look like Channing Tatum or David Beckham, but we still think that's what a "real man" looks like.

Revisiting the Question

 If the gender binary doesn't describe a large number of the people we know, where does the idea come from?

It's everywhere! It's everywhere because we all have a pair of gender binary glasses. We don't all have identical prescriptions, or ones that are equally strong, but we all look through those lenses and see a gendered world. There is nothing unusual about this. Gender is a common way of making meaning out of the world around us. We use the gender binary to understand things, ideas, objects, activities, places, and more. We also apply it to our bodies and, believing that our bodies should conform to the binary, we work hard to in-crease the chances that they do. In this way, we create societies in which people conform more to the gender binary than they otherwise would. Meanwhile, we define as deviant the 1 percent of people who present a biological challenge to the idea at its most basic level.

When we apply a gender ideology to the world, however, what we end up seeing is false on many fronts. One clue is that the categories fail to fit most people we know well, including ourselves. This is partly because the categories are rigid and predetermined, but also because they are random and contradictory. Still, because we wear gender binary glasses, we don't notice the ubiquitous counterevidence. We subdivide the binary to keep it in place even when reality doesn't conform to our expectations or we forget or misremember experiences that challenge the gender binary. Our glasses distort our cognition.

Next . . .

The idea that gender is a social construction might resonate with you, but it also likely bumps up against things you've heard about pink and blue brains, the male sex drive, or women's intuition, all seemingly irrefutable biological differences between men and women. With this in mind, we'll tackle this question next:

 The gender binary might be an ideology, but there are real differences between men and women, right?

This question is so much harder to answer than you might think.

FOR FURTHER READING

Dworkin, Shari. "A Woman's Place is in the . . . Cardiovascular Room?: Gender Relations, the Body, and the Gym." In *Athletic Intruders: Ethnographic Research on Women, Culture, and Exercise*, edited by Anne Bolin and Jane Granskog, 313–158. Albany, NY: State University of New York Press, 2003.

Fausto-Sterling, Anne. "The Five Sexes: Why Male and Female Are Not Enough." *The Sciences* March/April (1993): 20–24.

Martin, Carol, and Diane Ruble. "Children's Search for Gender Cues." *Current Directions in Psychological Science* 13, no. 2 (2004): 67–70.

Martin, Emily. "The Egg and the Sperm: How Science has Constructed a Romance Based on Stereotypical Male-Female Roles." *Signs* 16, no. 3 (1991): 485–501.

Paoletti, Jo. *Pink and Blue: Telling the Boys from the Girls in America.* Bloomington and Indianapolis: Indiana University Press, 2012.

Rupp, Leila. "Toward a Global History of Same-Sex Sexuality." *Journal of the History of Sexuality* 10, no. 2 (2001): 287–302.

MEN ARE FROM NORTH DAKOTA,
WOMEN ARE FROM SOUTH DAKOTA.

—KATHRYN DINDIA[1]

3

Bodies

In a part of the ocean so deep that no light can reach it, an anglerfish hunts. She attracts prey with a glowing lure that springs from her forehead and looks suspiciously like something other creatures would like to eat. No matter if they are bigger than she is; she can swallow prey up to twice her body size.

She pays no attention to her male counterpart, who is relatively tiny. Females can grow up to 3.3 feet long, but males are never longer than a few centimeters. He, in contrast, needs her desperately. Born without a lure, a male anglerfish can't catch prey, a small concern given that he doesn't have a digestive system. A male's only chance at survival is finding a female before he dies of starvation. If he's so lucky, he'll latch onto her with his mouth, initiating a chemical reaction that slowly dissolves his face into her body. Eventually he will lose all his internal organs, except his testicles. A healthy female anglerfish will carry many pairs of testicles on her body, adding to her ominous appearance.

This is what **sexual dimorphism** looks like. The phrase refers to differences between males and females in appearance and behavior. Across the range of species on Earth, some are highly sexually dimorphic and some are less so. The high end includes the green spoonworm (like the anglerfish, the male lives its entire

In some species, males and females appear very different than each other; in other species less so. Elephant seals, lions, and anglerfish are all species that are more sexually dimorphic than humans.

adult life on a female, or *inside* her if she accidentally eats him); peacocks (males carry a resplendent tail with which to dazzle the relatively drab females); and elephant seals (males outweigh females by about 4,600 pounds). Despite our curiosity about gender differences, humans are on the low end of the spectrum when it comes to sexual dimorphism.

Highly sexually dimorphic animals help us put human gender difference in perspective. Given the range of sexual dimorphism in nature, we should be rather impressed by how obviously similar we are. If humans were as dimorphic by size as elephant seals, for example, the average male would weigh 550 pounds. If we were anglerfish, the very tallest men would be lucky to be two inches high. Men don't come in elaborate colors or have tails to get the ladies' attention. Alas, we're just not that kind of species. As Dorothy Sayers once said, "Women are more like men than anything else in the world."[2]

But we're not *totally* alike. A man will never sprout antlers like a moose or a mane like a lion, no matter how badly he wants to impress his date, but a male-bodied person will also never menstruate or gestate a fetus in his uterus. We *are* different. Accordingly, it is understandable that people are curious about the answer to the question that we posed at the end of the last chapter:

The gender binary might be an ideology, but there are real differences between men and women, right?

This chapter reviews the research on gender differences and similarities and explores how biology contributes to them. Anticipate, however, an answer to this question that is simultaneously disappointing and inspiring. The truth is that despite our best efforts, it is much more difficult to answer than you might imagine. It involves a model of the relationship between biology and society that is far more complex than even scientists once imagined, one that has changed dramatically even in your lifetime.

RESEARCH ON GENDER DIFFERENCES AND SIMILARITIES

From a practical perspective, getting a clear understanding of how men and women are alike and different is an incredibly complex task. As you'll see, whether we find differences, what causes those differences, and how dramatic they are, varies over time and across cultures; these differences respond to psychological manipulation and practice and training; and they're sensitive to how we design studies and define measurements. We would have to amass a lot of evidence, and consider all the possible influences, in order to determine which differences we find consistently and which we don't. And that's just what psychologist Janet Hyde did.

Hyde combined an impressive 7,084 studies by different researchers who collectively looked at 124 measures of possible differences between men and women in thoughts, feelings, behavior, intellectual abilities, communication styles and skills, personality traits, measures of happiness and well-being, physical abilities, and more.[3] She separated the variables into ones for which there appeared to be no differences between men and women, and those for which there was evidence for small, medium, or large differences. The leftmost columns of Table 3.1 show the percentage of variables that fall into each category and the rightmost columns offer ways to think about the size of the difference. The second column from the right reveals the percentage of one sex that outscores the average for the other sex and the far-right column shows what percentage of men's and women's scores overlap.[4]

As Table 3.1 shows, Hyde found no differences between men and women for 30 percent of the traits examined. On an additional 48 percent, there was

TABLE 3.1 | INTERPRETING THE SIZE OF OBSERVED
GENDER DIFFERENCES

Size of the Difference	% of Variables in each Category[a]	% of One Sex Scoring Higher than 50% of the Other	% of Scores that Overlap
Zero	30%	50–54%	93–100%
Small	48%	55–64%	76–92%
Medium	15%	65–74%	59–75%
Large	6%	75–84%	45–58%
Extra Large	2%	85–100%	0–44%

[a]*Percentages do not add up to 100 due to rounding.*

evidence for a small gender difference. Figure 3.1 below demonstrates what a small difference looks like. The bottom of the graph represents levels of self-esteem (from low on the left to high on the right) and the height of the curve represents the number of people who reported each level. Few people have very low self-esteem (far left) or very high self-esteem (far right). While Hyde's analysis offered good evidence for a statistically significant difference between men and women, it's not a large one.[5]

Other variables that fall into the categories of no difference or small difference include reading comprehension and abstract reasoning; talkativeness, likelihood of self-disclosing to friends and strangers, tendency to interrupt others, and assertiveness of speech; willingness to help others; negotiation style, approach to leadership, and degree of impulsiveness; symptoms of depression, coping strategies, life satisfaction and happiness; vertical jumping ability, overall activity levels, balance, flexibility; willingness to delay gratification and attitudes about cheating; likelihood of wanting a career that makes money, offers security, is challenging, and brings prestige; and some measures of sexual attitudes and experiences (e.g., disapproval of extramarital sex, levels of sexual arousal, and sexual satisfaction).

As Table 3.1 shows, gender differences were medium or large for the remaining 22 percent of traits. Moderately sized differences included physical aggression (with 62–80 percent

FIGURE 3.1 | AN ILLUSTRATION OF A "SMALL" DIFFERENCE BETWEEN MEN AND WOMEN

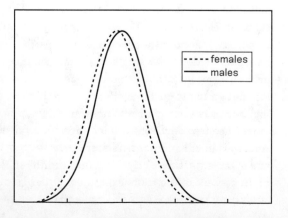

----- females
—— males

of men more aggressive than 50 percent of women) and visual-spatial abilities (72–77 percent of men are better at turning a two- or three-dimensional object around in their heads than 50 percent of women).

The largest gender differences were for some measures of physical ability, especially throwing; 80 percent of men can throw farther and faster than 50 percent of women (because these differences are related to size, they are particularly pronounced after puberty). Large differences were also found in some measures of sexuality. Eighty-three percent of men report masturbating more often than 50 percent of women, and 80 percent of men are more likely to approve of casual sex than 50 percent of women.[6] Two traits show especially strong sexual dimorphism: sexual identity (most men identify as male and most women identify as female) and sexual object choice (most men are sexually interested in women and most women in men).

Are these the "real differences" our opening question asked about? Let's consider some possible definitions of "real."

DEFINING "REAL"

Definition 1: Sex differences are real if we can measure them.

Scientists really do conduct experiments, and they really do find sex differences. By this definition, the 22 percent of variables on which Hyde found medium-sized or larger sex differences represent real sex differences, as do the 48 percent on which she found small differences. These are real **observed differences**: the results of surveys, experiments, and other ways of collecting information.

But is this what we mean by "real"?

One possible problem is that study subjects sometimes act or perform differently because they're being observed. Women smile more often than men and men are more likely to engage in heroic helping behavior than women, but only if they know they are being observed; when people think they are alone, the gender differences disappear.[7] People also lie on surveys. Men report higher rates of masturbation than women, a variable on which Hyde documented a large difference. But when scientists do studies in which they increase the motivation to be honest (by, say, hooking a man up to a fake lie detector) and decrease their motivation to lie (by ensuring that the answers are anonymous), the frequency with which men report masturbating drops to the same level as women's. We see similar patterns in reported number of sexual partners and age at first intercourse.

In other cases, psychologists have discovered that they can manipulate study results quite easily. If you remind study subjects of a stereotype right before the test, in a trick called **priming**, test scores will reflect that stereotype. Women asked to identify themselves by their gender immediately before a test of empathy will do better than those who didn't answer a gender question.[8] Because women expect themselves to be more empathic than men, priming them with their gender may give them more confidence, focus their attention, or motivate them to do better. For men, reminding them that they're male lowers their scores.

You can also depress women's scores on empathy tests simply by asking them to imagine themselves to be men for a few moments before they begin the experiment. In one study, women were asked to write a fictional story about a day in the life of a person named Paul.[9] Half were asked to write in the first person ("I") and the other half were asked to write in the third person ("he"). Women who wrote in the third person did better on the empathy test than their male counterparts (getting 72 percent of the test correct), but women who had imagined themselves to be men did just as badly as the real men (getting only 40 percent of the test right).

Does this mean that women have an ability to be empathic that men don't have, and they just need to be motivated to use it? Nope. Men can be motivated to score higher on tests of empathy, too. You can do that either by tricking them into thinking that the task they are performing is one that men are stereotypically good at (perhaps telling them that you're measuring leadership ability) or by offering a social or financial reward for doing well.[10] Similarly, men (presumably heterosexual ones) will do better on tests of empathy if they're told that women really dig a sensitive guy.[11]

The differences Hyde observed, then, are real in that we really observed them, but they don't necessarily stand up when we poke and prod at them. Perhaps what we need is a definition that is more robust.

Definition 2: Sex differences are real if they are observed in all or most contemporary and historical cultures.

By this definition, if we could find a gender difference that was observed around the world and throughout history, we would have a compelling reason to think it was real. The vast majority of traits discussed by Hyde, though, show significant cross-cultural variability.[12] Let's take math ability as an example.

In 1992 the toy company Mattel released a talking Barbie doll that said, among other things, "Math class is tough!" Then, and now, many people believe that girls and women struggle in mathematics more than boys and men.[13] At the time Barbie was making her confession, it was true. Disparities in skill emerged in high school, with boys scoring slightly higher than girls on the math portion of the SAT, a standardized test for college admissions.[14] In the intervening twenty years, however, the gap has narrowed as girls have started to take math classes at the same rate as boys. This equivalence in test results suggests that the difference in performance had more to do with training and practice than gender.[15]

If we look at mathematical abilities across developed nations—those with modern economies and educational systems—girls do about as well as boys in about half the countries.[16] In the other half, boys outperform girls. In a few outlier countries, such as Iceland, girls outshine boys significantly. Whether men or women appear to be better at math depends on what country you're looking at. Still, boys do better than girls more often than girls do better than boys.

If you look a bit closer at the data, you'll also discover that this is true only if you compare boys to the girls *in their own country*. Math ability varies so widely across societies that sometimes girls who are outshone by boys in their own country do significantly better than boys in other countries. For instance, though Japanese girls do less well than Japanese boys, they generally outperform American boys by a considerable margin.[17]

Gender differences in math ability, it turns out, are lowest in countries whose citizens are least likely to *believe* that men are better at it.[18] In fact, there is a strong correlation between gender differences in math ability and the level of gender inequality in a country (Figure 3.2).[19] The differences diminish, and then disappear, as men and women become more equal.

How we measure math ability also matters. Men and women are equally capable *on average*, but men are more likely to be math *geniuses*. Boys outnumber girls in the top 1 percent of math ability. Among twelve- to fourteen-year-olds, math prodigies are more likely to be male at a ratio of 3:1. So that's impressive. But, less impressively, they're also more likely than girls to struggle with math. In those populations where boys outnumber girls at the highest scoring levels, they also outnumber girls at the lowest scoring levels.[20] Boys are more likely than girls to get nearly all the answers on a math test wrong. So when boys do better, they are usually also doing worse.

But, this, of course, also varies by country, over time, and across subgroups. Even among the top 1 percent, boys outperform girls among only some parts of the U.S. population. White male students outperform white female students at this high level of ability, but among Asians in the United States, the trend is reversed. Looking cross-culturally, girls also dominate the top 1 percent in Iceland, Thailand, and the United Kingdom. Boys, then, do not always outnumber girls when we look at the highest-scoring students. And in the United States, as girls and women have closed the gap between the average ability of males and females, they've also been closing the gap at the highest levels of mathematical ability.[21] We mentioned above that today boys outnumber girls at the genius level 3:1; in the 1980s, the ratio was 13:1.[22] That's quite a remarkable catch-up.

FIGURE 3.2 | GENDER GAP IN MATH ACROSS COUNTRIES

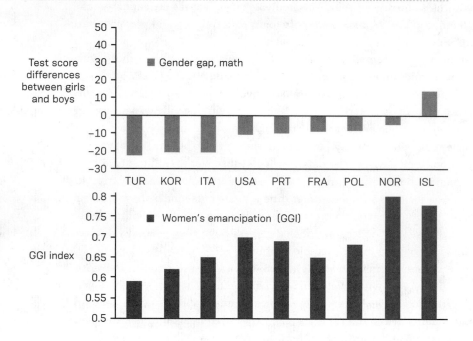

Note: With the exception of PRT (Portugal) and Iceland (ISL), the countries are abbreviated as their first three letters.
Source: Guiso Luigi, Fernando Monte, Paola Sapienza, and Luigi Zingales. "Culture, Gender, and Math." *Science* 320, no. 5880 (2009): 1164–65.

In any case, performance on the standardized tests used to evaluate ability doesn't predict who will get the highest grades in math classes. Girls in U.S. high schools and colleges get higher grades in math than boys.[23] While only a few decades ago most math majors were men, today they're about 50 percent female. The number of women receiving PhDs in math has also risen; it's more than tripled between 1976 and 2001.[24]

So, are men better at math than women? In part, it depends on how we test for math aptitude. If you go by standardized tests, sometimes boys outperform girls, but if you go by grades, girls outperform boys. If you test for genius-level math ability, boys in some populations outperform girls, but if you test for average level, girls and boys come out about even. And lastly, if you look at the most poorly performing students, girls come off looking much more capable than boys. But none of these generalizations about difference is consistent among groups in any given country, across countries, or even over time in a single population. Math ability is sensitive to cultural context, so whether we find differences, what direction they are in, and how dramatic they are var-

ies over time and across cultures. This complex story about math ability is jus
one example of the way that observed gender differences vary across time and
space. Findings of difference often fall apart as soon as you add a historical or
cross-cultural dimension.

Part of what scholars may be trying to get at by comparing different countries is the possibility that, underneath it all, gender difference has a biological foundation. This is what many people mean by "real," so let's consider that
definition.

Definition 3: Sex differences are real if they are biological.

Some readers might want to reject the idea that **learned differences**—ones that
are a result of how we're raised (like our religion or parenting) or our socio-
cultural environment (education or media consumption)—count as real. They
may want to restrict their definition to **biological differences**—ones caused by
hormones, brain morphology, or genetics. We have some evidence of biological
differences between men and women in traits and abilities, though not as many
as you might expect. Let's review the research on genes, hormones, and our
brains.

GENES Our **genes** are a set of instructions for building and maintaining our
bodies. Each of us has a unique set of genes, our **genotype**, and an observable
set of physical and behavioral traits, our **phenotype**. By our current working
definition, the differences described by Hyde are
biological if they are phenotypes shaped by our
genes.

Genetics contribute to gender differences in
three ways.[25] First, some traits are **sex-linked**,
tied to whether a person is a genetic female
(XX) or genetic male (XY). Surprisingly, this
isn't a large source of gender difference. As the
image to the right shows, there just isn't much
to the Y chromosome. It is significantly smaller
than the X chromosome, containing fewer than
50 genes compared to the 1,000 to 2,000 genes
on the X chromosome.[26] Accordingly, so far the
Y chromosome has turned out to be an unlikely
cause for observed gender differences. While
research is still ongoing, the tentative conclusion is that the Y chromosome does little more
than give XY fetuses functioning testes and

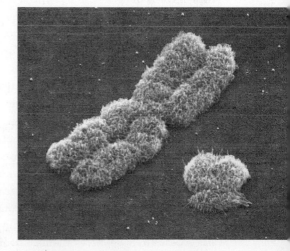

Despite its mighty reputation, the Y chromosome contains substantially less genetic
material than the X chromosome.

facilitate male fertility. That might be all. Well, that and the tendency to have hairy ears.[27]

The fact that women have two X chromosomes and men have only one seems to be a greater source of gender differences. In genetic females, one X is inactive in most cells. So women are essentially just like men: They both have only one functioning X chromosome. But women have a "backup" X that men do not. When a person has two Xs, if one is defective, the other one will be there to mediate the effect.

Because genetic men don't have a backup X, they are more vulnerable to problems caused by defective Xs.[28] For example, 60 of the 300 genes known to be involved in mental retardation are on the X chromosome and 500 of the 800 genes on the X chromosome are relevant to brain function. Accordingly, we might expect this difference to affect men's intelligence. In fact, men show greater variability in intelligence (that is, they are both dumber and smarter than women, on average) and their single X chromosome may be why.[29] Relatedly, if a trait carried on the X chromosome is recessive, men are more likely to show that trait, since they need to inherit only one recessive gene to express the trait, whereas women need to inherit two. Color blindness is an example of an X-linked recessive trait seen more commonly in men.

Sex-linked traits are the most obvious source of gender differences, but other chromosomal pairs are relevant, too. Some of these genes are **sex-limited**, meaning they are only expressed if they are in a male or female body. The genes that allow a woman to produce milk for an infant, for instance, are carried by both men and women, but they are only expressed in mothers. Likewise, some men have a genetic condition that causes their testicles to remain in their abdomen. Women can carry these genes, too, but it doesn't cause them any trouble. Their gonads are *supposed* to remain in their abdominal cavity. Sex-limited genes, then, mostly remain dormant if they're not relevant to the body they're in.

A final set of genes, called **sex-influenced**, do different things in male and female bodies (that is, what they do depends on the gender of the carrier). It is this type of gene that explains why men are more likely to go bald. The baldness gene has a strong influence on phenotype (hair loss) only in the presence of high levels of testosterone, so most women who carry the gene don't show signs of baldness. Another example involves our singing voices. The same genes that produce a high singing voice in women cause a low voice in men.

Genetic influences like these contribute to some physical differences between the genders, including singing voices and hairy ears. They also set us on paths to have male or female bodies, which are related to some of Hyde's measures, such as throwing ability. But we don't have good evidence that genes have gender-specific effects on the majority of items Hyde studied, traits like our cognitive abilities or personalities. The possible exception is potential for greater male variability on some traits as a result of their single X chromosome. To consider biological contributors to these other characteristics, we have to consider the influence of hormones and brain function.

HORMONES   Our **hormones** are messengers in a chemical communication system. Released by glands or cells in one part of the body, hormones carry instructions to the rest of the body. They trigger masculinization and feminization in utero and at puberty. They regulate basic physiological processes, like hunger and the reproductive cycle. And they influence our moods: feelings of happiness, confidence, and contentment. They are part of what inspires us to have sex, get into (or run away from) fights, and settle down and raise a baby.

Importantly, it's a mistake to use binary language and say that men have "male hormones" and women have "female hormones." All human hormones circulate in both men's and women's bodies, but some of them do so in different proportions. Men tend to have higher levels of androgens and women higher levels of estrogens. Moreover, research on other species shows that estrogen sometimes has the same masculinizing effects in females that testosterone has in males and vice versa for testosterone. So just as we are not "opposite sexes," our hormones are far from opposite in their chemical structure, presence, or function.

Still, while it's not true that we are hormonally "opposite," differing levels of these hormones might contribute to gender differences. Testosterone usually gets the most attention. In fact, testosterone is strongly related to sex drive in both women and men and may be weakly related to physical aggression in men.[30] Since men have more free testosterone than women, this fact might partially explain why men are, on average, more aggressive than women and report higher sex drives.[31] The relationship between hormone level and observed difference isn't straightforward, though. Men seem to respond similarly to wide variations in testosterone levels (between 20 percent and 200 percent of normal), and women have been shown to be more sensitive to lower levels of testosterone, so it might take less of the hormone to have an equivalent effect.[32]

There is good evidence, too, that the hormone cycles that regulate women's menstrual cycles correspond to mild changes in mood, sexual interest, and partner choice,[33] but we see no changes across the menstrual cycle in women's memory, creativity, problem-solving ability, or athletic, intellectual, or academic performance.[34] Men experience hormone fluctuations as well, on both daily and seasonal cycles (testosterone is higher in the morning than other times of day, and in the fall compared to other times of year for men in the Western Hemisphere). Interestingly, studies of mood fluctuations in men find that they are just as emotionally "unstable" as women.[35] In other words, men get "hormonal" sometimes, too. The lesson here, again, may be that men and women are more alike than different and, in both cases, these mood swings are small. That is, hormone fluctuations are a relatively minor force in determining our mood compared to, say, whether it's Monday morning or Friday afternoon.[36]

Testosterone levels also correlate with visual-spatial ability, such as **mental rotation**, the ability to imagine an object rotating in your mind.[37] Very high and very low levels of testosterone are correlated with poor visual-spatial ability, so high-testosterone women and low-testosterone men do best on visual-spatial tests because they both fall into the middle range. As men's and women's hormones fluctuate, their performance on tests fluctuates as well; women score better right before ovulation (when their testosterone levels are highest) and men score better in the spring (when their levels are lowest). All these differences are quite small, however, and have not been shown to have an impact on a person's ability to do related work.[38]

In sum, we find differing levels of androgens and estrogens in men's and women's bodies and those hormones have been linked to a limited number of observed differences: aggressiveness, sex drive, visual-spatial ability, and when (but not whether or how much) mood fluctuates. All the effects are small, with the possible exception of sex drive. Hormones, then, may contribute to some of the differences we see between men and women, but they are also responsible for many of the similarities. Next, we'll consider a biological candidate for gender difference getting a lot of attention lately: our brains.

BRAINS Scientists have documented quite a few gender differences in brain anatomy (the size and shape of its parts), composition (characteristics of the tissue), and function (rate of blood flow, metabolism of glucose, and neurotransmitter levels).[39] Women have smaller brains (largely explained by their overall smaller size), and men and women have different ratios of gray matter (brain tissue responsible for information processing) to white matter (brain tissue responsible for allowing the brain to communicate with itself) in some regions.[40] Though the idea that men are "left-brained" and women are "right-brained" is a popular one, there is no evidence for a gender difference; both men and women tend to be left dominant.[41]

Any differences between men's and women's brains are caused in part by the different hormone profiles of developing fetuses and elevated levels of hormones during the first six to twelve months of life. They may give men and women nonidentical preferences and talents. The idea that male and female brains may have different strengths and weaknesses is part of **brain organization theory**. To date, however, none of these average differences between male and female brains has been clearly linked to the types of differences observed by Hyde—with one exception.[42] The same prenatal hormone levels that are believed to masculinize and feminize the brain have been linked with girls preferring boys as playmates and slight toy preferences (though both male and female children tend to prefer boys' toys, boys and masculinized girls do somewhat more so).[43] Men and women may be predisposed to be interested in slightly different things, even if they are equally capable of successfully pursuing either interest.

Brain organization theory is in its infancy. We find differences, but we don't know what they mean, if anything. It's possible that these differences are inconsequential or, even, that these differences might function to produce sameness from difference. That is, one difference in the brain (say, neurotransmitter function) might exist specifically to compensate for another difference (say, proportion of gray to white matter). According to neuroendocrinologist Geert De Vries, gender differences in the brain might create observable difference, but they may "just as well do the exact opposite; that is, they may prevent sex differences in overt functions and behaviors by compensating for sex differences in physiology."[44]

THE REAL DIFFERENCES? Research on genes, hormones, and brain anatomy may explain some of the differences observed by Hyde, such as certain measures of sexual desire and behavior, physical aggression, visual-spatial ability, variation in intelligence, and toy choice among children. This tidy list of differences, short though it is, may satisfy some readers. These, you might conclude, seem to be good candidates for real differences in traits between men and women. But what if individuals could actively change things about their biology? In fact, many of the things that are biological are **mutable**, responsive to efforts to shift or disrupt them. Consider that your body can be flooded with adrenaline in a mere instant, only to dissipate entirely within two minutes. The flight-or-fight response that adrenaline facilitates, in other words, is a highly mutable biological state. If biologically based differences can be decreased in size, erased, or reversed quite easily, do they still count as real?

Consider mental rotation, our very best candidate for a large biological cognitive gender difference. It turns out that mental rotation skill can be taught,

FIGURE 3.3 | EXAMPLE OF A MENTAL ROTATION TASK

(a)   (b)

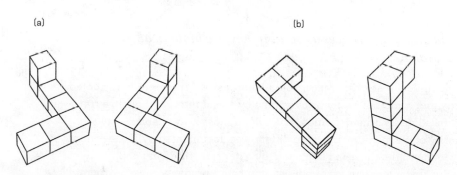

Mental-rotation tasks like this one measure how easily and accurately you can determine whether two figures are identical except for their orientation. Assembling jigsaw puzzles is one use of this skill.

and quickly. One study found that assigning women to a semester of *Tetris* (a simple video game that involves rotating and fitting various geometric shapes into one another) almost closed the gap between men's and women's scores.[45] In another study, just ten hours of video game play reduced the gap to statistical insignificance.[46] In a third study, five and a half hours of video game play erased the gender difference.[47] And in a fourth experiment, just two minutes of practice before the test erased the different performance levels of men and women.[48]

Both men and women benefit from these interventions. They show that whatever natural ability an individual has for mental rotation, both men and women can improve with a little bit of practice.[49] Indeed, the difference between the scores of people with training and people without training is larger than the difference between men and women.[50]

While this finding doesn't rule out an in-born biological advantage for boys, neuroscientist Lise Eliot argues that ultimately gender differences in mental rotation ability are probably the result of the fact that we don't teach mental rotation in school (so no one learns it there), and boys have a greater likelihood of learning it elsewhere (playing with building toys, spending lots of time with video games, and being involved in sports).[51] This theory gets added support from evidence that the gender differences in mental rotation ability that we see in elementary-school children from middle- and high-income backgrounds are not seen in children from low-income backgrounds, where boys don't have as much access to video games and building toys.[52]

It is quite remarkable that even the most robust cognitive sex difference we've ever measured can be strongly affected by instruction and practice. Whatever our predispositions, training and practice are key.[53] As two prominent cognitive scientists explained, "Simply put, your brain is what you do with it."[54] Even the largest and most significant sex difference can be significantly altered with just a few minutes of *Minecraft*. Lots of observed differences respond to intervention and we will discuss more examples below. For now, let's consider a final strict definition of real.

Definition 4: Sex differences are real if they are biological and immutable.

By this definition, a sex difference would count as real if it were both rooted in biology and could not easily be overcome by social interventions like training and tricking. By this definition, however, almost no variables—including the majority of the medium and large differences documented by Hyde—count as real. Gender differences in height and, by extension, throwing ability might qualify. But if you were an evil scientist, you could probably raise a group of girls to be taller than a group of boys simply by feeding all the girls a nutritious diet and starving the boys a bit. So by this definition, even height may not qualify as real. Gender identity and sexual orientation may be better candidates. These two variables do show significant sexual dimorphism: There is at least some evidence for a biological basis for both, and they are strongly resistant to change.

This is a good time to remember the anglerfish. There's no reason to think that we *should* be able to establish a whole host of large, immutable biological differences between men and women, beyond the very necessary physical differences required for sexual reproduction. We're just not that kind of species. "Opposite sexes" is a misnomer.

So what is the take-home message of this quixotic attempt to define "real"?

A DIFFERENT QUESTION ALTOGETHER

Novelist Thomas Pynchon once made a provocative claim: "If they can get you to ask the wrong questions," he said, "they don't have to worry about your answers."[55] The truth is that members of Western societies are rather tied up in knots these days trying to answer the question that began this chapter. Thus far, we've shown you that answering this question is far more difficult than one might imagine.

It's also the wrong question. It pulls us into a fruitless and largely discredited argument, often referred to as **the nature/nurture debate**: on the "nature" side are people who believe that observed differences between men and women are biological; on the "nurture" side are people who believe that these differences are acquired through socialization. The "nature" side is premised on the idea that men and women are *born* different, and the "nurture" side presupposes that male and female human beings are not very different biologically, but that men and women *become* different.

The argument is a seductive one, but ultimately both sides—nature *and* nurture—are wrong. This is for two reasons. First, if we're not careful, the nature/nurture debate escalates into an argument over how to explain something for which we don't have strong evidence: the gender binary. Both the nature and nurture sides of the debate *presuppose* that there are important differences between men and women that need explaining. As Hyde's research suggests, it's important to keep our degree of dimorphism in perspective.

Second, the nature/nurture debate is a dead-end argument because nature and nurture are always working together to produce whatever behavior or trait is being considered. The truth is that in just the last fifteen years, what scientists believed about the relationship between biology and society has undergone a change that can only be described as revolutionary. The revolution is happening on two fronts. First, we've learned that we can't understand human biology without paying attention to the physical and cultural environment of the bodies we study. Second, we've learned that we deeply underestimated the complexity of the human organism itself. In the remainder of this chapter, we'll provide you with an overview of this new biological frontier and discuss what it means for thinking about gender.

100 Percent Nature and 100 Percent Nurture[56]

Scholars from all disciplines now overwhelmingly reject **naturalism**, the idea that biology affects our behavior independently of our environment. Likewise, we reject **culturalism**, the idea that we are "blank slates" and that we become who we are purely through learning and socialization. These rejections should make sense. Any given gender difference can't purely be a result of "nurture" (a culturalist assumption) because it is only through our bodies that we encounter our social world. Nor can it purely be "nature" (a naturalist assumption) because our bodies don't exist in a vacuum. We begin interacting with the environment from the moment we are conceived, and all our biological functions evolve in the context of that interaction.

When we think about what is truly fundamental about the human animal, then, we always have to consider both our bodies and our environments. Each is equally important. As psychologist Donald Hebb once observed, asking whether nature or nurture is more fundamental is like asking which is more important to the area of a rectangle, its length or width. Without both pieces of information, *there is no rectangle.*[57] The evidence for Hebb's observation is so overwhelming that scientists now agree that it makes no sense to talk about "human nature," except insofar as "the social *is* the natural."[58]

In practice, this means that when we take away the social environment, we don't become true, unadulterated, *natural* human beings; instead, we don't quite become human beings at all, at least not ones that we recognize. The most compelling evidence for this may be the stories of children with little or no human contact of any kind. One tragic example involves a California girl named Genie, one of the most extreme cases of human neglect ever documented.[59] She spent the majority of the first thirteen years of her life tied onto a child's potty-training seat in a bedroom, abandoned:

> *Genie received a minimum of care and stimulation. She was fed only baby food and wore no clothing. There was no TV or radio in the home. The remainder of the family lived in a separate part of the house, so she heard little of any family conversations. As her bedroom was set in the back of the house, away from the street, she heard few noises from passersby. Her room contained only the potty and crib—no carpet, no pictures on the walls, certainly no toys. The room's two windows were covered up except for a few inches at the top.*[60]

Genie was malnourished, could not stand erect, and was not potty trained. She was afraid to make any noise at all, as she had been beaten when she vocalized, and she had never learned a language.

The girl was discovered in 1970 and rescued from her family, but the isolation stunted her ability to develop basic human traits. Genie didn't know how to smile and continued to spend large amounts of time being still in dark rooms. She eventually learned some words and some sign language but was never able to develop facility with spoken English. Her brain, isolated from the company of other people, hadn't developed the basic structures it needed. She had missed an important developmental window, and so there were some things—some basic *human* things—that she would simply never be able to do.

Cases like Genie's show us that we aren't spontaneously and naturally male or female in the absence of social interaction.[61] Studying her brain would not have taught us something about what "female brains," unspoiled by contact with culture, are really like. Instead, becoming human involves becoming a (female or male) member of a society. Additionally, *how* we are human is very much dependent on the society we are born into.[62]

Biology-Society Interactions

Our bodies are actually *designed* to respond to our environment. For example, our genotype doesn't dictate our phenotype in a simple, one-directional way. Instead, each gene can express itself in many, sometimes thousands of different ways and the environment is an important determining factor, telling our genes what to do and when. Scientists describe this as **gene-environment interaction**.[63] The genes we inherit only begin to determine who we are. Each gene's level and type of activity are also important, and these variables are strongly influenced by everything from the cellular environment to the global one. Even identical twins become both genotypically and phenotypically different over time.[64]

A neuroscientist named James Fallon learned this lesson the hard way.[65] After many years of studying the brains of psychopaths, typically violent individuals who show an extreme lack of empathy, he became curious about his own family tree. He turned out to be descended from what he called a "whole lineage of very violent people," including the famous ax-murderer Lizzie Borden. So he decided to test family members for a gene related to aggression. No one in his family carried the gene except for him. A subsequent brain scan confirmed that his neural activity closely resembled that of known psychopaths. "In a sense," he explained, "I'm a born killer." For quite a while, Fallon kept the news to himself.

Luckily, Fallon had a "terrific childhood" and grew up to be a scientist instead of a psychopath. Having a gene for violence doesn't, in itself, make a person violent; the gene needs to be triggered by trauma. A body of research

FIGURE 3.4 | SOCIETY AND BIOLOGY CONTINUOUSLY INFLUENCE EACH OTHER

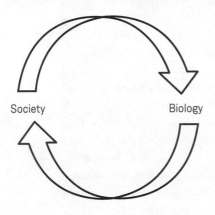

Society   Biology

has confirmed this finding.[66] Living in a happy home with loving parents decreases the likelihood that a person genetically predisposed to aggression will become aggressive. In contrast, poverty, a dysfunctional family life, and abuse all increase the chances that the genes for aggression will be "turned on" and lead to violent behavior. Genes matter in that a person without a genetic predisposition for violence probably won't grow up to be violent, even if that individual suffers trauma.[67] A person with the genetic predisposition may or may not; it all depends on the quality of his or her life.

As with genes, our hormones don't simply cause us to act in certain ways. Instead, the production of hormones in our bodies is closely tied to the experiences we're having with others through **hormonal feedback loops**. Hormone levels don't just influence us to do things; the things we do also influence our hormone levels. Testosterone, for instance, rises and falls in response to our interactions. If we are anticipating a competition, our levels will rise. If we win the contest, they'll go up further; if we lose, they'll go down.[68] This is true for sports games and games like chess, too.[69] It also works if we're just sitting on the couch watching our favorite team win or lose.[70] If we do something we think is cool—like drive a sports car—our testosterone gets a bump; if we do it in front of other people, it bumps even higher.[71]

The feedback loop is different for everyone. If we don't particularly care about sports or sports cars, the experience won't have the same effect.[72] Neither will the experience of competition if, it turns out, we're not particularly competitive.[73] Our interactions with (real and imaginary) others, then, influence our testosterone levels, which pump us up for competition and make us feel good if we win. If we care, that is. A neuroscientist summarizing the research on the effects of our experiences on testosterone levels concludes that the levels are so dependent on other things that hormonal "responses to victory or defeat are highly idiosyncratic."[74] Idiosyncratic but gendered; because certain symbols for cool are socially constructed in gendered ways, things like sports cars have different types of meaning to men and women on average.

A man's social environment can depress his testosterone levels, too. Single men have higher levels of testosterone than men in stable, committed relationships. This isn't because men with high testosterone levels are less interested in

If fathers are actively involved with their children, their bodies respond in ways that help them be good dads.

settling down. Instead, the settling down produces a decline in testosterone.[75] Having a baby can bring that testosterone level down even more.[76] A study of two communities in Tanzania found that such hormonal shifts can happen at the group level, too.[77] Hadza men were involved fathers, taking care of children alongside women. Datoga men did not parent, leaving the work to mothers. The difference in behavior was reflected in their testosterone levels: On average, Datoga men had higher levels than Hadza men.

Genes and hormones also contribute to the greater size and strength of men's bones and muscles, but even these building blocks of our bodies are dependent on the environment. Muscularity is determined, biologically, by the number and size of muscle fibers. While the number of fibers is fixed in childhood, the size and strength of muscle fibers respond to training, and most of the difference in men's and women's musculature is related to the latter.[78] Growth is determined, in part, by hormones, which contribute to men's larger muscles, but also by use. Without the proper physical activity, muscles will remain small. The anthropologist Margaret Mead, observing Balinese men in 1949, wrote that while they had the same potential to build muscle as other men, their cultural practices left their arm muscles undeveloped:

The arms of the men are almost as free of heavy muscle as those of the women....
They prefer to carry rather than lift, and to summon many hands to every task....
If we knew no other people than the Balinese we would never guess that men were
so made that they could develop heavy muscles.[79]

Just as men can live in ways that leave their arm muscles small, regardless of their biological predisposition, what women do with their muscles is also dependent on their societies. Consider marathons. Women were formally excluded from competing in marathons for almost 100 years. In that time, men got much faster (the current record holder beat the winner of the first marathon, held in 1896, by almost an hour). When women were first allowed to compete, they were much slower than men, but they've gotten faster, too. In fact, they've gotten faster much faster than the men. Men took approximately thirty years to shave thirty minutes off their best time; it took women only five.[80] Today the men's record is still faster than the women's record, but by less than ten minutes (Figure 3.5).

And, yes, we are gendered to the bone.[81] Men have 20 to 30 percent greater bone mass and strength than women, making women twice as likely to break a bone and four times as likely to be diagnosed with osteoporosis.[82] Genes and hormones contribute to this discrepancy, but an individual's bone health is also strongly related to other things about their lives: social class, race, gender, and culture as well as diet, leisure activities, and type of work.[83] Among ultra-Orthodox Jewish adolescent boys, for example, the gender pattern is reversed.

FIGURE 3.5 | MARATHON WORLD RECORDS BY GENDER

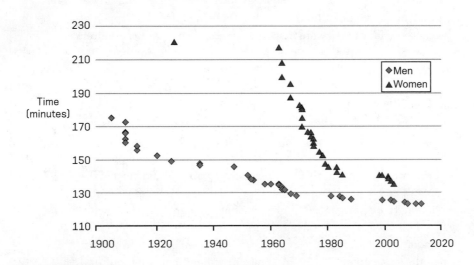

Source: International Association of Athletics Federations

Boys in these communities are tasked with intensive study of religious documents from a young age, so they spend much less time exercising than other boys their age. As a result, their bones never grow as strong as even those of their sisters, who have lighter study loads. If women have, on average, weaker bones, it is because we *embody* our culture. Biology is, literally, the flesh and blood (and bones) of society.

All this is true of our brains, too.[84] Our brains change dramatically over our life span in response to whatever challenges and opportunities we give them. Our brain's ability to respond to the environment is called **brain plasticity**. The development of our senses is a great example. We aren't born with the ability to process sight, sound, and touch. Instead, our brain has to learn how to interpret the data from our senses; it has to be trained. The brain of a person who is born deaf, for example, won't develop the ability to process sound. Even if, as an adult, they are given a cochlear implant that allows them to hear, their brain will not be able to make sense of sound—the sound will register as undifferentiated noise—because it's never been trained to do so.[85]

A person with a sensory deficit, however, may use the part of the brain originally allocated for that task to do something else. The part of the brain devoted to sight in a blind person will simply be devoted to some other task, like memorizing the spatial layout of rooms, reading Braille, or maximizing the ability to attend to sounds and smells. In some instances, people can teach the brain to do remarkable things. A boy named Ben Underwood learned to see like a bat. After losing his sight at the age of three, he trained his brain to echolocate, clicking with his tongue and listening for the echoes off the objects around him.[86] Using echolocation, Underwood could safely skateboard through crowded streets and play team sports. Others have also developed this extraordinary ability.

Remember those kids playing *Tetris*? Consistent with what we know about brain plasticity, the change in ability manifests itself in our neuroanatomy. In one study, the brains of twelve- to fifteen-year-old girls were measured before and after a three-month period during which they played *Tetris* for an hour and a half each week.[87] At the end, their brains were heavier and showed enhanced cortical thickness, with heightened blood flow to the area. Changes in the brain have been documented in response to a wide range of activities: juggling, dancing, singing, meditating, and even driving a taxi.[88] The ability of the brain to respond to the demands of its environment may also help explain the Flynn effect, a strong and consistent rise in IQ scores all over the world.[89]

In sum, the two important variables defining our humanity might not be male and female but complexity and flexibility. It's the ability of our bodies to adapt and respond, sometimes in surprising ways, to whatever environment we encounter. This adaptability helps explain why it's so difficult to establish biological causes of observed gender differences as well as their immutability. Gendered bodies contribute to (at least some of) those differences, but gendered

Fifteen-year-old Ben Underwood is blind but skillfully roller-blades around his neighborhood without incident thanks to his developed use of echolocation. His self-training is a fascinating example of brain plasticity at work.

bodies are also the result of the social conditions in which we find ourselves. And these differences and similarities between women's and men's bodies and environments—and any relationship between them—is also filtered through life experiences that are not centrally about gender, like social class; race and ethnicity; whether you live in the country or the city; the quality of your education; your diet and health; and whether you have parents who help you with your schoolwork, play ball with you, or neither. Biology matters, gender matters, society matters, and they all work together to make us the people we are.

Revisiting the Question

 The gender binary might be an ideology, but there are real differences between men and women, right?

As H. L. Mencken famously observed: "There is always an easy solution to every human problem—neat, plausible, and wrong."[90] It would be easy to say that the gender differences we observe are biological and immutable. It would be equally easy to say that they are cultural and easily undone. Neither is true.

Instead, both the gender differences and similarities we see are the result of a complex interplay between biology and society. These dynamic intersections are progressive (each moment we are someone slightly different than the moment before), contingent (what happens is dependent on what is happening both inside and around us), and probabilistic (making it more likely for some outcomes to occur and less likely for others but never entirely determining the future). To paraphrase Edward O. Wilson, biology has us on a leash, but the leash is very, very long.[91]

The gender binary—the one that characterizes men and women as "opposite sexes"—simply doesn't do justice to what we know about human beings. For the remainder of this book, then, it's important not to fall back on "plausible" biological explanations that offer simple answers. We're an extraordinary species with a rich sociocultural life, and our bodies have been designed to respond to it.

Next . . .

While the focus on human possibility in this chapter may be inspiring, it still seems like there is quite a bit of gender conformity out there in the real world. In the next chapter, we'll address one of the mechanisms that contributes to the gendered patterns that you see. We'll ask:

If men and women aren't naturally opposite, then why do they act so differently so much of the time?

It's time to put the "social" in social theory.

FOR FURTHER READING

Cherney, Isabelle D. "Mom, Let Me Play More Computer Games: They Improve My Mental Rotation Skills." *Sex Roles* 59 (2008): 776–86.

Fine, Cordelia. *Delusions of Gender: How Our Minds, Society, and Neurosexism Create Difference*. London, UK: Icon Books, 2011.

Guiso, Luigi, Ferdinando Monte, Paola Sapienza, and Luigi Zingales. "Culture, Gender, and Math." *Science* 320, no. 5880 (2009): 1164–65.

Hyde, Janet. "The Gender Similarities Hypothesis." *American Psychologist* 60, no. 6 (2005): 581–92.

Wade, Lisa. "Sex Shocker: Men and Women Aren't That Different." *Salon*, September 18, 2013.

AS FAR AS I'M CONCERNED,
BEING ANY GENDER IS A DRAG.

—PATTI SMITH

4

Performances

In the last chapter, we reviewed what we know about the role of biology in contributing to the gender binary. After searching our genes, hormones, and brains for the source of our differences, we concluded that while men and women may not be biologically identical, we're not particularly dimorphic either. We've also conceded that we do act in gendered ways much of the time, leading us to pose the question:

 Q+A   **If men and women aren't naturally opposite, then why do they act so differently so much of the time?**

Indeed, men and women do seem to be quite different in their *choices* about how to use their time and effort, often in ways that match stereotypical expectations. Women, for example, are four times as likely to major in education as men, while men are five times more likely to major in engineering.[1] Likewise, women are more likely than men to learn to dance and sing. Men tend to stick to sports and, if they become musicians, they're more likely to pick up an instrument than use their voice.

Even though we are rather similar, then, we make divergent choices much of the time. These choices apply to an amazing range of activities and are both obvious and subtle. There are gender differences even in how people look at their fingernails (with their hand held out or with the palm turned toward the face and the fingers curled in), how one holds a cigarette (between the thumb and forefinger or between two forefingers with the palm facing in), and how we hold hands with a partner of the other sex (men's palms are usually pointed backward and women's pointed forward such that her body is placed just slightly behind his as they walk). So, there are many differences between men and women in *practice*.

This chapter explains such gendered social patterns as a consequence of social interaction instead of biological or psychological predisposition. We learn complex sets of gendered expectations that tell us how to behave as men and women in varying situations. While we sometimes act in gendered ways out of habit, we also come to understand that if we fail to do so, others may tease, hassle, or hurt us. We aren't, then, simply socialized as children into gendered roles that we then passively perform as adults. Instead, the process of acquiring a gendered sense of self is an active and ongoing one. We will negotiate gender with other people throughout our lives.

None of us, however, simply follows gendered expectations blindly. We become crafty manipulators. We make exceptions (for ourselves and others), and we apply very different standards depending on the situation and the person. In response, we each develop a way of managing gendered expectations that works for us as unique individuals.

Still, because it's easier to obey gender rules than break them—and life is challenging enough as it is—many of us behave in gendered ways most of the time. Whatever strategy we choose, we all contribute to those gendered patterns that we see around us. These patterns sustain the illusion that gender stereotypes are "real," but they also frequently create the impetus for social change.

HOW TO DO GENDER

Psychologist Sandra Bem's four-year-old son, Jeremy, decided to wear barrettes to preschool one day. Bem recalls:

> *Several times that day, another little boy insisted that Jeremy must be a girl because "only girls wear barrettes." After repeatedly insisting that "wearing barrettes doesn't matter; being a boy means having a penis and testicles," Jeremy finally pulled down his pants to make his point more convincingly. The other boy was not impressed. He simply said, "Everybody has a penis; only girls wear barrettes."*[2]

Jeremy's schoolmate stated his objection in the form of a general rule. It wasn't that *he* didn't like it when boys wore barrettes, or that *Jeremy specifically* didn't look fetching in a barrette, it was: *Only girls wear barrettes.* Jeremy's schoolmate articulated a rule for all boys that Jeremy had unwittingly broken.

Sociologists use the phrase **doing gender** to describe the ways in which we actively obey and break gender rules. **Gender rules** are instructions for how to appear and behave as a man or a woman. They are, essentially, the social construction of gender re-stated in the form of an instruction. You could likely brainstorm dozens or hundreds of such rules if you tried. They apply to every area of our lives, specifying how we should decorate our homes, what hobbies and careers we should pursue, with whom we should socialize and how, and much more. Some rules are relatively rigid (e.g., men do not wear makeup), while others are more flexible (e.g., men take showers instead of baths).

Cross- and Intra-Cultural Variation in Gender Rules

Most gender rules are simple cultural agreements. For instance, whereas grown men in the United States are supposed to physically touch each other only in very ritualized ways (e.g., the back slap in the "man hug" or the butt slap in football that means a job well done), in France and Argentina, among other places,

President George W. Bush welcomes Saudi Crown Prince Abdullah to his Texas ranch. Holding hands is not an accepted way for two adult men to touch in the United States but is a common practice in some Middle Eastern cultures.

heterosexual men exchange friendly kisses of greeting. In some Middle Eastern societies, men even hold hands.

Likewise, whereas skirts are strongly feminized in the United States, men wear kilts in Scotland and, in Arab countries, mean wear a white robe called a *thawb*, often with a pink-and-white head covering. The color pink doesn't have feminine connotations in Arab countries the way it does in the West. And in Belgium, pink isn't gender neutral; it's for boys. Flowers are another icon of femininity in the West, but certain floral patterns on a kimono clearly signal masculinity in Japan.

What women and men *don't* wear is also dictated by gender rules. In the United States, it is against the rules for women to expose their breasts in public. We take this so seriously that whether women should be allowed to breastfeed in public is still a hot debate. This obsession with hiding women's nipples seems unduly conservative from a European standpoint; in some parts of Europe, it is perfectly acceptable for women to sunbathe topless. Americans might be surprised to hear that Europeans describe Americans as irrationally prudish. Many Americans, as well as Europeans, in turn, condemn the "veiling" practices associated with Islam. Of course, many U.S. subcultures—like the Amish and Orthodox Jews—also value modesty for women, requiring that they cover their hair and arms and wear long dresses. Only because the idiosyncrasies of our own culture tend to be invisible to us does it seem obvious that women should cover some parts of their bodies, like their breasts, but not other parts, like their faces or hair.

It often isn't until we travel to or read about a new society or alternative subculture that we encounter rules that are unfamiliar to us, revealing our own rules as culturally contingent. This is the very definition of culture shock.

Historical Variation in Gender Rules

No matter how severe our culture shock, we can often adjust to new gender rules without too much trouble. We are good at such adjustments because we get practice throughout our lives. Gender rules are constantly undergoing both subtle and dramatic shifts.

Consider the earring. An American girl born in the 1930s would likely have worn clip-on earrings.[3] Pierced ears fell out of favor in the 1920s and were, at the time, preferred only by Italian and Spanish women (for whom it was an ethnic practice, similar to the small dot or *bindi* that Hindu women wear on their foreheads) and, oddly, male sailors (who hoped that a gold earring might serve as payment for a proper burial were they to sink, wash ashore, and be found by strangers). Clip-on earrings, however, were passé by the 1960s when pierced ears came back into fashion. Our hypothetical girl, then, might not have gotten her ears pierced until about the age of thirty.

If our hypothetical girl were a boy, he probably wouldn't have worn earrings of any kind. When his sister and all her friends were getting their ears pierced, the only men doing so were hippies and homosexuals. Twenty years later, during the '80s, male musicians and athletes popularized wearing earrings, but only in the left ear. If our now-fifty-year-old man decided to get an ear pierced, he would have gotten it in the left ear if he were straight and the right ear if he were gay. By the time our hypothetical man was seventy, though, the side of the head would be irrelevant: Young men around him would be piercing their left, their right, and even both ears. And these piercings would have signified, essentially, nothing.

Today, both men and women pierce their ears, but *how* we do so is quite different (reflecting a subdivision of the gender binary). Whereas women are more likely to wear either elaborate or dainty earrings to signify femininity, men typically wear simple studs or ear plugs. And now we pierce other things, too—in gendered ways, of course. Belly-button piercings are found almost exclusively on women, whereas men are more likely to stretch their earlobes with plugs.

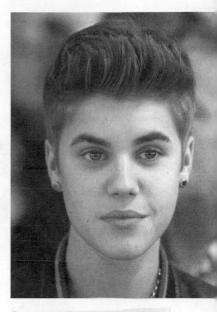

Justin Bieber debuted earrings at the 2011 MTV awards. At one time this would have led to speculation about his sexual orientation, but pierced ears have lost their cultural association with homosexuality.

Earrings are a great example of the way that gender rules change, sometimes in ways that seem quite arbitrary. Rules also change from context to context.

Contextual Variation in Gender Rules

Many of us take for granted the rules that guide our own gender display and easily adapt to cultural change. Our flexibility tends to mask the fact that the United States itself is a turbulent mixture of subcultures. Accordingly, doing gender, even in our daily lives, requires that we simultaneously know the rules of the cultural mainstream as well as those of the subcultures we visit. In other words, we need more than one pair of gender binary glasses.

Goths are a striking example. Ann Wilkins, who studied a group of self-identified Goths in the northeastern United States, explains that they flout conventional gender expectations. Both women and men strive to attain a distinctive, even frightening appearance:

> Goths tell the world and each other who they are by making their bodies freaky. Goth bodies are cloaked in black, pierced, tattooed, dyed, powdered white. The Goth style juxtaposes medieval romanticism with bondage wear; puffy velvet

Attendees at a Gothic festival in Poland congregate, showing off their unique fashion. They likely tone down their appearance when in less Goth-tolerant settings.

with skin-tight PVC. Goths may sport dog collars and spikes, or fishnets and corsets—all in somber colors: black or blood red.[4]

Goths cultivate a countercultural appearance, but they also go to work at places like banks and elementary schools. Some of them "do Goth" all the time, but most will adjust to more mainstream expectations when necessary, washing off the white powder and covering their tattoos with a cardigan when at work.

Goths are an extreme example of **cultural traveling**, moving from one cultural or subcultural context to another and sometimes back. Many of us adjust our look for different audiences. We all make cultural adjustments throughout our day and week. A guy driving home from a night at the sports bar with his buddies, during which he yelled at the TV, threw back beers, and pounded the table, will likely resort to a polite and professional manner when pulled over by a cop. Both of these self-presentations are versions of masculinity. Likewise, a college student may comfort crying children at her job at a day care center, look to hook up at a party that night, and drag herself to class the next morning prepared to discuss the week's reading. In each context, she does a different version of femininity: the nurturer, the flirt, the smart girl.

The gender rules that apply to varying contexts can be quite nuanced. Knowing exactly what style and behavior rules are appropriate for a wedding (is it a day or night wedding?), a first date (is it coffee or dinner?), and a job interview (do you want to project creativity or reliability?) requires sophisticated calculations. Nevertheless, most of us make these cultural transitions easily, often flawlessly. And thank goodness. People who are incapable of "tuning" their behavior are at risk of coming off as psychologically disturbed or willfully deviant. The same glowing, silver gown that made an actress seem so glamorous on the red carpet at the Oscars would make her look drunk or deranged if she were to wear it at the grocery store the next morning.

We learn a set of gender rules that are specific to our societies. We also learn how that set of gender rules varies—from the funeral home to the classroom, from Savannah to San Francisco, and from age eight to eighty—and how to adjust to those changes. We don't just get a pair of gender binary glasses when we're kids; we get many pairs. And we're constantly getting new prescriptions as needed.

LEARNING THE RULES

Our First Prescription

Since different gender rules apply to different situations and change over time, learning how to do gender appropriately is not easy. Children learn gender from infancy.[5] They can tell the difference between male and female voices by six months old and between men and women in photographs by nine months old. By the time they're one, they know to associate deep voices with men and high voices with women. By two and a half, most children know what sex they are and are "reaching out to social norms"; they are trying to learn the rules and their brains are built to absorb everything around them.[6] By three years old, they tend to prefer play partners of their own sex and think more positively about their own group compared to the other.

Parents show children that gender matters by teaching them that they are a boy or a girl. Teachers separate school activities and games into boys vs. girls; community and school sports are usually sex segregated, such that girls and boys rarely play alongside or against each other.[7] All these things affirm for children that the distinction is important and meaningful. This is a child's first pair of gender binary glasses. "By the age of 5," psychologists Carol Martin and Diane Ruble write, "children develop an impressive constellation of stereotypes about gender (often amusing and incorrect) that they apply to themselves and others."[8]

Once children have a pair of gender binary glasses, they begin to act in ways that reflect the view, especially if their parents reward gender-stereotype-consistent behavior.[9] They orient themselves to toys they believe are gender appropriate and begin to make assumptions about other people based on their gender. Divisions between boys and girls in play become more strict and defined. Understanding the logic of the gender binary, they try to apply it even to gender-neutral items on the assumption that everything must be gendered. "Men eat pizza and women don't," announced a four-year-old to his parents on the way home from an Italian restaurant.[10]

As children absorb (or invent) new ideas about how girls and boys are supposed to act, they become increasingly rigid about doing things "right." This rigidity peaks around age six, which is exactly when many parents throw their hands up and give their daughters Barbie dolls and sons toy guns. Though this rigidity is often used as evidence that gender is biological, psychologists have shown that it is largely because children aren't yet capable of absorbing and negotiating the rules in their complexity.[11] Childhood rigidity is a learning phase more than proof of biological predispositions toward firepower and fashion.[12] As children learn that gender norms are not quite so strict, they become much more flexible about their own and others' conformity to gender expectations.

Even so, children are not passive recipients of gender socialization. They also actively resist it and, as the story about Jeremy's barrette suggests, they teach each other the rules they (think they) know. Children, then, are participants in their own and others' socialization. We are all negotiating gender rules from the get-go and setting up consequences for one another.

Lifelong Learning

Later, as adults, we navigate gender rules in more sophisticated ways. We become more tolerant of ambiguity and contradictions. But we continue to reach out to gender norms, continually learning and adjusting to new sets of gender rules that we encounter as we interact with new people, in new places, and across a changing social terrain. When we interact with children, we inevitably model and teach gender rules and, as we will explain next, we model and teach gender rules to adults around us as well.

Learning the rules, then, is a lifelong process that we actively negotiate. This means that an **injection model of socialization**, in which genderless children are "dosed" with a gender role in their childhood, never to fully recover, is wrong. Media commentators, when they bemoan the influence of violent video games and skinny actresses on young people, are using this culturalist model of socialization, one that assumes that children are victims of their environment, infected with rigid versions of masculinity or femininity. Children, it is presumed, are exposed to gender roles by "sick" adults and a "diseased" media when their immune system is weak; then they live with the virus for the rest of their lives.

Tess, shown here among her many pink possessions, plays out the learned gender norm of girls preferring that color to all others. Not every girl is as over the top as Tess in defining herself through pink possessions, but today young girls learn that pink is for girls.

This model of socialization fails on three fronts. First, it suggests that socialization is somehow finished by the time we're adults and doesn't account for our ability to learn new sets of rules and adjust to changing ones. Second, it leaves no room for the possibility that we actively consider and resist gender rules, something that Jeremy was doing even in preschool. Third, because the model fails to give people credit for actively resisting and changing gender rules, the injection model can't explain cultural changes, such as the ones that made pierced ears acceptable at different times for women and men.

Accordingly, sociologists prefer a **learning model of socialization** that suggests that socialization is a lifelong process of learning and re-learning gendered expectations as well as how to negotiate them. Unlike the injection model, the learning model reflects the need to adjust constantly to new contexts as we age, travel, and try new things. We don't *get* socialized once and for all but are constantly *being* socialized to a shifting social terrain.

The learning model gives us credit for being *smart* members of our culture. Because it recognizes that we are socialized to know the rules instead of to act out a role, it acknowledges our ability to think critically about and even reject rules. We aren't cultural dupes; we are cultural *experts* who consciously and strategically adapt our behavior to changes in the social fabric. We do this in negotiation with others who also have some intellectual autonomy from the rules. This is a much more social understanding of socialization than the injection model, which posits a one-way communication from adult to child. We do gender together, learning to manage conflict along the way (usually without resorting to dropping our pants like Jeremy).

Like the contents of the gender binary, then, the rules only *seem* simple and stable over time. Rather, they are complicated, constantly shifting, and even contradictory. Their complexity, however, provides us with little excuse when we do not conform to what others expect.

WHY WE FOLLOW THE RULES

We follow gender rules for a wide range of reasons, including habit, pleasure, and, importantly, the reactions we expect or receive from others.

Habit

Sometimes we follow gender rules simply because they are part of our culture. We become habituated to them. We get used to walking and sitting in a certain way, own a wardrobe of already appropriately gendered clothes, and have experiences in rewarding gendered activities. Practice allows us to do gender with-out even thinking about it. Psychologists call such behaviors "over-learned"; they are learned not only by our minds but by our bodies—like riding a bike or typing on a keyboard—so we no longer need to think about them. Men's shirts, for example, are typically made so that the buttons are along the right and the button holes along the left; women's shirts are typically made in the opposite way. When is the last time you had to stop and think about the relative location of the buttons and button holes on your clothes while getting dressed? Your hands just automatically go to the right places.

Once we have over-learned a rule, we don't experience it as oppressive but as natural, however arbitrary it may be. Accordingly, it's often *easy* to follow gender rules, especially ones that are fundamental in our culture; we mostly do so unconsciously. American men don't often deliberate, for instance, about whether to pee sitting down or standing up. This is something they have learned (only after being potty trained in the sitting position), but now mostly take for granted. Men in Germany and Japan are much more likely to pee sitting down and whether to do so is more of a conscious choice.

On the flip side, it never occurs to most American women to pee standing up, even though, with enough practice, the majority could probably do so with little mess (or, at least, no more mess than that frequently left behind by men). In some parts of the world, such as Ghana, women do stand up to pee. Many of the gender rules that we follow are simply a matter of habit.

Pleasure

More than simply being habitual, following gender rules can be quite pleasur-able. For a man who has over-learned conventional American masculinity, it is rewarding to enact that masculinity at a sports bar with the guys. He knows the script, the beer tastes great, and his team might win. The same is true for enacting those aspects of femininity that are over-learned. Many women, for instance, enjoy dressing up, dancing, and flirting at a club.

For just this reason, we may especially enjoy opportunities to do gender elaborately. You may relish formal events like quinceañeras, bar and bat mitz-vahs, your high school prom, and weddings. These events all call for strongly gendered displays: suits or tuxedos for men, dresses or gowns for women. It can be fun to pamper yourself at the salon, bring flowers to your date, and open doors or have them opened for you. It feels great to know that you look especially beautiful in your dress or unusually dashing in your tux. Success is intrinsically rewarding, and that is no less true when the success comes from performing gender.

A group of high schoolers in New Orleans performs gender with flair. Their floor-length gowns and pressed suits reflect the heightened salience of gender at prom.

However, there is a dark side to these success stories. Following rules creates cultural boundaries that are often painful for the people who are on the wrong side of them, by choice or circumstance. Sociologist Michael Kimmel says it beautifully:

> *For some of us, becoming adult men and women in our society is a smooth and almost effortless drifting into behaviors and attitudes that feel as familiar to us as our skin. And for others of us, becoming masculine or feminine is an interminable torture, a nightmare in which we must brutally suppress some parts of ourselves to please others—or, simply, to survive. For most of us, though, the experience falls somewhere in between.*[13]

The American guy who hates football or has a gluten allergy to beer sometimes feels like an outsider. So, too, does the woman who wants to wear a tux to the prom or can't walk in heels. The American man whose body is limber and powerful and who loves to dance to classical music may in fact train rigorously to be a ballet dancer, but he follows these pleasures at the risk of critical assessments from others that question his gender, his nationality, or his sexuality: He's not a real man, or a real American, and he's probably gay. Likewise, women who are tall and strong and enjoy playing basketball sometimes find that the pleasures of their own bodies can come at a cost to their social life if others judge them to be "unfeminine." We follow the rules voluntarily both out of habit and for pleasure, but also because there are consequences for breaking them.

Policing

Jeremy's schoolmate felt confident that he was entitled to enforce an unwritten rule about barrettes. Despite Jeremy's protestations, his schoolmate remained insistent that boys don't wear barrettes. Breaking the rules can attract negative attention. Sociologists use the term **gender policing** to describe responses to the violation of gender rules aimed at promoting conformity.

When we are policed, we are being taught that we should learn the rules, that these rules warrant conformity, and that we can expect consequences for breaking them. Gender policing happens every day. It comes from our friends, our love interests, our parents, bosses, and mentors. It's part of our daily lives. Some of it can be brutal and painful (especially for people who don't fit in binary boxes), but much of it is friendly and humorous or takes the form of teasing. Consider these stories from our students:

- As James came in from a Saturday night with friends, his father warned, "Get to bed. We're going to the woods tomorrow." "Nah, Dad," the son replied. "I can't." His dad began to tease him, saying: "What? You too good to go huntin' with your dad now?"
- Chandra goes to her economics class wearing sweats, a ponytail, and no makeup. A guy with whom she has been flirting all semester says to her, humorously, "I guess I'm not important enough to dress up for!"
- Sun, waiting in line to use a single-stall bathroom, sees that the men's bathroom is open and starts toward it. As she walks in, her friend says, "You're not going to use the *men's* bathroom, are you!?"

In each of these stories, a person breaks a culturally and historically specific gender rule and is then subjected to policing. In the first example, James's disinterest in going to the woods with his dad broke a rule common in rural working-class communities: *Men should want to hunt.* When Chandra's guy friend used her appearance to remind her that he was interested in her, he affirmed a rule common among young singles: *Women should dress up for men they want to impress.* Sun's friend expressed surprise that she would dare to use a restroom labeled "Men." Whenever there are two bathrooms, even if they each include only one toilet, the rule is clear: *Use the appropriate gender designated bathroom.*

A raised eyebrow, a derisive laugh, or a comment like "Are you sure you want to wear that?" are small prices to pay for the freedom to be ourselves. But policing isn't always so mild or so fleeting. When women are called "dyke" or "bitch," they are often being policed for being strong or assertive, characteristics that a binary lens sees as masculine and unacceptable for women. Conversely, when men are called "pussy" or "girl," they are often being accused of not being strong or assertive, and in the logic of the gender binary, that means not masculine. The phrase "nice guys finish last" refers, in part, to women's participation in this same gender policing by showing a preference for dating men who practice emotional unavailability. Guys who work hard to have a muscular upper body, like women who hide their strength or act deferential when men are around, are using the rules to win friends and protect themselves from censure.

The risks of nonconformity may be much higher than attracting ridicule or being unpopular. We may fear losing friends, lovers, or the support of our parents. We may be fired or passed over for jobs or promotions because our gender display doesn't please clients or co-workers. Gender policing can also be emotionally and physically brutal. The FBI reported 1,572 victims of hate crimes against gays, lesbians, and transgender people in 2011.[14] Gays and lesbians break the rule: *Men should have sex with women and women should have sex with men.* Transgender people break the rule: *People's gender performance should match their apparent biological sex.* It may be odd to think that hate crimes against transgender, gay, and lesbian people are a form of *gender* policing, but they often are. People who cross-dress earnestly, with the intent to pass as the other sex, challenge gender rules and undermine other people's ability to determine their sex in a binary way. People who are committed to a gender binary *trust* these signs as markers of something real and important about others, so they may feel betrayed and act violently to punish people whom they feel are essentially lying to them. Violent gender policing may also aim to produce conformity to the rules by those unwilling to follow them.

Because the rules themselves vary situationally, so does their policing. It is certainly dangerous to be queer in some contexts, but it can be quite fun at Halloween or at friendly gay bars. Middle school boys who study hard may be subjected to constant taunts of "fag," but if they adopt the tough guy performance those taunts are designed to elicit, they may be policed by their teachers and parents. Female athletes may be told to be aggressive on the field but policed toward more traditional gender performances off it. Girls may be pushed to concentrate on their school work and aspire to high-powered careers while at the same time be expected not to be overbearing around their male peers. What happens later when they're asked to deprioritize their own careers in favor of their husbands'?

We, like Jeremy, are policed into multiple and even contradictory gender displays by people with various, often clashing agendas. Some people have more

In this still from makeover show *What Not to Wear*, fashion consultant Stacy London makes a face as her co-host, Clinton Kelly, holds up a "frumpy" item from the wardrobe of actress Mayim Bialik. TV shows like this one teach us all that others will judge us if we don't do femininity or masculinity "right."

influence than others: Policing is more influential if it comes from someone you care for (like your girlfriend or boyfriend) or who has power over you (such as your boss). We also police ourselves, kindly and cruelly. We watch TV and read fashion blogs to learn how, and how not, to dress. We read the sports section to make sure we can talk about who won the big game last night and why. We stand in front of the mirror and inspect our faces, scrutinize our bodies for too much or not enough hair, and hope for bumps and bulges in gender-appropriate places.

We inspect our behavior no less than our bodies: Were we too loud or forward? Too meek or agreeable? Sometimes we call ourselves ugly names or feel shame or disgust. We punish our bodies with overexercise or starvation. We police our words and our tone of voice, watching to ensure that we don't sound too opinionated (if we're women) or too emotional (if we're men). We may force ourselves to major in engineering when we'd really like to take more literature classes because we know we'll later be judged by the size of our paycheck; or we may choose to stay single because our guy friends will never let us hear the end of it if we let them know we're actually in love with that girl or that we're gay; or we may not say anything to the guy we like about the other women he's sleeping with because we fear being called "needy."

We even recruit others to help us police ourselves. We ask each other to evaluate our bodies, our clothes, and our interactions with others: Do I look fat in this dress? Do these shoes look gay? When women get ready for a party together, they frequently ask one another to assess their outfits, looking for a second opinion as to whether they are wearing just the right clothes. Many women try to follow this tricky rule: *Women should dress sexy but not slutty*. "You can wear a short skirt or a low-cut top," we hear, "but not both." There is nothing malevolent in this type of policing; it is simply women trying to help their friends follow the rules that they know apply to them.

We also use media, often unconsciously, to advertise and test gender rules with our friends and family. If you are commented *to*, but not commented *on*, you are still being instructed as to what is and is not acceptable, and these moments help clarify the (ever-changing) rules. When friends get together to watch the Oscars and snark at the outfits on the red carpet or take pleasure in laughing at the women on *Real Housewives*, they are telling one another what makes a person look good or be likeable. Often, our evaluations are gendered. Through these routines, we learn what our friends think is ugly, slutty, sloppy, gay, bitchy, weak, and gross and, accordingly, how we should and should not dress and act around them. Collective reactions to celebrity fashions and personalities, then, can serve to clarify and affirm rules.

And, of course, we participate in policing others directly. We create consequences for those who break the rules. We police others in the name of kindness. We feel we know the rules well and can cue in our friends and family members that they are at risk of being policed by someone less benevolent than we are. Other times we are more deeply disconcerted by rule breaking. We may give in to the temptation to be mean spirited or cruel in our policing when we are personally invested in the rule. We may even feel a sense of injustice or unfairness if the rules we follow—sometimes at a sacrifice—are broken by others who can do so without censure.

Because of policing, our choices about following the rules have real social consequences. Some are mild, some are severe, but they all shape the distribution of rewards and punishments. But—and this is a big "but"—we don't *always* choose to follow the rules; we also break the rules. In fact, we break them all the time.

So the complicated truth is that while we all know the rules, and often follow them, we also break them. How do we do this?

HOW TO BREAK THE RULES

All of us get away with some rule breaking. Breaking rules *is* doing gender. That is, doing gender is about more than just conformity. It's also about negotiating with the rules. In fact, people who *rigidly* conform to a single set of gender rules aren't often considered ideal men or women. Instead, they're often the butt of jokes (a dumb jock or ditzy blonde) or pitied for their one-dimensional lives (the ruthless CEO who never knew his kids or the full-time housewife who never discovered her other talents). Likewise, those who are vicious policers of others' behavior are called rude, intolerant, or worse.

We also break the rules because sometimes it is impossible to follow them, no matter how badly we would like to. The mother undergoing chemotherapy, for example, may not be able to care for her husband and children the way she feels she should; the man with a spinal cord injury, similarly, may not be able to perform sexually the way men are told they must. Likewise, the guy who is five foot two simply can't be taller than most women.

Other times, rules are downright contradictory, like the one that says that men should be able to drink a lot of alcohol but also remain in control. Or maybe we're part of a subculture that requires breaking the rules endorsed by the mainstream, like female farmers. Sometimes we literally can't afford to follow a rule, like the man who doesn't have the extra income to treat women on dates. Sometimes we break a particular rule just because following it is undesirable, like the man who loves romantic comedies. Or perhaps we don't like rules in general and rebel on principle.

So we need a mechanism that allows us to break rules with little or no consequence. How do we do it?

We have a creative way to get around the rules. Remember the three stories of policing discussed earlier in this chapter? In each case, it turns out, the rule breaker got away with breaking the rule, despite being policed. Each rule breaker avoided a greater penalty by offering an **account**, or an explanation for why they broke the rule that then excused their behavior. Let's revisit the stories, this time following them through to the end:

- As James came in from a Saturday night with friends, his father warned, "Get to bed. We're going to the woods tomorrow." "Nah, Dad," the son replied. "I can't." His dad began to tease him, saying: "What? You too good to go huntin' with your dad now?" James just said, "No, football tryouts are next week and I was gonna run drills with Mike in the morning." "Go get 'em, son," said his father.
- Chandra goes to her economics class wearing sweats, a ponytail, and no makeup. A guy with whom she has been flirting all semester says to her, humorously, "I guess I'm not important enough to dress up for!" And she smiles and replies, "Hey! I just came from the gym." He reassures her, "I figured. I was just kidding."
- Sun, waiting in line to use a single-stall bathroom, sees that the men's bathroom is open and starts toward it. As she walks in, her friend says,

"You're not going to use the *men's* bathroom, are you!?" Sun says, "I wouldn't, but I really have to go!" Her friend nods sympathetically.

As these stories illustrate, we can get away with breaking rules if we have a good excuse.

When the characters above say, "Football tryouts are next week," "I just came from the gym," or "I really have to go," they are offering an account to justify why they are breaking the rule. These accounts may or may not be true, but they offer a sufficient explanation to others that makes gender nonconformity *incidental* rather than *intentional*. If a person has a good account, he or she is likely to get away with it. In all these stories, the "policer" accepts the explanation, responding with "Go get 'em, son," "I was just kidding," or a sympathetic nod.

Accounting does more than excuse one's behavior. In these examples, as often happens, the speakers affirm the rule at the same time that they are explaining why an exception should be made in their specific case. So James is *really* saying: "[Of course I would go hunting], it's just that football tryouts are next week." Chandra is saying: "I [would have dressed up for class, but I] just came from the gym." And Sun is saying, "I wouldn't [use the men's bathroom normally], but I really have to go!"

These speakers didn't respond, "Actually I don't like hunting" or "Who says I can't come to class sloppy!" or "It's stupid that I can't use the men's bathroom!" Such responses reject the rules altogether. Confronting the rules head-on can cause conflict. Instead, if the rule breaker affirms the legitimacy of the rule, the policer is usually satisfied, and conflict can be avoided. Interestingly, affirmation of the rule often works just as well as a change in behavior; infractions are punished only when they aren't excused. That's why transsexuals are more likely to be victims of hate crimes than guys dressed up like women at Halloween. Halloween is an account. It is a way for men to say, "[I would never dress like a woman normally], but it's Halloween!" A transsexual has no such excuse. The Halloween reveler is an exception that proves the rule; the transsexual is an attack on the rule itself.

Accounting is a skill. Jeremy, our intrepid pants dropper, had not yet mastered the art of accounting. He wasn't sophisticated enough to negotiate his gender with his schoolmate and resorted instead to a rather primitive way of proving he was a boy. Explicit conflict over gender rule breaking is typical of younger kids who have just begun to learn the rules and haven't yet mastered the act of explaining violations away. In contrast, because we learn how to do it by watching others and practicing, adults tend to be quite good at offering accounts, though some of us are better at it than others.

In addition to learning the rules in all their variety, then, part of gender socialization is learning what exceptions and accounts are acceptable in the different social circles in which we move. We may tend to over-conform when we are in an unfamiliar setting, break lots of rules in a familiar setting, and even provide accounts for others when we know them or the setting well. "Ron must have lost his job," we might surmise. "I wonder how he feels being a stay-at-home dad." "Sandra is taking up the trumpet just like her big brother," we might comment. "Maybe the family can't afford another instrument."

Yet even when we have learned the art of accounting, there is always the risk that our accounts will fail. Our student Jeff told of his failed account:

> I told my guy friends I couldn't hang out with them because I was going to a movie with my girlfriend. They asked me what movie and I said, sheepishly, because I knew they were going to laugh at me: Sweet Home Alabama. They laughed hysterically because I was going to see a "chick flick."

Jeff broke a rule: *Guys don't watch chick flicks.* And his friends policed him by laughing. So Jeff offered an account, but it didn't work:

> Even though I really did want to see the movie, I said: "Because [my girlfriend] wants to see it, and if she's not happy, then I'm not happy." This just made them laugh at me more. "You're totally whipped!" they cried.

Jeff's account failed to excuse his rule breaking (seeing a chick flick) because it broke another gender rule about heterosexual relationships: *Men don't submit to their girlfriends' desires.* While Jeff's account might have worked in an all-girl or mixed-gender group, his account didn't work with this particular group of young, single men.

Higher social status usually provides greater immunity from others' policing. Those of us who think more quickly on our feet, are opinion leaders among our peers, or are exceptionally well liked or charismatic can get away with an amazing amount of rule breaking. You probably know someone who gets a pass on rules. And some people like to test the rules more than others, trying to see how much they can get away with. We all probably know someone like this, too, just as we know people who are extremely risk averse. All of us, though, break the rules at least a little bit. We sometimes make strategic gambles, breaking the rules in situations where we suspect we won't get ribbed too hard or when the stakes are low.

Like following the rules, breaking the rules can be fun, empowering, and rewarding. The risks of breaking a rule may be outweighed by the value of doing something you want or nudging the world toward a future society you'd like to see. When a woman wears sweats and a baggy T-shirt to class, she sends the message that she doesn't care what anyone else thinks, and that can be empowering. Wearing sweats and a baggy T-shirt, however, is only defiant in the context of a rule against doing so. So breaking rules doesn't mean you're "free" from

Thanks to her lovable personality, comedienne and talk show host Ellen DeGeneres gets a pass on strict gender rules. Her talk show continues to attract record numbers of audience members, even as she dons menswear and keeps her hair short.

them. It is as much a reaction to the rules as following them. Even the shape of rebellion, then, is determined by the gender binary and its dictates.

Because we can't or don't want to follow gender rules, we break them quite frequently. We can get away with breaking gender rules fairly easily most of the time, so long as we offer a good excuse for doing so, one that affirms the rule that is being broken. All of this affirmation, then, makes the rules seem legitimate and true. That is, we manage to simultaneously break and affirm the rules, making it seem like everyone buys into them, while still accommodating a wide range of both male and female behavior.

THE NO. 1 GENDER RULE

The rules vary across cultures, subcultures, and history; intersect with other identities; and vary in strength. But one rule transcends all identities and is true across cultures and subcultures and throughout recent history. That rule is *do gender*. No matter how you do gender, doing it is compulsory if you want to be treated like an integrated member of society, a person whom others want to know, work with, play with, and love. In the West, this generally means that you *must* identify as male or female, not both, and not something else. And you *must* perform a culturally recognizable form of masculinity or femininity that matches your genitals, especially if you could conceivably pass as the other sex and/or naturally look a little androgynous.

If you do not do gender, you become **culturally unintelligible**. You will be so outside the symbolic-meaning system that people will not know how to interact with you. This is the experience of one sociologist, Betsy Lucal, an androgynous-looking woman who doesn't do femininity. She writes:

> *Using my credit cards sometimes is a challenge. Some clerks subtly indicate their disbelief, looking from the card to me and back at the card and checking my signature carefully. Others challenge my use of the card, asking whose it is or demanding identification. One cashier asked to see my driver's license and then asked me whether I was the son of the cardholder. Another clerk told me that my signature on the receipt "had better match" the one on the card.*[15]

What Lucal understands all too well is that if you really don't or can't do gender, it is a serious communicative crisis for everyone interacting with you. Accordingly, most of us do gender at least a little bit. It preserves our membership in our cultural community and ensures that those around us treat us with a modicum of benevolence.

This need to be culturally intelligible is why we see gendered social patterns. We see them because everyone is doing gender. We may not do it all the time, we may not do it enthusiastically, and we may not do it in the same way, but we do it. And while the weak rules are followed inconsistently, the strong rules are followed by almost everyone who is capable of following them. And the strongest rule of all—the rule to do gender—has nearly 100 percent compliance.

Thus, while the contents of the gender binary are constantly jumbled as we move across time and space, the binary itself persists. It persists in our minds (because we fashion our perception of the world to match it); it persists in our bodies (because we adorn and manipulate them to reflect it); and it persists in our society (because we perform it in interaction with others).

Revisiting the Question

Q+A   If men and women aren't naturally opposite, then why do they act so differently so much of the time?

We see gendered patterns in society because we learn rules for gendered performances through lifelong processes of socialization. The gender rules themselves are incredibly complex, varying across time, cultures, subcultures, and even contexts. We adjust our gendered performances, often seamlessly and unconsciously, as we encounter different situations and audiences.

Sometimes we follow these rules because it is enjoyable to do gender well. Much of the time, however, we follow them out of habit. We often do gender like we ride a bicycle, use a keyboard, or play the piano. At other times, we quite consciously follow rules in order to avoid policing. Policing serves to remind us of the importance of following rules and promotes compliance by offering mild to severe punishments. Policing others gives us the satisfaction of feeling our power; having the power to enforce rules creates feelings of superiority and entitlement, while being policed may make us feel humiliated, stupid, or excluded.

Policing is necessary to produce and protect the gender binary in the face of bodies, personalities, interests, and inclinations that are diverse, regardless of the gender label we hang on ourselves. If we *just were* feminine or masculine in this binary way, there would be no need to police gender performances. Because the rules are complex, and even contradictory, we often must respond to equally complex and contradictory policing. The fact that we can know, concurrently, different sets of rules for different contexts is another indication that gender is not a part of our biology over which we have no control.

Even rule breaking has a way of affirming the binary. If we can offer a good account, we can break rules without consequence; the account assures the policer that we are committed to the rules, just like he or she is, in all cases but this one. As long as most people, most of the time, can offer satisfactory accounts for rule breaking, breaking them will not undermine our collective belief in the rules and the gender binary they uphold.

Somewhere between reaching out to learn the rules, learning how to follow them flexibly, accounting for the many instances in which we break them, and seeking subcultures that share our sense of what rules were "made to be broken," we manage to develop a way of doing gender that works for us, given our opportunities and constraints. We grow up into culturally adept, gendered adults and leave some portion of the rigidities of childhood behind.

Next...

Our strategy for managing gendered expectations, of course, is also shaped by other personal characteristics, such as our social class and residential location, race and ethnicity, immigration status, sexual orientation, age and attractiveness, and our physical abilities and disabilities. It is to this fact that we turn next, asking:

 If gender is just one part of who we are, why isn't it crowded out by all the other things about us that are meaningful and consequential?

The answer will add many more layers of complexity to our theory of gender.

FOR FURTHER READING

Bridges, Tristan. "Doing Gender with Wallets and Purses." *Inequality by (Interior) Design*, April 2, 2013.

Jacques, Juliet. "What Sort of Woman Do I Want to Be?" *The Guardian*, February 9, 2011.

Lucal, Betsy. "What It Means to Be Gendered Me." In *The Kaleidoscope of Gender: Prisms, Patterns, and Possibilities*, 18–28. Thousand Oaks, CA: Sage Publications, 2014.

Saint Louis, Catherine. "Black Hair, Still Tangled in Politics." *New York Times*, August 26, 2009.

West, Candace, and Don Zimmerman. "Doing Gender." *Gender & Society* 1, no. 2 (1987):125–51.

> **EVER SINCE I'VE BEEN IN A WHEELCHAIR, I'VE STOPPED GETTING CATCALLED.**
>
> —FEM KORSTEN[1]

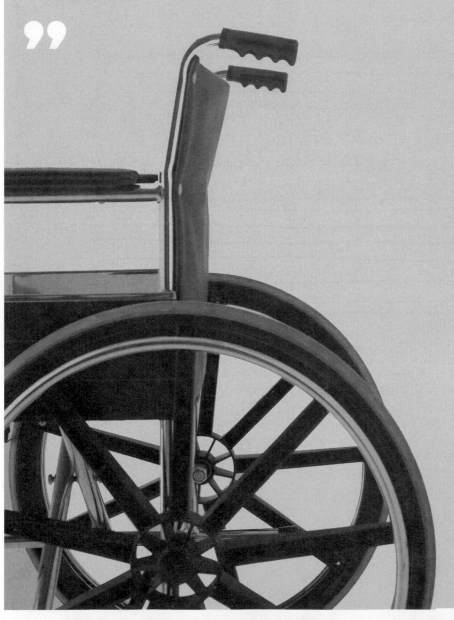

5

Intersections

By now you've been introduced to the idea that gender isn't something we are, but something we do. People we interact with push us to follow or break gender rules. And we often do break them, but usually in ways that affirm the rule itself. As a result, gendered social patterns emerge both in reality and in our minds.

One might observe, however, that gender is just one of many things about us that make us who we are. Some of us are gay, others heterosexual; some bodies bring admiration, other bodies bring pity or derision; some of us have economic resources with which to shape our lives, others have fewer choices available to them. Our gender, then, sits alongside many other socially salient facts about us. Accordingly, we asked:

Q+A | If gender is just one part of who we are, why isn't it crowded out by all the other things about us that are meaningful and consequential?

Instead of being crowded out by these other things, gender *inflects* all the other things about us. For example, it's not that gender is more important than age, or age more important than gender. Instead, there is *a gendered way to age*. Likewise, there is a gendered way to manage being rich or poor, and we experience our race in gendered ways. Similarly, the experiences of being gay, disabled, or an immigrant are all gendered.

In this chapter we will discuss how gender inflects other parts of our identities. We will first introduce a term to describe this phenomenon and then consider how we negotiate this complex social terrain. We will then explore how different kinds of people do gender differently. Our aim is to get you thinking about how gender intersects with our other qualities in ways that preserve the centrality of gender.

INTERSECTIONALITY

When asked to imagine a "real man" and a "real woman," most people think of a white person first. This tendency reveals that the mythical inhabitants of the gender binary are implicitly white. They are also implicitly middle or upper class, heterosexual, able bodied, and Christian. Our ideas about the "perfect" man and woman—the ones that we often use biology to suggest are natural—are actually ideals shaped by the decentering of people of color and the poor and by the invisibility of the gay, the disabled, and the old. The gender binary *normalizes*, then, one kind of man and one kind of woman, erasing or marginalizing other types of men or women. This is good for the binary because excluding various populations keeps things simple, but it doesn't reflect the way that men and women vary in reality.

In real life, we're complicated individuals with unique and layered identities. The fact that gender is not an isolated social fact about us, but instead intersects with our other identities, is called **intersectionality**.[2] We are not just men or women. We are a white, middle-class, married woman—once Catholic, now Evangelical Christian—with a two-year-old (and one on the way), who loves karaoke and votes Democratic. Or maybe we're an Eastern European immigrant who joined a Hasidic Jewish community in New York City at age twelve only to lose his faith, move to New Orleans, and fall in love with jazz and bourbon. Or perhaps we are a purposefully childfree bisexual Texan who works for the Girl Scouts, manages her epilepsy, and likes to spoil her quirky nephew.

These individuals are all responding not only to gender rules, but also to cultural rules governing how to "do" marital status, immigration status, religion or atheism, political affiliation, and parenthood. How they follow or break these rules is further shaped by what is possible given their income, marital status, and health as well as whether they are at risk of discrimination due to their race, sexual orientation, or religion. In the end, they all hope to build lives that are consistent with their values and goals. Like them, we are all adapting to the unique positions we occupy on a *complicated* cultural map.

If this sounds fraught with difficulty, it is—and more so for some than others. Still, all of us try our best to manage these many expectations, opportunities, and constraints in ways that allow us to assert a socially valued identity that reflects our personality, is consistent with our moral beliefs, and responds to our reality. And as we discussed in the previous chapter, this identity must be recognizably masculine or feminine. Finding a way of doing gender that works for us as unique individuals who are also shaped by other parts of our identity and the realities of our lives is called a **gender strategy**.[3]

Varying strategies add up to many culturally recognizable masculinities and femininities. There is the Girly Girl who emphasizes her femininity most of the time; the Tomboy who rejects many feminine characteristics; the Jock whose identity revolves around sports; and the Dork who hates sports and plays *World of Warcraft*. These recognizable stereotypes (no less socially constructed, of course, than "man" and "woman") help us begin to carve out an identity that we like and can feel good about. From there, we try to "be ourselves," breaking the rules associated with these subcategories of masculinity and femininity in order to try to be recognized as not *just* a Jewish Princess, Jersey Girl, Farm Boy, or Science Geek.

In the remainder of this chapter we will look at how some of our personal characteristics and social locations shape our gender strategies, including our economic class; the countries, states, and cities where we live; our race and ethnicity; our immigrant status and whether the native language is our first language; our sexual orientation; and what our body looks like and can or can't do.

ECONOMIC CLASS AND PLACE OF RESIDENCE

Our lives and opportunities are shaped by where we grow up and the resources of our families. Many countries, including capitalist ones, are characterized by significant gaps between the richest and poorest members of society. This means that children and adults from families with higher incomes and greater wealth have more resources to shape their lives to match their ideals. Many middle- and upper-class families live in cities and suburbs surrounded by excellent social services, educational opportunities, and employment options. In contrast, many poor and working-class people live in small communities in rural America, modest suburban developments with fewer opportunities, or inner-city neighborhoods. These variables—economic class and place of residence—intersect with gender, making certain strategies more available to some than others.

Many men in high-pay, high-status occupations, for instance—men who work as lawyers, doctors, account executives, and managers—often invest heavily in

FIGURE 5.1 | MEAN HOUSEHOLD INCOME IN THE U.S., 1967–2012

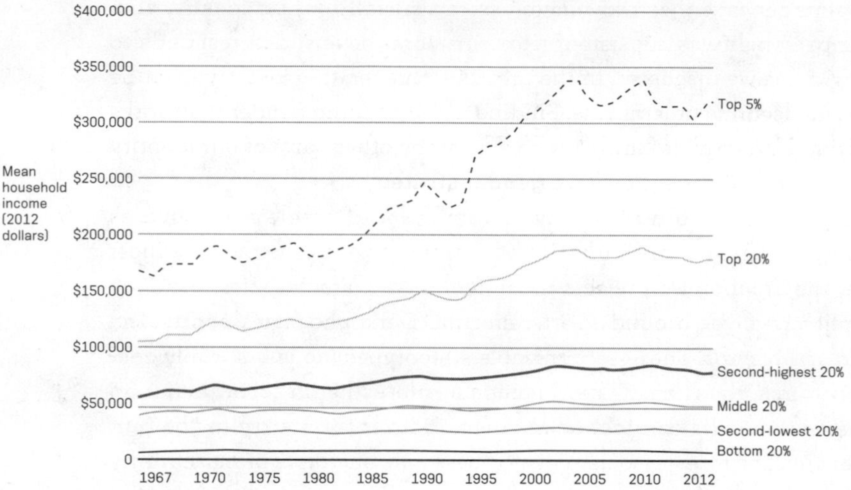

Source: U.S. Bureau of the Census. (2014). "Mean Household Income Received by Each Fifth and Top 5 Percent." Historical Income Tables: Income Inequality, Table H-3, census.gov/hhes/www/income /data/historical/inequality/index.html

their career and identify strongly with their job. Sociologist Arlie Hochschild, who studied the formal and informal workplace norms at a large company, profiled Bill, a senior personnel manager. Bill's life was focused almost exclusively on work, and he argued that no one can get ahead without putting in at least fifty or sixty hours per week. Emily, his wife, stayed home and took care of their house and four children. Of his marriage, Bill said:

> We made a bargain. If I was going to be as successful as we both wanted, I was going to have to spend tremendous amounts of time at it. Her end of the bargain was that she wouldn't go out to work. So I was able to take the good stuff and she did the hard work—the car pools, dinner, gymnastics lessons. . . . Emily left Oakmont College after two years when we got married. . . . I really had it made. I worked very long hours and Emily just managed things.[4]

Earning more than enough money to support his family on one income, and married to a woman whom he believes is happy to manage things at home, Bill's gender strategy was to excel in the masculine pursuit of extraordinary career success. He was a Breadwinner.

Because Emily was married to a Breadwinner, she had the option of choosing a Wonderful Wife and Mother strategy that allowed her to focus exclusively on raising children, being a good partner to her husband, and keeping a beautiful home. Some upper-class married women embrace this strategy. They may feel pressure to invest in their children's future and husbands' careers, be relieved to be out of the income-earning "rat race," or experience great pleasure in nurturing a successful family.

Other affluent married women may reject the binary division of labor and instead adopt a Career Woman strategy in which they nurture their own careers alongside their husbands'. These couples often replace the housework and child care that a Wonderful Wife and Mother would do with paid help. This was the strategy adopted by another family profiled by Hochschild. Both lawyers, Seth and Jessica identified strongly with their jobs and, because they were upper class, they could afford to hire a nanny, a housekeeper, a gardener, a driver, and a neighborhood boy to play with their son, allowing them to put in a combined 120 hours of work each week.

Our gender strategies are not only a reflection of our personalities but also of the twists and turns of our lives. Women are more likely to adopt a Wonderful Wife and Mother strategy if they encounter limited job opportunities and marry a man with a high-paying job, while men find the Breadwinner identity increasingly appealing as their actual income rises.[5] Similarly, men who decide to be stay-at-home dads very rarely leave high-paying, high-status careers. Instead, they are primarily men who have an unsatisfying or excessively demanding job and are married to a high-achieving Career Woman.[6] Other men abandon a Breadwinner strategy when they have children and discover, often to their own surprise, that they absolutely love parenting.[7] In other words, the strategies that we plan for as teenagers and young adults often turn out to be maladaptive or otherwise unsatisfying, so sometimes we end up in places we never intended to go.

Our strategies, though, are never just a result of personality and chance; they are also contingent on our class status. The gender strategies adopted by the men and women profiled by Hochschild were available to them primarily because they had sufficient income. In fact, most two-parent families need both incomes to make ends meet, and few families can afford to hire as much domestic help as Seth and Jessica. Most men can't afford to support a family by themselves, so measuring their masculinity by their ability to do so is self-destructive. Most women, accordingly, can't afford to be either a Wonderful Wife and Mother or a Career Woman. Instead, if they have children, their only option is to try to be a Supermom. Supermoms take on the challenging task of working a full-time job, being a full-time mother, and supporting their husbands. Most single mothers are pushed into the Supermom strategy by default; they must do it all because there is no one else.

Importantly, there are a lot more Supermoms than Super Dads and many fewer female Breadwinners than male ones. This is because women are still held disproportionately responsible for housework and child care. Meanwhile, men whose peers or family think that being a househusband is unmanly or irresponsible may feel uncomfortable taking on that role. Of course, when conditions are right, some men will choose a Super Dad strategy. One study of working-class emergency medical technicians (EMTs) showed that these men prioritized their families alongside their work.[8] They had particular skills that allowed them to have jobs where they could spend time at home providing family care, something they really enjoyed. As one explained: "[I]t's long hours at times, but honestly, I get four days off in a row with my kids. How many people get that much?"[9] Implicitly contrasting himself with the Breadwinner who can't take off much time from work, this Super Dad has embraced active parenting as part of his gender strategy.

Like this EMT, most men try to carve out a masculinity that both feels good and is possible, given their circumstances. Working-class men, such as those who work in factories, in construction, or with cars, sometimes actively contrast their own form of masculinity with that of the Breadwinner, arguing that white-collar workers are "wimps" and "paper-push[ers]."[10] Real men, they argue, the manliest men, do hard physical labor with a degree of personal risk. Construction workers sometimes articulate a similar gender strategy. While they may be subordinate to their more class-advantaged managers (who stay in air-conditioned trailers in front of computers most of the day), some feel sure that they are the "real men." He may "not know what fork is used for salad," but he knows "which drill bit is used for different forms of masonry under different and varying conditions"; he may not "know what sort of wine goes best with

Sociologist Matt Desmond spent time with wildland firefighters in Arizona, studying how these rural Blue-Collar Guys related to each other and to (hyper)masculinity.

salmon, but he knows what grade of motor oil is needed for each piece of the workplace machinery."[11] Construction workers may not have much money, but their masculinity, as they construct it, is more natural and raw. With this logic, these Blue-Collar Guys can embrace a strategy that is available to them *and* feel good about themselves as men.

A boy who grew up in the country may feel out of place in the fancy companies populated by Breadwinners, the suburban parks where we find Super Dads, and the local pubs frequented by Blue-Collar Guys. This was the case in a study of Arizona forest firefighters.[12] These men thought of themselves, specifically, as Country Boys. They distinguished themselves from City Boys, who failed to understand basic guy stuff, like how to spot poison ivy, find a good fishing spot, or pick up a snake. Because these men grew up farming, ranching, fishing, and hunting, identifying as a Country Boy was a gender strategy they could pull off and feel good about. And like the Blue-Collar Guys who dismissed Breadwinners as "wimps," these firefighters enjoyed the particular brand of masculinity that stemmed from their rural upbringing.

The examples discussed thus far demonstrate that our gender strategies aren't simply products of our individual personalities and luck. They are also shaped by the constraints and opportunities afforded by our class status and the types of neighborhoods in which we find ourselves. In the next section, we'll discuss how these identities intersect with race.

RACE

Like our economic class and place of residence, race shapes our gender strategies. Some racial groups are denigrated, others valorized; all are subject to advantages and disadvantages related to their unique histories. This is a sensitive and complicated topic that deserves careful attention. In this section, we're going to look at three examples: the experiences of gender for blacks, whites, and Asians in the United States.

African American Men and Women

The United States sustained a system of racialized slavery for over 200 years. White elites framed themselves as caretakers, not captors. Black men were stereotyped as jolly buffoons who were helpless to take care of themselves, let alone anyone else. Like children, it was argued, they needed a "master" to take care of them; the complicated responsibilities of freedom were simply too much for a black man's simple mind.[13] Slavery was framed as a kindness, a way to support a race that, left to its own devices, would go extinct out of pure haplessness.

This stereotype of black men is likely unfamiliar today. In fact, it would change quickly once African Americans won emancipation in 1865. After slavery was abolished, the stereotype of black men as weak and ineffectual no longer served a useful purpose. Much more useful to white supremacists was the idea that black men were aggressive, prone to criminality, and sexually violent. With this justification, a segment of the white population terrorized the black community. Black men and their allies were potential targets of **lynching**, a murder carried out by citizens in the absence of due process, most notoriously by hanging. Though these murders were motivated by a desire to keep black people "in their place," false accusations that these men had raped white women were the most common excuse.[14]

Beliefs about black people in the United States still reflect these strategic stereotypes designed to shore up white power. Black people are stereotyped as tougher and more athletic than white people; sometimes they are even portrayed as meaner, more aggressive, and prone to criminal behavior and sexual promiscuity.[15] These characteristics, notably, are also stereotypes of masculinity. Black men, then, are frequently stereotyped as *hyper*masculine: super aggressive (as athletes or criminals) and super sexual (as players, philanderers, and potential rapists). In other words, for black men, being black *intensifies* expectations based on their gender, and being male intensifies expectations based on their race.

This stereotyping starts when black boys are children. Sociologist Ann Ferguson showed how both white and black teachers interpret the bad behavior of white and black boys differently.[16] White boys are seen as inherently innocent; they may misbehave, but it is not out of malice. Their behavior would be excused with the idea that "boys will be boys." When black boys misbehave, however, some of these teachers—both black and white—see it as a sign that they are criminals in the making. Ferguson writes about how black boys' "transgressions are made to take on a sinister, intentional, fully conscious tone that is stripped of any element of childish naïveté."[17] At the schools Ferguson studied, if black boys wanted to be seen as "good," they had to perform an *extreme* degree of deference. In other words, in order to avoid negative racial stereotypes, black boys often need to adopt behaviors that would be considered "sissy" if performed by white boys.

As Ferguson observed, this "enactment of docility is a preparation for *adult* racialized survival rituals."[18] Indeed, some adult black men report adopting strategies designed to manage the negative hypermasculine stereotypes that others attribute to them. Some take care to never raise their voice. Others wear glasses (even if they don't have to) or make a point to always dress in khakis and button-down shirts. This Gentle Black Man strategy is a way of doing masculinity that some black men use to avoid being stereotyped as a Dangerous Black Man.

Journalist Brent Staples adopts just this strategy. As a "youngish" six-foot-two black man with "billowing hair," Staples is aware that he is frequently seen as a potential threat. Staples recounts watching women scamper to the other side of the street and hearing the *thunk* of car doors being locked when he comes into sight. More than simply hurtful, though, others' perceptions of him are inconvenient, as he is sometimes harassed by doormen, bouncers, and security guards. One facet of Staples' gender strategy, then, is to "take precautions to make [him]self less threatening." Of one of these precautions, he writes:

> *I employ what has proved to be an excellent tension-reducing measure: I whistle melodies from Beethoven and Vivaldi. . . . Even steely New Yorkers hunching toward nighttime destinations seem to relax, and occasionally even join the tune. Virtually everybody seems to sense that a mugger wouldn't be warbling bright, sunny selections from Vivaldi's Four Seasons.*[19]

By whistling Vivaldi, Staples disrupts others' initial perceptions of him because classical music is associated with upper-class masculinity, invoking ideas of wealth and intelligence, two things that black men are assumed to lack. "Doing" upper class is one way that black men can mediate the intersection of race and gender that makes people believe they are dangerous.[20]

This strategy can do more than just interrupt racist narratives. Because black men are frequently perceived as threatening, they are often targeted and sometimes injured or killed by overly zealous police or citizens who find them threatening. Staples's Gentle Black Man strategy is not only a gender strategy; it's a survival strategy: "It is my equivalent of the cowbell that hikers wear when they know they are in bear country." The murder of seventeen-year-old Trayvon Martin, who was walking home with Skittles and an Arizona juice drink, is a poignant example. George Zimmerman's claim that he was assaulted by Martin and acted in self-defense was found credible by a jury in 2013. We'll never know what really happened in that case, but we do know that juries are most likely to find self-defense arguments believable when the victim is identified as black and the person who used lethal force appears white.[21] We see similar disparities by race throughout the criminal justice system.[22]

If black men are imagined to be more masculine than white people, so are black women. Slave captors required both men and women to do hard labor and suffer harsh punishments, and female slaves were sometimes forced into sexual relations with their captors and required to produce children. The way black women were treated conflicted with cultural beliefs about feminine fragility and purity. In order to rationalize their treatment, black women were characterized as masculine: hypersexual and physically tough.[23] Post-slavery, this same stereotype served the strategic purpose of defining only white women as

How Beyoncé chooses to wear her hair has implications far beyond style.

vulnerable to rape, ignoring assaults that black women faced from both white and black men.

The stereotype that black women are unfeminine persists today, such that black women are frequently confronted with the perception that they are less feminine than white women, regardless of how they act.[24] That is, a black woman's race *interferes* with people's perception of her as a feminine person. Because of this, the Girly Girl strategy is harder for some black women to pull off. This is especially true if they have tightly curled hair (worn "natural," in cornrows, an afro, or dreadlocks), darker skin, or features that appear more "African." Black women, then, must contend with the need to *over*-compensate by doing more femininity in order to counter stereotypical beliefs. For example, long, light-colored, straight, or gently wavy hair is associated with femininity. Accordingly, black women with curly or kinky dark hair sometimes straighten it, lighten it, get extensions to lengthen it, or wear wigs. Many successful black models, musicians, and actresses, such as Tyra Banks and Beyoncé, adopt this strategy.

Because femininity is implicitly white, doing femininity can feel like doing whiteness. So some black women may feel that the Girly Girl strategy is a capitulation to or an internalization of racism. In response, some black women embrace a Black Is Beautiful strategy. This strategy rejects the idealization of white femininity in favor of reframing characteristically black features as both feminine and beautiful. Lauryn Hill, originally of the Fugees, performs culturally African American music and wears her hair in characteristically "black" ways (afros and dreadlocks). This style of doing gender as a black woman works with her deliberately countercultural image and likely fits with her identity and politics. This was certainly true for Jenny, an African American woman interviewed for a study about hair, who explained her decision to wear hers in dreadlocks, or "a natural":

> *I consider myself in a constant state of protest about the realities of cultural alienation, cultural marginalization, cultural invisibility, discrimination, injustice, all of that. And I feel that my hairstyle has always allowed me, since I started wearing it in a natural, to voice that nonverbally.*[25]

While black women can choose to wear their hair in ways that reflect their own personal values and aesthetics, they must also contend with the way others respond to them. Black women who straighten their hair may be judged as "sellouts," whereas those who wear their hair naturally may be seen as unattractive or unprofessional. For black women, then, both the Girly Girl and the Black Is Beautiful strategies come with costs as well as benefits, ones that white women with naturally straight or wavy hair do not have to balance.

Singer-songwriter and rapper Lauryn Hill, in embracing the Black Is Beautiful aesthetic, wears her hair "natural."

Asian American Men and Women

Asian American men face a predicament similar to that of African American women. American stereotypes about Asians attribute characteristics associated with femininity to both Asian men and women.[26] Asians are assumed to be smaller, lighter, and less muscular than whites and are often portrayed as passive and reserved. Asian women are taken to be extremely shy and deferential, and Asian men are often depicted as less masculine than other races, even deficiently sexual.

These stereotypes don't come out of thin air, but, like the stereotypes of African Americans, are tied to history.[27] During the gold rush of the 1800s, the United States brought Chinese men as laborers, often against their will. Tens of thousands of men, living in all-male groups, had to learn how to perform domestic tasks for themselves. Later, when they were forced out of their jobs in farming, mining, and manufacturing, they became servants or opened businesses offering domestic services to the wider population. By virtue of doing "women's work," Asian men were feminized in the cultural imagination.

For Asian men, then, racial stereotypes interfere with their ability to conform to gender expectations. This is part of why the word *Linsanity* resonated as a description of the Chinese American professional athlete Jeremy Lin's success on the basketball court. His feats were remarkable because of his skill and athleticism, but also because Asian stereotypes are incompatible with being that good at such a strongly masculinized sport. People felt that what they were seeing was just "insane."

Because of the stereotypes, some Asian men try to compensate for others' perceptions by acting more aggressively than they otherwise would.[28] Gary, a Chinese American lawyer who describes himself as a "jockish type," explains: "Well, I think the stereotype is that Asian men are docile.... That is the reason I decided to be a trial attorney—to cut against that." Being a trial attorney requires Gary to *fight* on behalf of his clients, a behavior that is inconsistent with the Asian stereotype.

The first American of Chinese or Taiwanese heritage to play in the NBA, Jeremy Lin's success defied a number of Asian male stereotypes and whipped basketball fans into a frenzy of "Linsanity."

Gary's Outgoing Asian gender strategy—being gregarious, dating frequently, excelling in athletics, and achieving in a job that requires him to be aggressive—has worked out well for him: He is a very successful lawyer. But it is also a daily battle. Most of his potential clients, he explains, have never encountered a Chinese lawyer and worry that he won't be able to represent them well. "Do I have to overcome [the stereotype] every day?" Gary asks himself out loud. "Yes, I do." He has to prove to others, continually, that he is not passive in the courtroom.

Asian women are also racially feminized. In the 1870s and 1880s, Chinese and Japanese women were brought to the United States to work as sex slaves. A trader might pay a starving family in China $40 for a daughter and then sell her to a brothel in San Francisco for $2,500. The large numbers of Asian prostitutes, alongside the Japanese geisha stereotype, hyperfeminized Asian women as demure, passive, and sexually available.

The stereotype lives on as Asian women continue to face a *hyper*feminization relative to other women, an intensification of gender expectations like that experienced by black men. Asian women are often expected to be *extremely* passive and may receive unwelcome attention for this presumed trait.[29] Karen Eng, a Japanese American, describes the stereotypical Asian woman:

> The fantasy Asian is intelligent yet pliable, mysterious yet ornamental. She's also perpetually prepubescent—ageless and petite, hairless, high-pitched, girly.... As I once overheard someone saying, she's "tuckable" under the arm.[30]

This fantasy Asian girl appeals, particularly, to men who want a submissive girlfriend or wife, but Eng has no interest in being "tuckable." She doesn't want to be anyone's geisha or china doll, but some men assume that she will be: "No matter how many combinations of combat boots, 501s, and ratty Goodwill coats you wear," she says, "they still see a little Oriental flower."[31]

Eng doesn't adopt an "Oriental Flower" strategy because it conflicts with who she feels she really is. Instead, she uses an Outgoing Asian strategy of her own. Lisa, an eighteen-year-old Korean American, has adopted this strategy, too:

> *I feel like I have to prove myself to everybody and maybe that's why I'm always vocal. I'm quite aware of that stereotype of Asian women all being taught to be submissive. . . . I don't want that to be labeled on me.*[32]

These women, like Gary, have adopted an Outgoing Asian strategy. But, while Gary can use his identity as a man to account for behavior inconsistent with the Asian stereotype, Asian women don't have that excuse. Accordingly, some Asian women use different strategies for different audiences. An drea, a twenty-three-year-old Vietnamese American, describes her strategy switching:

> *When I'm with my boyfriend and we're over at his family's house or at a church function, I tend to find myself being a little submissive. . . . But I know that when I get home, he and I have that understanding that I'm not a submissive person. I speak my own mind and he likes the fact that I'm strong.*[33]

With racy jokes and a brash personality, Korean American comedienne Margaret Cho seems neither passive nor fragile. When she was hired to play herself on a sitcom, producers hired coaches to teach her how to be more "Asian."

Asian women and men, then, like black men and women, face challenges because of the way gender stereotypes intersect with beliefs about their race.

White American Men and Women

In contrast to African and Asian Americans, white Americans are racially *un*-marked. This is because "American" and "white American" are typically synonymous in American society. White men and women are never seen as too masculine or too feminine, or not masculine or feminine enough, based on their race alone. This means that if they have the personality and resources for it, white men and women can rather easily adopt mainstream gender identities. A young woman who is born into the middle class with genes that give her light skin and a petite, thin body type can, if she wants, be an All-American Girl, while the young man who is athletically gifted, racially white, and class privileged can be an All-American Guy.

By virtue of seeming "normal," notice that being white and middle class also carries the stigma of being "regular," "plain," and "uninteresting." Boring sex is "vanilla," clean-cut people are "white bread," and an acceptable but ultimately unimportant lie is a "white lie." This is why the Nerd, the Librarian, and the Soccer Mom are implicitly white: They are imagined to be the opposite of cool, exciting, or dangerous.

Accordingly, some middle-class white people try to differentiate themselves from the respectable but bland image that is bestowed on them by virtue of their race and class. The Goths discussed in Chapter 4 were doing just that. Most were white, middle-class, self-identified geeks. Being Goth (that is, doing freakiness) was a way for them to "renounce humiliation, invisibility, and boredom," "become a little cooler," and "differentiate themselves from the mainstream"—to be, by definition, not normal.[34] Somehow, the idea of seeming scary is less appealing to, say, black men, who find such a persona forced upon them.

Likewise, when being white intersects with being poor and living in a violent urban neighborhood, being marginal isn't a choice; it's a reality despite one's white privilege. Sociologist Amy Wilkins studied poor, urban, white women who identified with the blacks and Puerto Ricans who lived alongside them.[35] These women adopted the "street" fashion, mannerisms, and language of their neighbors of color with whom they shared a class but not a racial background. This Urban White Girl strategy offered freedom from the more restrictive gender rules for middle- and upper-class women. They could act tough and be outspoken and openly sexual. The strategy also came at a cost, though: the women of color in their neighborhoods sometimes called them "wannabes" and described them as imposters:

> White girls who "don't know who they are." They're loud, annoying, always fighting, too proud of having sex. They wear the wrong clothes. They smoke the wrong cigarettes. They talk wrong, have the wrong attitudes, and have the wrong priorities. And they have the wrong boyfriends.[36]

In other words, these women were critiqued for doing gender wrong. From the perspective of the poor white women who adopted this strategy, however, being a "wannabe" was one of their best options. Without class privilege, these women didn't have the option to be an All-American Girl so being an Urban White Girl gave them "an inhabitable, if stereotyped and degraded, persona" that was better than the alternative: White Trash.[37]

All of us, including white people, carry racialized physical features that are "read" by others trying to figure out who we are and, simultaneously, who we should be. These racial designations intersect with gender and class, leading us to develop different strategies to fend off stigmatizing identities and assert esteemed ones.

SEXUAL ORIENTATION

The lives of gay, lesbian, and bisexual people, also called **sexual minorities**, are similarly shaped by gender. In Western societies, gay men are stereotyped as effeminate and lesbians as masculine. Indeed, some of us claim to have excellent "gaydar," or the ability to detect, radar-like, gay men and lesbians in our presence. In fact, what we are looking for is neither the presence nor the absence of sexual desire for people of the same sex, but gender deviance: swishy men and manly women. That is, we are looking for people who are breaking gender rules.

This assumption that one's sexual orientation is linked to one's gender display in predictable ways is not universal across societies. And even in societies in which the assumption is common, gays, bisexuals, and lesbians "do gender" in a variety of ways, just like heterosexual people. Still, taking on an openly gay or lesbian identity in societies that make this assumption means negotiating with this specific social construction of gayness. How one does so depends in part on whether one wants to "pass" as heterosexual or be visibly homosexual.

Many gay men, lesbians, and bisexuals want to keep their sexual orientation a secret because of **homophobia**, the fear and hatred of sexual minorities. Since our gaydar is tuned to detect gender deviance, gender conformity is an excellent way to hide in plain sight. Brandon, a gay man living in rural Colorado, explained how he tries to pass as heterosexual: "I try to live as straight a life as possible. Whether it's dressing, the car I drive, the area I'm in. When I fill up at a gas station, my greatest fear is to look at another guy the wrong way."[38]

Brandon feels compelled to hide his sexual orientation because of **compulsory heterosexuality**, a rule that all men be attracted to women and all women to men. Following gender rules can be advantageous, however, even for sexual minorities living in places where living openly is an increasingly viable option. Many people are more tolerant of sexual minorities who are gender-conforming than those who are gender-deviant. Asked how she would feel about having a lesbian roommate, a college student expressed just this sentiment:

> If my roommate was a lesbian and she was more feminine, I think I would be more comfortable. . . . [If she was] like me—she looked girly—it wouldn't matter if she liked guys or girls. But if it was someone that was really boyish, I think it would be hard for me to feel comfortable.[39]

When he was drafted by the St. Louis Rams in May 2014, Michael Sam became the first openly gay player to be picked up by an NFL team. The live-broadcast kiss he shared with his boyfriend after receiving the news swiftly received both support and backlash.

Because some people's discomfort with gay people is related to their gender performance, some lesbians adopt an All but Heterosexual strategy, often described as the Lipstick Lesbian. Many do this because they feel feminine, and so it is a gender strategy that they enjoy, but some do so because presenting a feminine appearance brings rewards, while failing to do so brings costs. One tall, forty-one-year-old lesbian copywriter named Rebecca, for example, explained that she uses makeup to mute her "difference" from heterosexual co-workers and clients: "I even try to take a little bit of that threat off, you know, by saying you don't have to worry about me being different."[40] Some gay men and bisexuals, too, adopt an All but Heterosexual strategy. This strategy likely appeals to gay men who feel comfortable with masculinity. Several studies of gay athletes document this approach to fitting in.[41]

One challenge for women and men who adopt an All but Heterosexual strategy is recognizability. In a **heteronormative** society, one in which it is assumed that everyone is heterosexual unless there are signs indicating otherwise, gender conformity may make same-sex sexual orientation *invisible*, even to other sexual minorities.[42] Gay men, lesbians, and bisexuals may want to be visible for multiple reasons: They may want to upset heteronormativity, find people to date or marry, or ward off unwanted attention from the other sex. Gay men and lesbians, then, may challenge **homonormativity**—a term used to describe sexual minorities who try to be as "normal" as possible—in favor of a Recognizably Butch or Queer strategy.[43] For women, this strategy might involve adopting more masculine clothes and mannerisms and avoiding makeup and long hair. One forty-year-old woman explained:

> I have a dyke look that I assume when I want to fit in more with lesbian social settings, and I think I've been more careful about keeping my haircut very crisp and clean so I can look more dyke-y when I want to.[44]

Race matters here, too, affecting how much femininity needs to be performed if lesbians and bisexual women want to be seen as less "different." Because stereotypes about Asians include the idea that they are more feminine than white people, Asian lesbians may not need to work as hard to seem "normal," but they may have a harder time being recognizably lesbian or bi. One Cambodian American lesbian explained:

> I guess that's one reason why I'm so in your face and out about being a dyke. . . . I'm invisible as a lesbian because I look in [an Asian] cultural way—that is, where I have long hair, you know—and I despise that invisibility.[45]

For Asian lesbians and bisexuals, doing femininity makes them extra invisible and may be a less viable strategy, depending on how visible they want to be. So they may emphasize their deviation from femininity to "compensate" for other people's assumptions. Conversely, to be seen as feminine, black lesbians and bisexuals have to overcome stereotypes applied to both black people and lesbians, both of which masculinize them.[46] Meanwhile, black women may face more pressure than either white or Asian women to perform femininity, since appearing heterosexual may be one of the few nonstigmatizing identities that they carry, especially if they are also working class or poor.

The way that others use our gender performance to guess our sexual orientation has implications for heterosexual people as well. Because we artificially conflate sexual orientation with inverted gender display—that is, we expect gay men to act feminine and lesbians to act masculine—gender-bending strategies carry serious consequences for heterosexual men and women who want to attract the romantic or sexual attention of the other sex. A heterosexual woman who performs masculinity, for example, risks being seen as a lesbian. She may despise makeup, love the feel of a short haircut, and prefer wearing her Canucks jersey over anything else, but being herself in this way might get her mistaken for gay. Likewise, a naturally effeminate man may try to act more masculine to avoid sending the wrong signals to women he likes. Gender strategies that push the boundaries of gender conformity have different consequences depending on one's sexual orientation.

Being openly gay is about more than just parades. How sexual minorities do gender affects whether their sexual orientation is visible to others around them on a daily basis.

It should be noted that the All but Heterosexual and Recognizably Queer or Butch gender strategies are specific to societies and subcultures in which "gay" and "lesbian" are acknowledged categories. In some societies, and historically in the United States and Europe, there is no such thing as sexual orientation. In China, for instance, most men over the age of forty do not recognize a gay identity, even those that have frequent sexual liaisons with other men.[47] Younger Chinese men are more likely to adopt a Western-style gay identity, but they do not necessarily value "coming out" to everyone. Instead, some feel that family harmony and respecting Chinese culture is more important than getting social acknowledgement for one's gayness.

Similarly, in France, making a big deal about coming out as gay is seen as overly theatrical. In France, one is encouraged to identify as French and just French. Being gay is supposed to be only a small part of one's identity, eclipsed by one's Frenchness. What's important, as one man explained, "is that you're French before anything and we don't care if you're anything else."[48] Wearing your identity on your sleeve—that is, being Recognizably Butch or Queer—is considered rude.

Research suggests that many African American men and rural white men think about their same-sex desire more like the Chinese and the French than their white, Western, urban counterparts. Gay-positive spaces in the United States tend to be dominated by white people and restricted to urban places;

both urban black and rural white men often do not have access to the same identity-strengthening communities available to urban whites. This, combined with other factors, often means that these groups tend to experience same-sex attraction as a *desire*, but not an *identity*, even when they act on it.[49] There are also plenty of white men in urban spaces who do not identify as gay or bi but still engage in significant amounts of same-sex sexual activity.[50]

Adopting a gender strategy that emphasizes sexual orientation is considered psychologically healthy by many in the United States. In other countries—such as China, or even within the United States if you are black or rural—doing so may seem inappropriate or be unfamiliar. In many places, negotiating gendered expectations by being "out" may not be an available or desirable strategy; other identities might be more salient or the notion of a gay *person* (as opposed to same-sex *practices*) simply might not exist at all. In these cases, the gender strategies familiar to Americans may seem inappropriate or be culturally unintelligible. In other cases, as with men and women in rural America, being gay may be far too stigmatizing. In these cases, acting heterosexual is not a social strategy so much as a survival strategy.

IMMIGRATION

When people move from one country to another, the gender strategies they employed in their place of origin may suddenly be impossible or undesirable. Immigrants may find themselves in an entirely different social class or a strange new living environment; meanwhile, in their new country, immigrants may suddenly be an ethnic or racial minority facing unfamiliar stereotypes even as they struggle to learn a new language and face discrimination based on their status as a foreigner.

Reconfigured Families

Some immigrants, prior to immigration, enjoy lifestyles that allow them to comfortably adopt Breadwinner/Wonderful Wife and Mother strategies. Upon arrival in another country, though, many immigrants experience **downward mobility**, a decline in their socioeconomic position. Wealth, occupational status, or educational degrees often do not translate into the same privileges in their new country, while discrimination, lack of social networks, and language barriers limit job choices.[51] For some immigrants, this shift in circumstances prevents them from continuing with the strategies that they enjoyed back home and, accordingly, requires that they adjust their ideas of masculinity and femininity and establish an economic *inter*dependence: The husbands and wives depend on each other to pay the bills.

In one study of couples who emigrated from Guatemala and El Salvador to California, many wives reported discovering that they enjoyed working. In response, they began to change their ideas about what kind of woman they wanted to be and what kind of husband they preferred. One interviewee, Rosa, explained:

> *Maybe it's the lifestyle. Here, the man and the woman, both have to work to be able to pay the rent, the food, the clothes, a lot of expenses. Probably that . . . makes us, the women, a little freer in the United States. . . . In this country if you are courageous and have strength, you can get ahead by yourself, with or without [a husband]. . . . I would say that's why here the woman doesn't follow the man more.*[52]

When women like Rosa embrace a new gender strategy, more akin to the Supermom, they often ask their husbands to embrace a new gender strategy, too, one more like the Super Dad. This sort of shift in a couple's gender strategy is facilitated by new cultural ideas and different economic realities. Ricardo talked about the adjustment:

> *Here we both work equally, we both work full-time. . . . If she is asked to stay at work late, I have to stay with the children. . . . In El Salvador it was different. I never touched a broom there [laughing]. . . . Here, no. If she quits, we don't eat. It's equal.*[53]

Jacobo, enthusiastic about his wife working, has high hopes for her future:

> *There are many opportunities here and she is smart in business and she can learn English quickly. . . . It upsets me to find her at home all the time [babysitting], when she could be doing something better.*[54]

Some men, like Ricardo and Jacobo, respond positively to the change that comes with economic interdependence. Other husbands resist. And some women pine for the days when they could focus on being a Wonderful Wife and Mother.

Reconfigured Sexualities

Like heterosexual immigrants, gay and lesbian immigrants encounter new cultural rules about how to do gender that intersect with the unique approach to sexual orientation in each country. Accordingly, just like married immigrants may begin rethinking what it means to be married, gay and lesbian immigrants may begin rethinking what it means to be sexually attracted to members of their own sex.

We've already discussed how the French consider highlighting one's difference from other French people to be in poor taste.[55] In contrast, Americans tend to endorse group identities and subcultural cohesion based on one's interests or membership in political, religious, and ethnic groups. Therefore, there is support, at least among some, for an "out" identity in the United States.

Gay men and lesbians who move from the United States to France, or vice versa, have to negotiate these differences. When Xavier moved to the United States, he welcomed the opportunity to adopt a gay identity. "I don't feel there is one way to be an American," he explained. "You can hyphenate your identity in the U.S. while you can't really in France." Danielle, who emigrated from the United States to France, enjoys her new country for just the opposite reason: "[I]n the U.S., people want to know your label immediately," she explained. She prefers things the French way.

Some immigrants have a hard time acclimating to new strategies designed to bring together their gender identities; sexual desires; and national, racial, and ethnic backgrounds. A study of men who immigrated to London from sub-Saharan Africa found that many were happy to be living in a society that was, overall, more accepting of homosexuality, but they still resisted identifying as "gay."[56] The term implied a lifestyle that they did not embrace. One African immigrant explained:

> If I say gay, it comes with lots of associations and ideas in terms of how you live your life, what kind of culture you are into, what kind of music and kind of the whole construct around that label that most of us, even me, I don't associate myself with.[57]

This man was still trying to find a gender strategy that bridged the gap between his cultural background and the gender rules and gay culture he encountered in London.

Stories of immigration reveal that we adopt gender strategies in response to our social context. In the final two sections, we explore the impact of age and disability on gender strategies.

ABILITY AND DISABILITY

Physical disabilities can interfere with one of our most potent resources for doing gender: our bodies. Thomas Gerschick, a disabilities theorist, explains:

> Bodies operate socially as canvases on which gender is displayed and kinesthetically as the mechanisms by which it is physically enacted. Thus, the bodies of

people with disabilities make them vulnerable to being denied recognition as women and men.[58]

What kind of challenges do women and men with physical disabilities face in designing strategies with which to do gender?

Disability and Masculinity

Newly disabled men may have to adjust to a sudden inability to be physically and sexually assertive. One study documented the struggles of young black and Latino men adapting to degrees of paralysis due to spinal cord injuries.[59] Because they came from impoverished inner cities that often required men to adopt a Tough Guy strategy for survival, their injuries dramatically challenged their identities. They explained that they felt like "half a man," pointing to the inability to enact the same highly physical masculine strategy that they had once enjoyed. "No longer could the men walk with a swagger and stand tall in a way that emanated power; no longer could the men have sex anywhere at any time; no longer could the men physically fight a potential threat."[60]

Some disabled men adopt a hypermasculine Still a Man strategy designed to remind others that they still have a distinctly masculine sexuality.[61] Roger, in Norway, experienced problems with memory, speech, and motor control caused by brain injuries sustained in a car accident. He embraced the sexual objectification of women, plastering his living space with images of "bikini-clad women lying on cars and motorbikes."[62] When the female sociologist who interviewed him entered his home, he immediately winked at her and asked her to do his dishes. His humor emphasized the fact that while he was disabled and she was not, he was still a man and she still a woman. Enacting a more youthful version of this strategy, a young man named Dag who was paralyzed at twenty-two used a programmed speaking device to whistle at women.[63] Dag's Still a Man strategy, like Roger's, was a way to remind others that he was still very much male.

Sports are another arena that offers disabled men the opportunity to assert their masculinity. Wheelchair rugby, originally called murderball, is an aggressive contact sport that enables players to prove their athletic prowess and fearlessness in the face of danger. The fact that they play through their disability suggests an extraordinary degree of manliness, counteracting the loss of masculinity they experienced when they were injured.

Class-privileged men with disabilities can use their money to preserve their sense of themselves as men. If they have the resources to live alone and pay for renovations, technologies, and human assistance, then they can retain much of the independence they enjoyed before they were injured. Damon, for example, a

Wheelchair rugby allows disabled men to reclaim their masculinity by proving that they are just as assertive and competitive as they were before their injury.

quadriplegic who requires twenty-four-hour personal care, was able to feel independent because he could afford to be so:

> I direct all of my activities around my home where people have to help me to maintain my apartment, my transportation, which I own, and direction in where I go. I direct people how to get there, and I tell them what my needs will be when I am going and coming, and when to get where I am going. . . . I don't see any reason why [I can't] get my life on just as I was having it before.[64]

For Damon and some other disabled men, regaining independence is an Able-Disabled strategy that preserves and even enhances a sense of masculinity, given that one must overcome such great obstacles to have what other men may take for granted.

Independence, or the opportunity to enact an Able-Disabled strategy, was one of the most challenging obstacles for the disadvantaged black and Latino men. Since they didn't have wealth, health insurance, money to hire lawyers, or a sense of empowerment with which to gain access to social services, they usually remained dependent on their families. "I can only do so much," one man said resignedly. "I'm always gonna need help."[65] The strategies available to disabled men to recover their identities as men, then, strongly intersect with class.

Disability and Femininity

If men's identities are troubled by the sense that they can no longer be *assertive* with their bodies, women's identities are more often tied up with their ability to be physically *attractive*. Disabled women are exposed to the idea that it is important to be sexy at the same time that stereotypes about the disabled portray them as unsexy, even asexual.[66] Some women with disabilities, then, are denied the Girly Girl strategy and other strategies that involve emphasizing their sexual attractiveness in exchange for men's attention. Beth, a woman with multiple sclerosis, writes: "I am sure that other people see a wheelchair first, me second, and a woman third, if at all."[67] For Beth, and others, a little bit of sexual objectification would be welcome. Disability rights activist Judy Heumann explains:

> You know, I use a wheelchair, and when I go down the street I do not get to be sexually harassed. I hear nondisabled women complaining about it, but I don't ever get treated as a sexual object.[68]

For Beth and Judy, it is a struggle to be seen as a woman at all.

Some women may respond by trying to conform to gendered expectations as rigidly as possible. Harilyn was one of these women. She writes:

> I was determined to prove I was a "normal" woman. I deliberately sought the most handsome man to parade around. . . . I became pregnant out of wedlock at seventeen, which was extremely affirming for me. One of my proud moments was parading around the supermarket with my belly sticking out for all to see that I was indeed a woman, and that my body worked like a normal woman's body.[69]

Occupying a position in "no woman's land" can inspire women to hyperconform, as Harilyn did, but it can also give them permission to resist cultural definitions of femininity.[70] Some disabled women find that their injury or illness gives them the insight and permission they need to escape from rigid standards of beauty. As one disabled woman with some difficulty with motor control explained: "If I tried to put on mascara, I'd put my eye out, you know; I could never physically do it."[71] For her, being unable to enact the Girly Girl strategy has been liberating:

> It's meant that I'm dealing with having a better balance in life as a person, not just as a person with a disability. So I think that we're able to be who we are as women 'cause we don't fit the stereotype maybe.[72]

Class also plays a role. Siv had adopted a Wonderful Wife and Mother strategy before an accident left her paralyzed from the chest down with only some arm movement.[73] Fortunately for her, this didn't disrupt her gender strategy very much; with her husband's income and her disability check helping to pay for help around the house—a housekeeper and nurse—she was able to continue on as the emotional center of her family. Siv "came out with her femininity intact."[74]

Disability interacts with masculinity and femininity, as well as other things about us, making the transition to a life with a disability different for men and women.

AGE AND ATTRACTIVENESS

As we grow older, our ability to "pull off" different gender strategies changes. This is because our appearance and physiology no longer support certain strategies and also because society has strict age-related rules that pressure us to "act our age."[75] Says sociologist Cheryl Laz:

> *"Act your age. You're a big kid now," we say to children to encourage indepen-*
> *dence (or obedience). "Act your age. Stop being so childish," we say to other*
> *adults when we think they are being irresponsible. "Act your age; you're not as*
> *young as you used to be," we say to an old person pursuing "youthful" activities.[76]*

Staying up all night at clubs is typically seen as fun-loving for young adults; among forty-somethings, pathetic and irresponsible. Becoming a parent is believed to be a blessing at thirty, a curse at thirteen. Learning to snowboard seems typical for a twenty-eight-year-old, but downright dangerous for a seventy-eight-year-old. Just as there are gender rules, then, there are age rules. These rules press us to "do" our age by doing things that are judged as neither "too immature" nor "too old" for the number on our birthday cake.

These age-related rules are gendered. In a social sense, men and women age at different rates and in different ways. Playing with dolls may be tolerated in a two-year-old boy who isn't expected to know the rules, but it is often considered maladaptive in a twelve-year-old boy who, by then, is seen as flouting a rule that he is supposed to want to obey. Girls, in contrast, can play with dolls throughout childhood and even collect them in adulthood with little to no scrutiny.

People learn early on that age matters. Consider three Swedish eleven-year-olds, already well versed in the intersection of age and gender rules.[77] One of the girls, Anna-Clara, explains:

> *Frankly it's ridiculous to wear thong [underwear] at our age. Eighth, ninth grade,*
> *that's when girls start to be mature enough for it. When you are, like, in the fifth*
> *grade, it looks ridiculous if you walk around with thongs.*

Anna-Clara's friends, Fanny and Angelica, may admire high heels, but they understand that they're not yet ready for them. Angelica recalls: "I saw these beige boots, which I thought were nice. But I wouldn't buy them. They had rather high heels." Fanny concurred, remarking that she'd be more than happy to police Angelica if she were to break this rule: "If Angelica wears such shoes, I tell her that they're adults' shoes."

These eleven-year-olds will eventually age into thongs and high heels, but they should expect to age back out again. As soon as their bodies are socially defined as unattractive, the rules change again, requiring them to adopt a strategy of invisibility. Duncan Kennedy, who studied British and American fashion-advice TV shows, explains:

> Old women . . . are expected to accept the conventional social assessment that they are sexually unattractive, and dress so as to minimize their sexuality. If they dress sexily . . . [they] are likely to be interpreted as rebels or eccentrics or "desperate," and sanctioned accordingly.[78]

As they get older, both men and women may face **ageism**, a prejudice based on a preference for the young and the equating of signs of aging with decreased social value.[79] Because more emphasis is placed on women's physical attractiveness than men's, however, women lose more esteem as they age.[80] Men may replace the admiration they enjoyed for their looks and physical fitness with the admiration that comes with building a successful career and its attendant gain in money, skill, and wisdom. So, while he may no longer be able to adopt an All-American Boy strategy dependent on golden locks and a hard, tanned physique, he can comfortably transition into a Breadwinner and, later, a Distinguished Gentleman.

Women, too, can attain occupational success that allows them to mediate the social consequences of aging, but the importance of women's appearance will make her mediation less effective than that of men. For women, writer Susan Sontag explains, beauty is tightly tied to youth: "Only one standard of female beauty is sanctioned: the girl."[81] In other words, women, as they age, are pushed to try to preserve youthfulness in order to preserve attractiveness. For men, she argues, there are two standards of beauty: the boy and the man. This allows men to transition to a different kind of attractiveness as they age, one not available to women. She writes:

> The beauty of a boy resembles the beauty of a girl. In both sexes it is a fragile kind of beauty and flourishes naturally only in the early part of the life-cycle. Happily, men are able to accept themselves under another standard of good looks—heavier, rougher, more thickly built. A man does not grieve when he loses

the smooth, unlined, hairless skin of a boy. For he has only exchanged one form of attractiveness for another: the darker skin of a man's face, roughened by daily shaving, showing the marks of emotion and the normal lines of age. There is no equivalent of this second standard for women. The single standard of beauty for women dictates that they must go on having clear skin. Every wrinkle, every line, every gray hair, is a defeat.[82]

Aging takes more of a toll on some groups than others. An aging body may be harder on a Blue-Collar Guy or Country Boy who relies on his body to do physical labor, compared to an upper-class man whose occupation requires him to be cognitively sharp but not physically able. Likewise, working-class women are more likely to be in occupations that trade more directly on their attractiveness. Waitresses and secretaries, for example, may see their employability slip or their tips decline; they don't have the class privilege that enables them to trade occupational success for their fading looks. Moreover, working-class women are less likely to have the resources to fight aging. Women with financial resources can look younger longer with excellent nutrition, good medical care, expensive beauty products, well-made and well-fitting clothes, gym memberships, personal trainers, and even cosmetic procedures (from Botox to face-lifts). It's a cruel reality: Working-class women, on average, lose their looks more quickly than middle- and upper-class women at the same time that losing their looks carries greater costs.

Eventually, of course, all women will fail to look like girls, and at some point, aging will diminish a man's masculinity to the point where he is hardly seen as a man at all.

Revisiting the Question

 If gender is just one part of who we are, why isn't it crowded out by all the other things about us that are meaningful and consequential?

Gender isn't crowded out by other characteristics because it doesn't compete with those things so much as collude with them. Gender intersects with our other socially salient identities, inflecting them with gendered meaning. As we carve out a masculine or feminine identity, we develop a strategy designed to manage all these expectations, constraints, and opportunities. Some gender strategies are more realistic for us than others. Our individual characteristics, and the organization of our societies, affect what we can pull off and shape the consequences for deviation from and conformity to gender rules in complicated ways. In other words, we don't all have the same choices.

Given our lot in life, we all try to adopt a gender strategy that recognizes and accommodates all our identities and opportunities while maximizing our own well-being and life chances. We try to distance ourselves from stigmatizing identities such as Dangerous Black Man, Deadbeat Dad, and Desperate Housewife, but we don't all have the same resources to claim an unproblematic, widely admired identity. So we choose the least stigmatizing identity we can, like the "Wannabes"; or we adopt multiple strategies, like the girls who oscillate between Oriental Flower and Outgoing Asian; or we hold on as tightly as possible to a valorized identity so as to push away a stigmatized one, like the disabled Still a Man and the All but Heterosexual gay guy. We accept that others may accuse us of de-emphasizing parts of ourselves, like the black woman who does Girly Girl or the Career Woman who hires help to take care of her children; or we try to be everything to everyone, like the Supermom. These struggles are intertwined with the pleasure of doing gender, but this is more of a struggle for some of us than it is for others.

Next . . .

We all face various cultural rules that dictate our behavior and limit our options. Yet, there is a tradition of women, but not men, protesting gender rules and the necessity of developing a gender strategy. This seems like a good time to pose the question:

If both men and women are constrained by a binary gender system, why is it that more women than men find this system unfair?

This question brings us to the part of the book where we tackle the issue of inequality.

FOR FURTHER READING

Anzaldúa, Gloria. "La Conciencia de la Mestiza." *Borderlands/La Frontera: The New Mestiza*. San Francisco: Spinsters/Aunt Lute, 1987.

Espiritu, Yen Le. *Asian American Women and Men: Labor, Laws and Love*. Lanham, MD: Rowman and Littlefield, 2008.

Hoang, Kimberly. "Transnational Gender Vertigo." *Contexts* 12, no. 2 (2013): 22–26.

Hunter, Margaret. "The Persistent Problem of Colorism: Skin Tone, Status, and Inequality." *Sociology Compass* 1, no. 1 (2007): 237–54.

Spade, Joan, and Catherine Valentine, eds. *The Kaleidoscope of Gender: Prisms, Patterns, and Possibilities*. Thousand Oaks, CA: Pine Forge Press, 2008.

Williams, L. Susan. "Doing Culture with Girls Like Me: Why Trying on Gender and Intersectionality Matters." *Sociology Compass* 3, no. 2 (2009): 217–33.

"DUDES," HE SAID,
"DO *NOT* FOLLOW OTHER
DUDES TO THE BATHROOM.

—*CITY OF FALLEN ANGELS*

6

Inequality:

MEN AND MASCULINITIES

D oing gender, as we have seen, is not optional for either men or women. Even those who attempt to subvert the system cannot completely escape its rules and sanctions. This makes some people unhappy or angry about the way this system works. You may be one of them. Yet it is also obvious that more women than men object to gender relations in their societies. This leads us to our question:

Q+A **If both men and women are constrained by a binary gender system, why is it that more women than men find this system unfair?**

We begin to resolve this question by looking at how the costs and rewards of doing gender are distributed unequally. We will show that while men and women both need to do gender in order to be seen as sane and competent members of society, we do not do gender in symmetrical ways, and the consequences of our gender performances are not the same. This is because the gender binary is *hierarchical*. It places men above women, values masculinity above femininity, and routinely brings men and women together into relationships in which women are positioned as helpers to men.

This is bad for both men and women, but in different ways. For men more than women, it narrows the range of life experiences that seem acceptable and right. For women more than men, it results in reduced social status, lower material rewards, and an expectation that men's needs and interests should take priority. Gender inequality, then, isn't just about preferring men over women. It involves a far more complex calculus. Let's begin with an example.

THE GENDER OF CHEERLEADING

At its inception in the mid-1800s, cheerleading was an all-male sport. Characterized by gymnastics, stunts, and crowd leadership, it was considered equivalent in prestige to an American flagship of masculinity—football. As the editors of the *Nation* saw it in 1911:

> *The reputation of having been a valiant "cheer-leader" is one of the most valuable things a boy can take away from college. As a title to promotion in professional or public life, it ranks hardly second to that of having been a quarterback.*[1]

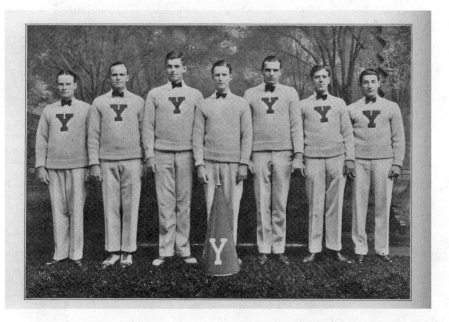

The men of the Yale University cheerleading team stand proud in 1927.

Indeed, cheerleading helped launch the political careers of three U.S. presidents: Dwight D. Eisenhower, Franklin Roosevelt, and Ronald Reagan were cheerleaders.[2] Actor Jimmy Stewart was head cheerleader at Princeton. Republican Tom DeLay was a noted cheerleader at the University of Mississippi.

Women were first given the opportunity to join squads when large numbers of young men were deployed to fight World War I, leaving open spots that women were happy to fill. When the men returned from the war, however, there was an effort to push women back out of cheerleading. Some schools even banned female cheerleaders. Argued one opponent in 1938:

> *[Women cheerleaders] frequently became too masculine for their own good. We find the development of loud, raucous voices . . . and the consequent development of slang and profanity by their necessary association with [male] squad members.*[3]

Cheerleading was too masculine for women.

Ultimately the effort to preserve cheer as an exclusively male activity was unsuccessful. With a second mass deployment of men during World War II, women cheerleaders were here to stay. The presence of women changed how

By the sixties and seventies, cheerleaders were primarily female and the activity became less about leadership and more about support and sexiness.

people thought about cheering. Because women were stereotyped as cute instead of "valiant," the reputation of cheerleaders changed. Instead of a pursuit that "ranks hardly second" to quarterbacking, cheerleading's association with women led to its trivialization. By the 1950s, the ideal cheerleader was no longer a strong athlete with leadership skills; it was someone with "manners, cheerfulness, and good disposition." In response, boys pretty much turned away from cheerleading altogether. So, by the 1960s, men with megaphones had been replaced by perky girls with pom-poms:

> *Cheerleading in the sixties consisted of cutesy chants, big smiles and revealing uniforms. There were no gymnastic tumbling runs. No complicated stunting. Never any injuries. About the most athletic thing sixties cheerleaders did was a cartwheel followed by the splits.*[4]

The demotion of cheerleading from a respected pursuit to a trivialized show on the sidelines has everything to do with gender.

GENDERED POWER

Patriarchy: Then and Now

The literal meaning of the word **patriarchy** is the rule of the father. It refers to the control of female and younger male family members by select adult men, or patriarchs. America and many European societies were patriarchies well into the 1800s and, in some cases, the 1900s. In a patriarchy, young and low-status men, as well as women, are subordinated to high-status men. In these societies, only patriarchs have rights. Women cannot have custody of their children and have no right to divorce. Men decide where the family lives and whom their children marry. If a woman works outside the home, she does so only with the permission of the head of household (a father, brother, or husband), and her earnings are given directly to him. A patriarch may have social and legal permission to physically punish both his wife or wives and children, brutally if he chooses. He is "the king of the castle," so his word is law at home. Meanwhile, because men alone have the right to enter contracts and make claims on the state, only men are entitled to act freely in the outside world. A patriarch can choose whether and how to represent the interests of his wife and children.

Life really was like this for a long time. As states evolved from monarchies to democracies, though, the relationship among citizens changed. Democratic states offered a new political bargain that increasingly brought a wider range of men together as equals. White land-owning men, primarily, shook off the power of kings, shahs, pharaohs, and fathers to act freely as equal citizens. A limited **brotherhood**—the distribution of power to a certain class of men—replaced patriarchy.

Women had to fight for the rights of citizenship offered to elite men in these early democracies. Only slowly, in struggle after struggle, did women win the right to vote, hold office, keep their own earnings, control their own property, choose their profession, establish their own home, seek a divorce, and keep their own children.[5] These struggles have changed both laws and customs so that **formal gender equality**—the legal requirement that men and women be treated more or less the same—has come to be seen as common sense. Most people in most countries today, that is, would object to both classic patriarchies and democratic brotherhoods as unfair.

Nevertheless, these long, hard political struggles reflect an underlying and still-relevant way of *thinking* about gender. First, whereas one no longer needs to be male to count as an autonomous person in the world, men continue to be conceived of as the generic human, with women as deviant from the norm. Consider the fact that political concerns are often divvied up into *issues* and *women's issues*; the way that the bathroom symbol for *men's* is the same one you see virtually everywhere representing *person*; or the way that classes on gender are often assumed to be primarily about women, as if men aren't gendered. Men's identity as men is often invisible, while women's identity as women is usually centrally important. In other words, men are seen as people first and men second, whereas women are seen as women first and people second.

The salience of women's but not men's gender is reflected in the way our brains process language. Studies show that the words *he*, *his*, and *man* (when used generically to refer to individuals or the human race) and the words *human*, *individual*, and *person* tend to conjure up images of men, not men and women.[6] As a comparison, these examples work kind of like the word *kid*. The word is used to describe the pre-adult version of both humans and goats but, in most contexts (that is, off the farm or petting zoo), the word is believed to unambiguously refer to a child. We know that the word *kid* can refer to goats, but in practice, when it's used, goats don't come to mind. It's the same with male pronouns and nouns. Women are all too often excluded from the terms, even if they're in the definition. One sign that we live in a modified patriarchy, then, is the persistent centering of men as normal or neutral and the marginalizing of women as a modified, non-neutral type of person, a relative of a real (male) person.

Second, most of us still live in societies that symbolically equate the exercise of power with masculinity. In both patriarchies and brotherhoods the right of an individual to act in the world authoritatively was contingent on being male. To have power was to be a man. In other words, power itself was gendered.

It's still that way. In contemporary American English, masculinity and femininity are synonyms for power and powerlessness, respectively. According to thesaurus.com, synonyms for the word *power* include *male*, *manful*, *manlike*, *manly*, and *masculine*, while synonyms for *weakness* include *effeminate*, *effete*, *emasculate*, and *womanly*.[7]

Likewise, the word *femininity* is synonymous with the terms *docility*, *delicacy*, and *softness*, whereas the word *masculine* is synonymous with the terms *courageous*, *hardy*, *muscular*, *potent*, *powerful*, *robust*, *strong*, *vigorous*, and *well-built*.[8] These synonyms reveal that "gender is a primary way of signifying relationships of power."[9] Whether you are male or female, to be weaker or subordinate is to be seen as less masculine, to run the risk of social *emasculation*. Whereas, to be powerful or exercise authority is to invoke the aura of masculinity, to *have balls*, to *man up*. If we want to communicate that a person, idea, or institution is weak or strong, we often do so with gendered language.

We live, then, in a **modified patriarchy**. On the one hand, gender egalitarianism is the default in modern societies. Part of being "modern," many people believe, is accepting the basic political equality of individuals. This is a far cry from the classic political model of fathers as little kings. On the other hand, despite the many modifications made to patriarchal practices, the patriarchal conflation of power and masculinity remains a central part of contemporary life.

In other words, we still live in societies that are characterized by patriarchal relations. Specifically, three relations of inequality shape the hierarchical nature of contemporary gender dynamics: sexism, androcentrism, and subordination.

Relations of Inequality

Sexism is prejudice against people based on their biological sex. It is the best word to describe valuing male over female children, the belief that men are naturally better at math, or the conviction that men are better suited for public office.[10] Many studies have shown that both men and women tend to hold sexist beliefs. In a study published in 2012, for example, 127 professors of biology, chemistry, and physics were asked to evaluate the application materials of a fictional person seeking a laboratory manager position.[11] Half the professors received a résumé with a female name; the other half received the exact same résumé with a male name. On average, compared to male applicants, females were rated as less competent, less hirable, and deserving of less mentorship and a lower salary. Both male and female professors showed this bias.

This is a common finding. Psychologist Janet Swim and colleagues reviewed 123 experimental studies asking study subjects to evaluate writing, artwork, behavior, job applications, and biographies attributed to fictional men or women.[12] The aggregated study results show that holding everything else constant, women are evaluated less positively than men by virtue of their sex alone. The same résumé, piece of art, or life's work may be seen as less impressive if the evaluator thinks it belongs to a woman instead of a man.

If sexism is sex-based prejudice, then **androcentrism** is gender based prejudice: the granting of higher status, respect, value, reward, and power to the masculine compared to the feminine. We've discussed the practice of dividing and subdividing the world into gendered categories already. Using music, sports, food, work, and animals as examples, we argued that our gender binary glasses encourage us to divide everything into the masculine and the feminine. Because of androcentrism, we don't simply divide the world; we order it hierarchically. So we do more than say that dogs are masculine and cats feminine; we also suggest that dogs and "dog people" are somehow cooler than cats and "cat people." If you're a guy who prefers cats, it's best to prepare a set of accounts to explain why ("it's my parents' cat," "the landlord doesn't allow dogs," "I'm just waiting till I have a yard," "I'm a hipster; it's ironic," etc.). And while it's OK for women to have a cat, having too many cats makes you a "crazy cat lady."

Androcentrism is very different than sexism because the rewards are not limited to people with one body or another. Instead, in a society characterized by androcentrism, rewards accrue to *anyone* who can do masculinity. This explains why women tend to embrace masculine traits and activities, but men tend to avoid feminine ones. We'll explain later in more detail; for now, notice that in practice, androcentrism means what is good for men (masculinity) is believed to be good for everyone, but what is good for women (femininity) is considered only good for women. This is why women wear pants and men don't wear skirts, why women become doctors but men have resisted becoming nurses, and why women have pushed their way into soccer and ski jumping, but men are leaving synchronized swimming and softball to the ladies.

In a third relation of power, men and women are brought together into hierarchical relationships, often through conformity with gendered expectations. This placing of women into positions that make them subservient to or dependent on men is called **subordination**. Nursing, for instance, is a feminized occupation dominated by women. But it is not just feminine and female; it also puts nurses into a subordinate relationship with doctors. Doctors tell nurses what to do; nurses "help" doctors do their job. The same is true for the gendered relationships between managers and secretaries, dentists and dental hygienists, and lawyers and paralegals.[13] These occupational roles are gendered. In the United States, women represent 90 percent of registered nurses, 92 percent of receptionists, 94 percent of administrative assistants, 98 percent of dental hygienists, and 86 percent of paralegals.[14] Men become secretaries and paralegals, of course, but this doesn't change the underlying understanding that it is "women's work." Likewise, women become managers and dentists, but typically

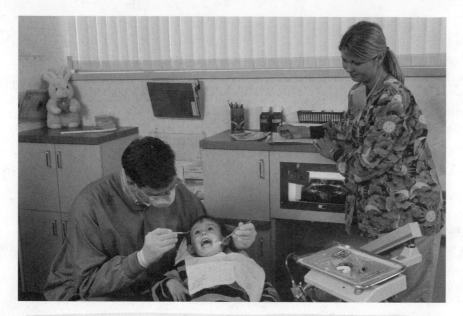

Dental hygienist is a gendered occupation that puts women in a subordinate relationship with dentists. In 2013, women made up 98 percent of dental hygienists.

the support they receive—from their secretaries and assistants—is still provided by women.

When occupational and other roles are gendered, then, they often place a woman in a position subordinate to a man, helping him and cheering him on as he does the high-profile, exciting, well-rewarded work. Meanwhile, the boss often has more control over who serves, helps, or assists him, making the woman's role dependent on his ongoing approval. Being support staff on a civic project or an aide to a diplomat are both examples of how women's interests in certain kinds of work (city planning and politics) are channeled into subordinate roles. Women are so frequently found in such roles that it often feels natural for women to be "the wind beneath his wings" rather than "top dog," and unnatural when it's otherwise. The supporting role is a distinctly feminine one, and it brings men and women—or masculine and feminine people—into a distinctly close yet unmistakably hierarchical relationship.

We do not live in a world that simply insists upon gender difference; we live in one that imbues men, masculine people, and masculinized activities with more status, value, and power than women, feminine people, and feminized activities. These asymmetries in the gender binary—and the relations between men and women that emerge—make doing gender a *different* challenge for men and women. Next, we talk about how men negotiate the hierarchical gender binary.

GENDER FOR MEN

Sociologist Emily Kane interviewed parents about their children's gender-conforming and nonconforming behavior.[15] Parents of boys, she found, were highly ambivalent about their sons participating in "girly" activities. Generally they tolerated their interest in learning how to cook and clean, but there was near universal distress over boys' interest in the "icons of femininity."[16] Kane explains:

> Parents of sons reported negative responses to their sons' wearing pink or frilly clothing; wearing skirts, dresses, or tights; and playing dress up in any kind of feminine attire. Nail polish elicited concern from a number of parents, too, as they reported young sons wanting to have their fingernails or toenails polished. Dance, especially ballet, and Barbie dolls were also among the traditionally female activities often noted negatively by parents of sons.[17]

Parents' negative reaction to boys' "feminine sides" reflects androcentrism and reveals the stigmatizing nature of femininity for men. Taking for granted that feminine interests and behaviors were inappropriate for boys, parents were confused when their boys acted this way. It suggested that something was *wrong*. The behavior demanded explanation. "Is he going to grow up to be gay? A transsexual? Is his relationship with his father too weak? Is his mother too overbearing? What is going on!?" Kane found that even parents who were tolerant of gender deviance themselves often sought to protect their sons from social disapproval by discouraging their adoption of femininity.

Doing Masculinity, Avoiding Femininity

Because of these lessons, boys tend to grow up learning that they should avoid femininity. Sociologist Michael Kimmel claims that one can start a fight on any playground by asking a group of boys, "Who's a sissy around here?"[18] *Sissy* is just one of the many slurs that enter the vocabulary of young boys as they learn to police one another's gender display. All these terms essentially instruct boys and men to avoid being in any way feminine. This is true with insults like *girl* and *woman*, which literally use a female identity to disparage a man. Other common slurs applied to both men and women reference women or femininity (like *douche*, *skirt*, *pussy*, and *bitch*). All these terms reflect a sexist and androcentric world, telling both boys and girls, in no uncertain terms, that being feminine makes you a girl and being a girl is bad.

The slurs related to homosexuality (e.g., *fag*, *homo*, *gay*) send the same message.[19] Being gay is actually rather incidental. Any man or boy who is perceived to be feminine attracts these slurs.[20] In fact, studies have shown that boys and men often actively avoid calling *known* homosexuals by these terms, even when they otherwise liberally pepper their language with them. In one study of college athletes, "everything was fag this and fag that," but after some of their teammates revealed their sexual orientation, the athletes stopped using it in reference to the *gay* players.[21] "They say, 'this is gay,' and 'that's gay,'" one gay athlete explained, "but they don't mean it like that."[22] In other words, they don't mean "gay" as in *gay*; they mean "gay" as in *feminine*. Accusations of homosexuality can be understood as a form of gender policing. This is true, also, of slurs like *cocksucker* and the phrase *suck my dick*; each denigrates someone who sexually services a man—male or female—and thereby inhabits the feminine side of the binary.

The chorus of slurs stigmatizing men who perform femininity sends a consistent message, a rule designed to guide all men's behavior: *Guys, whatever you do, avoid acting like a girl*. Ironically, as sociologist Gwen Sharp suggests, it is as if "masculinity is so fragile that apparently even the slightest brush with the feminine destroys it."[23] This imperative means that men, in at least some parts of their lives, face enormous pressure to avoid doing anything associated with women.

Avoiding femininity can be extremely constraining, requires constant vigilance, and extends to the most trivial of things. Here's a fun example: a series of online slideshows with titles like "Drinks Men Should Never Order."[24] The list of drinks that men must avoid includes (take a deep breath) anything blended or slushy; Jell-O shots or anything "neon"; white zinfandel; drinks with "an obscene amount of garnish"; anything with whipped cream; anything that ends with "tini" (except an "honest martini"); malt beverages (unless they are "'40s"); anything with Diet Coke; cosmopolitans (they're "downright girly"); wine coolers; anything that comes with an umbrella; anything fruity (including fuzzy navels, Bacardi breezes, mai tais, screwdrivers, margaritas, daiquiris, and Alabama slammers); all mixed drinks (seriously, all of them); and anything with a straw.

One slideshow concludes with the insistence that, above all else, a guy can't have anything that "she's having" on the assumption that anything a woman drinks is immediately off-limits for men. Men are abandoning the bar drink by drink. What will happen when women are sipping from *all* the bottles?

We are being tongue in cheek, but this dynamic has serious social consequences, too. Because of androcentrism, when women successfully integrate a masculine domain, their growing presence makes it unappealing to men. One result is **male flight**, a phenomenon in which men abandon feminizing arenas of life. This is what happened with cheerleading. The same happens in professional occupations. As women join a profession, men leave it.[25] A study of veterinary school applications, for example, found that for every 1 percent increase in the proportion of women in the student body, 1.7 fewer men applied.[26] One more woman was a greater deterrent than $1,000 in extra tuition. Male flight exacerbates the trend toward feminization, quickly ramping up the pace at which a given domain seems inappropriate for men.

This is no trivial matter. Consider education: Women are now outperforming men at all levels of schooling. They are more likely to be identified as "gifted and talented" in elementary school, about half as likely to be held back a year in middle school, and less likely to drop out of high school.[27] There is no level of higher education in which men dominate. Women earn 62 percent of associate's, 57 percent of bachelor's, and 63 percent of master's degrees. They even earn 53 percent of PhDs.[28] And they get better grades all along the way.[29]

As girls and women have increasingly excelled in school, boys and men have begun to associate education with femininity. Thinking studiousness is for girls, they don't study or, if they do, they hide their hard work.[30] Underachievement is seen as cool for men, especially if they pretend not to care. Accordingly, men are less interested in studying and getting good grades than women, especially if they've strongly internalized the rules of masculinity.[31] Working-class men who decide not to pursue higher education sometimes frame their disinterest in terms of masculinity.[32] Will men abandon education because women are getting too good at it? It is understandable why men might flee feminizing areas of life, given the very real constraints they face, but they are effectively backing themselves into a smaller and smaller corner of society. What else will they let go? What happens when all that's left is football, beer, and man caves?

And what could possibly be the advantage of limiting one's life options in order to be a perfectly manly man who only drinks beer, honest martinis, and other stuff women supposedly don't drink? The answer has to do with a concept we call hegemony.

Hegemonic Masculinity

Hegemony is a sociological concept used to help us understand the persistence of social inequality. It refers to a state of collective consent to inequality that is secured by the idea that it is inevitable, natural, or desirable. An idea is hegemonic only when it is widely endorsed by both those who benefit from the social conditions it supports and those who do not. Hegemony, then, means widespread consent to the social disadvantage of some.

Capitalism is a great example of a hegemonic ideology. Most Americans will argue that capitalism is a fair and effective economic system. You might agree. But it's hard to deny that it works better for some than for others. It's not working very well for the parents of the 22 percent of American children who live in

Known for womanizing, whiskey, good looks, and good copy, Don Draper of *Mad Men* is the embodiment of hegemonic masculinity. Like all hegemonic heroes, he struggles with the contradictions faced by anyone attempting to be the perfect man.

poverty or the 53 million people who have fallen out of the middle class as it has shrunk over the last four decades.[33] Still, instead of banding together and saying, "this may be working for *you*, but this isn't working for *us*," even the poorest of Americans will typically defend capitalism as the best and most just option for the United States. This is hegemony.

The phrase **hegemonic masculinity** refers to a type of man, idealized by men and women alike, who functions to justify and naturalize gender inequality.[34] The hegemonic man is the "real man" in our collective imagination who theoretically embodies all the most positive traits on the masculine side of the gender binary. He has the athlete's speed and strength, the CEO's income, the politician's power, the Hollywood heartthrob's charm, the family man's loyalty, the construction worker's manual skills, the frat boy's tolerance for alcohol, and the playboy's virility. We then attribute these individual traits to the category "man" (overlooking, of course, the ways that women sometimes embody these traits and men sometimes don't).

All men, by virtue of being men, have some claim to all these traits, even if they don't themselves possess them. A married father who loves his wife may nod approvingly at the playboy and say, "*We men* just like women." Meanwhile, the playboy, who is a struggling musician, can point to the politician and say, "*We men* are in control," while the politician points to the frat boy and says, "*We men* like to party hard." That frat boy may be getting solid Cs, but he can point to the doctor and say, "*We men* are ambitious," while the doctor, who may never have punched anyone in his life, can cheer on the professional boxer and say, "*We men* know how to fight." The boxer, who voluntarily risks getting hit in the face, can point to the scientist and say, "*We men* are logical." You get the idea. Just by virtue of their membership in the category, all men get some claim to the characteristics we attribute to men in general. In this way, men benefit from the hegemony of masculinity. They can lay a socially valid claim to the positive traits attributed to men in a society that imagines men and women to be opposites.

Importantly, however, the benefits of masculinity are not awarded equally to all men. *Some* men will be able to approximate and lay claim to ideal masculinity more successfully than others.

The Measure of Men

In many ways, men who fail to embody hegemonic masculinity are seen as lesser men. These judgments matter. They are used to establish a **hierarchy of men,** a rough ranking of men from most to least masculine, with the assumption that more masculine is better. Men who are subordinated in other hierarchies, for instance, are vulnerable to being judged as failing to embody the hegemonic ideal and, thus, tend to fall lower on the hierarchy than men who don't carry marginalized identities. This is because the hegemonic man, implicitly, embodies the positive end of *all* hierarchies in a society, not just the gender hierarchy. In Western societies, then, he is typically a well-educated, tall, affluent, white, heterosexual, able-bodied, fit, Christian, nonimmigrant with hair.

This is why the Asian and black men discussed in Chapter 5 are imagined to be not manly enough and too manly, respectively. It is also why disabled and aging men sometimes feel like they're losing their masculinity; society defines "real men" as something they're not. Working-class men are often portrayed as particularly strong with hard-working bodies, but they are simultaneously seen as somehow too manly: tough to the point of brutishness and, thus, unintelligent and prone to violence. Men who are physically weak ("wimps"), emotional ("sissies"), uncool ("nerds"), or who break important gender rules ("fags") are all vulnerable to being defined in gender terms as lesser men.

Even men who are blessed with the physical bodies, cultural identities, social circumstances, and personalities that allow them to most closely approximate the hegemonic man will never be able to rest assured that they are "real" men. Men's ability to perform hegemonic masculinity is always at risk, no matter how privileged they seem. And all men *will* fail sooner or later. They will fail, first, because the hegemonic man is an impossible fiction, a jumble of idealized, contradictory elements. A person can't be both a perfect husband and a playboy, responsible and devil-may-care, or hard bodied and hard drinking. No single man will ever be able to approximate the full scope of hegemonic masculinity. They will fail, second, because no one can win all the time. A man's masculinity is potentially undermined by competitive losses (at sports, jobs, fights, fathering children, or any other masculinity-defining activity), and aging and disability always threaten to rob men of the body of a "real man."

Accordingly, all men will at times find themselves lacking in some way, leading every man "to view himself—during moments at least—as unworthy, incomplete, and inferior."[35] As Michael Kaufman, a scholar of masculinity, puts it:

Whatever power might be associated with dominant masculinities, they also can be the source of enormous pain. Because the images are, ultimately, childhood pictures of omnipotence, they are impossible to obtain. Surface appearances aside, no man is completely able to live up to these ideas and images.[36]

But many men try. They try to "stay in control," "conquer . . . and call the shots"; they try to "tough it out, provide, and achieve" and, in the meantime, they have to repress the things about them that conflict with hegemonic masculinity.[37] They have to try not to feel, need, or desire the things they're not supposed to feel, need, or desire. Because hegemonic masculinity pressures men to be a particular kind of impossible person, it is a significant source of oppression for men.

Accordingly, to many men, gender rules *do* feel like oppression. When prompted, some will talk about the requirement that they wear a mask or "guise" that projects masculinity and hides the things about them that are off-limits. In a set of interviews with men in college, students explained that masculinity meant acting homophobic, being competitive with other men, and hiding emotional vulnerability. One interviewee, Chauncey, explained: "I am more of an emotional person. . . . I never really felt much like who I [pretended to be] because I felt that maybe it was like—I guess, maybe me putting my man face on."[38] Jason reported that he only listened to R&B music when he was alone, for fear of being policed. Kumar would do "stupid hook-up things . . . just to kind of prove yourself."[39] Chet talked about the difficulty he had being open with even his closest friends: "If a guy starts opening up to another guy, he will joke around like, 'You look like you are ready to make out with me.' . . . I have done it."[40]

As Chet's example suggests, much of the time men follow gender rules not to impress women but to avoid the censure of other men. In this way, men may be granted the privilege of looking down on women, but they also know that other men may be looking down on them. Classical patriarchy was always as much about relations among men as it was about relations between women and men; modified, modernized patriarchal relations still are. Hegemonic masculinity, then—and this is important—doesn't simply position men above women, it arranges men in *a hierarchy all their own.*

This means that it's simply not true to say that all men have more power than all women. Being male is an advantage, yes, and being a *masculine* male is a greater advantage, for sure. But men who can't or won't do masculinity can fall in the masculine hierarchy such that women with other kinds of privilege—like race or class privilege—may enjoy greater social esteem. And because gender is not the only game in town, men's disadvantages can significantly outweigh their gender advantage. Because of **colorism**, a racist preference for light skin, for example, a light-skinned black woman may have more social power than a dark-skinned black man; because we are also arranged in a class hierarchy, a male gardener likely has significantly less social power than the rich woman whose flowers he cultivates; because of disability stigma, an able-bodied woman may be taken more seriously than a man with a spinal cord injury. It's important to remember that some women may have significantly more power, resources, and status than some men, even if men, on average, have more power and prestige than women. As Kaufman explains: "Within each group, men usually have privileges and power relative to the women in that group, but in society as a whole, things are not always so straightforward."[41]

As a result of the expectation that men live up to an impossible ideal, the uneven way in which masculine power is distributed, and the pressure upon men to be someone they're not, many individual men do not *feel* particularly powerful at all. Many feel downright powerless in many areas of their lives: at work, in their relationships, and in relation to other men, on whose judgment their status in the hierarchy depends. Men, it turns out, often feel a disconnect between who they are and the power that "men" are said to have. There is a good reason for this, but it is not, as some like to argue, because we no longer live in a society characterized by gender inequality. Instead, the idea of the hegemonic man holds up both men's power over women and men's power over other men.

For men, then, there are also costs to pay. And because gendered hierarchies are strongly and even violently policed, both conformity and resistance can be dangerous.

The Danger of Masculinity

HARMING OTHERS Extreme conformity to the more aggressive rules of masculinity, or **hypermasculinity**, is glorified in many corners of our culture. We particularly idealize it in some music genres (such as rap and heavy metal) and in action movies and video games that glamorize male violence and ignore its real-life consequences. We also see such performances by some athletes (especially in highly masculinized sports like football and hockey). These performances naturalize men's violence, aggression, and anger. So even though most men we know are not violent at all, hypermasculine performances take on a heightened reality and construct men as emotionally hard and physically aggressive. Because of androcentrism, men's aggression may even seem good or right, such as when they protect women, go after "bad guys," or defend their country.

Despite the prevalence of hypermasculinity, men are *not* naturally violent. Instead, men must be trained to resist "impulses to empathize with victims" of verbal and physical violence and encouraged to enter dangerous situations enthusiastically.[42] We see hypermasculinity nurtured, especially, in some fraternities, military units, police squads, gangs, and prisons. We see it among some poor, urban men and some male politicians or CEOs whose masculine

The movie poster for *300: Rise of an Empire* glamorizes hypermasculine violence.

performances often include aggressive posturing and bullying. We see it, too, among some athletes in especially physical sports.[43] Men in these situations may avoid demonstrating feminized qualities like empathy, nurturance, kindness, and conflict avoidance in favor of exaggerated performances of verbal and physical aggression. And almost no man does it all of the time, though sometimes his mother, girlfriend, or wife is the only person who ever sees him without his hypermasculine mask.

Partly as a result of this anti-empathy training, we see gender differences in who commits violent acts. In 2012, men accounted for 89 percent of those convicted of murder and nonnegligent manslaughter, 77 percent of those arrested for aggravated assault, 73 percent of those arrested for family violence, 99 percent of those arrested for rape, 82 percent of those arrested for arson, and 92 percent of those arrested for unlawful carrying of weapons (Table 6.1).[44] Gang violence, suicide bombings, serial killings, and school shootings are all overwhelmingly perpetuated by men.

HARM TO THE SELF Taking masculinity to such an extreme makes men dangerous to others, but it also threatens to make men dangerous to themselves.[45] Men are significantly more likely than women to disregard their own safety. They are more likely than women to break seat belt laws, drive dangerously, smoke cigarettes, take sexual risks, and abuse drugs and alcohol; they compose 75 percent of those arrested for drunken driving and 82 percent of those arrested for public drunkenness. They go into dangerous jobs and then resist safety rules, accounting for 93 percent of occupational deaths. They are almost three times more likely to die in a car accident.[46] They are less likely than women to undergo regular health screenings, take vitamins, get regular exercise, see a doctor if they feel sick, and treat existing illnesses and injuries.[47] The association of lotion and body care with women leads men to dismiss the im-

TABLE 6.1 | ARRESTS BY SEX, 2012

Offense charged	Percent male
Murder and nonnegligent manslaughter	88.7
Forcible rape	99.1
Robbery	87.0
Aggravated assault	77.1
Burglary	83.6
Arson	82.0
Larceny-theft	56.9
Motor vehicle theft	81.1
Fraud	59.5
Embezzlement	51.6
Vandalism	79.8
Weapons, carrying, possessing, etc.	91.7
Drug abuse violations	79.7
Driving under the influence	75.3

Source: Federal Bureau of Investigation, Crime in the U.S., 2012, fbi.gov/about-us/cjis/ucr/crime-in-the-U.S/2012/crime-in-the -U.S.-2012, accessed 5/6/14.

portance of sunscreen; they are two to three times more likely to be diagnosed with skin cancer.[48] Some argue that being male is the strongest predictor of whether a person will take risks with their health.[49]

Likewise, high school and college athletes sometimes exercise so hard that they overheat and collapse on the field, while body builders sometimes die from the damage done to their bodies with steroids and diuretics. The image above shows Ronnie Coleman breathing through an oxygen mask, immediately after walking off the stage at the Mr. Olympia competition. He would take first place. Photographer Zed Nelson explains that oxygen is frequently administered to contestants: "The strain of intense dieting, dehydration, and muscle-flexing places high levels of strain on the heart and lungs, rendering many contestants dizzy, light-headed, and weak."[50]

Men also take physical risks in their personal lives. They are far more likely to engage in fist fights than women. Sociologists Douglas Schrock and Michael Schwalbe summarize:

> As with crime, much of this health damaging behavior may be symbolic, intended to signify capacities to control one's own life, to be invulnerable and needless of

Professional bodybuilder Ronnie Coleman breathes pure oxygen immediately after competing in Mr. Olympia. Organizers make oxygen available backstage because contestants are frequently lightheaded after their performance.

help, and to be fearless and hence not easily intimidated by others. The effort to signify a masculine self ... can be toxic.[51]

Meanwhile, these same rules of masculinity discourage men from reaching out and forming strong, intimate friendships with other men.[52] To be close friends, men need to be willing to confess their insecurities, be kind to each other, have empathy, and sometimes sacrifice their own self-interest. This, though, is incompatible with the rules of masculinity. So as boys grow up to be men, they learn to resist the impulse to connect with other men.

Psychologist Niobe Way interviewed boys about their friendships in each year of high school. She found that younger boys spoke eloquently about their love for their male friends but, at about age fifteen, this began to change. One boy, for example, said this as a freshman:

[My best friend and I] love each other ... that's it ... you have this thing that is deep, so deep, it's within you, you can't explain it. It's just a thing that you know that person is that person. .... I guess in life, sometimes two people can really, really understand each other and really have a trust, respect and love for each other.[53]

Studies find that young boys form and maintain friendships that are similar to those between young girls, but these skills tend to whither, or be put to less use, among older boys and men.

By his senior year, he had changed his mind:

> [My friend and I] we mostly joke around. It's not like really anything serious or whatever.... I don't talk to nobody about serious stuff.... I don't talk to nobody. I don't share my feelings really. Not that kind of person or whatever.... It's just something that I don't do.

In part because of the rules of masculinity, adult, white heterosexual men have fewer friends than women and other men.[54] Since friendship strongly correlates with physical and mental health, this is another way in which closely following the rules of masculinity is bad for men.[55] Even as the imperative to hide emotions and deny psychological weakness makes it more likely for men to feel a deep sense of loneliness, women are more likely than men to seek help and be diagnosed for depression. Men are significantly more likely to commit suicide.

HYPERMASCULINITY IN INTERACTION Because gender is something we do with others, hypermasculinity isn't something men perform simply because they have internalized its values. Instead, it is enforced by others who police men's gender performances. Matthew Desmond's research on wildland firefighters, discussed in Chapter 5, is a study of a group of men collectively performing and enforcing hypermasculinity. To be accepted among the firefighters, the men had to suppress both their own emotions and empathy for others.

Desmond documented a constant and brutal trading of insults designed to constantly test men's willingness to conform to these rules: "Every day brings new derisive clashes, and loud, quick, crude, and abrasive crewmembers . . . prey on the shyer types."[56]

The battle of wits often involved policing the boundaries of masculinity with attempts to humiliate others with accusations of homosexuality or anger them with threats to harm people they loved. Desmond quoted a firefighter describing why he enjoyed the repartee:

> *It's fun to give your coworkers shit, you know. It's like, everybody does it and I like to piss everybody off, so I do it. It's a fun thing to do. To upset people out here is hilarious. To piss somebody off is the greatest thing ever out here, dude. When you know you're getting under somebody's skin, it's like, yes, I'm there. I love to do it. It's awesome.*[57]

The verbal beatings, Desmond argued, functioned as hazing rituals. The men were required to give and take physical jostling, cruel insults, and threats of violence to be a part of the group. But the insults and obscenities didn't function simply to facilitate group bonding and the exclusion of others; it also created a hierarchy within the group. The sharper your wit, the meaner your jokes, and the less you cared about anyone, the more status and dominance you accrued. If a firefighter lost his cool, got angry, or felt hurt, he failed in the eyes of the other men, attracting even more policing. Self-protection, in this system, meant conforming to expectations of hypermasculinity, enforcing it in others, and never stepping in to protect someone being targeted.

Sometimes it can be dangerous to refuse to participate. This was exactly the case for one of our students, Rick. Recently out of the army and enrolled in community college, Rick loudly and proudly confessed to his classmates that he participated in gang rapes of fellow male soldiers. The rapes functioned as an enactment of the extreme form of masculinity valued in their unit. It was a way for them to prove to their fellow soldiers that they were a particular kind of man, one physically and emotionally hard enough to victimize others without hesitation. The men who were targeted, Rick explained, were "pussies" and "fags" who "deserved it." Sodomizing them was a way to affirm their subordinate status. The sexual assault of men is not uncommon. One in thirty-three adult men will be a victim of sexual assault; the vast majority are assaulted by other men.[58]

Rick's classmates expressed outrage and disgust, condemning him for the rapes. But his response stunned them. He explained that participating in the gang rapes was a form of self-defense. "If I hadn't done it," he shouted, "I would have been next!" So he raped to avoid being raped. This story illustrates the role of violence in enforcing a male hierarchy, one in which the ability to be violent and unfeeling is treated with respect because it represents the opposite of femininity. It is defended by high-status men who have the most to lose, but also by men who are trying to avoid victimization themselves.

Hegemonic masculinity—this single standard of esteem for men—makes the position of even the most advantaged men perilous. Meanwhile, it sometimes presses them to put themselves or others in danger. So why don't men just say no to hegemonic masculinity?

Bargaining with Patriarchy

Instead of repudiating hegemonic masculinity, many men embrace strategies that allow them to benefit from being men, even if it simultaneously gives other men status over them. In other words, being *girly* places one at the bottom of the male hierarchy, and that's bad, but being *a girl* would be even worse. Accordingly, many men, even those who populate the bottom rungs of this hierarchy, will defend hegemonic masculinity. This is called a **patriarchal bargain**: a deal in which an individual or group accepts or even legitimates some of the costs of patriarchy in exchange for receiving some of its rewards.[59] Both men and women make patriarchal bargains. When men make such bargains, they accept some degree of subordination in the masculine hierarchy in exchange for the right to claim a higher status than women and some other men.

Few men make these bargains out of a simple desire to exert power over others. Instead, they make them because status translates into resources that raise one's quality of life and protect them from stigma and physical harm. Esteem from others—and the intimacies, connections, and jobs into which it translates— offers people autonomy, safety, and life satisfaction. Men make patriarchal bargains, then, because they want to maximize their happiness, not necessarily because they desire to dominate other men and women.

Sociologist Michael Messner described a moment during his boyhood when he made a patriarchal bargain. He sensed early on that sports were a "proving ground for masculinity" and that excelling would bring approval in the eyes of other men and women. Attracting this esteem, however, also meant participating in enforcing the hierarchy as he ascended it. In particular, he recounts teasing and bullying a nonathletic boy. This, he explains, was "a moment of engagement with hegemonic masculinity" where he upheld a masculine hierarchy that empowered him but disempowered others.[60]

Many men make patriarchal bargains. Gay men, for example, are disadvantaged in a system that defines masculinity in part through the successful pursuit of women. Frequently considered lesser men, gay men have a choice: They can either emphasize their masculinity so as to maximize the power that comes with being men or align themselves with women and other marginalized men against the gender binary.

Gay men sometimes choose the former. In one instance a group of gay men formed a fraternity in an attempt to benefit from membership in an association that affirms men as men.[61] Though they had two relevant identities—they were *gay* and they were *men*—they allowed heterosexual *men* to be members, but not *gay* women. In this way, they sought to highlight the more socially valuable identity. Women were allowed to participate in the fraternity only insofar as they affirmed the gay brothers' identity as men. To this end, the frat brothers welcomed "little sisters," the ostensibly heterosexual women who play a supportive role in Greek life, but rejected lesbians because the brothers believed they would expect to be treated as equals. One brother explained:

> I would prefer straight women because the lesbians would try and take over. A straight woman might enjoy being a little sister and attending functions and hanging out, while a lesbian would consider the role subordinate and get tired of it quickly, trying to dominate and manipulate the program. Basically, a straight woman might understand the role while a lesbian would not. . . . I see their role as supportive and basically helping out.[62]

As this quote illustrates, the gay men in these fraternities welcomed women into their fraternity, but only as subordinates. Meanwhile, they were enthusiastic about making alliances with men of all sexual orientations. In other words, by being gay and "out" they were actively *breaking* the association between fraternities and the sexual pursuit of women, but they were equally enthusiastic about *enforcing* the rule that fraternities bring men gendered privilege.

Nerds, dorks, and geeks form a trifecta of subordinated masculinities that are marginalized by some combination of social awkwardness, socially inappropriate interests, and physical weakness. One community of self-identified "nerds" revealed how some men will embrace their low position in the masculine hierarchy in exchange for the right to exclude women.[63] These men knew that they fell far below Brad Pitt in the masculine hierarchy, but instead of rejecting hegemonic masculinity as a fair measure of their own and others' worth, they pushed women away through denigration and sexual objectification, placing all women in the role of sex objects. In other words, like the gay fraternity brothers, they prioritized their identity as men and tried to grab whatever male privilege this offered by treating women as fundamentally different from and inferior to themselves. The ubiquitous and extreme sexualization of women in video games and comic books is part of this dynamic.

Fans in Tokyo line up to play the new *Grand Theft Auto* videogame. The game's advertising prominently features a buxom blonde in a bikini.

This bonding among men as men crosses racial and class lines, as illustrated by the career of the white rapper Eminem. Masculinities scholar Jackson Katz observes that Eminem has aligned himself with black people, both musically and politically, at the same time that his persona is intimately tied with vicious misogyny and virulent homophobia.[64] In his eighth album, released in 2013, he sings of pulling a woman through the window of a car and throwing her onto the street: "*I body slam her onto the cement, until the concrete gave and created a sinkhole / Bury this stink ho in it, then paid to have the street re-paved.*" On another track, he sings of killing a woman with a machine gun and throwing a party. Elsewhere women are "fucking pigs."

As the quote above illustrates, Eminem's antiracist politics do not extend to black *women*. Other lyrics make it clear that they also don't extend to black men who are gay. Eminem has made a patriarchal bargain. Representing a subordinated masculinity (he grew up poor), he aligns with men who also represent a subordinated masculinity (black men from similar backgrounds), and together they differentiate themselves from and claim superiority to all women and gay men.

Patriarchal bargains are ways for men to try to enhance or protect their well-being in a system that, in fact, is pretty hard on most of them. Even if they are low in the hierarchy, though, patriarchal bargains often offer them a little bit of status and, at the very least, protect them from the negative consequences of challenging the system. This is one important reason why so many men conspire to defend the rules of masculinity.

Revisiting the Question

 If both men and women are constrained by a binary gender system, why is it that more women than men find this system unfair?

There are good reasons for men to find the system unfair. Being male doesn't mean being free from gender; nor does it mean that life is easy. Because femininity is designated as only for women, men must avoid performing it; their daily lives are constrained by this imperative. As a result, men may repress those parts of themselves that do not reflect hegemonic masculinity and emphasize those that do, sticking only to man-approved masculine things and ways of being, at least in public or around certain kinds of people. In doing so, they miss out on lots of great things.

Moreover, preserving the privileges that come with maleness—both for individual men and the group—means preserving the hierarchical gender binary that gives hegemonic masculinity its power. This means rough policing of the boundaries of masculinity, which in turn can make masculinity dangerous, creating circumstances in which men are pushed to make dangerous choices, exposed to violence, or incited to harm others.

It's no surprise, then, that men sometimes find the rules of masculinity to be strict and arbitrary, but they often defend instead of challenge them because each man's position in the hierarchy depends on upholding them. They have to choose between following the rules or being seen as a failure. Other men are automatically excluded from the top of the masculine hierarchy by virtue of their race, class, immigration status, or some other disadvantage. For these men, especially, holding onto male privilege can be important; it may be the only kind of privilege they have. Accordingly, most men make patriarchal bargains in at least parts of their lives. No amount of bargaining protects them from the fear of emasculation, however. Wherever they fall in the hierarchy, all men have to live with some fear of losing the traction they've gained and sliding down to join the men on whose disadvantage their advantage depends.

Many men suffer greatly under this system and almost all men suffer at least a little bit. Ironically, men who may have the most to gain by rejecting the gender binary—those who fail to approximate the hegemonic ideal, live miserably under its rules, or are victimized by others for their rule breaking—are often the ones who are the most defensive about it because they are constantly worried about falling even lower. They defend hegemonic masculinity because at the very least it guarantees them superiority over somebody: women.

This helps explain why so few men actively challenge the gender binary, but we have yet to tackle why so many women do. To fully answer our question, we need to understand women's experiences.

FOR FURTHER READING

Edwards, Keith, and Susan Jones. "'Putting My Man Face On'": A Grounded Theory of College Men's Gender Identity Development." *Journal of College Student Development* 50 (2009): 210–28.

Halberstam, Judith. "An Introduction to Female Masculinity: Masculinity without Men." In *Female Masculinity*, 1–43. Durham: Duke University Press, 1998.

Kimmel, Michael. "Masculinity as Homophobia: Fear, Shame and Silence in the Construction of Gender Identity." In *Theorizing Masculinities*, edited by H. Brod and M. Kaufman, 119–142. Thousand Oaks, CA: Sage Publications, 1994.

Moss-Racusin, Corinne, John Dovidio, Victoria Brescoll, Mark Graham, and Jo Handelsman. "Science Faculty's Subtle Gender Biases Favor Male Students." *Proceedings of the National Academy of Sciences* 109, no. 41: (2012) 16474–79.

Richardson, Laurel. "Gender Stereotyping in the English Language." In *Feminist Frontiers* (6th ed.), edited by Laurel Richardson, Verta Taylor, and Nancy Whittier, 89–93. New York: McGraw Hill, 2004.

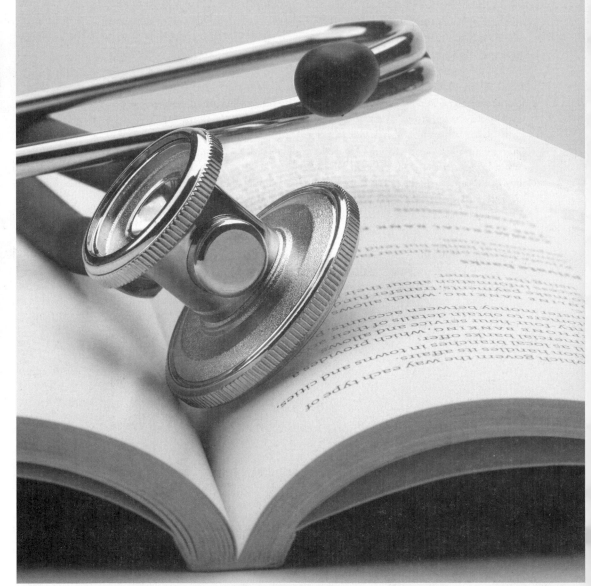

Inequality:

WOMEN AND FEMININITIES

The last chapter focused on how gendered power shapes men's experiences. In this chapter, we discuss women's lives. On the one hand, women have a lot more freedom than men to enjoy both masculine- and feminine-coded parts of life, a freedom that offers women many exciting opportunities and simple pleasures. On the other hand, because doing femininity is at least somewhat compulsory, and we live in an androcentric society, women also have to adopt gender performances that harm them as individuals and guarantee group disadvantage. After reviewing the realities facing women, we'll offer an overview of the big picture. But first, let's start this chapter the way we did the last: with cheerleading.

CHEERLEADING TODAY

As you now know, in the 1800s male cheerleaders were respected for their ability to lead a crowd. Women joined teams during World War II, prompting men to eventually abandon the activity. By the 1960s, cheerleading teams were essentially all female and served simply to support male athletes. No longer equivalent to being a quarterback, cheerleading was now a cute sideshow to the main event.

It wouldn't stay this way. Eventually, women re-masculinized cheerleading. By the 1990s, cheer involved intense athleticism. Gymnastics were back and stunts became increasingly complicated, difficult, and dangerous. Cheerleaders began to compete against one another, leading to an entire industry that revolves around fierce cheer competition.[1]

Despite these changes, cheer retains feminine dimensions. A cheerleader's primary job is still to root for football and basketball teams. That is, it remains largely a "feminine auxiliary to sport," not the serious main event.[2] Cheer also retains a performative aspect that seems unsuited to men. Sociologists Laura Grindstaff and Emily West, who did research on cheerleaders, explain:

> *Appearing before a crowd requires that cheerleaders be enthusiastic, energetic, and entertaining. This is accomplished not just through dancing, tumbling, or eye-catching stunts, but also through the bubbly, peppy, performance of "spirit." . . . It includes smiling, "facials" (exaggerated facial expressions), being in constant motion, jumping, and executing dynamic arm, hand, and head motions— all considered feminine terrain.*[3]

As one male cheerleader said, somewhat embarrassed, "a game face for a cheerleader is a big smile," not exactly the threatening grimace or strained expres-

Cheerleaders at a University of Nevada, Las Vegas basketball game blend feminine grace, peppy enthusiasm, and impressive athleticism.

sion associated with the competitiveness or exertion believed to characterize "real" sports.[4]

The association of cheerleading with femininity means that many of us take it less seriously than other physical activities. As a result, despite the high-impact athleticism that now characterizes many squads, less than half of U.S. high school athletic associations define high school cheerleading as a sport and neither the U.S. Department of Education nor the National Collegiate Athletic Association (NCAA) categorizes it as one. Instead, cheerleading is frequently labeled an "activity," akin to the chess club. Accordingly, cheerleading remains unregulated by organizations responsible for ensuring the safety of athletes, leading to higher rates of injury among cheerleaders than those among American football players.[5] Among all types of teenage athletes, cheerleading accounts for a whopping 66 percent of injuries with the potential to result in permanent disability.[6]

Cheerleading is somehow simultaneously masculine and feminine. This is not unusual for women. In fact, cheer today is a great example of the contradictions women face throughout all aspects of contemporary life in the global West. Unlike men, who are encouraged to avoid femininity, women are strongly encouraged to embrace *both* femininity and masculinity.

GENDER FOR WOMEN

In many ways the daily lives of women are much less constrained than those of men. Unlike men, who face policing when they do gender in ways that are associated with the other sex, women's performances of masculinity are generally regarded positively, such that women today are doing almost everything men do. Emily Kane, the sociologist who documented parents' nervousness about their sons' performances of femininity, found that parents weren't at all troubled by their girls' gender-nonconforming behavior. In fact, they were downright tickled if their daughters wanted to wear a dinosaur backpack or collect bugs in the backyard. They even endorsed their girls' interest in "icons of masculinity" like trucks and tools.[7] Kane writes:

> *Mothers and fathers . . . reported enjoying dressing their daughters in sports-themed clothing, as well as buying them toy cars, trucks, trains, and building toys. Some described their efforts to encourage, and pleased reactions to, what they considered traditionally male activities such as T-ball, football, fishing, and learning to use tools. Several noted that they make an effort to encourage their young daughters to aspire to traditionally male occupations and commented favorably on their daughters as "tomboyish," "rough and tumble," and "competitive athletically."*[8]

Enrolling girls in martial arts training encourages them to be assertive and build strength, both coded masculine, but most boys are discouraged from feminine hobbies like dance and fine arts.

As this example shows, whereas parents don't typically approve of their sons being "sissies," they often embrace the idea of their daughters being "tomboys." And, while they felt a need to explain their sons' preference for girly things, their daughters' interest in masculine things needed no such explanation. Since masculine activities are highly valued, it makes perfect sense that girls would be drawn to them and parents would be proud.

Adult women benefit from this greatly. Today, many choose "masculine" pursuits: Women have the freedom to enjoy the complex flavors of scotch, the rigorous training of law school or the military, the risks and rewards of casual sex, and the thrill of learning to fly an airplane. They can become construction workers or architects and feel the deep satisfaction of watching one's work materialize; they can become surgeons or CEOs and choose to take responsibility for human life and corporate profits. In fact, in 2013 it was announced that the very last occupation off-limits to women in the United States—combat positions in the military—will be opened officially in 2016.[9] These are all rightly interpreted as signs that women have gained equality with men, a state of affairs that most Americans endorse and most parents want for their daughters. Measured by the scope of gender rules, then, the life options of women in contemporary Western societies are undoubtedly more open than men's. But there's a catch.

The Importance of Balance

While women are allowed and even encouraged to do masculinity, a woman who performs *too much* masculinity attracts the same policing as a man who does even *a little* femininity. Women who perform only masculinity violate the gender binary and break the number 1 gender rule, the rule that one has to identify as male or female and perform gender in a way that's consistent with that identity. They face an imperative, in other words, to *balance* masculinity and femininity. Women who balance masculinity are often seen as more than just OK—they are the new female ideal. This is why parents are excited when their little girls don't mind getting dirty. The model woman, the one all women are supposed to try to be these days, is *not* the perfect picture of femininity; she is both feminine and masculine.

Media coverage of women often fawns over those who do both gracefully. Candace Parker, a professional basketball player for the Women's National Basketball Association (WNBA), is a good example. In 2009 Parker appeared on the cover of *ESPN* magazine after a record-setting first year in which she was awarded the Rookie of the Year and Most Valuable Player awards, was named the Associated Press Female Athlete of the Year, and made both the All-Rookie WNBA and the All-WNBA teams. The photo of her that was chosen for the cover, however, did not show this extraordinary athlete playing basketball.[10] Instead, she stood in a white dress, visibly pregnant, smiling into the camera, alongside a pregnancy pun: "How big can Candace Parker get?"

The associated story, by journalist Allison Glock, was about the stunningly good start to Parker's professional career, but it also heavily highlighted her "feminine side." It began:

This ESPN cover featuring pro basketball player Candace Parker balances her success on the court with her embrace of motherhood.

> *Candace Parker is beautiful. Breathtaking, really, with flawless skin, endless legs and a C cup she is proud of but never flaunts. She is also the best at what she does, a record-setter, a rule breaker, a redefiner. She is a woman who plays like a man, one of the boys, if the boys had C cups and flawless skin. She's nice, too. Sweet, even. Kind to animals and children.*[11]

Notice how the coverage strongly emphasizes her perfect balance of masculine and feminine attributes. This theme of balance is repeated throughout the article: Elsewhere it is written that she is a "combination of game, generosity and gorgeous," "a saint in high-tops," and "one of the guys, albeit with flat-ironed hair and pink lipstick."[12] It is not her ability to perform masculinity, nor her ability to successfully perform femininity, that is touted in this article; it is her supposedly remarkable ability to do both. When asked about her plans for after the baby is born, Parker explained: "The baby will be along for the ride with me on trips, at the court. You don't hear about male players doing that, do you? Women, we just have to balance more things."[13] Indeed.

Women have the opportunity to do masculinity and get the esteem that comes with valued traits and activities, and that's nice for them. But women must also do femininity. Being intelligent, ambitious, outspoken, and sporty, in other words, is great, but being properly feminine is essential.

Doing femininity can be understood as an account for breaking the rule that requires women to leave the guy stuff to guys. It's a way of saying: "I know it looks like I'm encroaching on men's territory, but be assured that I know my place as a woman." In other words, when women acquiesce to the requirement that they perform femininity, it is a way of letting others around them know that *they know* that they are still first and foremost female.

The requirement that women balance their appropriation of masculine interests, traits, and activities with feminine performance is called the **feminine apologetic**. The term points to how a woman's performance of femininity can be a way to soothe others' concerns about her appropriation of masculinity. One manifestation of the ubiquity of the feminine apologetic is the tendency for women who are highly respected for accomplishments in masculine fields to pose for fashion and beauty magazines. Recently, Yahoo President and CEO Marissa Mayer, a woman *Fortune* considered the eighth most powerful businesswoman in America in 2013, did a photo shoot for *Vogue* magazine. Sociologist Pepper Schwartz, reflecting on Mayer's fashion spread, asked:

> What does [it] say to all the women who would never be beautiful enough to do that, but might be brainy enough to have her job? Should they feel "less than Marissa" because they can't qualify for the Vogue slot?[14]

Schwartz's comments reflect the exhaustion women sometimes feel at the imperative to balance masculine achievements with feminine performances:

> We women would like to feel that for at least some of us sheer competence would make looks a non-issue in our lives. We would like to think that a brainiac like Marissa Mayer wouldn't need, perhaps would not want, to have a very public glamor shot as a career capstone. Unfortunately, it is not an exaggeration to say that Marissa Mayer is kind of saying, even though I am sure she did not

mean to, that to have it all, sure, you have to be smart, but, let's face it, you also need to be beautiful.

This is the lesson that Barbie teaches us so well: Barbie can do anything—she can be a doctor, an astronaut, an athlete, or a presidential candidate—but everyone knows that the important thing is that she look damn good while doing it.

Powerful men, even rather attractive ones, are rarely the focus of men's lifestyle magazines. We don't see them gracing the pages of *Maxim* or *Men's Fitness*. They get to *just* be CEOs. When they are featured in magazines, they get to just look like themselves, not supermodels. They wear relatively minimal makeup, receive much less retouching aimed at making them look young, and are posed in businesslike instead of high-fashion or sexy poses. Likewise, when was the last time a male athlete was described as "nice to animals and children"? What would be the male equivalent of commenting on a woman's breast size?

Marissa Mayer, president and CEO of Yahoo, was the first CEO of a Fortune 500 company to be featured in a fashion spread. Here she signs a copy of the issue of *Vogue* in which she appeared.

Men are subjected to this kind of scrutiny less often because there's no need to assure onlookers that they're not straying too far from their place. Many know that they can be reasonably attractive, or even rather unattractive, and still be at the top of the most powerful companies in the world. Unless they are a racial minority, have a disability, or are otherwise stigmatized, they are less likely to ask themselves: "Can I be successful, given how I look?" "Will I not be taken seriously as a manager because I'm too fat?" "Am I good-looking enough to speak publicly about my expertise?" "Will clients respond to me like they do my prettier co-worker?" "Would I be a better lawyer if jurors thought I was more attractive?" "Would I get better tips if I lost ten pounds?"

A certain set of slurs are typically aimed at women who don't perform the feminine apologetic: *bitch, dyke,* and *feminist* are among them. Women's constraint is of a different sort than men's: She can do anything she likes, so long as she also acts to affirm the hierarchical gender binary on which men's privilege and power depend.

The requirement that women do femininity, combined with the more recent option to also do masculinity, gives women a great deal more behavioral freedom than men today. Women can adopt a wider range of interests, activities, and behaviors, while men are constrained by the imperative to eschew femininity most of the time. As we will see, though, women are disadvantaged compared to men because they are required to do something society does not value: femininity.

Doing More, Winning Less

The feminine apologetic is useful for women; it allows them to gain some of the benefits that come with doing masculine things without attracting harsh or violent policing. Doing femininity, however, also disadvantages women because femininity is overtly disparaged and disempowering; meanwhile, they're subjected to a form of sexism that masquerades as admiration and praise. Let's take each in turn.

First, many traits associated with femininity are quite actively disparaged in our societies. Some of us think that women consumed with the feminized task of raising children, for example, are boring or unambitious. Some are condescending toward mom-related activities—like scrapbooking, recipe swapping, and attending PTA meetings—or they make fun of "mom jeans" and "mom hair." On the flip side, some of us think women who spend "too much" time on their hair and makeup are vain, that an obsession with fashion is shallow, that women who display their bodies are slutty, and that getting cosmetic surgery is sad. "In spite of relenting pressure to 'make the most of what they have,'" philosopher Sandra Lee Bartky writes, "women are ridiculed and dismissed for . . . their interest in such 'trivial' things as clothes and make-up."[15] Some of the things women are expected to do, then, simultaneously detract from our evaluation of them as interesting and dignified human beings.

Second, because power is gendered, the requirement to do femininity is also the requirement to do powerlessness: passivity, deference, submission, fragility, and weakness. A feminine person (someone trying to do perfect femininity) smiles at others sweetly, keeps her voice melodic, and asks questions instead of making declarations. A feminine person defers to hegemonic masculinity by letting men take care of her: She lets others open her doors and pay her tab. A feminine sexuality is one that waits and responds, never acts or initiates. He makes the first move. She is kissed; she does not kiss. She is pulled to him, pushed against the wall, and thrown on the bed, but she does not pull, push, or throw. A feminine body is small and contained; "[m]assiveness, power, or abundance in a woman's body is met with distaste."[16]

This is not pure theory. Research has shown that expansive body postures that take up more room than necessary instill a psychological sense of power and entitlement.[17] Indeed, the bodily comportment that we associate with femininity is, in fact, more widely associated with deference. Bartky uses hierarchies among men as an example:

In her photo series "Switcheroo," photographer Hana Pesut demonstrates the differences between Jillian and Andrew's performance of gender. Notice how their body language changes along with their clothes.

> *In groups of men, those with higher status typically assume looser and more relaxed postures; the boss lounges comfortably behind the desk while the applicant sits tense and rigid on the edge of his seat. Higher-status individuals may touch their subordinates more than they themselves get touched; they initiate more eye contact and are smiled at by their inferiors more than they are observed to smile in return. What is announced in the comportment of superiors is confidence and ease.*[18]

It's significant that the performance of femininity overlaps with performances of others who are interacting with people with power over them: job applicants with their interviewers, enlisted soldiers with their superiors, and students in the offices of their professors. Femininity is, as Bartky says, "a language of subordination" and we know this because we see it used to indicate subordinate status in other contexts.[19] By being required to perform femininity, women routinely advertise their subordinate status with their body language.

Lastly, women are subjected to a "benevolent" form of sexism. **Benevolent sexism** is the attribution of positive traits to women that, nonetheless, justify women's subordination to men. We may put women on pedestals and revere them on the assumption that they are supportive, loving, patient, and kind, but this reverence is a double-edged sword. Women's ability to love others, in this narrative, is beautiful, but it's also an emotional weakness that threatens their ability to compete and dominate in work, sports, or politics. Being nice doesn't win games, promotions, or elections. The female temperament, it is believed, is at odds with what is required in the power-driven arenas still associated with men.

Combined with women's supposedly natural desire to care for children, this makes them dependent on someone else economically. Women, then, need husbands to support them and help discipline the children, behaviors precluded by a feminine demeanor. Likewise, women are admired for their graceful and small bodies, but it is also believed that these bodies leave them incapable of strenuous physical tasks and vulnerable to attack. This leaves them in need of assistance and protection from stronger, more physically powerful men. Benevolent sexism, by making women more dependent on men by virtue of expressing positive characteristics, ultimately positions women as inferior.

Moreover, those areas in which women are seen as naturally better than men are also viewed as self-sacrificial. Women, it is believed, are better suited than men to forgo their leisure time, educational trajectories, and career aspirations in order to help others. The role icons of femininity—mother, wife, nurse, secretary, teacher—are supportive, not leading roles. Disinvesting in oneself in favor of nurturing others may be honorable, but it is also assumed to leave women less developed, less accomplished, and less impressive than men. Accordingly, women are often dismissed when it comes to acknowledging the most important, unique, and valuable people in society. Law professor Deborah Rhode explains it this way:

> *The difficulty here is that many traits traditionally valued in women also perpetuate women's inequality. These traits include sensitivity, warmth, self-sacrifice, nurturance, and physical attractiveness. Most Americans believe that women should exhibit those qualities, and a majority of women view "being feminine" as central to how they define themselves. Yet ... [p]ersonal qualities that attract workplace rewards—drive, competitiveness, and self-promotion—are at odds with the characteristics that men most value in women, and that many women value in themselves.*[20]

For these reasons, we can't speak of a hegemonic femininity the way we speak of a hegemonic masculinity. Recall that the hegemonic man carries all the traits that we value in an ideal *person*. That's why both men and women tend to seek to emulate him. There is no hegemonic femininity because feminine traits and activities are seen as desirable only for women. There are idealized femininities, certainly, that women can strive to attain, but feminine traits and activities are not *universally* desirable. No version of femininity is seen as good for everyone, male and female alike.

Women have more freedom than men to do gender as they like. They can do both masculinity and femininity. But the requirement that they do feminin- ity, combined with androcentrism and subordination, means that women are required to adopt features and behaviors that are actively disparaged, indicate weakness, or naturalize service to others. This adoption, in turn, interrupts women's ability to succeed in masculine arenas where power, prestige, and per- sonal accomplishment are the valued currency.

When Being a Woman Gets Dangerous

In 2009, forty-eight-year-old George Sodini walked into an aerobics class and sprayed bullets into a crowd of exercising women. His online journal detailed his plan to murder women and kill himself. He complained of being repeatedly sexually "rejected" by women. In his mind, women owed him sexual access and, by not offering it freely, they were breaking an implicit contract between men and women. His rage toward women came across clearly in his journal:

> *It seems many teenage girls have sex frequently. One 16 year old does it usually three times a day with her boyfriend. So . . . after a month of that, this little ho has had more sex than ME in my LIFE, and I am 48. One more reason. Thanks for nada, bitches!*[21]

He felt angry when women rejected him because he did not believe, deep down, that women had the right to deny him their bodies and affection. He was not only *disappointed* in his lack of success, he felt *entitled* to women's attention and sexual availability. His desire to kill women, in other words, was motivated by the belief that women were not obeying the rules.

For Sodini, all women were complicit in denying him. He complained that 30 million women, his estimate of the entire female population of the United States, had rejected him. From his perspective, taking his anger out on female strangers made perfect sense. All women were to blame for his feelings. He injured eleven, killed three, and then killed himself.

Male mass violence inspired by hatred of women is not uncommon. In 1989 Marc Lepine killed fourteen women in a forty-five-minute killing spree at the École Polytechnique in Montreal, during which he repeatedly screamed, "I want women!" Segregating the female from the male engineering stu- dents, he screamed, "I hate feminists!" and opened fire. In 1996, Darrell David

Rice murdered two women camping in Virginia. He explained that they "deserved to die because they were lesbian whores."[22] In 1998, a teacher and four
female students, chosen because of their sex, were killed by Arkansas middle
schoolers Mitchell Johnson and Andrew Golden. In 2006 Charles Roberts IV
went to an Amish schoolhouse, separated the boys from the girls, and shot ten
girls, killing five. In 2010 Gerardo Regalado killed his wife and then shot six
more women at a Florida restaurant, sparing the men. Many serial killers target
women. Jack the Ripper, Ted Bundy, and the Hillside Stranglers (Kenneth Bianchi and Angelo Buono Jr.) all killed only girls and women.

As this book was going to print, the news broke of a mass shooting at the
University of California, Santa Barbara. This case highlights both the hatred
of women and the self-hatred of a man who felt he had failed at hegemonic
masculinity.

Elliot Rodger's particular twisted rage was stoked by a sense of entitlement
to sex and affection from the most socially desirable women (white, blonde, and
attractive). Rodger was mixed Chinese-British ancestry, but he thought himself
superior to Asian men by virtue of being half-white. He was especially infuri-
ated when men he considered lesser (black and Asian men) "won" the "prizes"
to which he believed he was entitled. In his video manifesto, he proclaimed:

> *I am going to enter the hottest sorority house at UCSB and I will slaughter every*
> *single spoiled, stuck-up, blond slut I see inside there. All those girls I've desired*
> *so much. They have all rejected me and looked down on me as an inferior man if*
> *I ever made a sexual advance toward them.*[23]

He murdered three Asian men before setting out to revenge himself on women.
He injured thirteen, murdered six, and then killed himself.

Mass killings are devastating, but they are rare compared to the abuse and
homicide that we see daily. One out of six women will be the victim of an attempted or completed sexual assault.[24] Approximately 25 percent of women
have been victims of intimate partner violence, compared to 8 percent of men.[25]
Boyfriends and husbands commit about 30 percent of female homicides; in
contrast, girlfriends and wives commit 3 percent of male homicides.[26]

These forms of violence are all designed, in part, to enforce women's subordination to men or to punish women who refuse to submit. This is where benevolent sexism comes together with its more overt cousin, **hostile sexism**, the
condemnation of women with negative instead of positive stereotypes and the
use of threats and violence to enforce women's subservience to men. Benevolent sexism rewards women who perform a degree of subservience with protection and support from men (sometimes called "chivalry"), but if women fall or
jump from their pedestal, hostile sexism takes its place. Protection and support
are revoked in favor of verbal or physical assault.

Consider street hassling as an example. Some people argue that men who comment favorably on a woman's appearance as she walks down the sidewalk are just offering a compliment. But often these remarks oscillate between niceties and sexualized hostile sexism. The compliments are often quick to turn into insults and threats if they are not met with the response that the men think they deserve: a feminine apologetic in the form of a smile, a "thank you," or another polite response. Women who ignore or reject men's compliments are often subjected to a vicious onslaught of insults or threats. These men have something in common with Sodini and Rodger: They both think they're entitled to women's attention and will act aggressively if they don't get it.

Compared to hostile sexism, it's easy to interpret benevolent sexism as a step toward a more female-friendly society, but that's not how it works. Societies with low rates of hostile sexism also have low rates of benevolent sexism and societies with high rates of one have high rates of the other.[27] As the comic strip to the right illustrates, a woman's day can be filled with a constant oscillation between compliments and insults from men who think that it's their right to call out to strange women and judge their appearance, comment on their demeanor, or simply intrude on their solitude. These types of sexism go hand in hand. Benevolent sexism is Plan A for ensuring women's subordination. If it fails, hostile sexism is Plan B.

Violence is part of the way that male dominance is upheld, but it's also a measure of the cracks in the system. If women never challenged male authority, there would be no need to reassert patriarchy by force. In fact, women are more likely to be victimized when they challenge male

Cartoonist B. Deutsch illustrates what it feels like to be sandwiched between both hostile and benevolent sexism.

dominance. In one study of 800 employees at five companies, 44 percent of women who performed a convincing feminine apologetic reported that they had attracted sexually harassing behaviors, while all of the women who did not—100 percent of them—reported being targeted.[28] This suggests that sexually charged taunts, insults, pranks, and violence are about gender policing: putting uppity women back "in their place."

Benevolent sexism isn't a kindness; it's a trap. If both the risk and protection are at the hands of men—that is, if *men* are the threat and *gentlemen* are the solution—then women are always positioned such that they need men in order to be safe. Moreover, it's difficult to know which men are threats and which are protectors. Should a woman accept a man's offer to walk her home? Who is more dangerous to her: the man in the alley or the man she's suddenly alone with on the street at night? The latter is a friend but, then again, three-quarters of women who are sexually victimized are assaulted by someone they know.[29] What to do? This is the type of difficult calculation women make routinely as they try to keep themselves safe in a society characterized by benevolent and hostile sexism.

Bargaining with Patriarchy

Just like men, women make patriarchal bargains in order to maximize their autonomy and well-being in the face of sexism, androcentrism, and subordination. Whereas men are presented with essentially one bargain, adopting hegemonic masculinity as much as one is able and can tolerate, women can choose among three types of bargains.

One bargain involves trading power for protection and support. To do so, some women perform **emphasized femininity**, an exaggerated form of femininity "oriented to accommodating the interests and desires of men."[30] Emphasized femininity is an adaptation to the fact that men, in general, have more power and resources than women. With this strategy, a woman attempts to offer feminized traits in exchange for the support of a high-status man who will share his privilege with her. Stay-at-home moms, for example, have struck a patriarchal bargain. They do feminized, unpaid work in the home for their husband and children. In return, their husbands share their income and status: providing a well-stocked kitchen, vacations, and a secure retirement. Other women—disparagingly called "gold diggers"—offer their beauty to economically successful men. In exchange for his financial support, these women promise to keep their bodies taut, their clothes flattering, and their hair and faces attractive. He has a lovely companion, then, to appreciate and display.

Both the housewife and the lovely companion are making a traditional patriarchal bargain. In both cases, they contribute to men's status and quality of life and the men, in turn, give the women material support. Both are performing (very different) femininities that are recognized as legitimate in Western societies but, like the characteristics attributed to women in a benevolently sexist society, do not empower them. Neither raising kids nor being beautiful pays your rent, ensures you won't be destitute as an old woman, or makes your voice heard. Instead, to varying degrees, these women trade the direct attainment of their *own* power for the indirect attainment of *his*.

The position of those who perform emphasized femininity is always precarious; they can't control how much reward men offer and on what terms. They are dependent on men's ongoing willingness to support them, even as the things they have to offer decrease in value. Children grow up and leave the house, and beautiful faces and bodies face the march of time. It's a risky bargain for women: What upper-class men have to offer (money and status) likely builds over their lifetime, whereas what women who are capitalizing on their femininity have to offer inevitably fades.

To this day, Marilyn Monroe remains an icon of emphasized femininity.

Being a doctor's wife is one way to get a little bit of the prestige and financial independence that comes with excelling in masculine arenas—being a doctor is another. Rather than performing emphasized femininity, some women try to be "just one of the guys"—a strategy sociologist Michael Kimmel refers to as **emphatic sameness**. In his study of the first women to integrate military schools, Kimmel found that some women tried to make the fact that they were female as invisible as possible.[31] Distancing themselves from other women, they tried to be "cadets" instead of "female cadets." Many women do emphatic sameness, downplaying the feminine in themselves in exchange for the right to do quite a bit of masculinity. These women may declare majors associated with men and deride women who major in femininized subjects like literature or elementary education. They may make sports a central part of their lives and dismiss cheerleaders as not real athletes. They may choose not to have children and decide that women who do are not serious about pursuing personal or professional accomplishments.

Doing emphatic sameness is a way for some women to gain power as individuals in a society that values masculinity. This strategy has limited

An emphasized sameness approach allows this woman to blend in with male recruits to the New York Police Department.

advantages, though, because it depends on the denigration of femininity in general. Because the majority of women who do emphatic sameness both reject femininity and perform it, the strategy backfires: They end up being the very thing they agree is valueless.

More, the strategy reinforces the idea that women and girly stuff are trivial and worthless. This strategy thus undermines attempts to empower women *as a group*, even if it allows one woman to have a bit more power than she would otherwise have. Notice that the most successful women (surgeons, judges, and politicians) usually rely on a team of other less advantaged women (housekeepers, nannies, nurses, and secretaries). The surgeon may have achieved a level of prestige usually reserved for a man, but she does so on the backs of other women who do devalued, still-feminized work on her behalf.

Most women alternate between emphasized femininity and emphatic sameness in a strategy called **gender equivocation**, using both strategies when they're useful and culturally expected. This is the strategy adopted by Candace Parker in her role as a professional basketball player: doing enough masculinity to gain some esteem and power and enough femininity to avoid harmful policing.

These patriarchal bargains—emphasized femininity, emphatic sameness, and gender equivocation—are not equally available to everyone. The ability to use feminine wiles to land a rich husband, for instance, depends in part on a person's particular body and face. Not everyone is born with a conventionally attractive, physically able body that they can train to be slim and graceful. Conversely, some women may not have the temperament to be a stay-at-home parent or the ambition or opportunity to pursue a career. Still, most women manage to develop strategies that they find appealing and practical, if not ideal.

Just as women have more choices than men in deciding how to do gender, women have more socially acceptable strategies for negotiating hegemonic masculinity. Men are forced to contend with an idealized masculinity by which they're measured. Period. Women, in contrast, are allowed to adopt different versions of femininity, so long as they perform it at least a little. However, no matter which strategy they adopt, women face a double bind.

Damned if You Do . . .

A **double bind** is a situation in which cultural expectations are contradictory. Satisfying only one or the other expectation inevitably means failure, and it is impossible to do both. In the case of women in contemporary Western societies, the double bind refers to the idea that to be powerful is to fail as a woman and to succeed as a woman is to give up power.

Women can and do fall from grace in either direction. We see this phenomenon in sports. South African Olympian sprinter Caster Semenya is an example of a woman who was attacked for doing too little femininity, whereas tennis player Anna Kournikova is an example of an athlete who did too much. Semenya's physical body, surprisingly fast races, and refusal to do femininity both on and off the track led to an investigation of her biological sex that threatened her career. Under this pressure, she submitted to a public makeover—a last-ditch attempt at an apologetic. Ultimately, she was cleared to keep competing as a woman.

In contrast, Kournikova's successful embodiment of femininity pushed her—with both a carrot and a stick—out of her tennis career and into modeling. Today she is frequently castigated as one of the worst professional athletes of all time; the fact that she was once ranked eighth in the world is eclipsed by her sex appeal. She still frequently graces the cover of men's magazines.

Likewise, while negative attacks are common in politics, backlash against female politicians often reflects the double bind. On the one hand, women are criticized for not being sufficiently feminine. In 2012, Geun-hye Park, then a candidate for the president of South Korea, was criticized by her opponent for not having children. Her opponent's spokesman said that she "has no femininity" because she wasn't "agonizing over childbirth, childcare, education and grocery prices."[32] She won anyway. Both Julia Gillard, who served as the prime minister of Australia from 2010 to 2013, and Angela Merkel, the current chancellor of Germany, have faced similar charges. Because these female leaders

Caster Semenya's astonishingly fast times on the track and disinterest in performing gender while she raced prompted the International Association of Athletics to investigate her biological gender in 2009. Her makeover for *You* magazine (right) was an effort to assure others of her femininity.

don't have children, critics said, "they've got no idea what life's about" and are not "real women."[33]

On the other hand, if female candidates do femininity well, this, too, becomes a part of how they are evaluated. They face constant scrutiny of their appearance.[34] In 2012 the French housing minister, Cecile Duflot, received wolf-whistles from the opposition while delivering a speech in the national assembly.[35] The next year President Obama called Kamala Harris "the best *looking* attorney general in the country."[36]

An excellent example of the double bind is the different treatment of Hillary Clinton, who ran for the 2008 Democratic presidential nomination in the United States, and Sarah Palin, the Republican choice for vice president. Comedian Tina Fey, speaking of Clinton and Palin, characterized public reaction to both politicians: "In real life these women experienced different sides of the same sexism coin. People who didn't like Hillary called her a ballbuster. People who didn't like Sarah called her Caribou Barbie."[37] Indeed, Clinton campaigned on the basis of her experience and was repeatedly skewered by the media for being too masculine. She was heckled to go back to the kitchen and "make a sandwich," depicted as a holiday nut cracker (pun intended), and repeatedly called a *cunt, nag, witch,* and worse.

In contrast, Palin emphasized her femininity with long hair, stylish clothes that hugged her body, and a cheerful demeanor. Because she performed the feminine apologetic, Palin escaped the type of policing that Clinton faced, but her performance was incompatible with the masculinized image of a smart, strong, and effective politician.[38] A pundit for CNBC claimed that she was politically successful only because "men want to mate with her." It wasn't long before she became a joke to much of America. While she certainly had her faults, Palin's downfall was distinctly gendered, featuring MILF jokes and look-alike stripper contests in Las Vegas.

Women, like men, make patriarchal bargains to maximize their autonomy and well-being. Men face substantially tighter restrictions than women, but the strategies available to them—while fewer than those available to women—offer greater rewards. Women enjoy more flexibility because there are more socially endorsed options for them than for men, but no matter what strategy women choose, they are faced with a double bind.

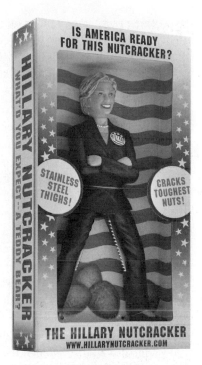

This joke gift, sold at stores like Urban Outfitters, draws on the widespread media presentation of Hillary Clinton as too masculine.

THE BIG PICTURE

Feminism, most simply, is the belief that all men and women should have equal rights and opportunities. The word was borrowed from the French in the late 1800s, when many women around the world were still the property of men by law. It has been used ever since to describe efforts to reduce women's disadvantage relative to men and free both men and women from harmful and oppressive gender stereotypes.

While feminism is principally concerned with gender inequality, differences among men and among women—intersectionality—have become central to the conversation. Especially since the 1970s, scholars and activists have been theorizing what it means to include a wide range of women in their mission.[39] Ultimately, it became clear that if one cared *strictly* about gender inequality, a feminist utopia was entirely compatible with other types of injustice. In this imaginary world, women would simply be equal to "their" men—ones of the same race, class, and so on. If those men were disadvantaged by other forms of injustice, then women would be, too. Ultimately, this utopia was intuitively unpleasing and morally objectionable to most feminists; it charted a feminism only for rich, white, and otherwise privileged women. Many argued that this was not feminism at all.

Feminists weren't alone in learning the importance of thinking intersectionally. Today, members of social justice movements of all types find it important to consider not just one injustice at a time, but all of them together at once. The target of their work is the **matrix of domination**, a structure in which multiple hierarchies intersect to create a pyramid of privilege, leaving on top only those people who are advantaged in every hierarchy.[40] As a result, when someone identifies themselves as feminist today, they often mean to say that they are part of a network of activists targeting a wide range of injustices.

Feminists have also been on the forefront of theorizing masculinity and the way the gender binary might be harmful to men. Many men today identify as feminist or pro-feminist, and they have formed organizations aimed at fighting gender inequality and its harmful effects on both men and women.[41] After the 1989 massacre at the École Polytechnique in Montreal, for example, some Canadian men began the White Ribbon Campaign, an effort by men to end men's violence against women that is now active in sixty countries.[42] Likewise, the National Organization of Men against Sexism works toward gender equality on the belief that "men can live as happier and more fulfilled human beings by challenging the old-fashioned rules of masculinity that embody the assumption of male superiority."[43]

Even in the very early years of feminism, people understood that it had the potential to change men's lives for the better as well as women's. Floyd Dell, writing in 1917, argued: "Feminism will make it possible for the first time for men to be free." He believed that feminism was the path to full humanity and the only hope for true love between men and women. Criticizing the elite marriages he saw around him, he wrote:

> *When you have got a woman in a box, and you pay rent on the box, her relationship to you insensibly changes character. . . . It is no longer a sharing of life together—it is a breaking of life apart. Half a life—cooking, clothes and children; half a life—business, politics and baseball. It doesn't make much difference which is the poorer half. Any half, when it comes to life, is very near to none at all.*[44]

Dell would likely be impressed at the lives women are leading today, thanks to a real reduction in both legal and interpersonal forms of explicit sexism. But he'd be deeply troubled by the continued pressure that men face to live half a life. This pressure has, in fact, been getting worse, not better. Since the

'70s, both men and women have become increasingly androcentric.[45] Men are feeling more pressure than ever to conform to a narrowing range of acceptable masculinities. Feminism has yet to deliver on the promise to men that Dell envisioned.

As we've seen, contemporary gender relations are not ideal for women either. It will become increasingly clear in the coming chapters that women continue to be limited. The increase in women's participation in male domains stalled out in the '90s and hasn't budged much since.[46] There can only be so much progress when women alone are offered the opportunity and incentive to embrace their full humanity.

This state of affairs has inspired scholars to argue that the United States and other similar Western countries are in the middle of a **stalled revolution**, a sweeping change in gender relations that is stuck halfway through. Women have increasingly embraced opportunities that masculinity and masculine arenas provide, but few men have moved toward feminine options. This new gender order hurts both men and women, but differently; men suffer more from gender inequality *as individuals*, while women are harmed more *as a group*.

Men are harmed as individuals because they have narrower life options, thanks to androcentrism. Paradoxically, it makes some men feel good because of a social agreement that masculine things are better than feminine things, but it's not the same thing as freedom. It's oppression dressed up as superiority. Androcentrism restricts men's lives, asking them to destroy or hide parts of themselves that don't fit the hegemonic model.

As a group, however, men benefit because the arenas of life to which they are constrained tend to be socially and economically rewarded. Men face less pressure to bother with things we've learned to belittle, to defer to others, or to sacrifice their own needs. In fact, because men are required to eschew femininity as much as possible, men are free to be brazenly strong, self-interested, and successful. Unless, of course, they are positioned at the lower end of a different hierarchy, like race or class, which requires that they perform deference at the cost of feeling masculine.

Women, in contrast, benefit as individuals but are harmed as a group. Individual women have more freedom to balance masculinity and femininity, mixing and matching. But the requirement to mix in some femininity means adopting gender performances that prevent them from maximizing their life chances and often place them in subordinate positions. Women as a group pay more of the costs of the hierarchical gender binary, measured in part by economic vulnerability and physical danger.

We may be accustomed to the options we're offered, but comfort and familiarity aren't the same thing as freedom and equality. The revolution is yet unfinished.

Revisiting the Question

 If both men and women are constrained by a binary gender system, why is it that more women than men find this system unfair?

Most women agree that the gender binary system is unfair. Men are less likely to think so. This is because the binary isn't just about difference; it's about hierarchy. Most of us have learned to devalue the feminine side, at least a little bit. The masculine side of the binary is presumed to be not just different but *better than* the feminine side.

This gender binary system means that we tend to value men over women. We require women to perform a devalued identity, and women's subordination to men in both public and private is naturalized. Though women can fight against these mechanisms of oppression by doing masculinity and appropriating masculine roles, powerlessness and subordination will nevertheless be coded feminine. Because they are female and required to do femininity, women as a group come out the losers compared to men.

Men face a similar imperative to do gender, but in their case they are compelled to adopt traits and activities associated with the more highly valued side of the binary. They know very well that femininity is disparaged, and so most avoid it much of the time. A lot of men are OK with this; they aren't that upset, it turns out, by being told they shouldn't do something they learned to not want to do. Many men mostly think it's OK to leave high heels, dirty diapers, and salads to women. They may feel that this is unfair, but they can enjoy the privilege of shrugging it off. Still, it's not the same thing as feeling free to do whatever they wish.

Ultimately, this binary harms both men and women, men more so as individuals and women more so as a group. The real story about gender and power, then, isn't a simple one about women's disadvantage but a complicated one that reveals that the vast majority of us are oppressed by the gender binary system.

Next . . .

Thus far in this book we've discussed the social construction of gender, policing of gendered performances, and relations of inequality. These are all very powerful forces. You might still feel, though, that if people really wanted to, they could reject the gender binary; ignore what other people say; refuse to accept or enact sexism, androcentrism, and subordination; and live a life free of all this gender stuff. That line of inquiry is how we're getting to the next chapter:

 When it comes down to it, regardless of social construction and social pressure, don't we live in a society in which it's possible to just be an individual?

It turns out, no. You'll see why in the next chapter.

FOR FURTHER READING

Glick, Peter, and Susan Fiske. "An Ambivalent Alliance: Hostile and Benevolent Sexism as Complementary Justifications for Gender Inequality." *American Psychologist* 56, no. 2 (2001): 109–118.

Friedman, Hilary Levey. "Soccer Isn't for Girly Girls? How Parents Pick the Sports their Daughters Play." *The Atlantic*, August 6, 2013.

Stephens-Davidowitz, Seth. "Google, Tell Me. Is My Son a Genius?" *New York Times*, January 18, 2014.

Wade, Lisa. "Miley Cyrus' Patriarchal Bargain." *Sociological Images*, December 28, 2013.

Weston, Kath. "Do Clothes Make the Woman? Gender, Performance Theory, and Lesbian Eroticism." *Genders* 17 (1993): 1–21.

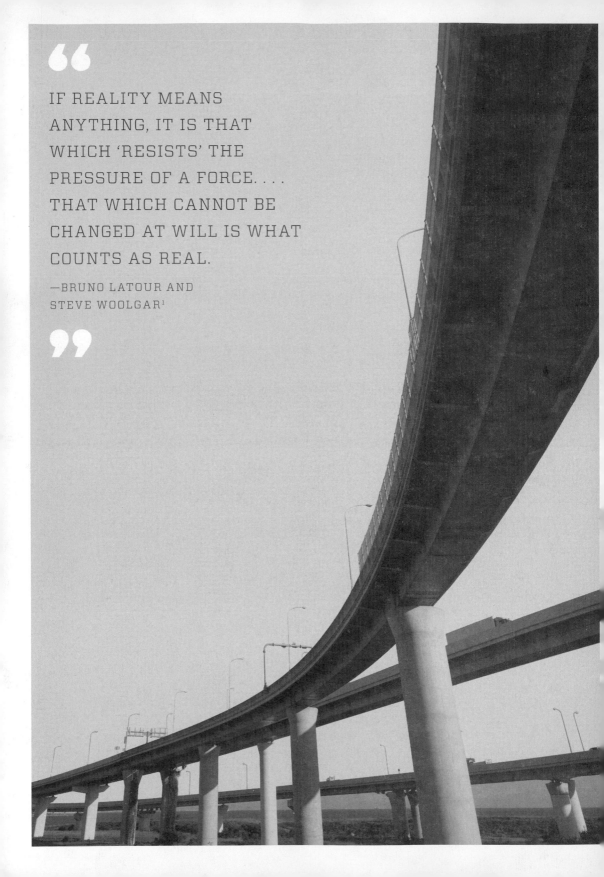

> IF REALITY MEANS
> ANYTHING, IT IS THAT
> WHICH 'RESISTS' THE
> PRESSURE OF A FORCE....
> THAT WHICH CANNOT BE
> CHANGED AT WILL IS WHAT
> COUNTS AS REAL.
>
> —BRUNO LATOUR AND
> STEVE WOOLGAR[1]

8

Institutions

Thus far we've talked about the way that individuals see the world in gender binary terms, internalize gender norms, and police their own and others' gender performances. We've also discussed how our ideas about men and women—and our expectations for male and female behavior—aren't just different, they're unequal. Finally, we've considered the ways that people can get away with breaking gender rules and form communities that support only the particular gender rules they endorse. This makes it seem like, no matter how pervasive the gender binary lens and how strong the pressure to do gender, an individual *can* make the difficult decision to live a gender-neutral life if he or she wants to. In other words:

Q+A **When it comes down to it, regardless of social construction and social pressure, don't we live in a society in which it's possible to just be an individual?**

In this chapter, we'll show that the answer to this question is, in fact, no. Gender is a set of ideas and something one does when interacting with other people, but it's also an organizing principle that permeates our social institutions. Because ideas about gender shape the environments in which we live, these ideas exert an influence on our lives independent of our own beliefs, personalities, and interactions. It's simply not true that if we reject the gender binary as individuals, and refuse to let others police us, that we'll be free of gender. Gender and gender inequality are part of the fabric of our lives.

THE ORGANIZATION OF DAILY LIFE

Most schools in the United States—from kindergarten to college—take a three-month break during the summer. Most kids enjoy the break without asking why, but there is a reason why we do it this way. Before the beginning of the twentieth century, urban schools met year-round while rural schools met for only six months, letting students off to help on their families' farms.[2] Urban schools eventually decided to break during the summer because that was when the wealthy liked to travel and also because, before the invention of air-conditioning, schools were oppressively hot and stuffy during those months. As education became more important and fewer kids were growing up on farms, rural schools increased the length of their school year to match that of urban schools. Our precious summer vacation was born.

Summer vacation has a history, then, but today we mostly just accept that this is how things are done. The idea of free public school—that the government rather than parents should provide for children's education—and the ways in which we organize education are part of how Americans "do" their schooling. In this sense, American education is an example of what sociologists call an **institution**, persistent patterns of social interaction aimed at meeting the needs of a society that can't easily be met by individuals alone.

Let's elaborate: Education is an institution because giving the next generation the knowledge and skills that they will need to be productive workers and responsible citizens is difficult or impossible for today's parents. In response, we take on education collectively, creating a systematic way to achieve the goal of an educated citizenry. The institution of education dictates the when, where, and how of teaching: the standards, curricula, and credentials that students and teachers are held to; special occasions and routines for enacting them (like the first day of school, graduation, field trips, and snow days); and teachers' unions that negotiate with districts and states to determine pay. It involves organizations: primary and secondary schools, colleges, and universities as well as federal and state departments of education, private and charter schools, and companies (like those running the SAT, ACT, and other tests). There are also commonly accepted routines—parents helping with homework, organizing carpools, and holding fund-raising events—and spectacles like swim meets, senior prom, and graduation.

American high school students toss their caps in celebration of their completion of one stage of education as it is institutionalized in this country.

For the most part, all these organizations and routines are taken for granted as just what school is like. In this sense, much of how we achieve institutionalized tasks is simply normative. **Norms** are beliefs and practices that, by being institutionalized, are well known, widely followed, and culturally approved (like back-to-school shopping trips). Conformity with institutionalized ways of doing things is also secured with formal **policies**, which are explicit and codified expectations, often with stated consequences for deviance (like school dress codes). Many policies elaborate on and reinforce norms, transforming common sense into regulations (like rules against cheating on tests); some policies are explicitly intended to override and change beliefs and practices that have become the norm (like texting in class). Some norms and policies are strongly enforced while others are enforced only weakly.

Because institutions are about *collectively* meeting the important societal needs of individuals, they are very different from the social forces we've discussed so far. We can try to get cultural ideas we don't like out of our brains, surround ourselves with people who support our personal choices, and accept whatever consequences come with breaking social rules, but it is essentially impossible to avoid institutions. They impose themselves on our lives. If you didn't have a stay-at-home parent or a parent who is a teacher, for example, your summer vacation may have been spectacularly inconvenient or considerably expensive for them. Child care during those months may have strained their budget while, depending on your age, leaving you at home to fend for yourself might have been considered neglect. Yet the trouble it caused your parents didn't make the institution magically transform. Summer vacation is summer vacation. Institutions affect your life whether you like it or not. This reality is captured by our opening quote: Our institutions are social inventions, but they are so pervasively and persistently part of our lives that they seem like concrete, unmovable, non-negotiable facts of life.

We can't just "be an individual," then, because we are part of a *society* that is replete with institutions. We have institutions designed to promote global peace and prosperity (involving, but not limited to the United Nations and World Health Organization); defend the country (the military, the Department of Homeland Security); keep citizens safe from violent crime (neighborhood watch programs, prisons, law enforcement, and the judiciary); enable transportation (airlines, public buses and trains, road construction, highway patrol, waterways); promote social welfare (food-stamp programs and Social Security, psychiatric institutions, child social services); raise the next generation (marriage and families); deliver and monitor health care (hospitals, insurance companies, the American Medical Association); promote national economic prosperity (regulations on printing money, incorporating businesses, borrowing and lending, insuring property, discharging debt); entertain, inform, and make life meaningful (newspapers, organized religion, professional sports, art, Hollywood); and shape the overall conditions of life and the future of our societies (advocacy organizations, nonprofit groups, and legislative bodies).

Sociologists use the phrase **social structure** to describe the entire set of institutions within which we live our lives. We call it a "structure" because institutions, in concert, create a relatively stable *scaffolding* on which we build our lives. If we want to be a doctor, for instance, we know that we have to go to college and then medical school. The path, or structure, already exists. We know we are expected to follow it and we *trust* that a medical degree will still be a requirement to begin a career in medicine when we finish our schooling eight years later. The stability of institutions, and the relationships between them, provide a framework that makes it possible to make rational decisions about our future. Structures are helpful because they help us know what we wish to accomplish, as well as how to do so.

And yet, the social structure is also a source of constraint. Sometimes climbing the scaffolding requires resources we don't have. If we can't afford the combination of tuition and eight years out of the workforce required to become a doctor, we probably won't become one. Or we may not have access to the right scaffolding at the right time. In the 1960s and early 1970s, many medical schools did not accept women or they set a 5 to 10 percent cap on female admissions, so many women who were interested in medicine did not apply to medical school, thinking it unrealistic, or didn't get in if they did. So, if you were a woman born in the 1930s, it wouldn't matter how much medical knowledge and experience you had, you'd still be a criminal if you practiced without a license.

Until quite recently, medical schools limited the number of women they allowed to enter degree programs in any given year.

Institutions inevitably enable and constrain us because there is no opting out. You can condemn state and federal governments as incompetent and corrupt, spread the word about anarchism, and stay home on voting day, but Congress is still going to pass legislation to which you will be held accountable. And if you break the law and get caught, you'll face legal penalties even if you personally object to the law. You could go "off the grid" to avoid capitalism, find an isolated spot in the wilderness, cut down some trees, build a hut, and live off roots and berries. Then again, where did you get the ax? Will you bring a book on poisonous mushrooms? Even the hermit will buy a few things to get along and, in any case, he or she can't help but draw on knowledge acquired through institutions like schools, families, publishing, and the mass media.

We live in, through, and with institutions and, by shaping our opportunities, they shape our lives. These institutions are gendered.

GENDERED INSTITUTIONS

A **gendered institution** is one in which gender is used as an organizing principle. In a gendered institution, men and women are channeled into different, and often differently valued, social spaces or activities and their choices have different and often unequal consequences.

Education is a gendered institution. If you were to observe an American elementary school playground, you would likely see children organized strongly (but not exclusively) by sex into different spaces and activities. Sociologist Barrie Thorne describes the typical scene she observed while doing research on playgrounds:

> Boys controlled the large fixed spaces designated for team sports: baseball diamonds, grassy fields used for football or soccer, and basketball courts.... There was also a skateboard area where boys played, with an occasional girl joining in. The fixed spaces where girls predominated—bars and jungle gyms and painted cement areas for playing foursquare, jump rope, and hopscotch—were closer to the building and much smaller, taking up perhaps a tenth of the territory that boys controlled. In addition, more movable activities—episodes of chasing, groups of younger children playing various kinds of "pretend," and groups milling around and talking—were often, although by no means always, divided by gender.[3]

The playgrounds Thorne observed all featured this "geography of gender," but the importance of gender often faded once students returned to the classroom.[4] Thorne found that students were rarely seated by gender—with a boys' and a girls' side of the room—but instead were seated alphabetically or arranged in other ways conducive to an orderly classroom. When students were working

Gender tends to be less salient in elementary school classrooms than it is on the playground.

on skills like reading or math, the teacher would typically arrange them in mixed-sex groups by skill level. In these moments, the importance of gender receded; it was "neutralized."[5] **Gender salience**—the relevance of gender across contexts, activities, and spaces—rose and fell across different parts of the elementary school experience.

The ebb and flow of gender is a persistent feature of elementary education, making it a gendered institution. When new students arrive, they are inserted into an already-existing system. The system is reproduced and enforced by a collection of others who assign esteem and stigma, or success and failure, according to how well new students follow or otherwise contend with the existing norms and policies. If you, an intrepid first grader, were to arrive at one of these schools, you would quickly learn when and how gender was important. No matter how precocious you might be at six years old (knowing already, perhaps, that gender is a social construction), the gendered geography of your elementary school is bigger than you. You can't escape it. You can choose to either conform or deviate, but you *will* contend with it.

Gendered institutions are interesting from a sociological point of view because they affirm and enforce both gender difference and inequality. In the next two sections we'll talk about why gendered institutions matter, starting with an intimate example: our plumbing.

THE INSTITUTIONALIZATION OF GENDER DIFFERENCE

A Room of Her Own

It is obviously impossible for all individuals in a complex society to build and maintain a personal toilet in every location in which they might find themselves. Providing a safe and sanitary way to eliminate personal waste is a social task. The provision of bathroom facilities in workplaces, schools, restaurants, department stores, government buildings, airports, and elsewhere is part of the institution of sanitation.

You typically find men's and women's rooms in these locations, requiring you to pick one or the other. This makes sanitation a gendered institution. You may be comfortable and familiar with this arrangement but, just like summer vacation, sex-segregated bathrooms have a history. The idea emerged during the 1800s when women and men were first brought together as workers in factories, threatening to upset cherished Victorian beliefs about the differences between men and women.

One such belief was that women were more fragile than men and, therefore, less suited to working for pay. One Department of Labor study published in

Nurses rest in a women's "restroom."

1903, for example, reported that "[w]omen suffer even more than men from the stress of [working], and more readily degenerate. A woman's body is unable to withstand strains, fatigues, and [de]privations as well as a man's."[6] Another report recommended the provision of "rest or emergency rooms" on the finding that "it is probable that there are a number of [women] likely to have sudden attacks of dizziness, fainting or other symptoms of illness."[7] *Restrooms*, a word you likely recognize, were small private rooms with a bed or chair, available to women workers suddenly struck by "the vapors" or some other feminine malady.

By reasserting women's fragility, the provision of restrooms eased the threat that women's presence in the workplace posed to the Victorian gender ideology. They served a second purpose, too. Employers placed them between the factory floor and the women's toilets so women were required to pass through them on their way to the bathroom. Whenever a woman went into the restroom, then, men could pretend that she was just going to *rest*; they could be in happy denial that women ever went in to *poop*. In other words, sex-segregated bathrooms, with the restroom as a buffer, allowed Victorian women to carefully conceal any sign of bodily functions and allowed men to pretend that women never used the bathroom at all.

The idea caught on. In 1887, Massachusetts enacted the first law mandating sex-segregated toilets.[8] By 1920, forty-three states had followed suit.

Gender and Bathrooms Today

Today every state in the United States requires the provision of separate bathrooms for men and women in every public building and private business with a certain amount of foot traffic.[9] It is a policy that has also become an invisible but powerful norm, and most of us use the "correct" bathroom in public if at all possible. This is often true even when the bathrooms in question are stand-alone rooms with a single toilet and a door that locks. Even when privacy can be assured, using the wrong bathroom seems *wrong*. Accordingly, most of us have likely found ourselves waiting patiently in line to use the restroom while open toilets designated for the other sex sit empty.

Of course, sex-segregated bathrooms are not a biological necessity. A little stick figure man on the door will deter women and stick figures with skirts will do so the same for men. However, if there *isn't* a stick figure on the door, we will use the same restroom as someone of the other sex without hesitation. This is true in many smaller businesses and workplaces with only one bathroom. It's also true on airplanes. The multiple bathrooms in the back of the plane *could* be designated male- or female-only but, out of a concern that passengers get back to their seats as soon as possible, they aren't. Nobody seems to mind. Men and women also use the same bathrooms at home. Having men's and women's bathrooms in your house would be a novelty, a gag. Everyone knows it's completely unnecessary.

Just as in the Victorian era, today's sex-segregated bathrooms serve *social*, not biological functions. It's no longer commonplace to think that women need a fainting couch within arm's reach, but the idea that women, more than men, should conceal their bodily functions (such as spitting, burping, farting, stinking, urinating, and defecating) is a persistent one. Different bathrooms allow women to keep "unladylike" bodily functions away from men. To a lesser extent, perhaps, the same is true for men. Likewise, gender-specific bathrooms allow women to do body work that is supposed to remain invisible; when done in public, fixing one's hair, smoothing one's clothes, checking for blemishes, and re-applying lipstick all reveal to the viewer that appearing effortlessly feminine requires a lot of work and surveillance. Sex segregation of bathrooms gives women a sex segregated space in which to do this.

Different bathrooms for men and women also assume that everyone needs to protect their dirty business from the other sex, but not the same sex. In other words, it assumes that everyone is heterosexual. That bathrooms are designed without the possibility of homo- or bisexuality in mind is obvious when we consider that bathrooms not only separate men from women, but are actually designed with the expectation that men will expose their penises to one another when urinating. This approach to bathrooms was obviously institutionalized before a concern with homosexuality became a part of popular consciousness.

And, of course, sex-segregated bathrooms uphold the gender binary itself. They don't allow for the possibility that some people don't identify as either male or female, appear male but look female (or vice versa), appear altogether gender ambiguous, or are in the process of transitioning from female to male (or vice versa). Betsy Lucal, the gender-ambiguous sociologist we discussed earlier, described the challenge of using bathrooms in public places:

> Encounters in public rest rooms are an adventure. I have been told countless times that "This is the ladies' room." Other women say nothing to me, but their stares and conversations with others let me know what they think. I will hear them say, for example, "There was a man in there."[10]

In response, Lucal has to make efforts to try to reduce the chances that she will be stared at, insulted, or even confronted by managers or police:

> If I must use a public rest room, I try to make myself look as nonthreatening as possible. I do not wear a hat, and I try to rearrange my clothing to make my breasts more obvious. . . . While in the rest room, I never make eye contact, and I get in and out as quickly as possible. Going in with a woman friend also is helpful; her presence legitimizes my own. People are less likely to think I am entering a space where I do not belong when I am with someone who looks like she does.[11]

People like Lucal can be significantly inconvenienced by our insistence on separating bathrooms into "male" and "female," but this binary approach to sanitation can cause everyone problems from time to time (like when we really, really, really have to go and there's a long line for one bathroom but not the other, or when we're trying to help a child or elderly person of the other sex use a public toilet). Eliminating sex-segregated bathrooms, or requiring the provision of at least some gender-neutral ones, is helpful to all of us some of the time and some of us all of the time. In fact, we increasingly see "family care" bathrooms in airports and "unisex" bathrooms in schools. There is, of course, resistance to change, as we'll see below.

The example of sex-segregated bathrooms shows how institutions can be gendered in ways that affirm differences. Institutions also contribute to gender inequality. To understand this latter point better, let's turn to an institution that many of us first encounter on the school playground: sports.

THE INSTITUTIONALIZATION OF GENDER INEQUALITY

How individuals experience sports varies tremendously. Some find it intimidating, some exhilarating; some shrink from the competition, others come alive under pressure. Some of us are blessed with strong and graceful bodies that bound, bend, and twist; others of us struggle to gain quickness, coordination, and endurance. We all struggle as we get older and our bodies become less spry.

Regardless of whether we like sports, they're part of an institution that shapes our experiences. Little Leagues and after-school programs for youth are complex organizations that engage children in sports in prescribed ways. Once American children start school, they may be required to take physical education classes that teach certain sports and not others; schools are also sites where team play and competition are taught and encouraged. Our teams need someone with whom to have matches, bouts, or games, so other schools nearby also need to field teams for the same sports. The space and equipment requirements for various sports—tracks; basketball courts; fields for baseball, football, soccer, and field hockey; balls, bats, mitts, and sticks—are provided by schools and city and state parks departments and manufactured and sold by companies for profit.

Colleges and universities also allocate money, space, and time to athletics. They are driven not just by enjoyment but by the public exposure and potential

This aerial view of a high school in Idaho is a testament to the infrastructure required to support the institutionalization of popular American sports.

alumni dollars that accrue to schools with successful or otherwise beloved teams. They have relationships with middle and high schools that funnel talented students into colleges that offer scholarships. The mass media follow certain college sports, making games lucrative for colleges and networks alike. Companies, in turn, can count on televised or streamed sporting events to find audiences to which they can advertise their goods and services. Regulatory bodies, such as the NCAA, define the rewards that sports can offer to athletes and the standards of the competition.

In fact, the entire economy benefits from the institution of sport. In the United States, revenues for sports equipment sales exceeded $74 billion in 2010.[12] Major League Baseball and the National Football League (the two most lucrative sports in the United States) earned $7 billion and $9 billion, respectively. The American sports industry, put together, is worth $422 billion. Individuals who profit—a list too vast to compile here, but one that includes not just owners, athletes, sports journalists, merchandisers, and marketing executives, but also cashiers, janitors, vendors, ticket takers, and owners and employees of nearby souvenir shops, bars, and restaurants—are all invested in the industry. Meanwhile, there is a vast infrastructure (stadiums, arenas, tracks) and media empire (an ever multiplying number of ESPN channels along with at least seventeen other sports networks).

Sports are an impressive behemoth of institutionalization. And they are also strongly gendered, making them an institution that works to establish a hierarchy among men and demonstrate the supposed inferiority of women.

Separating the Men from the Boys

Despite the millions of women who play sports around the world, sports are squarely on the masculine side of the gender binary.[13] While many girls like sports, for boys they are basic "manhood training."[14] Playing sports—and thinking, watching, and talking about sports—is "astonishingly important" for young men.[15] Most boys get involved with sports at some level. Their first plush toy may be a soccer ball; their first T-shirt may feature a baseball and bat. A boy's first memories of bonding with his father may involve watching football on TV or playing T-ball in the backyard. Informal games in the neighborhood may transition into Little League and then participation on school-based teams.

Because sports are so strongly associated with masculinity, excelling in sports is one way for young boys to show that they are "real boys" and, later, "real men." Sports, though, don't simply offer boys and men an avenue through which to claim esteem; they place individual boys and men into the hierarchy of masculinity. Recall that sociologist Michael Messner described his decision to embrace sports as his first "engagement with hegemonic masculinity," a moment in which he accepted that he would have to belittle other men if he was to ascend the hierarchy.[16] Importantly, he notes that sports aren't just about individual accomplishment; they are also about competition: "It is being better than the other guys—*beating them*—that is the key to acceptance."[17] As Messner argues, sport "serves partly to socialize boys and young men to hierarchical, competitive, and aggressive values."[18] While some men excel, others end up at what Barrie Thorne calls "the other end of the pecking order."[19] In this sense, sports separate "the men from the boys."

Most men, of course, eventually turn their energies elsewhere. This, too, is how institutions work. As men recognize that it is unlikely that they will become professional athletes, many turn their attention to their educations, careers outside of athletics, or the daily rhythms of raising a family. Still, the institution of sport continues to play a symbolic role in many men's lives even after they stop playing. Some men trade the physical competition for a more passive consumption of televised sports and sports news. Men on couches cheer for their respective teams on big flat-screen TVs, engaging in friendly (or not so friendly) trash-talking of opposing teams and their fans. They jostle for relative position by owning better paraphernalia, holding season tickets with better seats, knowing sports history and statistics more thoroughly or, of course, bragging when their team wins. In this sense, sports retain a competitive aspect, and men still bond and jostle over games. Men who aren't interested in sports suffer many of the same disadvantages as men who don't play well.

Sports is intensely competitive from both the court to the crowd, but it is also a culture-wide, feel-good, male-bonding extravaganza. Because they are men, even couch potatoes can point to the game and claim that they share something important and meaningful with LeBron James, Peyton Manning, or Rafael Nadal.[20] As one male fan said: "A woman can do the same job I can do—maybe even be my boss. But I'll be damned if she can go on the football field and take a hit!"[21] Of course, the vast majority of men couldn't "take a hit" either, but this is beside the point. Instead, sports like football serve as a *cultural* testament to the idea that no matter what happens, men are men and women are women. As Mariah Nelson notes: "The stronger women get, the more men love football."[22]

A Team of Her Own

We can imagine a different world of sports, one that is centered on, worships, and rewards the physical skills in which women, on average, excel more than men. Jane English tried such a thought experiment. She pondered:

> Speed, size, and strength seem to be the essence of sports. Women are naturally inferior at "sports" so conceived. But if women had been the historically dominant sex, our concept of sport would no doubt have evolved differently. Competitions

emphasizing flexibility, balance, strength, timing, and small size might domi-
nate Sunday afternoon television and offer salaries in [the] six figures.[23]

This is not our world. Instead, media coverage of sports keeps a raw, grimacing, bulging, powerful male body front and center in our culture.[24] It's no accident, argues Messner, that the most popular sports in America are also ones based on what he terms "the most extreme possibilities of the male body."[25] Using American football as an example, he explains:

Football ... is clearly a world apart from women.... In contrast to the bare and vul-
nerable bodies of the cheerleaders, the armored male bodies of the football play-
ers are elevated to mythical status, and as such, give testimony to the undeniable
"fact" that there is at least one place where men are clearly superior to women.[26]

The bodies of these professional athletes serve as icons of masculine physical achievement. Their extraordinary feats of athleticism tell a story about men and male bodies. In this way, the symbolic link between the male spectator and the male athlete establishes men's supposed superiority over women.

Organizing sports according to the gender binary protects the idea that women are inferior athletes. There are some exceptions to sex segregation—equestrianism and synchronized swimming are sex integrated (though we see few men in the latter)—but, in general, sex segregation in sports is the rule. Almost all team sports feature sex-segregated teams, leagues, meets, and games that ensure that men and women never compete with or against one another. Likewise, individual sports like long-distance running or swimming usually do not put men and women in direct competition. They rank records separately, making comparison more difficult.

Both those on the political left and political right tend to think this is a good way to organize sports, given the assumption that men are stronger, faster, and bigger than women. If women played with or against men, it is argued, they may get hurt; if they competed against men, they'd usually lose; and if they went out for the same team, they'd rarely get on. Accordingly, sex-segregated teams are supported by both conservatives who think women are more fragile than men and liberals who want women to have the same opportunities.

Sorting by sex, however, also organizes sports in ways that affirm cultural beliefs in gender difference and inequality. We will explore two different ways that sex segregation is used to affirm a hierarchical gender binary.

What Is Sex Segregation For?

DIFFERENT BUT EQUAL? First, sorting allows us to require—with both policies and norms—that men and women perform the same sports differently, often in ways that make it *seem like* women couldn't compete with men. Both women and

Learning gymnastics is also a lesson in gender, as boys are less likely to sign up and, if they do, will learn a different set of skills and exercises.

men play hockey, for instance, but whereas men are allowed to "check" (body slam) one another, it is against the rules for women to do so and punishable with penalties. Likewise, tackle football is the province of "real men"; women (and "lesser men") are allowed to play "flag" (also sometimes called "powder puff") football. These differing policies—especially those that forbid women to be as physically aggressive—mean that women and men play hockey and football differently. In the case of baseball, women are sorted into a related but different game, softball, with its own equipment and rules. Each of these alterations to the game changes the nature of the sport such that women play a different game, one that is usually seen as not "real" baseball, hockey, or football. While these various adjustments may protect women from some types of aggressive play (on the assumption that they need or desire such protection and men do not), they also ensure that we never know if women and girls *could* play the games the way men and boys do.

The different aesthetic expectations for male and female athletes, sometimes encoded in judging guidelines, create sports that reinforce beliefs about men's and women's talents and abilities. Writing about the feminine apologetic in figure skating, sociologist Abigail Feder keenly observed that one of a female skater's most useful talents is the ability to disguise the incredible athleticism required and, instead, make it look effortless.[27] Whereas male figure skaters are valued for appearing powerful and aggressive on the ice, female figure skaters are not. Instead of athleticism, an ability to look beautiful and graceful is valued in women—no matter that she is launching herself into the air at 20 miles an hour or rotating so quickly through a flying sit-spin that she might give herself a nosebleed. Women figure skaters risk losing competitions if they fail to do femininity successfully on the ice.

Bodybuilding is on the flip side of the gender binary but has the same gendered expectations. Judges are instructed to evaluate men only on how muscular they are, but to judge women on both their muscle development and their femininity. The International Federation of Bodybuilding and Fitness, the organization that sets the rules for judging competitions, specifies the following for women's bodybuilding contests:

> First and foremost, the judge must bear in mind that this is a women's bodybuilding competition, and that the goal is to find an ideal female physique. Therefore, the most important aspect is shape—a muscular yet feminine shape. . . . Muscular development must not be carried to such an excess that it resembles the massive muscularity of the male physique. . . . Competitors shall also be assessed on whether or not they carry themselves in a graceful manner while walking to and from their position onstage.[28]

Female bodybuilders at the 2009 European Women's Bodybuilding & Fitness Championships perform a feminine apologetic by smiling and wearing bejeweled bikinis and makeup.

One judge confessed to a bodybuilder who had taken a disappointing eighth place: "As a bodybuilder you were the best, but in a *women's* bodybuilding competition I just felt that I couldn't vote for you."[29] Emma, also a bodybuilder, explained: "A lot of [the women] just get too big."[30] Men, of course, can never get "too big."

Notice that there would be no need for a policy discouraging women from having such muscles if, in fact, they were biologically incapable of doing so. It is the very fact that women *can* build bodies that resemble the "massive muscularity of the male physique" that prompted the International Federation to define it as "excess" and write rules penalizing women for doing so.

The examples of figure skating and bodybuilding show that separating women and men allows us to require that even the most elite of athletic performances conform to gendered expectations. It's circular logic: The idea that men and women have fundamentally different physical abilities is used to institutionalize policies that ensure women and men don't participate in the same sports in the same way. And because they don't, we can easily go on believing that men and women have fundamentally different physical abilities.

Who Loses if Women Lose to Men?

A second way that sex segregation in sports protects a belief in the hierarchical gender binary is by ensuring that men and women never compete against one another. This longstanding segregation relies on the assumption that women would rarely win and that this would be demoralizing or used as proof that women are inferior.

Who really stands to lose if we desegregate sports? Messner argues that it's men. Reflecting on primary school, he writes:

> The best athlete in my classes never got to play with us. She was a girl. Somehow we boys all knew that she was the fastest runner, could hit a baseball further than any of us, yet we never had to confront that reality directly. Our teachers, by enforcing strict sex segregation on the playground, protected our fragile male egos from the humiliation that presumably would result from losing to a girl.[31]

Because we already assume that men would win any competition with women, it is men, not women, who have the most to lose from desegregated sports. If women lose, the status quo—believing women are physically inferior to men—simply remains in place. They haven't actually lost anything but the game or race. But if men lose, they lose much more than the match; their loss undermines the assumption of male superiority.

Many young boys and their parents intuit this. In 2011 a high school threatened to forfeit a junior varsity football game unless a girl on the opposing team, Mina Johnson, sat out.[32] Johnson, a five-foot-two-inch 172-pound linebacker on the opposing team, had "gain[ed] a reputation in the league as a standout junior varsity player"; she sacked a six-foot quarterback in her very first game. Nevertheless, not wanting to be the cause of a lost opportunity for her team to play, Johnson sat out. The opposing team still lost 60 to 0, but apparently that was less humiliating than losing to a girl.

Sex segregation structurally protects men from losing face. As one mother of a boy wrestler put it: It's "unfair for girls to compete against boys. . . . [It puts boys] in a no-win situation. . . . If he wins, it's just a girl, and if he loses, his life is over."[33] It's important to be empathetic to the experiences of men in a world characterized by sexism and androcentrism, but unfair to boys? Hardly. It's extra humiliating to lose to a girl only because we've already decided that women *should* lose.

Still, you might object, doesn't segregating sports by sex protect women and give them an opportunity to play that they might otherwise not have? Not really. Gender is neither a necessary nor logical way to organize sports and make competitions fair.[34] Any justification for this criterion is based on using gender as an imprecise substitute for some features of individuals that might actually be relevant to the particular competition. Remember, there's a great deal of overlap between men and women on most physical characteristics.

Consider wrestling, the sport causing the mother above such angst. Wrestling matches have traditionally been organized by weight class. People in the same weight class, considered equally matched, wrestle each other. The relevant characteristic here isn't gender at all; it's weight. So men and women of the same weight class should be considered good competitors. By this logic, girls and women have been pressing coaches to allow them to wrestle and have been joining previously all-male high school wrestling teams since the 1990s. Today, there are thousands of female wrestlers on teams. In fact, in 2006 Michaela Hutchison from Alaska became the first girl to win a state high school mixed-sex wrestling championship.[35] She wasn't the last.

Basketball could also be organized according to size instead of sex. Instead of sex-segregated teams, it would make more sense to have two teams with taller and shorter players. Really tall women could play with the really tall men, and shorter women could play with shorter men. Now everyone gets to play, short and tall women *and* men. The same logic applies to American football, where being big and heavy is an advantage in several positions. Women are almost entirely excluded from football on the logic that they're small and would get hurt. But, as we've already suggested, most men are also "too small" to play football. Football *isn't* a man's game; it's a game for exceptionally large, strong, athletic, and pain-tolerant men. As it is played now, football excludes not just women, but all the men who are too small to play (that is, most men). Having two or more teams organized by size would give everyone a chance to play.

If the issue is ability, why not divide up the competition that way? Foot races are already organized according to qualifying times, so why is it necessary to

Proving that wrestling is not just for men, Sara Dosho of Japan and Aline Focken of Germany compete in a bronze medal match.

further break it down by gender? If a woman *can* lift as much weight as a man, why stop her from competing against him? If we integrated these sports by sex, men may overpopulate the fastest races and most extreme weight-lifting competitions, but the fact that some women are extraordinarily fast and strong—faster and stronger than plenty of men—would be far more obvious to us.

If we organized sports by weight, height, or some other criteria like qualifying times, it'd be more difficult to claim that all women were too small, weak, slow, or fragile to compete with men. There'd always be some women who would outperform even some of the best men (as there already are). If we allowed this fact to become clear, the belief that women are lesser athletes than men would be much more difficult to justify.

Sex-segregated sports, then, affirm the hierarchical gender binary. The effects are more than just ideological; they also make it possible to justify paying female athletes less than male ones. The assumption is that women are inferior athletes and less interesting and impressive to watch, so fans don't support them and media companies don't feature them or put much effort or money into broadcasts. As a result, prize monies and salaries for male athletes far exceed those for female athletes. The minimum salary for players in the National Basketball Association in 2010, for example, was $457,588 a

Tennis star Maria Sharapova, like many female athletes, makes most of her money through commercial endorsements.

season. In contrast, the minimum salary for the Women's National Basketball Association was less than 10 percent of that, at $35,190. The highest-paid professional male basketball player that year earned over $23 million. The highest-paid female earned $99,500—less than one-fifth of the *minimum* salary for a male player.

Forbes listed the highest-paid athletes in 2013 and only three women made the top 100: Maria Sharapova (the only one to break the top fifty), Serena Williams, and Li Na, all tennis players.[36] All three have made more money in endorsements than salary and prize winnings; four-fifths of Sharapova's income, for example, comes from contracts with companies to endorse their products. In contrast, only fifteen of the ninety-seven men on the list made more money from endorsements than they did directly from their athletic abilities.

These disparities in income are pervasive throughout the sports world and not at all commensurate with the skills men and women display, even once we account for gender differences in performances. Concluding a study of pay in professional golfing, professor of sport management Todd Crosset acknowledged that male golfers outperform female golfers on average, but these differences are, all things considered, very small.[37] Both sets of golfers are remarkably dedicated, skilled, and talented. To Crosset, the vast differences in prize money—regularly over $250 million for the men's Professional Golf Association Tour and around $50 million for the Ladies Professional Golf Association Tour—largely reflect the "social significance" of male versus female athletics.[38]

Sports fans, he explained, often argue that men's sports get more support and attention because male athletes are better. But, he countered:

> If it was truly skill that fans were going to see, how can we explain the lack of fan support for women's college teams that could easily handle boys' high school teams, which draw more fans. Quite simply, sports have more significance for men regardless of skill level.[39]

It's the social significance—not the skill—that drives the unequal attention and rewards that accrue to male and female athletes. Sex segregation is the foundation on which such unequal attention and rewards rest.

The policy of sex-segregating sports, supported by a widespread infrastructure, makes sports an arena in which beliefs in gender difference and inequality are routinely and ritualistically rehearsed. This is part of the institution of sport, one you can opt into or out of but can't ignore or overrule. If you want to be an athlete, you have to play by these rules. If you're a girl and you want to play baseball, you are up against more than the discomfort that sometimes comes with breaking gender rules and the policing that follows; you're also confronted by the fact that there isn't a girls' baseball team at your school. Even if there *were* girls' baseball team, though, who would you play? Girls' baseball teams haven't been institutionalized and, since it takes a community to field an entire league, changing this is very difficult. We discuss the difficulty of changing institutionalized ways of doing things in the final section of this chapter.

INSTITUTIONAL INERTIA AND CHANGE

As individuals we may wish to change or ignore the institutions we confront, but this is far more difficult with institutions than it is with cultural ideas or social interactions. Institutions are more resistant to change and more difficult to ignore because institutional patterns reflect widespread norms and are often encoded in formal policy. A return trip to the restroom offers a case study.

Sociologist Harvey Molotch was part of a failed effort to install a gender-neutral bathroom during the renovation of a space designed for the edgy New York University Department of Social and Cultural Analysis.[40] While the department included transgender faculty members who would clearly benefit from a gender-neutral bathroom and other faculty members were intrigued by the opportunity to push gender boundaries, they nevertheless ended up with conventional sex-segregated toilets. Why?

The first reason was related to inconvenience and expense. The administration was reluctant to spend extra time and money on a brand new restroom design. It was much *easier* to rely on a tried-and-true approach. Molotch wrote:

In creating new buildings and remodeling old ones, there is a set pattern for how to do things. Staying on pattern allows a lot of people to perform their duties across a range of specialties. Everyone "knows" what a building restroom should be like, that it will involve toilets and sinks, signs and separations, some spaces with urinals and some not. Access to plumbing of specific sorts at precise locations needs to be designed or captured in already existing facilities. To innovate means going back to the drawing boards, rethinking architectural opportunities and constraints, and checking continuously to make sure everyone is aware of the plan now being implemented. This is a hassle, one with financial implications and new potentials for error. . . . Working through details of restroom innovation was an extra, one that burdened an already crowded agenda.[41]

The second reason the initiative failed had to do with discomfort with the very idea. The NYC Department of Buildings required all large new buildings to install sex-segregated facilities, so the university had to submit a petition for an exemption. New York City turned them down. The university appealed and lost. The building commissioner expressed "concerns about security and liability."[42]

This result suited many of the future inhabitants of the building just fine, it turned out. Not everyone actually liked the idea of gender-neutral restrooms. Some of the female faculty cited the belief that men were messy, a discomfort with potential for male nudity, and a fear of meeting strange men in close quarters during off-hours. Meanwhile, the non-faculty staff generally was not on board with radically rethinking gender. They just wanted to pee in peace. Molotch's hopes for urinary utopia were crushed.

As this example shows, doing things differently can be challenging on multiple fronts. This isn't to say that institutions can't be changed, but changing them requires a *collective* shift in organizations and routines. Sometimes this simply means a slow but steady disinvestment in policies and norms that make the old ways seem out of date, like when school and workplace dress codes began to allow girls and women to wear pants.

Other times, institutions change in response to shifts in the broader social structure. The preponderance of African American male athletes in professional basketball is a great example. Whereas today African Americans are stereotyped as particularly suited to basketball, in the first half of the twentieth century, it was Jews who dominated the sport. In both cases, the pull into basketball was largely institutional. Just like many African Americans today, in the first half of the 1900s, immigrant Jewish families found themselves isolated in dense, economically strained, urban neighborhoods. Basketball requires only a little space, a ball, and a hoop on a pole. It's a sport that "fits" the tight space and budgets faced by inner-city families. Sounding like he could be talking about young black men today, retired Jewish professional basketball player Dave Dabrow said: "It was absolutely a way out of the ghetto."[43] Basketball scholarships were one of the few ways low-income urban Jews could afford college.

Today we draw on stereotypes about black men to explain their dominance in basketball, but this is an after-the-fact justification. Very different characteristics, stereotypes associated with Jews, were used to explain Jewish dominance of the sport. Paul Gallico, sports editor of the *New York Daily News* in the 1930s, explained that basketball was great for Jews because "the game places a premium on an alert, scheming mind, flashy trickiness, artful dodging and general smart aleckness."[44] Moreover, he argued, Jews were rather short and so had "God-given better balance and speed." Yep, there was a time when we thought being short was an advantage in the sport of basketball. Never underestimate how much things can change.

Who invests heavily in developing skill with a basketball, then—and how we socially construct the skills of athletes—is driven in part by the organization of our cities, patterns of immigration, the availability of teams, and an economic system in which some people are poorer than others. All these factors push some boys into basketball (and keep other boys and many girls out).

In contrast to the historical shifts that changed the face of basketball, it was activism that opened up organized sports to women, showing how collective action is another way to bring about institutional change. Title IX, an amendment to the Civil Rights Act of 1964, states, "No person in the United States shall, on the basis of sex, be excluded from participation in, be denied the benefits of, or be subjected to discrimination under any education program or activity

FIGURE 8.1 | MEN'S AND WOMEN'S PARTICIPATION IN NCAA CHAMPIONSHIP SPORTS

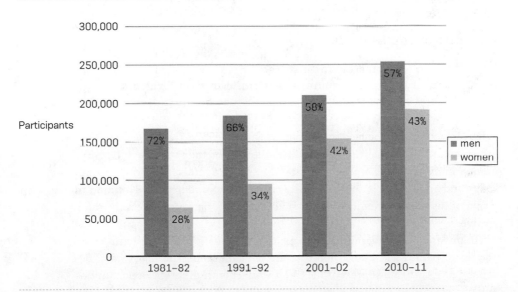

Source: Wilson, Amy. "The Status of Women in Intercollegiate Athletics as Title IX Turns 40," 2012, ncaapublications.com/productdownloads/TITLEIX.pdf.

receiving Federal financial assistance."[45] Passed in 1972, Title IX meant that schools and colleges receiving federal funding could not legally give preference to men. Instead, they had to allocate their resources to men and women in proportion to their interest and enrollment.

The intention of the policy was to change the norms that gave preference to men in all sorts of fields, from medical schools to sports teams. Because most schools and colleges have extensive athletics departments, sports were included among the resources that schools were required to dole out fairly. Eventually, even grudging and partial compliance with the requirements of Title IX dramatically increased the opportunity for women to play sports (Figure 8.1). In the forty years since its passage, the number of female athletes climbed more than tenfold among high school girls and sixfold among college women. Today, 41 percent of high school athletes and 43 percent of college athletes are female.[46] The remarkable increase in the number of women playing sports reveals the power of institutions to shape the experience of individuals and change social ideas. As this policy works to shift norms, women's participation in sports can be credited with eroding the Victorian idea that once made employers think that working women were so weak that they needed a room to rest.

Institutions often resist change, but they are never seamlessly constructed and impenetrable. Contradictions expose institutional practices as socially constructed ways of doing things. When even a minority of people recognize that institutionalized practices are cultural and changeable, not natural and inevitable, they open opportunities for themselves and others who want to do things differently. This isn't always easy, but it's always possible.

Revisiting the Question

When it comes down to it, regardless of social construction and social pressure, don't we live in a society in which it's possible to just be an individual?

When someone is so focused on the details that they miss the big picture, they are sometimes told that they can't see the forest for the trees. Each tree is a unique individual well worth understanding, but together they form a landscape and an ecosystem that is equally important to understand. Thinking in terms of institutions reminds us to zoom out and look at the forest in which we live.

To understand gender we need to examine the institutional structures and persistent patterns of interaction that are *our* landscape and ecosystem. Because these sometimes present men and women with different opportunities and obstacles, they produce gender difference and inequality regardless of the inclination or attitudes of the people who move through them. It's not possible, then, to be just an individual. Some things simply resist our personal volition.

Once we recognize that some of the institutions that are central to our daily lives are strongly gendered, it becomes clear that, as sociologist Raewyn Connell once argued, there are "gender phenomena of major importance which simply cannot be grasped as properties of individuals."[47] Societies are bigger than the sum of their individuals. They present *real* opportunities and obstacles that cannot be "changed at will," as the quotation that opened this chapter suggests.[48]

Next . . .

The end of this chapter marks the halfway point of this book. By now you have a strong understanding of how sociologists theorize gender as a set of ideas, ongoing actions and interactions, and interconnected institutions. Together they form the **gender order**, the social organization of gender relations in a society. The gender order is pervasive, expanding horizontally to affect all dimensions of a society and vertically to shape everything from the individual to the whole society. It intersects with other social hierarchies, establishing a matrix of domination that includes gender difference and inequality.

We hope you feel like you've gained a set of theoretical tools to help you better understand what is going on around you and how your participation both affirms and disrupts gendered ideas, interactions, and institutions. In the second half of this book, we will take a different approach. Using the theory you now know, we'll take a closer look at some important parts of life: sexuality, family, the workplace, and politics. Before we talk about where we are, however, we're going to talk about how we got here. The next chapter is about change.

FOR FURTHER READING

Anthony, Kathryn, and Megan Dufresne. "Potty Parity: Gender and Family Issues in Designing Public Restrooms." *Journal of Planning Literature* 21, no. 3 (2007): 267–94.

Berger, Peter, and Thomas Luckmann. "Society as Objective Reality." In *The Social Construction of Reality: A Treatise on the Sociology of Knowledge*, 63–146. Garden City, NY: Doubleday, 1966.

Birrell, Susan, and Diana Richter. "Is a Diamond Forever? Feminist Transformations of Sport." *Women's Studies International Forum* 10, no. 4 (1987): 395–409.

Britton, Dana. "Gendered Organizational Logic: Policy and Practice in Men's and Women's Prisons." *Gender & Society* 11, no. 6 (1997): 796–818.

Johnson, Allan. "Patriarchy, the System: An It, not a He, a Them, or an Us." In *The Gender Knot: Unraveling Our Patriarchal Legacy*, 27–50. Philadelphia: Temple University Press, 1997.

THE PAST DOES NOT REPEAT
ITSELF, BUT IT RHYMES.

—MARK TWAIN

9

Change

You know the scene. He gets down on one knee in a restaurant that is a tad above his price range. The ladies at the next table, spying him kneeling, clasp their hands to their chests and inhale. The room is suddenly hushed. All eyes turn toward the couple. Out pops the box. Her eyes widen; the bottom lashes moisten with the first sign of tears. He pushes out his arms, meaningfully pressing the box upward in her direction, imploring as he pulls back the velvety lid to reveal a glimmering sewing thimble.

A small metal cap worn over the tip of one's finger to protect it from needle points was the engagement item of choice for early Americans.[1] It is just one of many items that have served as a symbol of a commitment to marry. Rings didn't become the standard sign of betrothal until the late 1800s and *diamond* rings only became standard later still, in the 1930s. Despite the hype about how "diamonds are forever," the diamond engagement ring isn't as old of a tradition as some might think.

In this chapter we'll ask you to think about marriage as an institution. While marriages today *are* about love, care, and commitment, they are also governed by informal norms and legal contracts that formalize the rights and responsibilities of spouses.

Marriage is also a gendered institution. It used to be much more so. And diamonds, for what it's worth, haven't always been a girl's best friend.

Marriage is changing. The same can be said for the other institutions we address in this chapter: sexuality, family, work, and politics. We offer a dynamic historical view of what often feel like static traditions. This overview will be helpful for understanding how we got here and how and why things are now evolving as they are. Let's begin with one undeniably transformative moment: the arrival of the Puritans on the rocky East Coast of the North American continent.

A CLASH OF CIVILIZATIONS

The notion of the puritanical—extraordinarily strict religious or moral laws—was named after the Puritans, and rightly so. They believed that sex should be restricted to intercourse in heterosexual marriage with the aim of making babies. All nonmarital and nonreproductive sexual activities were forbidden, including pre- and extramarital sex, homosexual sex, masturbation, and oral or anal sex (even if married). Violations of the rules were punished by fines, whipping, public shaming, ostracism, or even death.

The Puritans were downright scandalized by the sexual lives of American Indians,[2] who were quite permissive in comparison. Their practices and norms varied, as they were organized into several hundred ethno-linguistic groups. Most tribes, however, accepted intercourse outside of committed relationships and both monogamy and polygamy were practiced. Unions were formed and dissolved at will. Homosexuality and gender nonconformity were accepted, with many tribes allowing men to live as women and women to live as men.

American Indians also often cared very little about whose child was whose. After the arrival of the French in the early 1600s, one Naskapi Indian was warned by a missionary that his failure to police his wife's sexuality might result in her being impregnated by another man. He responded: "You French people love only your own children, but we all love all the children of our tribe."[3]

This Naskapi man could be rather nonchalant about both sexual behavior and parentage, in part, because his tribe didn't subscribe to the idea of private property. His attitude is typical of **hunter-gatherer** societies that migrate seasonally, following crops and game across the landscape. Anthropologists and archaeologists have shown that both private property and patriarchy consistently emerge as societies transition from gatherer-hunter to **agrarian** societies, ones that cultivate domesticated crops. The invention of agriculture allows groups to put down roots. This creates the conditions for ownership of land.

Once there is private property, certain members of a group can consolidate power by owning more property than others.

Patriarchy—like many forms of inequality—takes hold once power can be passed down from generation to generation. Only then does knowing whose child is whose become important. Since for most of human history the only way to prove paternity was to control women, female sexual freedom is often curtailed when societies transition from gatherer-hunter to agrarian economies. The immigrants who came from Europe in the 1600s had already undergone this transition and, accordingly, they had very different ideas about the function of sex than the millions of American Indians who populated North America at the time.

Sex Is for Babies

Differences like those between the American Indians and the Puritans are often described in cultural or religious terms, but there were concrete reasons, too, why the Puritans were so darn puritanical. First, while Indian tribes were well established, the colonizers lived a fragile existence: Many people were dying from exposure, starvation, illness, and war. Babies replenished the labor supply, motivating the Puritans to channel their sex drive toward the one sexual activity that made babies: penile-vaginal intercourse. Having intercourse with your spouse wasn't only allowed, it was essential; women could divorce men who proved impotent so they could marry a new husband who could impregnate them.[4]

Because of these population concerns, the Puritans could be quite forgiving when people broke the rules they held so dear. When there was survival in numbers, both ostracism and punishment by death harmed the community as well as the individual. So even though both men and women broke all the sexual rules routinely, the harsher penalties were rarely imposed. Instead, fines and public shaming served as a mechanism by which the Puritans could forgive sexual deviations; by institutionalizing a way to pay penance, they could preserve the unity of their colonies. In other instances, settlers bent the rules for reasons related to the sex ratio. In the Chesapeake-area colonies, for example, men outnumbered women four to one.[5] Women were sparse, so even a

PURITAN MORALITY ENFORCED.

Adherence to the Puritan moral code was often enforced by stringent punishments, such as being locked in stocks for the purpose of public humiliation.

"disgraced" woman could count on a man being happy to have her. For this reason, there was little incentive for women to obey the rules.

The colonists' devotion to their religious rules had other limits as well. They made it impossible for the African women and men they enslaved to follow these rules. Slaves were legally denied the right to marry and their families were often broken up by sales of their partners or children.[6] Denied the right to form and maintain stable families, enslaved Africans accepted non-marital sex and childbearing by necessity. In a cruel twist, white elites would claim that black "immorality" was "a natural inclination of the African race" in order to defend forced breeding and their rape of female slaves.[7] The colonists extolled godliness, but didn't extend the opportunity to be godly to everyone.

The colonists' belief in restricting sex to intercourse was compatible with their need to reproduce themselves. When it wasn't—when population sustainability or economic viability was at stake—they were happy to look the other way, forgive misdeeds, or even make following the rules impossible. Their sexual values and behaviors were shaped not only by religion but also by the rigors and culture of colonization and an economy based on the exploitation and dehumanization of Africans. The Puritans surely earned their reputation, but beneath the strict rules were human beings who were fallible, rebellious, and brutally strategic.

As we'll see in the remainder of this chapter, institutional demands and opportunities—derived from economic change, technological innovations, medical advances, and political upsets—continually shape and reshape American lives. The changes brought by the Industrial Revolution would spur surprising shifts.

THE CHANGING VALUE OF CHILDREN

Beginning in the 1700s and advancing through around 1900, the Industrial Revolution first brought metal tools and steam-powered manufacturing, then factories, mechanization of the production process, and assembly lines. The need for labor drew many people out of small communities and into cities, where people were more densely packed and more anonymous.

In agriculture-based societies, men and women both lived and worked at home, whether on their own farm or that of feudal lords. Industrialization separated work from home. No longer sitting on fertile land, people had to leave the house to "go to work" in factories, mines, and shops that belonged to others. In return, they received money, their **wage**, with which they would go out and buy the things they once made. The process by which goods transition from something a family provided for itself into something bought with a wage is called

commodification: the making of something into a **commodity**, a thing that can be bought and sold. The new industrial economy would dramatically change how people thought about reproduction.

Sex Is for Love

Though kids were useful on farms, they became a burden in cities, where lodging was expensive and overcrowded. This gave couples an incentive to have fewer children, and because industrial production had made condoms increasingly cheap and effective, they had the capacity to limit family size.[8] Marital fertility rates dropped precipitously between 1800 and 1900: from 6 or more children per woman to 3.5 in the United States, England, and Wales.[9]

In this context, a Puritan sexual ethic that restricted sex to efforts to make babies just didn't make sense. People needed a new logic to guide sexual activity.[10] Over the course of the 1800s, Victorians slowly abandoned the idea that sex was only for reproduction, embracing the now familiar idea that sex could be an expression of love.[11]

In the era of tenement housing, large families in cramped quarters often necessitated the storage of toddlers in wire cages attached to the windows.

We have the Victorians to thank for romance, in a sense. We can also credit them with the invention of the **gendered love/sex binary**, a projection of the gender binary onto the ideas of love and sex, such that women are believed to be motivated by love and men by sex.[12] This feminization of love and masculinization of sex would have been unfamiliar to the Puritans. They believed that women were more wantonly sexual than men because they were "weaker vessel[s]" with "less mastery over [their] passions."[13] In their reading of the Bible, Eve succumbed to the forbidden fruit because she couldn't control her desire. In contrast, men were believed to be in better control of their passions and concerned with more important things than sex.

Victorians reversed this stereotype. Early feminists were among those who advocated for the idea that women took more naturally to both sexual moderation and romantic love. They thought they could convince their contemporaries that women were men's equals, and perhaps even their superiors, if they could convince them that women had a more developed spirituality. In an effort to attract and support female members, Protestant churches agreed.

Woman never overpower men

Dualistic thinking about the opposition of body and spirit meant that if women were more spiritual than men, women were also less carnal.[14] During the Victorian era, women were re-imagined as *naturally* chaste, innocent of the vulgar sexual desires felt by men and motivated by love instead of lust.[15] Men, in contrast, were believed to be more deeply tied to their bodies, constantly torn between the carnal and the celestial. This is when the idea of "opposite sexes" really took hold.

The Victorians sustained the notion that women were free of sexual thoughts and men were dens of sexual depravity by giving men an outlet for their more perverse inclinations: prostitution. Early capitalism had created a new class of extremely impoverished, wage-dependent families.[16] Prostitution was a way for poor women to support themselves and their families. At the same time, it functioned to protect "the virgin of the wealthier classes and shield their married women from the grosser passions of their husbands."[17] By one estimate, London alone was home to 8,600 prostitutes in the mid-1800s. Manhattan had one prostitute for every sixty-four men, and there was one for every thirty-nine and twenty-six men in Savannah, Georgia, and Norfolk, Virginia, respectively (slaves are likely excluded from these estimates).[18] The Victorians, then, were responsible for introducing the **sexual double standard**, different rules for the sexual behavior of men and women.

Just as Puritans had used the (impossible to avoid) sexual transgressions of enslaved Africans as proof of their inferiority, Victorian intellectuals would champion the purity of middle- and upper-class women and scorn the "uncivilized" sexual behavior of poor women.[19] Today we know this as the **good girl/ bad girl dichotomy**, the idea that women who behave themselves sexually are worthy of respect and women who don't are not.

The Victorians introduced Americans to ideas that were, at the time, rather radically new. All these ideas still thrive today in most Western societies, though the idea that only men are interested in sex has had less staying power. The 1920s would push society even further from the Puritan ideal.

Sex Is for Pleasure

The 1920s was a period of economic prosperity, technological innovation, and artistic experimentation. Americans call this decade the Roaring Twenties; in France it is called the *Années Folles*, or the "Crazy Years."[20] This era saw the invention of "sexy," literally; the word was first recorded to mean "sexually attractive" in 1923.[21] The '20s were sexy because the city offered unsupervised mixed-sex socializing that lent itself easily to flirtation and romance. Urban life meant that young adults found themselves increasingly free from the surveillance that characterized highly controlled small community environments.

The Charleston, a jaunty dance invented during the 1920s, allowed men and women to dance side-by-side as equals instead of together as a lead and follow.

People with extra money, some free time, and the opportunity to socialize inspired the birth of modern marketing and entertainment. Entrepreneurs and advertisers quickly learned the power of sex. Amusement parks catered to flirtatious young people, "nickelodeons" showed newly invented moving pictures with larger-than-life seductions, and burlesque clubs kept the morality police at bay with pasties and G-strings. In Harlem and other centers of African American life, high-end clubs featuring black musicians attracted white patrons, encouraging racial integration and introducing them to a new form of music: jazz. Revelers danced the "hug me close" and the "hump-back rag" in dimly lit ballrooms where singers mastered the art of innuendo, singing "keep on churnin' till the butter come" and "it ain't the meat, it's the motion" (*not* songs about food). As historians John D'Emilio and Estelle Freedman wrote, "More and more of life, it seemed, was intent on keeping Americans in a state of constant sexual excitement."[22] And not just heterosexual excitement. As early as 1908 it was reported that "certain smart clubs [we]re well known for their homosexual atmosphere."[23]

People in small communities, as well as the upper classes, continued the Victorian tradition of "calling" in which young men were invited to chaperoned visits with young women in their own homes. In cities, though, young working people invented "dating."[24] This wasn't dating as we know it today. The idea was not to find Mr. or Mrs. Right but to be seen with as many high-status members of the other sex as possible. A successful dater would be out with a different person every night of the week.

Dating shifted the balance of power. Because courtship took place "safely within the warm bosom of the family,"[25] calling was an activity over which women had substantial control. Women decided who came over, when, and how they socialized, providing snacks or entertainments of their choice. As historian Beth Bailey writes, dating "moved courtship out of the home and into the man's sphere."[26] Whereas advice books during the Victorian era strongly discouraged men to call without being invited, advice books on dating scolded women who would dare "usurp the right of boys to choose their own dates."[27]

Part of the reason men were accorded such an exclusive right involved the expense. Unlike calling, dating required that someone pay for the transportation, food, drink, and entertainment that the couple enjoyed. With no equal-pay laws protecting women's wages, working women could barely afford rent; entertainment was an impossible luxury.[28] This was the basis for **treating**, a practice in which a man funds a woman's night on the town. One government vice investigator, horrified by this new development, reported, "Most of the girls quite frankly admit making 'dates' with strange men.... These 'dates' are made with no thought on the part of the girl beyond getting the good time which she cannot afford herself."[29] Meanwhile, the owners of establishments worked hard to convince the public that "treating" was not tantamount to prostitution.

The inequitable responsibility for the cost of dating was not lost on men. Some were resentful of the fact that women now expected to "go out" on expensive dates. Men were nostalgic for the good old days of calling, which cost them nothing. For their part, women tried to make themselves, literally, worth it. This meant being an attractive and pleasing companion. Whereas for most of American history a plump and voluptuous body had been conflated with health and fertility, "reducing diets" suddenly became all the rage.[30] Likewise, women began wearing makeup and nail polish, previously only worn by prostitutes. Advertisers, eager to catch the few dollars women had to spare, perfected the trick of making women feel inadequate if they didn't use their products. Claimed one ad:

> The first duty of woman is to attract. It does not matter how clever or independent you may be, if you fail to influence the men you meet, consciously or unconsciously, you are not fulfilling your fundamental duty as a woman.[31]

"Unless you are one woman in a thousand," threatened another, "you must use powder and rouge. Modern living has robbed women of much of their natural color."[32]

A lipstick advertisement from the 1930s emphasizes women's efforts to "fascinate" men while also stressing how "natural" rather than "theatrical" or "painted" she would appear.

Whereas women in previous eras had been valued for their fertility, purity, or productivity, as well as attractiveness, during the '20s, an attractive face and body, as well as a certain degree of sexual accessibility, became more central to their value. The cosmetics industry grew from $17 million in sales to $141 million in just ten years.[33]

There were ways in which the '20s, too, created new potential for gender equality. Women's growing freedom meant that men and women could mix socially and hold intimate conversations. Half of all women coming of age during the Roaring Twenties had premarital intercourse, and being a virgin at marriage was beginning to seem quaint. For men, this freedom meant that they could have sex within their own social groups instead of with poor women, slaves, and prostitutes. These changes brought both men and women pleasure and paved the way for more gender-egalitarian relationships. Many young people were excited by this development and liked the idea of finding a partner who would be a "soul mate," someone who brought them joy and happiness.

Still, the power of institutions designed to limit and punish sexual freedom ensured that sex remained dangerous for women. With birth control information limited by law and still condemned by most mainline churches, 28 percent

The Roaring Twenties provided ample opportunity for working-class men and women to mingle and play out from under the watchful eyes of their parents.

of women became pregnant before marriage, up from 10 percent in 1850, a rise seen disproportionately among the urban working class.[34] Without a community in place to force men to "do the right thing," and with abortion newly illegal (in all states but one by 1910), women were more likely than those of earlier eras to have a child out of wedlock.[35] Since women were still paid wages much below men's, raising a child alone could lead to a lifetime of poverty, assuming the mother was not forced to hand over the child to an orphanage to ensure the child didn't starve. In other words, while the 1920s was a time of rising sexual opportunities, these opportunities came with costs.

The combination of industrialization, urbanization, the commercialization of leisure, and new freedoms for women all increased the ability of unmarried men and women to congregate without supervision. This freedom altered the overall environment in which sexuality was experienced, as well as the norms for sexual behavior. Such a transformation did not occur overnight, but eventually the life-style first enjoyed by bawdy working-class youth would become "mainstream." With the exception of a short-lived detour in the 1950s (which we'll talk about in a bit), the sexual attitudes and behaviors of young people have become increasingly permissive.[36] Marital practices have changed just as dramatically.

HOW CITIES CHANGED MARRIAGE

For thousands of years, marriage served economic and political functions unrelated to love, happiness, or personal fulfillment.[37] Prior to the Victorian era, love was considered a trivial basis for marriage and a bad reason to marry. There were much bigger concerns afoot: gaining money and resources, building alliances between families, organizing the division of labor, and producing legitimate male heirs. For the wealthy and, to some extent, the middle classes, marriage was important for maintaining and increasing the power of families. The concerns of the working classes were surprisingly similar but operated at a lower level of grandeur: "Do I marry someone with fields near my fields?" "Will my prospective mate be approved by the neighbors and relatives on whom I depend?" "Would these in-laws be a help to our family or a hindrance?"[38] These marriages were not chosen but typically arranged by older family members. They thought it foolish to leave something as important as marriage to the whims of young people.

Such marriages were patriarchal in the original sense of the term. Men were heads of households and women were human property, equivalent to children, slaves, and servants. A woman was entered into a marriage by her father, who owned her until he "gave her away" at the wedding. We call these **patriarch/ property marriages**.

This logic—that marriage is a form of property ownership—led to many marital rules that seem outrageous today. If an unmarried woman was raped, for instance, the main concern was the harm to her father's property (she became less valuable when she lost her virginity); the rapist could make up for the bad deed by marrying her. It was a sort of "you break it, you buy it" rule. Her feelings about the matter were irrelevant. A wife who was believed to be infertile could be discarded, like a broken TV, as she was useless if she couldn't produce sons to pass on her husband's wealth, power, and legacy. If her husband died, she could be inherited like livestock. Often, she was passed onto her husband's brother; the important thing was that her future children would still carry her husband's name.

Feminist activists of the 1800s and early 1900s fought to end patriarch/property marriage. One of the earliest feminist demands was for women to have the legal right to *own* property rather than *be* property. This right would eventually make many other rights possible: the right to vote and decide one's own citizenship; the right to work (even if one's husband disapproved), keep one's own wages, and get financial credit; the right to have a voice in family decisions; and, if divorced, the right to ask for custody of one's children. All of these issues were part of early feminist struggles.

Ultimately, in response to feminist activism as well as other forces, marriage would change. By the 1950s, a new kind of marriage would be institutionalized, the one that we typically call "traditional" today. This form of marriage was ushered in on the heels of industrialization.

"Traditional" Marriage

Industrialization broke up the then-traditional family. The vast majority of men could no longer be heads of households with their own land on which they supported their dependents. Instead, all family members were pulled into the workplace and survival depended on everyone's income. This new dynamic caused intellectuals of the time to worry that capitalism would destroy the family completely. Capitalism valued cheap labor regardless of the costs to the family. Since the subordinate status of women and children made their labor especially inexpensive, capitalists were happy to employ them. This drove men's wages down, leading them to fear the end of their authority over their wives and children. If he was no more valuable at work than she was, then gender no longer organized day-to-day life and patriarchy would vanish.

Instead of abandoning patriarchal marriage altogether—an option advocated by some at the time—men organized to modify and modernize patriarchy. They did so, in part, through unionization. Pushing back against capitalism, labor unions argued that working men had the right to be able to support a "home and

After World War II, the U.S. government subsidized the building of the first suburbs, where
normative ideas of the family came to be signified by a married man and woman with two to
three fresh-faced, smiling children.

family" on their wages alone.[39] Through protests, strikes, and boycotts, unions
carved out a new way of life for adult white men. They instituted laws meant
to enhance their compensation (such as the minimum wage), laws meant to reduce competition among workers (restrictions on child labor and legislation that
barred women and men of color from well-paying jobs), and laws enabling wives
to stay at home (child-rearing allowances and maternity leaves). They eventually
succeeded in institutionalizing a **family wage**: an income paid to one male earner
that was large enough to support a home, a wife, and children.

Some societies had stronger unions and, therefore, stronger policies than
others. Europe went much further than the United States. West Germany and
the Netherlands, for example, paid women a wage for raising their children
during the early months (and sometimes years), gave tax breaks to married
couples with only one earner, and offered cash bonuses for each child. Weaker
"breadwinner policies" (in the United States) and stronger ones (in much of
Europe) made it more or less possible for men to support a housewife, while
pushing women out of the workforce with more or less force.

The Great Depression of the 1930s called the feasibility of capitalism into question, but the crisis was interrupted by World War II, an event that pulled the United States and other parts of the world out of an economic depression. Policies put in place in the aftermath of World War II further changed how Americans organized families. Most notably, during the '40s and '50s the U.S. government collaborated with private investors to build suburbs and facilitate homeownership in what historian Stephanie Coontz calls "the most massive government subsidization of young families in American history." This was the birth of the "American dream." The G.I. Bill—designed to reward soldiers and help them reintegrate into society—offered white male veterans college scholarships and cheap mortgages. Meanwhile, the government funded the building of an interstate highway system that connected the cities to the countryside much more efficiently. This led to a boom in housing developments, to which cities strung power lines and dug sewer tunnels. These government investments transformed America into a land of homeowners for the first time in history, but home was farther from work than ever.

SEPARATE SPHERES

With industrialization, unionization, and suburbanization the idea of **separate spheres**, a masculinized work world and a feminized home life, became the new common sense. For the first time in history, there was a thing called a "workplace" somewhere other than where the family lived, and the new division between home and work that emerged became understood as a "naturally" gendered division of labor.

At work, employees engaged in **production**, the making of goods for sale. Since capitalism is a competitive system, factory owners pushed workers to produce as efficiently as possible. Workers who couldn't keep up were fired. The logic of capitalism asked men to become the kind of people it found most useful: those who were interested more in work than family and concerned with climbing a corporate hierarchy and maximizing economic success. Living in such a world required that men master the qualities of competitiveness, aggression, and ruthlessness. "'It's a jungle out there,' says the stereotypical male provider when his wife and kids meet him at the door."[40]

Inside that door, he could expect a warm, comfortable space filled with people who cared for him. At least, this was the idea. At home there was supposedly no production, only **reproduction**, the making and nurturing of human beings. There would be his loving children and doting wife. Under the glow of their admiration, he could recharge to fight another day. The notion that women could and should wholeheartedly embrace the work of making a loving home

A housewife stops to feed her son while in the midst of ironing, as the Army–McCarthy hearings of 1954 play on television. The politics of the 1950s were aimed at rooting out "communist" ideas like child care and gender equality.

is called the **cult of domesticity**. It emerged as a dominant idea during the Victorian era—at the same time that we feminized the idea of love—and has had significant staying power.[41] Together with the ideology of separate spheres, it aimed to protect part of life from the harsh capitalist values of rationality and cost-benefit analysis.[42] Women were expected to specialize in a particular kind of supportive and loving emotional role that society needed in order to balance dog-eat-dog capitalism.

This new **breadwinner/housewife marriage** was of an entirely different kind. In the mixed-sex environments innovated in the 1920s and mainstreamed over the next several decades, men and women met and got to like one another. They married by choice and were expected to find comfort in their relationship. Unlike patriarch/property marriage, breadwinner/housewife marriage did not legally subordinate wives to husbands (that is, she was no longer his property). But, because this model of marriage was organized in a gender binary way, it continued to define the rights and responsibilities of husbands and wives differently. Women owed men domestic services (cleaning, cooking, child care, and sex); in return, men were legally required to support their wives financially.

This is the type of gendered marriage we typically mean when we use the phrase "traditional marriage" today. As we'll see, however, this type of marriage, and the era for which it is famous, was actually a short-lived and uneasy experiment.

THE FUNNY '50S

The icon of Rosie the Riveter signifies the work opportunities offered to women during World War II. During that time, women entered many occupations previously dominated by men but, after the war ended in 1945, American women were subject to a campaign designed to push them back into the home. Marketers, columnists, scientists, public intellectuals, and the U.S. government all began touting the societal benefits of gender-specific family roles. This resulted in a sudden turn toward the nuclear family. As Coontz explains:

> At the end of the 1940s, all the trends characterizing the rest of the twentieth century suddenly reversed themselves. For the first time in more than one hundred years, the [average] age for marriage and motherhood fell, fertility increased, divorce rates declined, and women's degree of educational parity with men dropped sharply. In a period of less than ten years, the proportion of never-married persons declined by as much as it had during the entire previous half century.[43]

All of these trends would reverse within a few decades. Historically speaking, then, middle-class marriages in the 1950s were *unusually* family oriented.

The era was unusually conservative in other ways, too. The government passed decency standards for Hollywood movies, ensuring that sex was kept off the screen and bad things always happened to "bad" girls. In 1952, books and magazines with sexual content were banned. Comic books were considered especially corrupting. In an official report, Congress argued that comic books give "short courses in . . . rape, cannibalism, carnage, necrophilia, sex, sadism, masochism, and virtually every other form of crime, degeneracy, bestiality, and horror."[44]

The rising visibility of male homosexuality would lead to public condemnation of gay men.[45] This concept of *being* gay was rather new. Homosexuals had been off the cultural radar for most of American history. The Puritans were familiar with homosexual *behavior*, but it had never occurred to them that individual *people* were distinctively homosexual. In their view, all humans were brimming with the potential for sin. Variation in how likely a person was to participate in homosexual sex was considered a measure of how godly they were, not an innate preference for one sex or the other.[46] While Puritans who felt same-sex desire may have experienced guilt and shame, they would not have paused to wonder if they were different kinds of people than anyone else.

Likewise, during much of the Victorian era the idea that women might feel for women what they were supposed to feel for men was unthinkable. Out from under any suspicion of lesbianism, women formed intimate and romantic relationships with each other that may or may not have been sexual but certainly were not imagined to be at the time. Correspondence between women during this time is full of language like the one found in this letter that Jeannie wrote to Sarah in 1864:

> Dear darling Sarah! How I love you & how happy I have been! You are the joy of my life . . . I cannot tell you how much happiness you gave me, nor how constantly it is all in my thoughts . . . My darling how I long for the time when I shall see you . . . Goodbye my dearest, dearest lover . . . A thousand kisses . . . I love you with my whole soul.[47]

It sounded like friendship at the time.

In the 1920s, college girls breathlessly described the girl on whom they were **smashing**, a term they used to describe a same-sex crush.[48] These crushes weren't all platonic. In a survey of 1,200 female college graduates from the 1920s, 28 percent of women enrolled in single-sex schools reported that they had been in a sexual relationship with another woman, along with 20 percent of women at mixed-sex schools.[49] They would write letters to their mothers about it. No one thought it odd. Instead, it was believed to be a normal developmental phase. So long as young women eventually married men, sexual and romantic relationships with other girls were considered harmless. Homosexual experimentation wasn't a cause for alarm because it didn't trigger an *identity* crisis. This should be at least somewhat familiar: It is how homosexuality is still experienced among older men in China, as well as some white men in rural America and black men on the "down low."

The idea of a homosexual *person*, as opposed to a person who engages in homosexual *practices*, didn't become a part of the collective consciousness until World War II. The war was so conducive to exploring same-sex attraction that it's been called "a nationwide 'coming out' experience."[50] One out of every eight American males—almost every young, fit male between eighteen and twenty-six years old—served in the war.[51] As a result, unmarried people on both the front lines and the home front found themselves largely in the company of the same sex. Indulging in homoerotic encounters became easier and more tempting. Wrote one young man: "The war is a tragedy to my mind and soul . . . but to my physical being, it is a memorable experience."[52]

With this newly imagined possibility, some soldiers rejected conventional heterosexuality and, after the war, instead pursued a gay "lifestyle."[53] The first gay bars in the United States opened in the 1940s and the first gay advocacy organization would be founded in 1951.[54] Notably, these new communities were mostly for men. Since women were effectively prohibited from earning enough money to support themselves, they didn't have the resources to socialize at bars, let alone live without a husband's or father's support. Gay women would remain less visible to the public and each other—at least for a while.

Growing awareness of homosexuality and more community among men who identified as gay invoked a backlash in the '50s. Cities passed laws saying alcohol couldn't be sold to homosexuals and they outlawed same-sex dancing and cross-dressing.[55] In response to the so-called "homosexual menace," the U.S. government sought to purge supposed homosexuals from public jobs on the assumption that they were "by definition morally bankrupt and, as such, politically suspect."[56] Much of the private sector followed suit. We often discuss this as a time when the government was focused on identifying and expelling Communists, but it was more common for men to lose their jobs for suspicion of homosexuality. Senator Joe McCarthy, famous for these efforts, said that anyone who opposed him was "either a Communist or a cocksucker."[57]

Far from being characteristic of American history, the 1950s were unusually family focused, pro-censorship, and intolerant of homosexual behavior. At least, this is how it appeared. What was happening behind closed doors?

Sex and Marriage in the '50s

A young woman in the 1950s might have been seriously concerned about her marriage prospects. In addition to the hundreds of thousands of men killed in the war, tens of thousands of soldiers married foreign women while abroad.[58] *The New York Times* reported that 750,000 young women would likely never marry. The process of securing a husband, then, became serious business. So while it may have made sense to go out with a different guy each night in the 1920s, flitting from guy to guy didn't seem so smart when there weren't enough guys to go around. Accordingly, during the 1950s dating was being edged out by a new practice, **going steady**, an often short-lived, but still exclusive, public pairing off. Going steady was "social security"; it ensured that a girl would always have a date on important nights and lessened the chances that she would end up an old maid.[59]

Ironically, this interest in marriage accelerated premarital sexual experimentation.[60] Compared to couples who might enjoy just one night together, couples that went steady were more likely to "neck" (contact above the neck for the purposes of sexual arousal), "pet" (contact below the neck), or "go all the way." Adults bemoaned the new system for just this reason (they also thought that going with just one person sounded boring), but necking and petting, if not intercourse, were becoming expected parts of any youthful romantic relationship. According to one 1952 advice manual, if a girl "wishes to be a member of the dating group," then "mild sexual contact" is "one of the requirements."[61] Meanwhile, the new ubiquity of the automobile did for suburban youth of the '50s what living in cities had done for the working-class youth of the '20s: It provided the opportunity to socialize without parental supervision. Hence the invention of "parking," driving off to a remote location, pulling off the road, and necking and petting in the backseat.

Emotionally intense relationships led to sex and the highest rate of teen pregnancy in American history. At its peak in 1957, one out of every ten women aged fifteen to nineteen gave birth.[62] But there was no teen pregnancy crisis. Instead of a rash of single teen mothers, the age of marriage dropped to a 100-year low (and babies born less than nine months after the wedding reached a 100-year high). At the end of the Victorian era, the median age at first marriage was twenty-six for men, twenty-two for women, and rising. By 1950, it had dropped to twenty-three for men and twenty for women, and it would remain this way throughout the decade (Figure 9.1).[63]

In the 1950s, the custom of going steady among teenagers guaranteed that girls would have companions to institutionally organized events, such as the senior prom, and facilitated both romantic and sexual experimentation.

Eventually it would be impossible to pretend that either the youth or the adults in the 1950s were sexual goody-goodies. The fable was dealt a heavy blow with the publication of sexologist Alfred Kinsey's reports on the sexual behavior of men and women.[64] Published in 1948 and 1953, his books detailing the sex lives of 18,000 people sold a quarter of a million copies. They roundly discredited the idea that it was only teenagers who were breaking the sexual rules, revealing that premarital "petting" was nearly universal, 90 percent of men and 50 percent of women had premarital sex, 90 percent of men and 60 percent of women masturbated, and half of men and a quarter of women had had extramarital sex. A third of men and 13 percent of women reported having homosexual sex, while a full 50 percent of men and 37 percent of women reported same-sex attraction. The cat was out of the bag.

It wasn't just sex that had been hiding behind the happy innocence of poodle skirts and saddle shoes; the realities of marriage were somewhere back there, too. In 1963 a book called *The Feminine Mystique* forever changed the way America thought of housewives. The title referred to a mythology—the idea

FIGURE 9.1 | MEDIAN AGE AT FIRST MARRIAGE, 1900–2010

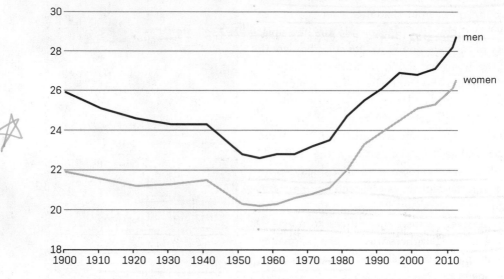

Source: U.S. Census Bureau, Current Population Survey, March and Annual Social and Economic Supplements, 2011 and earlier.

that women were gleefully happy as wives and mothers—that strongly contrasted with reality. The book, by feminist Betty Friedan, documented widespread un-happiness among middle-class married women in the 1950s and '60s. Writes Friedan:

> *Each suburban wife struggled with it alone. As she made the beds, shopped for groceries, matched slipcover material, ate peanut butter sandwiches with her children, chauffeured Cub Scouts and Brownies, lay beside her husband at night—she was afraid to ask even of herself the silent question—"Is this all?"*[65]

The book spent six weeks on *The New York Times* best-seller list; its first print-ing sold 1.4 million copies.[66] Women wept with recognition, claiming that it was like a "bolt of lightning," a "revelation," a "bombshell."[67] Friedan's book illustrated a number of cracks in the breadwinner/housewife model, fault lines that would contribute to its demise.

STRAINED BY SEPARATE SPHERES To begin, the separate roles of bread-winner and housewife—with the husband working overtime and the wife busy with children and housework—drained the life out of the friendships that cou-ples had built before marrying. The differences in their daily lives left them strangers to one another. Less than a third of spouses described their mar-riages as "happy" or "very happy."[68]

America's controversial best seller!

MARYA MANNES: "A damning indictment of the social, educational and commercial pressures which have caused a harmful discrepancy between what women really are and what they are told they should be."—Page-one review, *N. Y. Herald Tribune Book Review*

CUE Magazine: "Mrs. Friedan swings a cool and sharp-edged axe at the dolls' houses that all too many of her countrywomen have been conned into occupying almost a century after Ibsen's Nora slammed the door on hers.... In its candor and wit, Mrs. Friedan's book is immensely refreshing; in its suggestions for improving the situation, it is hopeful and inspiring."

FRED HECHINGER, N. Y. Times: "Confirms and drives home with editorial passion many dangers that educators themselves often warn against privately."

WASHINGTON POST: "Deserves cheers for daring women to take a more intelligent approach to life and work."

PHILADELPHIA BULLETIN: "Mrs. Friedan will have fur flying, hackles rising—quite possibly more women's than men's; the book may well win more enemies than friends, but it will be read — and it deserves to be."

PROFESSOR WILLIAM A. OWENS, Columbia University: "Written about women, for women, but should be required reading for men. Directly or indirectly, it touches on the contributions of American men to the problems of American women."

MILLICENT G. McINTOSH: "Its implications are terrifying — a 'must' for all who are concerned with marriage and family life, or who care about the future of our society."

LONDON OBSERVER: "Betty Friedan shows how the mystique of femininity has failed to deliver the goods in practice; she also kicks some penetrating holes in the theory.... It is not the drive to independence that has done harm to American women but the increasing compulsion to concentrate on getting a man rather than on becoming a human being."

ESTHER PETERSON, Asst. Secretary of Labor, Women's Bureau: "Mrs. Friedan's intelligent and sympathetic approach is refreshing. She has made a real contribution."

VIRGILIA PETERSON: "Absorbingly interesting, pertinent, relevant to my own problems and those of every woman I know."

LILLIAN SMITH: "Filled with startling and significant facts about modern women and the homes they are destroying through no fault of their own."

LIFE Magazine: "An angry, thoroughly documented book that in one way or another is going to provoke the daylights out of everyone who reads it."

The Feminine Mystique

By BETTY FRIEDAN

7th BIG PRINTING · $5.95 at all bookstores · W. W. NORTON & COMPANY, INC.

Betty Friedan's sociological and psychological study of American housewives' dissatisfaction with their lives spurned the second wave of feminist mobilization in the United States.

Stranded in the suburbs and with few other adults to talk to, privileged wives living the American dream often felt isolated, lonely, and bored. Many had earned college degrees and resented being pushed out of the workforce at the end of World War II.[69] Instead of finding housework and child care endlessly stimulating and enjoyable, many chafed under the expectation that they would find fulfillment this way.[70] Gleaming linoleum could only bring so much joy. Child care was exhausting. They worried that their brains were wasting away while they did endless rounds of shopping, cooking, and cleaning. When *Redbook* asked readers to write to them about "Why Young Mothers Feel Trapped," 24,000 women responded.[71] One 1950s housewife described her life as nothing but "booze, bowling, bridge, and boredom."[72]

There was, indeed, lots of drinking. Likewise, pharmaceutical companies developed tranquilizers—or "daytime sedatives for everyday situation stress"—in response to housewives' complaints.[73] Unheard of in the mid-fifties, in 1958 doctors prescribed 462,000 pounds of the stuff; that number more than doubled the next year.[74] White middle-class women—the group most likely to be in a breadwinner/housewife marriage—were four times more likely to take them than any other type of person.[75] "Many suburban housewives were taking tranquilizers like cough drops," wrote Friedan.[76] They were known, colloquially, as "mother's little helpers."

Wives weren't the only ones unhappy in breadwinner/housewife marriages. Marriage was essentially compulsory for men; often jobs and promotions depended on their ability to show that they were good family men. Bachelors were considered immature ("Why can't he settle down?") or deviant ("Is he a homosexual?"). Meanwhile, men were wary of women who saw them only as a "meal ticket" and often found it hard to be the only adult companion on whom their wives could rely for emotional support. A whole genre of humor emerged, designed to resonate with men's own sense of being trapped (hence the idea of the "ball and chain").

Hugh Hefner, the founder of *Playboy*, exemplifies a new ideal of masculinity that was becoming hegemonic in the supposedly staid 1950s.

Tapping into this sentiment, Hugh Hefner launched *Playboy* magazine in 1953. Hefner changed ideas about masculinity.[77] Encouraging men to stay single and avoid commitment, he mainstreamed the notion of a man who didn't marry but was anything but gay. As Barbara Ehrenreich explained, "The playboy didn't avoid marriage because he was a little bit 'queer,' but, on the contrary, because he was so ebulliently, even compulsively heterosexual."[78] Hefner introduced a new set of gender rules for men that rewarded men's resistance to marriage and monogamy, leading to the still-present myth that men must be dragged, kicking and screaming, to the altar.[79]

Both men and women, then, enjoyed fantasizing about a life without a spouse, kids, and a mortgage, but it was women who were truly vulnerable in marriage.

SEPARATE AND UNEQUAL SPHERES While both men and women had their dissatisfactions, women carried virtually all the risks of a breadwinner/housewife marriage. These marriages weren't overtly patriarchal—women were seen as men's moral equals, different and complementary, not better and worse—but women were still men's economic inferiors. In classic androcentric fashion, the masculine sphere of work was evaluated as important and admirable, while the feminine sphere of the home was seen as somehow less so.

The imbalance in the value attributed to work and home was literal. Men's work was *worth* something; they received a wage in exchange for it. In contrast, women were doing more or less the same work they'd been doing since agrarian times but getting less credit for it than ever. Capitalist rationality and the new golden rule—he who has the gold makes the rules—replaced explicit patriarchy. Determining power by paycheck size ensured a wife's economic subordination to the "head of household."

This was a peculiar invisibility. Prior to industrialization, women's labor—both the work of maintaining a household and the birthing and rearing of children—was understood to be *work*. After industrialization, however, with the separation of work from home, women's labor seemed to disappear, turning into something called *staying home*. Because women's work was invisible, housewives seemed dependent on men, but not vice versa. While her dependence on his wage was obvious to everyone, his dependence on her cooking, cleaning, shopping, and child care often was not. To be fair, a housewife would be in big trouble if she lost her breadwinner, but a breadwinner needed his housewife, too. Without her, he had hungry, dirty, misbehaving children who he couldn't leave alone, plus no clean clothes to wear, an empty belly, nothing in the fridge, and a filthy house. He either had to stay home (and lose his wage) or hire someone to replace his wife. Even a family wage wasn't designed to support a house, children, *and* a full-time babysitter and housekeeper. It relied on him getting the domestic work for free. The degree to which wives supported husbands' breadwinning activities was swept under the rug, so to speak.

In becoming housewives, women gave up incomes of their own, the likelihood of having a successful career in the future (employers often didn't want to hire women who had spent many years out of the workplace), and the status that comes with doing work deemed important. All this was theoretically fine *if* the marriage lasted, her husband valued her contribution, and he consistently earned a good income. If the marriage fell apart—if the husband couldn't hold up his end of the bargain or traded her in for a younger, more attractive, or more submissive woman—wives could end up divorced and destitute, often with children. This was not an unlikely scenario; between a quarter and a third of marriages in the 1950s ended in divorce.

The government tried to protect "displaced homemakers," as they were called, by institutionalizing alimony (monthly cash payments to ex-wives from their former husbands) and by making divorce legally difficult (by requiring proof that a spouse had broken the marriage contract, for example), but marriage remained an intrinsically risky bet for women. The often desperate financial situation of divorced women would serve as cautionary tales to younger women. Pretty soon the idea that they needed to secure their own future incomes and opportunities "just in case" carried quite a bit of weight.

Ultimately, the breadwinner/housewife model failed to offer women a practical, economic basis for equality. The workplace potentially did.

GOING TO WORK

At the same time that the breadwinner/housewife model was emerging as the ideal family form, women were leaving the home to go to work. Even at its height, the 1950s version of the traditional marriage was more of an ideal than a reality. Due to legal discrimination, the family wage was elusive for most men of color and immigrant men. Black soldiers were excluded from the G.I. Bill that made the American dream a reality for white soldiers. They didn't get the college loans and mortgages that launched white families into the middle class and, even if they could afford to move into the suburbs without government help, most of the communities did not allow black people. As a result, many black families were left behind in cities that governments neglected. Because they were married to men who were essentially prohibited from earning a family wage, poor women and women of color entered the wage economy from the beginning and stayed there. Soon middle-class white women were joining them. Before 1940, more than 80 percent of women who married left the labor force on their wedding day and never came back.[80] In the next twenty years, the proportion of married women who worked doubled.[81]

Women did not, generally speaking, enter the workforce in an effort to live out a feminist impulse to compete alongside men in paid work. They went to work out of necessity: Even among native-born, white families, only a third could survive on a single wage. The economy also needed more workers.[82] Recall that more than a quarter million men never came back from World War II.[83] Meanwhile, the low birthrate during the 1920s and '30s, a response to both the Depression and city life, meant that there were, literally, fewer people around. In order to keep churning, the economy had to incorporate all kinds of women, not just poor women (who had always worked) and young women (who often worked between high school graduation and marriage).[84]

Some policies that limited women's workplace participation were discarded due to the demand for workers. This was true of **marriage bans**, policies against employing married women. Beginning in the late 1800s, marriage bans were common in banking, teaching, office work, and government jobs. A majority of school districts (87 percent) had bans against hiring married women, as did over half of all firms employing office workers.[85] Bans were expanded to manufacturing work during the 1930s in an effort to save jobs for men during the turmoil of the Great Depression. By the late '40s, however, these bans were harmful to the American economy. By 1951, only 18 percent of school districts had a marriage ban. Other types of work followed suit.

Although marriage bans were being discarded by most industries, many other politics were more resistant to change. These included **protective legislation**, policies designed to protect women from exploitation by restricting their workplace participation. Beginning in the mid-1800s, almost every American state had passed some protectionist laws.[86] These laws were passed alongside child labor laws. Since middle-class women workers tended to be young

FIGURE 9.2 | WOMEN'S PARTICIPATION IN THE LABOR FORCE IN THE UNITED STATES, 1948–2012*

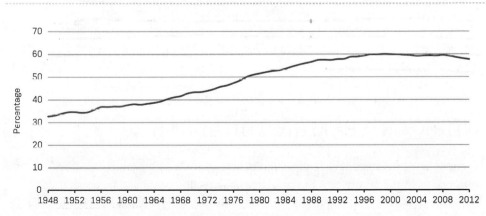

*Labor force participants as a percentage of all civilian women age sixteen and over.
Source: U.S. Bureau of Labor Statistics. 2011. "Women in the Labor Force: A Databook," www.bls.gov/cps/wlf-databook-2012.pdf

and many still lived with their parents, reformers saw women as like children: liable to be exploited by employers and guardians who controlled their employment and confiscated their earnings. Accordingly, women were often banned from working long hours, doing night work, or taking dangerous jobs. Meanwhile, defenders of the family wage and the breadwinner/housewife model of marriage excluded women from occupations like law, medicine, and aviation.[87]

Despite the protective language, these policies slotted women into largely dead-end jobs. The assumption that women would quit or be fired upon marriage was a disincentive to both women and employers.[88] For women, extended schooling and training might make it more likely that they would marry a man with a promising career, but it was unlikely to have any payoff in the workplace. Meanwhile, employers were loath to put any time into on-the-job training for women on the assumption that they'd work, at best, five to seven years and then quit upon marriage. Instead, women were largely hired into jobs that offered them little or no chance of building skills or moving up a promotion ladder. Training them for professions was pretty much out of the question.

In 1964 this type of discrimination against women would become illegal in the United States. In a last-ditch effort to ensure that a bill mandating equal treatment of African Americans would fail, Virginia Democrat Howard Smith added "sex" to the Civil Rights Act, thus including sex in the list of characteristics against which workplace discrimination would be illegal: race, color, religion, and national origin.[89] He thought the idea of equal treatment for men and women was so preposterous that it would surely kill the bill. Much to his chagrin and surprise, it passed anyway. Only in part an accident—there were women in Congress who worked to make Smith's joke a reality—the Civil Rights Act made it illegal to discriminate against women in the workplace.[90]

As the economy grew and demographics changed, women were increasingly pulled into the workforce. As they were, though, they were pushed into low-paid occupations and, even after discrimination against women at work was outlawed by the government, the idea that women were best suited to low-status work persisted.

WORK AND FAMILY TODAY

In 2003, James Dobson Jr., founder of Focus on the Family, wrote: "Unless we act quickly, the family as it has been known for 5,000 years will be gone."[91] The truth is, the patriarch/property marriage was already gone and the breadwinner/housewife marriage was fading fast. Even in the 1950s, the strength of the family wage on which the breadwinner/housewife model depended was waning. The economy was changing in ways that made marriage less essential. First, it was becoming increasingly easy for a man of means to buy a housewife's services in the market. Dinner could be eaten at restaurants; maids could clean your house and wash your laundry; and female companionship (both free and paid) was a cocktail lounge away. If many of the services of a housewife could be obtained in the marketplace, why should men marry at all? For women, too, marriage was becoming less essential. If a woman could earn a wage herself, even if it meant living a little less well, then why would she enter into a state of financial dependence? Given how risky marriage was for women, holding out until she could find a husband with whom she could innovate a new model of marriage, or not marrying at all, seemed like a fine idea to many.

The United States was transitioning from an industrial economy founded on production to a **service and information economy**, one dependent on jobs focused on providing services for others (such as waiting tables and bartending, working in hair and nail salons, cashiering, providing administrative assistance, and operating phones) or working with ideas (including engineers, computer technicians, human resource managers, lawyers, doctors, and college professors).

On the one hand, service jobs are typically low paying and unstable and offer few or no benefits. The low wages that made it so difficult for African American husbands to be sole providers in the 1950s, in other words, have since become characteristic of the entire American working class. Many middle-class factory workers saw their children slide down the economic ladder; as factory jobs disappeared, they ended up as service workers. For working-class and most middle-class people today, two incomes are essential for making ends meet.

On the other hand, information jobs pay well, but they require significant investment in education up front. People who can get these jobs are situated in the upper-middle or upper classes and typically have health insurance, vacation pay, sick days, and other benefits. While a single earner with this type of job is more capable of supporting a spouse, most women who invest in college and begin a well-paid, high-status career are not eager to exchange the economic security they have won with the risky business of being a long-term, full-time housewife. Even among the upper classes, then, two-income families are the norm.

The breadwinner/housewife model of marriage makes even less sense now than it did in the 1950s. Both men and women are now increasingly educated and employed for longer periods of their lives. Age at marriage and first birth has bounced back up. The expectation that women leave the labor force permanently at marriage has vanished, as has the idea that a man becomes a good father merely by dropping his paycheck on the table. Fathers who are engaged with their wives in the day-to-day work of parenting and mothers who work are the norm rather than the exception.[92] If they need to, both men and women can do without marriage. If people want to marry today, it needs to be for reasons that fit with the more gender-egalitarian demands of the new economy.

In response, the breadwinner/housewife ideal has been replaced by an idealized **partnership marriage**, a model of marriage based on love and companionship between two equals who negotiate a division of labor unique to each couple. The law has cleared the way for such marriages. In response to over a century of feminist activism and demands, the marriage contract today is almost entirely gender neutral, providing the same rights and responsibilities to men and women. Both men and women are now responsible for paying alimony to a spouse who spent time out of the workforce taking care of the family. A widower can now collect his wife's Social Security check instead of his own if her lifetime earnings exceeded his (in the 1950s, '60s, and '70s, only widows could do this). The Equal Credit Act defines both wives and husbands as participating in borrowing and paying bills; men no longer have special rights to manage family investments. Nearly all states now confer equal standing to both spouses in issues of child custody.[93]

Because partnership marriage involves a gender-neutral contract, married couples are free to organize their lives however they wish. And they do. Coontz writes:

> Almost any separate way of organizing caregiving, childrearing, residential arrangements, sexual interactions, or interpersonal redistribution of resources has been tried by some society at some point in time. But the coexistence in one society of so many alternative ways of doing all of these different things—and the comparative legitimacy accorded to many of them—has never been seen before.[94]

Today we see family-focused dual-earner couples (working part-time and taking turns caring for kids) and work-focused dual-earner couples (working overtime and hiring gardeners, maids, and nannies). We see breadwinners married to housewives and, in small but growing numbers, breadwinners married to househusbands, too. Gay couples adopt all these family forms as well, though their marriages may not be recognized by their state's government. The idea of non-monogamous, polyamorous unions of more than two people and open relationships in which couples negotiate extra-pair sex, are increasingly part of the conversation about what relationships can look like.

Marriage no longer determines your living arrangements. While it remains the norm that couples will live together once married, some don't. Some live in separate cities either by choice or circumstance; others live in the same town but choose to live apart. In practice, of course, marriages are still gendered, but they are less so than ever.

While marriage is still normative, it is not so surprising anymore when people reach their thirties, forties, or fifties without marrying.[95] About 45 percent of

U.S. adults aren't married and about one in seven lives alone.[96] It's totally normal to be single, even as a "grown up." While it may be preferable to some, marriage is no longer necessary for entrance to adulthood, nor is it a prerequisite for having a child. It is certainly no longer a job requirement. It's rarely used, at least explicitly, to cement political alliances or hoard wealth. For these reasons, marriage itself is less necessary than it was in the past, so much so that we might ask whether it is still a major institution. Some people choose to live together without being married, others neither marry nor cohabit. Nearly half of Americans (44 percent) have lived with someone without being married.[97] Over a third (39 percent) of nonmarried people say they "don't want to marry" or are "not sure."[98] Parenting now occurs in the absence of marriage. Today almost half of children (41 percent) are born to unmarried parents.[99] A majority of Americans (86 percent) say that a single parent and a child "count" as a family. Meanwhile, about one in six Americans is freely choosing not to have children.

Since the primary reason to marry in Western cultures today is love, marriages are both more voluntary and less stable. As Stephanie Coontz explains, the "same things that made marriage become such a unique and treasured personal relationship during the last two hundred years, paved the way for it to become an optional and fragile one."[100] People divorce. When they do, they often take children with them, sometimes into new marriages, creating "blended families." A third (30 percent) of Americans have a step- or half-sibling and 13 percent are raising step-children.[101] The high rate of divorce does not signal a decline in the value of marriage. Instead, Americans engage in what sociologist Andrew Cherlin calls the "marriage-go-round": They both marry *and* divorce more frequently than people in other countries.

Since marriage is more about choice and pleasure than ever, it makes sense to some to further reduce the rules about who can marry whom. In 1967 the United States Supreme Court struck down laws against interracial marriage. A more recent contentious marriage debate was over same-sex marriage: 49 percent of the population is in favor. Sixty-three percent believe that two men or two women with children count as a family.[102]

Same-sex marriage is a reality today because our marriage contracts no longer legally demand a gendered division of labor.[103] If gender isn't a central organizing principle of marriage, why does it matter if it's between a man and a woman? American states began recognizing same-sex marriage in 2004 (Massachusetts was first) and in 2015 a Supreme Court ruling made same-sex marriage federal law. A growing number of countries around the world recognize such marriages: Argentina, Belgium, Brazil, Canada, Denmark, England and Wales, Finland, France, Greenland, Iceland, Ireland, Luxembourg, the Netherlands, New Zealand, Norway, Portugal, Scotland, South Africa, Spain, Sweden, and Uruguay. Other countries are likely to join soon.

After the Defense of Marriage Act was struck down by the Supreme Court in June 2013, same-sex couples in many states—such as Amber Weiss and Sharon Papo in California, pictured here—have exercised their right to marry.

The breadwinner/housewife model still echoes through our personal lives and political debates. It competes with and sometimes lives quietly alongside the partnership model, producing the types of trouble that contradictions cause. Still, despite the trouble, and despite the clamor to return to the breadwinner/housewife model of marriage, partnership marriage is here . . . maybe not to stay, but for now.

CONCLUSION

When you hear people defend the idea of "traditional marriage," you would be smart to ask which one they mean. The patriarch/property model of marriage reigned supreme for thousands of years, while the breadwinner/housewife model was but a blip on the historical timeline. Today's marriage contract reflects a partnership model that facilitates personalization. The unprecedented diversity in family forms found in Western societies today reflects the choices we are now able to make. The institution of marriage has changed not only because feminists insisted that it was unfair to women, but also because of shifts in the institutions with which marriage intersects: industrialization, the rise of cities, the demands of capitalism, global competition, technological innovation, and more. Political activism and changing socioeconomic relations have changed marriage as well as other institutions, warping and tweaking all of them separately and together.

All the other institutions we discussed in this chapter are also being changed deliberately and responding to changes around them. Even sexual practices aren't simply driven by values or nature, but respond to opportunity provided by technological, economic, political, and demographic change. Likewise, the workplace has evolved, pushing and pulling men and women into different kinds of work and changing their relationships in the home. Much of this evolution has been because of technological innovation, economic change, and more, but some has been due to activists who have targeted governments and social organizations to press for change. When we take the long view, we see tumultuous upheaval of social norms and institutions, making any natural and universal idea of gender relations—based on biology or religion—seem increasingly implausible.

Next . . .

In the next four chapters, we explore the on-the-ground realities that people face today. We start with sexuality. It is difficult to imagine, perhaps, that social forces shape this most intimate part of our personal selves. Desire for sexual and romantic connection is felt so deeply that it seems impervious to "outside" influences. We imagine you might ask, in a hopeful tone:

Gendered ideas, interactions, and institutions may affect almost every part of my life, but some things are personal and my sexuality is mine and mine alone. Isn't it?

Alas, dear reader, alas.

FOR FURTHER READING

Cancian, Francesca. "The Feminization of Love." *Signs* 11, no. 4 (1986): 692–709.

D'Emilio, John. "Capitalism and Gay Identity." In *The Lesbian and Gay Studies Reader*, edited by Henry Abelove, Michèle Barale, and David Halperin, 467–475. New York: Routledge, 1993.

Gerson, Kathleen. "Changing Lives, Resistant Institutions." *Sociological Forum* 24, no. 4 (2009): 735–44.

Goldin, Claudia "The Quiet Revolution that Transformed Women's Employment, Education, and Family." *The American Economic Review*, 96, no. 2 (2006): 1–21.

Hull, Kathleen, Ann Meier, and Timothy Ortyl. "The Changing Landscape of Love and Marriage." *Contexts* 9, no. 2 (2010): 32–37.

Strasser, Susan. *Never Done: A History of American Housework*. New York: Macmillan, 2000.

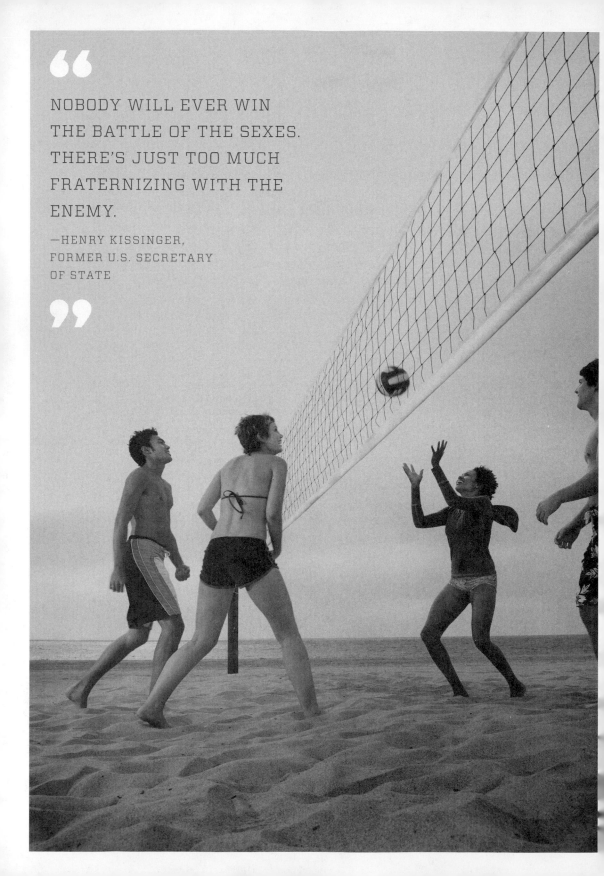

> NOBODY WILL EVER WIN
> THE BATTLE OF THE SEXES.
> THERE'S JUST TOO MUCH
> FRATERNIZING WITH THE
> ENEMY.
>
> —HENRY KISSINGER,
> FORMER U.S. SECRETARY
> OF STATE

10

Sexualities

Part of a "true college experience," many students say, involves going to parties, getting drunk, meeting someone new, and having sex.[1] As one student describes it: "There's this system that's like, you're gonna get drunk, randomly meet randoms, and just, like, whatever happens."[2] This is **hookup culture**, a new norm on college campuses in which casual sexual contact in the absence of romantic intentions is held up by many as an ideal. Over 90 percent of college students in America say their campus is characterized by a hookup culture.[3]

Most students are excited by the opportunity to experiment with their sexuality, and three-quarters of students will hook up at least once before graduation.[4] But many students also feel a great deal of pressure to participate. Kimbra, one of our students, was one of them. Tall and outspoken, with chin-length dark hair, radical politics, and a bisexual identity, she seemed the child of unapologetic hippies. She expressed concern, though, that she wasn't sexual *enough*. "Maybe I actually am a prude," she worried:

> I'm so embarrassed by that, and so I want to distance myself from it. I "know" that I should want to have sex all the time, and should take advantage of it when I get the chance. . . . [P]ressure to be sexual was and has been so constant for so long. . . . I feel as if by not voluntarily taking part in it, I am weird, abnormal, and a prude.[5]

Kimbra was articulating a sentiment that is widespread among college students. Hookup culture often feels like more than just an *opportunity* to engage in routine casual sexual encounters; it can feel like an *imperative*. As another student put it: "People ask, 'You're at college and you're not having sex? What's wrong with you?'"

This imperative is part of wider changes in sexual attitudes and behaviors. Instead of reflecting a sudden transformation of human nature, this increasing sexual permissiveness is a result of changes in the cultural and institutional context for sexuality. In order to understand the way we feel and the choices we make, we need to look beyond the individual. Accordingly, the answer to the following question is no:

Q+A Gendered ideas, interactions, and institutions may affect almost every part of my life, but some things are personal and my sexuality is mine and mine alone, isn't it?

Let us make the case.

We've already encountered the sexual regimes of the Puritans, the romantic Victorians, the revelers of the 1920s, and the experimental teenagers of the 1950s. In all cases, sexual attitudes and behaviors were strongly influenced by the societies in which these individuals lived. The same is true now. To understand how, we'll learn about the rebels of the sexual revolution, take a closer look at sexuality today, and end somewhere that might be familiar: hookup culture.

THE SEXUAL REVOLUTION

After World War II ended in 1945, people made babies. Lots of 'em. Birth rates increased in North America, Australia, New Zealand, and most European countries. In the United States, they rose from just over two children per woman during the Great Depression to a high of nearly four.[6] These kids, the "baby boomers," grew up during the 1950s and '60s, changing the demographics of the country. Between 1960 and 1970 the number of eighteen- to twenty-four-year-olds increased by over 50 percent.[7]

The Vietnam War began in 1955 and massively expanded in scope in the mid-1960s. It would last twenty years, during which time an active resistance would emerge. Anti-Vietnam activists would ally with the civil rights movement. Violent attacks by American government authorities—both on the Vietnamese during the war and on American anti-war and civil rights protesters—stirred a more general resistance to authority. Some boomers, now in their teens

FIGURE 10.1 | FERTILITY RATE IN THE UNITED STATES,* 1920–2012

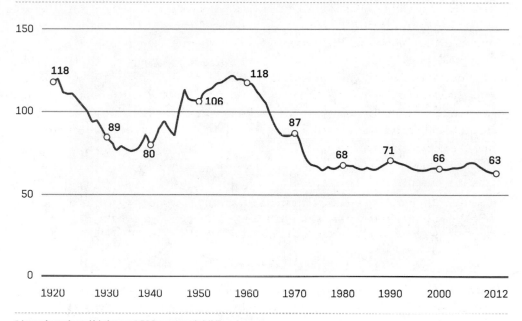

* Annual number of births per 1,000 women of childbearing age.
Source: Livingston, Gretchen and D'Vera Cohn. "Chart of the Week: Big drop in birth rate may be leveling off."
Pew Research Center (2013).

and twenties, rejected their parents' eager embrace of conformity, willingness to
turn a blind eye to injustices, and sexual conservatism.[8]

Youth often push boundaries set by adults and by 1970 there were more
young people than ever. Many things changed. This generation—with members
now in their sixties—brought us the civil rights, women's, gay liberation, and
anti-war movements. It also brought us the sexual revolution.

One aim of the sexual revolution was to liberate female sexuality, but what
does a liberated sexuality look like? Reflecting the androcentrism of the time,
women's sexuality was framed as "suppressed" and men's as "normal."[9] The
very definition of sexual liberation, in other words, came to be modeled on a
masculine version of sexuality that involved fewer restrictions on sexual behavior. Sexual attitudes and behaviors became more permissive as a result, especially for women.[10]

Women were "both excited by and resentful of this new world," wrote historian Angus McLaren.[11] Many wanted to say yes to sex, but doing so presented
its own set of problems. Comparing notes, women discovered that their sexual
encounters with men typically conformed to men's desires. Women were unhappy with men's lack of interest in women's sexual pleasure and the ongoing
risk of sexual violence.[12] McLaren concludes, "They wanted to say yes to sex and
no to sexism."[13] But that was easier said than done.

The killing of four students at Kent State University by the Ohio National Guard in 1970 spurred mobilization against the Vietnam War and a call for less violent policing. The youth movement of the 1960s and 1970s, which promoted peace and challenged repressive authority, also helped prompt the sexual revolution.

Just Say Yes?

It's tempting to pat ourselves on the back and conclude that the sexual revolution vanquished both sexual repression and the gendered double standard. However, today's context for sexual expression is not devoid of rules; rather, it involves a new set of expectations that bring both opportunities and imperatives. Consider the question regarding whether and when to lose your virginity. The majority of Americans think that waiting until marriage to lose your virginity is a romantic but silly idea. In fact, nearly two-thirds of young adult men and women say that it's simply not realistic to wait until marriage to have sex and only about 5 percent of Americans are now virgins on their (first) wedding night.[14]

This sentiment means that most people who want to have premarital sex don't feel a crushing amount of pressure to preserve their virginity, but it puts new pressure on many people to "lose it." In fact, today many men and plenty of women think that being a virgin, after a certain age, is *embarrassing*.[15] One student who sought to lose her virginity the summer before college explained: "The thing I feared the most about going off to college? Being a virgin. . . . I thought that only nerds, religious nuts, and momma's boys were untouched when they started college."[16] She's not alone. While previous generations protected their virginity, many people today go to great lengths to get rid of it, even if they're not sure they want to.[17] About a third of fifteen- to twenty-four-year-olds say that they feel pressure to have sex, and half of women and a third of men report they weren't sure they wanted to lose their virginity when they did.[18] Likewise, in a society that conflates virginity loss with penile-vaginal intercourse, some gay men and lesbians will have heterosexual sex because it seems like the only way to lose their virginity.

Put simply, the historical pressure to say no to sex has been replaced by a pressure to say yes. This creates anxiety and sometimes very negative experiences for people who don't want to have sex or participate in certain sexual activities. It can also contribute to depression and self-doubt among people who are, for whatever reason, unsuccessful in finding sexual partners. Meanwhile, gender rules and gendered hierarchies still shape how people experience their sexuality.

CONTEMPORARY RULES OF SEXUALITY

We've introduced the idea of doing gender; we also "do" sexuality. We learn the rules for whom we should be attracted to, what is attractive, how to be sexual, and what we should and shouldn't do with one another. Though we resist these rules as well as obey them, the result is that our sexual activities are far from spontaneous or natural. Instead, much of our behavior is carefully orchestrated, creating patterns in our sexual interactions. In the next three sections, we discuss the erotic marketplace, the gendered division of the sexual dynamic, and the sexual script.

The Erotic Marketplace

The term *market* is typically used to describe the abstract space in which goods and services are attributed economic value. Borrowing that idea, the phrase **erotic marketplace** refers to the ways in which people are organized and ordered according to their perceived sexual desirability. Some people have more erotic "capital" than others. This isn't about purely personal taste or human nature. It's part of a cultural value system that attributes more worth to some bodies than others.

Scarlett Johansson, like other darlings of Holly-wood, has been given titles attesting to her erotic capital, like "Sexiest Woman Alive" (*Esquire*), "Babe of the Year" (*GQ*), and "Sexiest Celebrity" (*Playboy*).

In this section we draw on data from over 7 million active users of the popular dating website OkCupid. Three-quarters of single people have used online dating sites.[19] It is the primary way in which people seeking same-sex relationships meet one another, and heterosexual couples are as likely to meet on the Internet as they are to meet through friends or at a bar.[20] Lots of people are using these sites, and analysis of their profiles and communications tells some interesting stories about gender, its intersection with race, and the "hot or not" game.

GENDER AND THE EROTIC MARKETPLACE Attractiveness is an important commodity in the erotic marketplace. OkCupid data shows that men are significantly more likely to message women who are judged to be of above-average attractiveness compared with women who are of average and less-than-average attractiveness.[21] *Much* more likely.

Two-thirds of men's messages go to women who are in the top third of attractiveness, such that a very attractive woman gets five times as many messages as the average woman and twenty-eight times as many as the least attractive.

Figure 10.2 shows that women tend to message more attractive men as well, suggesting that attractiveness matters to them, too, but not nearly as much as it does to men. The most attractive men receive ten times the average number of messages, but the most attractive women receive twenty-five times the average number.

This asymmetric emphasis on women's appearance suggests that, at least in the abstract, women's value in the erotic marketplace is less tied than men's to *who they are* and *what they do*, and more tied to *how they look*. Men's desirability is less centrally dependent on his appearance, such that he can make up for mediocre looks by being funny, smart, or rich. Women can't so easily do this. Why?

In the erotic marketplace there is a ceiling placed on women's level of success. With the noted exception of attractiveness, most of the variables at play in

FIGURE 10.2 | NUMBER OF MESSAGES RECEIVED VS. RECIPIENT'S ATTRACTIVENESS

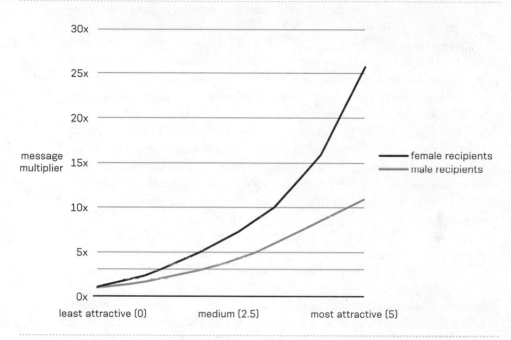

Source: Christian Rudder, "Your Looks and Your Inbox," *OkTrends*, November 17, 2009, http://blog.okcupid.com/index.php/your-looks-and-online-dating/.

the erotic marketplace—income, level of education, occupational prestige, age, height, weight, strength—fall into a pattern. Gendered matching rules suggest that men should be *more* than women. Cultural norms dictate that the man be taller, stronger, bigger, older, more educated, and have a higher-status job that brings in more income. It doesn't have to be a Cinderella story; that is, we don't expect him to necessarily be *a lot* more (most princes don't marry maids), but we've learned to feel comfortable with a gentle asymmetry. As a result, it makes sense to us that women would seek out men who are *just a little bit more* than them on each variable and, likewise, that men would feel most comfortable with women who are *just a little bit less*.

The OkCupid data on age puts this in stark relief. Age is an imperfect measure of both attractiveness and accomplishment. We tend to conflate aging with ugliness, so we should predict that women's value in the erotic marketplace would be harmed with age. This should be true for men as well, but we can imagine that it might be offset by other things we value in men. In fact, heterosexual male OkCupid users report that they will consider dating women who are significantly younger, but only a bit older.[22] More, as a man ages, his lower bracket goes lower relative to his own age. The average thirty-year-old man, for instance, says he's interested in dating a woman as old as thirty-five and as young as twenty-two. A man at forty will date a woman as old as forty-five but as young as twenty-seven.

This is what men *say*, anyway. In reality, men's messaging habits are even more skewed toward younger women.[23] In practice, men mostly seek contact with the youngest women in their reported preferred age brackets and women who fall *below* their lower bracket. Their willingness to date "down" suggests that they prefer or will accept a mate whose career is "behind" their own.

The average woman, conversely, prefers to date a man who is her age or older. The average thirty-year-old woman is interested in men up to seven years older and as much as three years younger. As women get older, they will accept about five years on either side. In actual messaging, they tend to focus on men their own age.

Gender inequality is at work in the erotic marketplace, then, placing a high value on men's accomplishments and women's appearance. For men, being bigger, stronger, and older, having advanced degrees and enjoying a high-prestige, well-paid occupation is always an advantage. For women, all these things carry both advantages and disadvantages. Gains may help her catch a highly valued man, but she might reasonably worry that too many gains could knock her out of the competition altogether. Meanwhile, her ability to attract men may decrease as she ages, while the men in her same age cohort become relatively *more* attractive. His achievements count more toward his attractiveness than hers do, and her fading looks harm her more than his.

Importantly, relationships that evolve off-line involve more complicated chemistry than the abstract ranking of OkCupid profiles, but these relationships still reflect the gentle asymmetry driven by gender inequality more so than they would in the absence of gendered matching rules. And even people who reject these rules are culturally competent enough to know when they're in violation of social norms. If they're not, the gender policing of relationships will likely tip them off sooner or later.

RACE IN THE EROTIC MARKETPLACE Race plays a role in the erotic marketplace, too. For black men, racial stereotypes are a double-edged sword. By virtue of being stereotyped as hypermasculine, black men are seen as especially sexy, sexual, and sexually skilled compared to white men. Though they may be sought out as sexual partners because of these stereotypes, the idea that they are *too* masculine—and, therefore, too sexual—may make them seem like frightening or inappropriate partners. For Asian men, stereotypes based on race are more straightforwardly negative. Asian men are seen by some as unmasculine and, therefore, sexually deficient. Research shows that even Asian women may think so.[24]

We see these patterns in the OkCupid data. In terms of compatibility, as measured by a mathematical algorithm, all races match with all other races rather equally.[25] But all races aren't equally valued in the online erotic marketplace. Table 10.1 lists the percent of the time that a man will receive a reply after he sends a message to either a woman seeking men or a man seeking men. In a society that centers and elevates whiteness, we would expect that white men would have an advantage, and they do. In fact, white men are more likely than men of any other race to get a response from women. Among men seeking men, white men get the second-highest amount of replies after Middle Eastern men. In both cases, Native American men follow close behind white men in popularity.

Conversely, black men are among the least likely to get a response from women and the least likely to get a response from men. Asians, too, are among the groups that get the least frequent responses. In another study of online dating behavior, college-educated white women were actually more likely to respond to a white man without a college degree than an Asian man with one.[26]

Racism both the kind that fetishizes and the kind that denigrates—also affects the desirability of women. Asian women, by virtue of being seen as extra-feminine, are seen by some as more sexually malleable than white women, which may make them appealing to men who are looking for subservient women. One white American man who prefers Asian women explained: "I'm kind of a soft guy. I really find American women overly aggressive."[27]

Table 10.2 shows that women typically seen as "Asian" (those who identify as Asian but also those who identify as Pacific Islander, East Indian, and Middle Eastern) do very well in the erotic market. These are the four groups

TABLE 10.1 | PERCENT CHANCE THAT A MAN IN EACH RACIAL GROUP WILL RECEIVE A RESPONSE FROM AN INQUIRY

Racial Group	Men Messaging Women	Men Messaging Men
White	29%	45%
Native American	28%	44%
Middle Eastern	26%	48%
Pacific Islander	25%	38%
Hispanic	23%	42%
Asian	22%	38%
Black	22%	35%
East Indian	21%	38%
Average	**28%**	**43%**

Source: Christian Rudder, "How Your Race Affects the Messages You Get," *OkTrends*, October 5, 2009, http://blog.okcupid.com/index.php/your-race-affects-whether-people-write-you-back/.

TABLE 10.2 | PERCENT CHANCE THAT A WOMAN IN EACH RACIAL GROUP WILL RECEIVE A RESPONSE FROM AN INQUIRY

Racial Group	Women Messaging Men	Women Messaging Women
Middle Eastern	50%	52%
Pacific Islander	46%	49%
Asian	44%	53%
Hispanic	43%	50%
East Indian	43%	63%
White	42%	51%
Native American	42%	49%
Black	34%	47%
Average	**42%**	**51%**

Source: Christian Rudder, "How Your Race Affects the Messages You Get" and "Same-Sex Data for Race vs. Reply Rates," OkTrends (blog).

most likely to receive a response from women messaging men, and three of the top four from women messaging women. In contrast, as in Table 10.1, black women are among the least likely to receive a response. Black women face a situation similar to that of Asian men. Racial stereotypes that masculinize African Americans relative to whites undermine a black woman's value in the erotic marketplace. When a black woman messages another woman, the response rate is four percentage points below the average; when she messages a man, it falls nine points below average. Black women—whether they are college educated or not—are least likely to be contacted or receive a response.[28]

While our individual preferences seem very personal, this data reveals that our aggregated preferences conform to social hierarchies.[29] Actual dating and marriage patterns reflect what we see online.[30] Whites are more likely to marry Latinos, Native Americans, or Asians than they are to marry blacks. White men are more likely to marry Asian women than black women, and white women are more likely to marry black men than Asian men.[31] Reflecting colorism, lighter-skinned racial minorities are more likely to intermarry with whites than darker-skinned minorities.

Evidence further suggests that people are more comfortable experimenting with interracial relationships than they are committing to them.[32] When white teenagers date white peers, they introduce them to their parents 71 percent of the time, but their nonwhite girlfriends or boyfriends get to meet the parents only 57 percent of the time. Black teenagers are also reluctant to introduce their boyfriends or girlfriends if they're in an interracial relationship, though the difference in likelihood of introduction is smaller. In any case, the rate of interracial dating tends to decrease as levels of commitment increase. People are more likely to date someone of a different race than they are to live with them and they're even less likely to interracially marry.

Gender and race hierarchies, then, clearly shape our ideas about who is an appropriate sexual and romantic partner. Social forces also affect how we think about our sexualities.

The Sexy and the Sexual

Paris Hilton once said: "My boyfriends always tell me I'm not sexual. Sexy but not sexual."[33] The difference is significant. To be *sexy* is to be an object of desire for others; to be *sexual* is have the capacity to experience sexual desire.[34] Most

of us want to both feel desire and be desired but, in practice, the lessons we learn about sexuality tend to divide and subdivide these phenomena by gender.

We get many of these lessons from the media. The sex education Americans encounter in schools largely focuses on reproduction and, outside of giving instructions to abstain or protect themselves from infections and pregnancy, parents rarely talk to their children about sex.[35] The media fills this void. Television programs, movies, advertising, and other media content, however, aren't very good teachers. Overwhelmingly, these media assume a **heterosexual male gaze**, meaning that the content is designed to appeal to a hypothetical heterosexual man.[36]

Plotlines and visuals intended to incite male sexual desire function to draw our attention to men's **subjectivity**, their internal thoughts and feelings. This is an acknowledgment that they are sexual, which is good, but it is also a prescription. Media images do more than *allow* men sexual subjectivities; they are *assigned* a very specific version of male heterosexuality. In this way, men undergo a process of **sexual**

Real women and girls are seen through lenses formed by omnipresent sexually explicit images of women's bodies presented as desirable objects for the gaze of the presumptively heterosexual male consumer.

subjectification: They are told what their internal thoughts and feelings should be. Advertisements, for example, consistently portray a particular kind of woman as sexually desirable, repetitively implying that she is the proper object of men's sexual attraction.

Men internalize this prescription to greater or lesser degrees, and no man is completely passive in the face of his subjectification. All of us, though, learn what this subjectivity looks like and all of us, regardless of our gender identification, have to contend with the cultural expectation that this version of male heterosexuality represents what men are really like.

For women, media made with the male gaze in mind means being exposed to constant scrutiny of female bodies. **Sexual objectification** is the reduction of a person to his or her sex appeal. To be clear, it's not the same thing as finding someone's body desirable; it's the *absence* of subjectivity, the total irrelevance of the internal life of the person portrayed. Both men and women are objectified in popular culture, but men are objectified much less often than women.[37] As a result, many of us internalize the idea that a woman's value is heavily dependent on her attractiveness, whereas a man's value is somewhat less so.[38] This is the same phenomenon we see reflected in the OkCupid data.

Many women **self-objectify**, internalizing the idea that their physical attractiveness determines their worth. During sex, habitual body monitoring may translate into a process called **spectating**, watching one's sexual performance from the outside.[39] A woman might try to stay in sexual positions she thinks are flattering, arrange her body and limbs to make herself look thinner or curvier, try to keep her face looking pretty, and ensure she doesn't make any embarrassing noises. She may even avoid orgasm because climaxing means losing control of these things. As a result of spectating, some women have "out-of-body sexual experiences" in which they don't focus much on how sex *feels*. And, sure enough, research has shown that the more a woman worries about how she looks, the less likely she'll experience sexual desire, pleasure, and orgasm.[40]

While heterosexual men are less likely to be sexually objectified, gay men can be positioned as either the objectifier or the objectified and, in fact, they report higher levels of self-objectification than heterosexual men.[41] A gay man interviewed about his experiences complained that sex often left him feeling "used" by men:

> You get tired of being used.... [I] was just nothing but this little receptacle.... It wasn't reciprocal.... I need to feel like some attention is to me and I'm not just this machine.... It makes me one dimensional. It just makes me an object.[42]

The discomfort of being sexually objectified may help explain why so many heterosexual men are uncomfortable in gay male spaces. Used to being the "predator," suddenly they are the "prey." Many women and gay men, in contrast, have grown accustomed to this feeling, even if they don't enjoy it.

The Scripting of Sexuality

Sociologists use the term **sexual script** to describe the rules that guide sexual interaction.[43] We know there's a script because, instead of randomly or experimentally progressing with a sexual encounter, most people do the same things in more or less the same order. It goes something like this: kissing (closed mouth), then close body contact, kissing (open mouth), then groping (first the butt, then the breasts). Once this all has occurred, the couple gets horizontal. Then there's more kissing and groping, including the touching of genitals through clothes. Clothes start coming off; first her shirt, then his, then her pants, then his, then her bra and underwear, finally his. It's a toss-up if it's a same-sex couple. Sexual activities are also tightly ordered. If it's a heterosexual couple, there's touching of naked genitals, oral sex on him, then penile-vaginal intercourse. Oral sex on the woman is a wild card these days, but it usually doesn't precede oral sex on the man. The scripts of same-sex couples aren't as straightforwardly gendered, but they still have a somewhat rigid ascending order of intimacy.

The sexual script is strongly institutionalized, especially when two people are first becoming sexual together. The rule that french kissing comes before fondling, for instance, isn't just a guideline; someone who moves straight to second base could be charged with sexual battery, a legal term for unwanted but nonviolent sexual touching. Even the body parts people are allowed to find sexy is carefully scripted. The guy who prefers feet, for instance, may be seen as a pervert.

We police one another around these sexual rules, requiring that others behave sexually in culturally competent and intelligible ways. This script creates predictability and helps ease social interaction—"Did she kiss me back? Aha, now I have clearance to try for second base"—but it is also gendered. Both difference and inequality become a part of our sexual scripts, with implications for interpersonal interactions. In the remainder of this section, we discuss how gendered social scripts contribute to high rates of sexual assault and an orgasm gap between men and women.

SEXUAL ASSAULT Written into the sexual script for heterosexual sex is the idea that men are supposed to initiate sexual activity and women are supposed to decide whether the couple should go forward with each "move." This is called the **push-and-resist dynamic**, a situation in which it is normal for men to press sexual activity consistently in the direction of increasing intimacy (whether he wants to or not) and for women to stop or slow down the accelerating intimacy when he's going "too far" (whether she wants to or not).

The push-and-resist dynamic may encourage and even require men to press women for sexual intimacy, and this is often uncomfortable or annoying, but it doesn't account for why one in six women will survive an attempted or completed sexual assault.[44] The majority of men, no matter how strongly they embrace their role as the initiator, will never commit a violent or coercive sexual crime. The push-and-resist dynamic doesn't make all men semi-rapists. Instead, it gives cover to the small proportion of men who are responsible for the vast majority of sexual assaults.

Research suggests that most assaults are committed by a small percentage of men. In one study, 6 percent of college men admitted to behavior that fit the description of rape or attempted rape.[45] Two-thirds of those men (4 percent of all men) were serial rapists, having committed an average of six rapes each. A study of navy enlistees found that a higher percentage admitted to rape or attempted rape (13 percent), but similarly found that about two-thirds of those men were serial offenders.[46]

These men are sexual predators. They plan their assaults, carefully choose their victims, use alcohol as a rape drug, and employ force when necessary. They are the minority, but in cultural context, they blend in. This cultural context is what scholars call **rape culture**, an environment that justifies, naturalizes, and even glorifies sexual pressure, coercion, and violence. The idea that men are naturally sexually aggressive is part of rape culture, as are jokes that trivialize sexual assault, advertisements that glamorize scenes of sexual force, sex scenes in which women say no and then change their minds, and the persistent belief that sexual crimes are falsely reported more often than other crimes (they're not).

Rape culture gives rapists plausible excuses for their actions and can also make it difficult for people who are targeted to understand that they can fight back. Indeed, rape culture makes us forget that men's bodies are at least as vulnerable as women's.[47] Maneuvers that take little strength—a thumb to the eye socket, a punch to the throat, an elbow to the nose, a quick kick to the knee cap, or a twist of the testicles—can often bring an attempted assault to an end. In fact, research has shown that hollering, fighting back, or fleeing reduces the likelihood of a completed rape by 81 percent, without increasing the severity of injuries sustained by victims.[48] Women rarely outrun men in the movies, but they often can in real life.

When men or women are assaulted—whether they successfully fight off their perpetrator or not—rape culture can make it difficult for them to recognize that what happened to them is a crime. Or, alternatively, it can make victims concerned that they won't be believed. This is understandable, as campaigns aimed at reducing rates of sexual assault frequently perpetuate rape culture, blaming victims for the actions of repeat sexual offenders. Anti-sexual assault campaigns on college campuses, for example, tend to focus extensively on what women can do to reduce their risk of sexual assault. This approach reinforces the idea that women could stop sexual assault if they just made different choices.

This is an odd way to think about crime. When we think of sexual assault as a matter of female risk taking, the perpetrator disappears from the equation.

This British police campaign that intends to reduce the incidence of rape does so by putting the onus of preventative action on the woman, as do campaigns on many U.S. college campuses.

People get robbed because there are robbers and get scammed because there are scammers, the logic goes, but women somehow "get themselves raped" by making the wrong choices. In reality, the only thing that causes rape is a perpetrator's decision to rape. In the absence of rapists, that is, none of women's choices results in sexual assault.

Also partly because of rape culture, the laws and prosecutions aimed at reducing sexual assault and penalizing perpetrators are, at best, weakly enforced. Rape myths frequently underlie the decisions and judgments of police officers, lawyers, judges, jurors, and the victims themselves. Partly for these reasons, it is estimated that only 10 percent of rapes are reported to law enforcement and 37 percent of these will proceed to prosecution.[49] Only 3.4 percent of rapes ultimately end in conviction.

THE ORGASM GAP   A large survey from the late '80s and early '90s found that 75 percent of men reported regularly having orgasms with their partners compared with 29 percent of women.[50] This is called the **orgasm gap**, a phenomenon in which heterosexual women report fewer orgasms than heterosexual men. The gap isn't a simple consequence of different anatomy or physiology. That is, despite what you may have heard, women are not somehow bad at having orgasms. When women are alone they reach orgasm between 80 and 96 percent of the time.[51] Women in same-sex relationships report having two to three times as many orgasms as women in heterosexual ones.[52] In pre-colonial Polynesia, women were expected to have about three times as many orgasms as men, and they did.[53]

The orgasm gap isn't natural; it's a social artifact related to the gendered sexual script. First, the script itself leads couples to penile-vaginal intercourse, an activity that regularly results in men's orgasm but not women's. Only 20 to 30 percent of women routinely have orgasms through intercourse alone.[54] Second, the gendered sexy/sexual binary justifies a focus on the male orgasm, since it's his desire that supposedly drives and is sated by sexual activity. This lets men off the hook for female orgasms, but it also discourages women from pursuing their own. Likewise, because the script puts women in the position of responding to sexual activity but not initiating it, women might not tell their partners how to give them orgasms.[55]

Just as we "do" gender, we "do" gendered sexualities. Our sexual script places men and women at odds, with men expected to push for sex and women expected to hold out for love. This dynamic makes manipulative and even coercive behavior seem normal, creating fertile ground for sexual violence. It also contributes to the orgasm gap between men and women. Expectations regarding women's attractiveness focus women's attention on their bodies, provoking anxiety and distracting them from the pleasure involved with sexual activity. Men, conversely, are prescribed a narrow heterosexuality and policed if they step outside its boundaries. For men especially, the imperative to be sexually active makes it difficult and disconcerting to opt out of sex altogether, at least without a good account to explain why. We see all of these dynamics, and more, on many college campuses today.

HOOKUP CULTURE

Joel "couldn't even begin to list" all the ways the media had prepared him for a "sexually overloaded college scene." This student had grown up in a small town just outside of Death Valley, California. He'd attended small schools all his life; there were sixty students total in his high school. These were intimate environments that made puberty extraordinarily awkward. "Everyone knew everything about everyone else," he explained, so sexual experimentation was rare and, when indulged, secretive. College promised to be a whole new world. That summer he anticipated the "imminent freedom that college presented." In his first week, he kissed four girls. Things were off to a great start.

Joel quickly discovered, however, that reality didn't exactly match the fantasy. "I soon realized," he wrote midyear, "that there was little resemblance to the college life that I saw on TV and in movies." After just one month of college, hookups had "lost their appeal." During the second semester of his freshman year, he didn't have any sexual contact with anyone at all. "I now know that the images in the media are only sloppily upheld by a handful of students," he wrote, "and for the most part are not an accurate indicator of actual college lifestyle."

Joel isn't wrong. Casual sex is not as common on college campuses as the media would lead us to believe. The average number of hookups for a graduating senior is seven.[56] This might seem low but, in fact, most students overestimate the frequency with which their peers hook up, as well as how "far" they go and the degree to which they enjoy it.[57] A quarter of students won't hook up at all; 20 percent of students will still be virgins when they graduate.

Only about 20 percent of students hook up more than ten times in four years and only half of those do so with pure enthusiasm.[58] Most students are ambivalent. The majority (70 percent of women and 73 percent of men) say they'd prefer to be in a relationship. Joel is one of them. If most people don't really like hookup culture, why does it dominate college campuses?

Why Hookup Culture? Why Now?

Since there have been colleges, there have been hookups, but hookup culture is new. The difference is crucial: It's the difference between a campus on which

College students collectively enact hookup culture, organizing and populating parties with the express purpose of facilitating casual sexual contact.

some people have casual sex and a campus on which casual sex is the most visible and widely embraced approach to sexuality.

A number of institutional forces have ushered in hookup culture. When women began attending universities in the 1920s, administrators considered themselves substitute parents. They set policies designed to minimize or eliminate sexual activity, especially that of women. Today, with the exception of sexual-assault programs, sexual-health information, and free condoms, most colleges do very little to direct the sexual activities (or non-activities) of their students.[59]

The students themselves, then, shape the cultural norms for sexual behavior on their campuses. To them, casual sex makes some sense. Many are busy preparing for careers and are in no hurry to "settle down." Students, especially those from wealthy backgrounds, speak about college as a place for personal growth, not interpersonal bonding. One student explained:

I've always looked at college as the only time in your life when you should be a hundred percent selfish. . . . I have the rest of my life to devote to a husband or kids or my job. . . . But right now, it's my time.[60]

Relationships can be time consuming and emotionally draining. Hooking up can be a good way for young people to gain some sexual experience and blow off steam while they ride out an **extended adolescence**: a significant period of time during which young people (who are no longer kids) prepare for a future (when they'll finally be "real" adults).[61]

As you might suspect, though, not all students are equally invested in hookup culture.

Who Likes Hookup Culture?

Hookup culture is disproportionately endorsed and enacted by the students with the most power to shape campus sexual culture: those who are white, wealthy, heterosexual, conventionally attractive, able-bodied, and socially adept.

Sexual-minority students, for example, are less likely to hook up than heterosexual students.[62] This is partly because parties and dances are not always gay-friendly. Many college students draw sharp boundaries around heterosexual activities. Girl-on-girl kissing for male attention, for example, is premised on the idea that both the women are heterosexual. While some women who are questioning their sexual orientation might use this as an opportunity to explore what it feels like to kiss another woman, others who participate in this activity report that they do it only if they're confident that the woman they are kissing is *not* a lesbian.[63] Accordingly, these women are invested in carving out heterosexual-only spaces and, in one study, reported more homophobic attitudes than women who don't kiss other women at parties.[64]

For students of color, embracing hookup culture can bring individual rewards, but these students also risk affirming harmful beliefs about their racial group. Many black people feel the need to perform a **politics of respectability**, a form of resistance to negative racial stereotypes that involves being "good" and following conservative norms of appearance and behavior.[65] The erotic marketplace plays a role here, too, racializing desirability and, therefore, rates of hooking up. Data show that black women and Latinas, as well as Asian men and women, are less likely to hook up than their counterparts.[66]

Research also suggests that class-privileged students hook up more often than other students.[67] Working-class women in college may be more focused on getting through school. One woman, reflecting on all the partying, observed:

> Some of these girls don't even go to class. It's like they just live here. They stay up until 4 in the morning. [I want to ask,] "Do you guys go to class? Like what's your deal? ... You're paying a lot of money for this. ... If you want to be here, then why aren't you trying harder?"[68]

Students from families with tight budgets are also likely to have a job outside of school and may live at home to save money. These students have less time to spend partying and less opportunity to do so. Sharing a small house with one's parents—which is often a car or bus ride from the party—isn't conducive to casual sex or heavy drinking.[69] For Shawn, an Asian student, it was just logistically difficult:

> *It's easier to party if you live somewhere on campus than off campus. If you're commuting, you may be able to do it every once in a while and crash and find a place to sleep, but if your parents are expecting you home, it's hard because you can't drink and drive.*[70]

Students who live at home, especially young women, are subject to surveillance from parents who may have rules against drinking, drug use, sexual activity, and staying out late. Lydia, for example, a Latina student, imagined that dorm life was more autonomous: "They don't have parents worrying about when they get home or calling them.... They do as they please."

The students with the greatest opportunity and interest in hookups are also the students with the most power to shape social life on college campuses. As a result, it can feel like "everyone is doing it," even if a significant proportion of the students dislike hookup culture or are excluded from it. In this way, hookup culture is a microcosm of our society. It reflects the same power dynamics we see outside of colleges.

Danger on Campus

Like the women of the 1970s, women in college want to say "yes to sex and no to sexism."[71] And it's still easier said than done.

Gender inequality shapes both the pain and pleasure that hookup culture can bring. Sexual manipulation and coercion are normal parts of college life. Women who attend college face a significantly higher risk of sexual assault than women who don't (one in four female college students experience a completed or attempted assault, compared with one in six women overall) and women who actively participate in hookup culture are more likely to be assaulted than women who opt out.[72]

Rape culture makes it difficult for campus activists fighting sexual violence to secure resources from administrators and ensure that colleges have proper reporting, fair policies, and proper management of cases. Its narratives also make the coercive behaviors that rapists engage in—plying women with alcohol or pulling them into secluded parts of a party—look "normal." And rape culture continues to obscure the most common source of sexual assault. Ninety percent of college victims know their attackers, but students still worry more about being raped by strangers.[73] Students asked to identify places on their campus map "where the danger of sexual assault is especially high" are more likely to point

These protestors are challenging the negative assumptions about women's sexuality in the word *slut* and arguing that a woman's appearance is never a justification for sexual assault.

to the woodsy paths and poorly lit parking lots than the fraternity houses and dorms where assault is far more likely.

It's difficult to change what's happening on campuses because they are shaped, in great part, by the wider social changes we've seen over the last 250 years and the more immediate institutional features of college life itself. But students can and do make a difference. Sexual culture is powerfully influenced by which students happen to be present and outspoken. **Bystander intervention programs**, for example—ones that educate students about sexual assault and teach them how to spot likely incidents and safely intervene—are effective in reducing rates of sexual violence.[74] Unlike programs that emphasize what women can do to reduce the likelihood of rape, these empower the entire college community. The success of these programs is proof that students can make colleges more inclusive, safer spaces for personal growth.

Pleasure on Campus

While both men and women often discover that they dislike or are ambivalent about hooking up, women's dissatisfaction is felt more acutely. The uneven distribution of pleasure—the orgasm gap between male and female college students—contributes to this dissatisfaction. In hookups, women have about half as many orgasms as men.[75]

Many men appear to differentiate between hookups and girlfriends. One male college student insisted in an interview that he always cared about "her" orgasm. However, when asked if he meant "the general her or the specific," he replied, "Girlfriend her. In a hookup her, I don't give a shit."[76] Some other men take a similar approach:

> *If it's just a random hookup, I don't think [her orgasm] matters as much to the guy.... But if you're with somebody for more than just that one night ... I know I feel personally responsible. I think it's essential that she has an orgasm during sexual activity.*[77]

Some men don't prioritize women's orgasm in hookups but, to be fair, women often don't prioritize their own pleasure either: "I will do everything in my power to, like whoever I'm with, to get [him] off," said one college student.[78] When women are worried about giving their male partners orgasms, it can distract them from their own pleasure: "My sexuality was filled with anxiety and my need to please the guy instead of worrying about my own pleasure," said one student."[79]

In contrast, women in relationships with men have 80 percent as many orgasms as their partners. Relationships in college typically begin with a series of hookups and it appears that a couple's attentiveness to the woman's orgasm escalates along with their interest in each other.[80] Women have orgasms in 11 percent of first hookups, 16 percent of second or third hookups, and 34 percent of hookups after that.[81]

Figure 10.4 shows just how widely a woman's chance of orgasm varies when considering the nature of the relationship and the activities the couple engages in. When partners incorporate a wide range of activities, especially oral sex and women's self-stimulation, the orgasm gap begins to shrink. The far right bar represents the chance of an orgasm alongside inclusion of intercourse, oral sex on her, and self-stimulation in the context of a relationship. When couples participate in all three activities, his chance of orgasm is 96 percent and hers is 92.

Looking at the data this way, college students are doing better than previous generations. Recall that the national survey found that 75 percent of men were regularly having orgasms, compared with only 29 percent of women.[82] These percentages were mostly from relationships. College women in relationships appear to be experiencing more orgasms than their mothers and grandmothers. Orgasm, however, is still gendered. Both men and women tend to believe that men are more entitled to orgasms, and women are still being divided into those women who men care about (girlfriends) and ones they don't (hookup partners).

FIGURE 10.4 | PERCENTAGE OF WOMEN HAVING AN ORGASM IN FOUR SEXUAL CONTEXTS, BY OCCURRENCE OF SELECTED SEXUAL BEHAVIORS

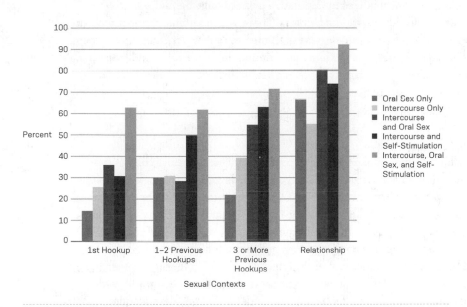

Note: Oral sex refers to receiving oral sex.

Source: E. A. Armstrong, P. England, and A. C. K. Fogarty, "Orgasm in college hook-ups and relationships," in *Families as They Really Are*, ed. Barbara Risman (New York: W. W. Norton, 2009).

Revisiting the Question

Gendered ideas, interactions, and institutions may affect almost every part of my life, but some things are personal and my sexuality is mine and mine alone, isn't it?

The sexual revolution changed the cultural context for sexuality, but it didn't usher in an era of liberation. Instead, there are new rules for sexuality. This means new opportunities to have sexual experiences but, because sexual liberation is modeled on a stereotypically masculine approach to sexuality, there is also a new imperative to say yes to sex.

Whether we gleefully embrace these new opportunities or struggle with the imperatives, our experiences are strongly colored by gender and other culturally meaningful social categories. Our race, gender, and other traits intersect with our sexuality, organizing us in an erotic marketplace that we don't control and can't easily escape. In this erotic marketplace, women's value is more closely tied to their appearance than men's, and certain racial groups are seen as more or less sexual and sexually desirable. Even our experiences of sexuality are gendered; the push-and-pull dynamic of the sexual script not only contributes to the orgasm gap, it normalizes manipulative and coercive behavior.

That said, individuals are not helpless. There is a great deal that people can do to change the ways in which gender shapes sexuality. As individuals, they can resist gender rules that enforce conventional sexual roles and, together, people can change the norms that govern sexual interactions as well as the institutions that structure them.

Next . . .

Hookup culture may make relationships seem passé, but most college graduates will eventually settle down. Nearly two-thirds will be married (and some divorced) by their thirtieth birthday.[83] These marriages have more potential to be true partnerships than any in history. For the first time in thousands of years, marriage law prescribes to men and women the same rights and responsibilities. One source of oppression for women appears to be crumbling.

And yet, despite changes aimed at giving women equal footing, women have become increasingly unhappy with their marriages over the last thirty years. The data show that women today experience significantly less wedded bliss than men.[84] In fact, despite the cultural messages that insist that women crave marriage and children more than men do, research shows us that the happiest women are single and childless. This prompts us to ask:

 If marriage is better for women than ever, why do married women report lower levels of happiness than married men and single women?

An answer awaits.

FOR FURTHER READING

Armstrong, Elizabeth, Laura Hamilton, and Beth Sweeney. "Sexual Assault on Campus: A Multilevel, Integrative Approach to Party Rape." *Social Problems*, 53 (2006): 483–99.

Eck, Beth. "Men are Much Harder: Gendered Viewing of Nude Images." *Gender & Society* 17, no. 5 (2003): 691–710.

Hennen, Peter. "Bear Bodies, Bear Masculinity: Recuperation, Resistance, or Retreat?" *Gender & Society* 19, no. 1 (2005): 25–43.

Pascoe, C. J. "Compulsive Heterosexuality: Masculinity and Dominance." In *The Politics of Women's Bodies: Sexuality, Appearance, and Behavior*, 3rd ed., edited by Rose Weitz, 318–28. New York: Oxford University Press, 2010.

Sanchez, Diana, Jennifer Crocker, and Karlee Boike. "Doing Gender in the Bedroom: Investing in Gender Norms and the Sexual Experience." *Personality and Social Psychology Bulletin* 31, no. 10 (2005): 1445–55.

Nagel, Joane. *Race, Ethnicity, and Sexuality: Intimate Intersections, Forbidden Frontiers*. New York: Oxford University Press, 2003.

"

OH, THIS WILL *REALLY*
INTEREST MY *WIFE*.

—A HUSBAND[1]

"

11

Families

T hanks to hundreds of years of legal reform and social
change, individuals have substantially more freedom to
arrange their relationships as they wish. This is what feminists have been fighting for and what many women want. Still,
women have a more troubled relationship to marriage than men.[2]
Men are more likely to believe in the idea of a "soul mate"; women
are more skeptical. Women are also less eager than men to marry.
Once married, wives are less happy than husbands. More than a
third of men (38 percent), but less than a quarter of women (22 percent), think that happiness comes more easily to married people
than singles.

Women are also more likely than men to file for divorce. This
is, in part, because they're significantly less likely than men to
think that a child needs both a mother and a father; 42 percent of
women think that being raised by a single parent does no harm
compared with 29 percent of men. After divorce, women are happier than they were when married; for men, the opposite is true.
Accordingly, divorced women are more likely than divorced men
to say they'd prefer never to remarry.

This has prompted us to ask:

Q+A   **If marriage is better for women than ever, why do married women report lower levels of happiness than married men and single women?**

The reasons have to do with how people arrange their family lives. In this chapter, we will explore the gendered nature of housework and child care in pop culture and conversation, then look at the surprising contrast between what people say they want and how they actually divide up paid and unpaid work in practice.

Moving past the averages, we'll review the wide variety of family arrangements, with an emphasis on how gender intersects with other features of families. In the end, we'll talk about how families produce and reproduce patterns of inequality, both gendered and otherwise.

GENDERED HOUSEWORK AND PARENTING

Today only about 12 percent of American households consist of a husband who financially supports a wife and children.[3] The majority of moms (80 percent, including 65 percent of moms with preschoolers) are in the workforce.[4] Accordingly, breadwinner/housewife marriages are outnumbered by both single-parent families and two-parent families in which both partners are engaged in paid work.

These families face a specific challenge: finding time to do the child care, cleaning, feeding, and errand-running that housewives do for breadwinner husbands. For single parents and families with two working parents, that work is a **second shift**, work that greets us when we come home from work.[5] After hours in the workplace, working parents without a stay-at-home spouse often face many more hours before they can fall into bed: Groceries must be bought, dinner must be cooked, messes must be cleaned up, chores must be supervised, cars must be gassed up, homework must be reviewed, budgets must be balanced, and kids must be bathed and put to bed.

Working two jobs—one paid at work and one unpaid at home—can be exhausting. In fact, as a result of their "double day," over half of married fathers and three-quarters of both married and single mothers say that they have too little time for themselves; a third of dads and over 40 percent of married and single moms say that they're always rushed.[6] These trends are true in most North American and Western European countries, but they are especially extreme in the United States among the middle and upper classes.[7]

The second shift, you might suspect, isn't a gender-neutral problem. Child care and housework still carry the gendered meanings they did when breadwinner/housewife families were considered ideal.[8] In the remainder of this section, we'll review the social construction of child care and housework and look at the actual and the ideal division of labor in families today.

Child Care and Housework in Pop Culture

There's a sneaky linguistic switcheroo that reveals that mothers are considered the primary parent and fathers the secondary one. While the male version of a term usually comes before the female—for example, "men and women," "his and hers," and "boys and girls"—writing about parenting usually uses the phrase "mom and dad."

We receive daily messages—linguistic and otherwise—that affirm the idea that women are, or should be, the main person in charge of the second shift. Advertisements for home décor, cleaning supplies, and food for families almost exclusively feature or target female consumers. Even when parenting guides, magazines, and newspaper articles don't make an explicit claim that mothers *should* be the primary parents, most assume they are.[9] They may address the reader as "you" but frequently reveal that they are imagining a female reader. "You've undoubtedly been smooching your baby and saying things like 'Give mommy a kiss!'" reads one parenting magazine.[10] Parenting websites sometimes feature a "Dad Zone," revealing that the rest of the website is *really* for

The assumption that child care is primarily for mothers shows up in advertisements for a variety of products.

The ABC comedy *Baby Daddy*, about a twentysomething who suddenly becomes a father after a one-night stand, uses the stereotype of fathers as incompetent caretakers to comedic effect.

moms.[11] The online retailer Amazon has an "Amazon Mom" site but no corresponding "Amazon Dad."[12]

When books, magazines, and websites about parenting do address fathers, they often aim to convince men that "babies can be fun" or that being an active parent is important. Mothers don't receive these messages on the assumption that they're already wholly invested in parenting. To make parenting seem fun and easy for dads, marketers offer them shortcuts. Whereas commercials and advertisements for elaborate or healthy meal options typically feature moms, advertisements that feature dads are often for fast food, microwaveable meals, or pizza delivery.

If dads are not portrayed as reluctant parents, they're often portrayed as incompetent ones. Fathers alone with their children are often played to comic effect: He'll burn the toast, dress his daughter in summer clothes on a winter day, or mix darks with lights and turn the family's clothes pink in the washer.[13] Exasperated women are often shown swooping in and relieving men of household duties on the understanding that it would be easier for them to just do it themselves.

Sitcoms, TV commercials, parenting advice books, and other pop cultural content represent women as the primary caretakers of the house and children and dads as backups. Real people seem to agree.

Housework and Child Care as Feminized Labor

"It's whatever," said Rick when asked about how he and his male roommates keep the house clean. "It doesn't really matter. I mean, it's not like something I consider. It's not like I'm caring about it if it happens or not."[14] Rick was interviewed by sociologist Kristin Natalier, who was interested in how all-male households divvied up chores.[15] Many of her interviewees felt that caring too much about cleanliness was "girly." Doing masculinity meant not caring, or at least pretending not to care, whether the house was clean.

Since caring about cleanliness is feminized and our society is androcentric, Natalier's interviewees avoided doing household tasks if they could. Jeremy explained what he did if there weren't any clean dishes: "We go 'nah' and leave it. We just get noodles up the road."[16] When these men did do housework, they had to come up with an account: some motivation *other* than a desire for cleanliness. They would put off doing laundry until there was absolutely nothing left to wear. Likewise, they wouldn't do dishes unless there were no clean ones left *and* they couldn't afford to eat out. Then they would only wash the dishes they needed, no more.

Manliness, of course, is a social construction. So, while some men were quite comfortable with this system, it frustrated other men who preferred cleanliness. If they said nothing, they ended up either living with the mess or doing the majority of the housework themselves. If they complained, they faced gender policing from their housemates. "I'm not his wife," grumbled one roommate, but a plea for a more equitable division of labor was unlikely to be recognized as legitimate.

Natalier's study of all-male households of roommates reveals that housework is gendered. Studies of gay fathers suggest that child care is, too. Gay dads use language associated with women to describe their desire for children and their role as a caretaker. They talk about listening to their "biological clocks," having "maternal instincts," and being "housewives" and "soccer moms."[17] An excerpt from a conversation between Nico and Drew, a couple with twin toddlers, shows just how much the "mother as true nurturer" idea pervades their thinking about parenting:[18]

Nico: *Since I don't work as often, I am more of the mom role. I am home more with them. I'm the one who takes them to the park during the week and I usually feed them and . . .*

Drew: *Wait, I am just as much a mommy as you! Just because my job is more lucrative does not automatically make me the dad, and besides, we both feed them dinner, read to them, get them to bed and I always do the dishes so that you can relax.*

Nico and Drew both used language that indicated that parenting was a woman's activity. This reflects a gendered understanding of household chores but, interestingly, both were competing over who got to be "mommy." Domestic work is gendered in ways that exclude or marginalize men, then, but is this how people really want it? And is this how labor is typically divided up?

Ideal and Actual Divisions of Labor

Sociologist Kathleen Gerson asked eighteen- to thirty-four-year-olds how they would ideally divide homemaking and breadwinning.[19] Only a minority of young people said that they wanted to do so by gender. The majority—about 80 percent of women and 70 percent of men across all races, classes, and family backgrounds—said that they wanted a relationship with "flexible gender boundaries" in which both partners do their fair share of breadwinning, housekeeping, and child-rearing.[20] In other words, they preferred **sharing** (doing more or less symmetrical amounts of paid and unpaid work) over **specialization** (splitting unpaid and paid work so that each partner does more of one than the other).

Reflecting these ideas, family life today is more balanced than it was in the '50s and '60s. Men do twice as much housework and three times as much child

FIGURE 11.1 | GENDER GAP IN DIVISION OF LABOR

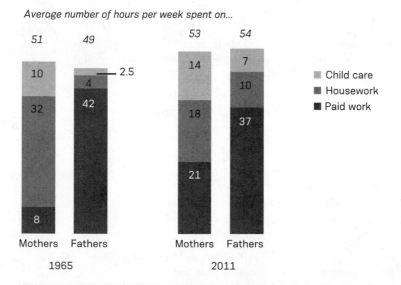

Average number of hours per week spent on...

Child care
Housework
Paid work

Mothers   Fathers
1965

Mothers   Fathers
2011

Source: Parker, Kim and Wendy Wang, "Modern Parenthood: Roles of Moms and Dads Converge as They Balance Work and Family," Pew Research Center, March 14, 2013.

care as their counterparts in 1965.[21] Meanwhile, women are working outside the home almost three times as many hours than they did in the '60s and spend about half as much time on household chores. As a result, men and women spend about the same amount of time on paid and unpaid work combined: Mothers spend about fifty-three hours a week, and fathers spend about fifty four (Figure 11.1).[22]

The proportion of time men and women spend in paid and unpaid work still differs, however, in gender-stereotypical ways. On average, women spend twenty-one hours per week working for pay and an additional thirty-two on housework and child care. Men, in contrast, spend an average of thirty-seven hours per week in paid work and seventeen on the house and kids. To put it more simply, men do about two-thirds of the paid work and one-third of the unpaid work and women do the inverse.

This data raises two questions. First, if men and women want relationships in which they share paid and unpaid work about equally, why do they specialize in practice? Second, why are women significantly less satisfied with the division of labor if men and women are working equally hard? Only 11 percent of wives say that the division of labor in their households is fair compared with 45 percent of husbands.[23] In the remainder of this chapter, we'll try to answer these questions.

IDEOLOGICAL AND INSTITUTIONAL BARRIERS TO EQUAL SHARING

Couples overwhelmingly want to share all the kinds of work required to sustain their families but, more often than not, they don't. This is partly for ideological reasons, but institutional forces also press couples into making decisions that reproduce asymmetry. In this section we show how couples get pushed into specialization by their spouses and their circumstances.

Ideological Barriers to Reorganizing the Second Shift

Both men and women face ideological pressures to specialize. Many men are still strongly attached to the breadwinner role and many women find themselves strongly drawn into parenting because they think it's best for their child.

"IF SOMEBODY'S GONNA BE THE BREADWINNER . . . " Reflecting a 1950s gender ideology, some men and women are **traditionalists**: They ascribe to the values of the breadwinner/housewife marriage that emerged with industrialization and came to be seen as "traditional." Traditionalists believe that men should be responsible for earning income and women should be responsible for housework and child care. Frank, for instance, ascribes to these values: "I look at myself as pretty much of a traditionalist. It's the way I am inside. I feel that the man should be the head of the house. He should have the final say."[24] Carmen, Frank's wife, agrees. She just wants to be "taken care of," she says.[25]

Unlike Carmen and Frank, **neo-traditionalists** embrace a modified version of traditionalism: They think that a woman should be able to work if she desires, but only if it doesn't interfere with her "real" duty to take care of her husband and children. Sam, for example, explains that he would accept a working wife, but, "[i]f she wanted to work, I would assume it's her responsibility to drop the kids off at grandma's house or something. She's in charge of the kids. If she's gonna work, fine, but you still have responsibilities."[26] These traditional and neo-traditional men and women resist reorganizing the second shift on principle; they believe that it is, in fact, a woman's job.

About one in three men and one in seven women are traditionalists or neo-traditionalists. Recall, though, that sociologist Kathleen Gerson found that the majority of men and women are **egalitarians**, preferring relationships in which both partners do their fair share of breadwinning, housekeeping, and childrearing. Looking at this data, Gerson wondered: What happens if people who prefer sharing discover that it isn't possible in practice? She asked her egalitarian respondents what type of family they would like if they couldn't sustain an equal partnership. Suddenly, the happy confluence of men and women's opinions disappeared: 70 percent of men chose a neo-traditional arrangement as their backup, but only about 25 percent of women did the same.

It turns out, if equal sharing proves too difficult, men overwhelmingly hope to convince their wives to de-prioritize their careers and focus on homemaking and raising children. Matthew exemplifies this plan:

> If I could have the ideal world, I'd like to have a partner who's making as much as I am—someone who's ambitious and likes to achieve. [But] if it can't be equal, I would be the breadwinner and be there for helping with homework at night.[27]

Most men value their role as workers too much—and perhaps homemaking too little—to imagine de-prioritizing their own career. "If somebody's gonna be the breadwinner," Jim said, "it's going to be me."[28]

Women are much less likely to prefer neo-traditionalism as a backup plan, but they may find themselves negotiating about how to divide labor with a husband who does. Simultaneously, they may find themselves the subject of a set of ideas about parenting that powerfully shapes their thinking about their role in the family.

"EVERY MINUTE OF THE DAY" Here is how one mother described her approach to child-rearing:

> *For me, I feel it is vital to be there for my children every day, to consistently tend to their needs, to grow their self-esteem, and to praise them when they're right, to guide them when they're not, and to be a loving, caring mom every minute of the day.*[29]

This mother believes that being a good parent means being actively engaged with her child "every minute" of "every day." She is articulating what sociologist Sharon Hays calls the **ideology of intensive motherhood**, the idea that (1) mothers should be the primary caretaker of their children, (2) child-rearing should include "copious amounts of time, energy, and material resources," and (3) giving children these things takes priority over all other interests, desires, and demands.[30]

At its root, intensive mothering is about putting children at the center of a woman's life. When children are small, this means letting them decide when to eat and sleep; avoiding the use of play pens or other restraining devices in favor of close supervision; providing constant interaction and stimulation; utilizing brain-stimulating toys and activities; and engaging in negotiation instead of instruction. Intensive mothering also means maximizing children's educational achievement (volunteering at school, meeting with teachers, helping with homework); keeping a close eye on their grades (ensuring they get good marks through cajoling, threatening, or helping); and organizing educational vacations and buying learning games (trips to zoos and children's museums, math- and science-based video games and apps). Finally, it means ensuring that children are well-rounded and have good self-esteem by enrolling them in activities for ideal physical and cultural development (piano lessons, Little League, dance classes); ferrying children to and from school as well as after-school and weekend activities; and giving them at least some of the material goods they want or need (the "right" clothes and accessories).

The ideology of intensive motherhood is a dominant model of parenting in the United States but, importantly, it's a rather unusual way of thinking about parenting in historical and cross-cultural contexts. Individual mothers are the primary caretakers in only 20 percent of cultures and, in most of these, children are given considerably more freedom and independence than we tend to think is wise today.[31] Indeed, according to historian Peter Stearns, for most of American history children were seen as "sturdy innocents who would grow up well unless corrupted by adult example and who were capable of considerable self-correction."[32] In other words, so long as they didn't encounter a person who set out to harm them deliberately, children could be expected to look after themselves, learn about life, and become well-adjusted adults.

Attachment parenting, or intensive motherhood, involves keeping one's child close at all times—perhaps even while checking e-mail.

In the 1800s, some experts even argued that *excessive* nurture was harmful. Women were given strict warnings not to over-love. "[M]other love is a dangerous instrument," cautioned John Watson, who wrote one of the best-selling child advice books of all time. According to Watson, a mother's love was:

> *An instrument which may inflict a never-healing wound, a wound which may make infancy unhappy, adolescence a nightmare, an instrument which may wreck your adult son or daughter's vocational future and their chances for marital happiness.*

As for affection, Watson advised: "[K]iss them once on the forehead when they say goodnight. Shake hands with them in the morning." But only, he said, "[i]f you must." Parents were advised against hugging, kissing, and letting a child sit in their lap.

Responding to the Watsons of the time, wealthy white Victorian wives embarked on a deliberate and self-interested effort to preserve their social standing in the face of the changes brought by their industrializing society. Pressing back against the devaluation of their separated sphere, and adjusting to men's disengagement from the home, these women claimed that mothering was an essential, delicate, and time-consuming enterprise. The more they could convince others of the importance of intensive mothering, the more esteem they could preserve alongside the androcentric reorganization of the economy.[33] This was the birth of intensive mothering.

Just like then, today the ideology is more common among upper- and upper-middle-class mothers than others, but the ideas of privileged groups tend to dominate cultural conversations. Today mommy bloggers, parenting experts, child psychologists, and advice-book authors tend to advocate for intensive parenting. Women are often held uniquely responsible for providing their child with experiences and support. In response to these demands, women often worry that the time they spend in paid work detracts from their role as a parent.[34] Men do not feel the same about their role as a father.

In this sense, mothers face a double bind that men do not. On the one hand, their paid employment may be necessary for paying the bills, or buying the house in a good school district, or saving for college tuition. On the other hand, their unpaid investments in intensive mothering are deemed crucial in giving their child "an edge" over the neighbor's kid. In an increasingly precarious economy, families often believe that careful cultivation of a child's skills and talents is essential to ensuring that their children enjoy the same class position as their parents. This escalating competition for maternal time has been called the "rug rat race": Fear of falling behind drives parents to do as much as they can and no amount is ever deemed too much. If they have the resources, many mothers will choose to disinvest in their careers, at least in the short term. Institutional forces often conspire with these inclinations.

Institutional Pressures toward Neo-traditionalism

TO SHARE OR SPECIALIZE? Both work and family are "greedy institutions," ones that take up an incredible amount of time and energy. High expectations for workers (which we'll talk about more in the next chapter) intersect with high expectations for parenting, making it difficult or impossible for people to be successful at work, feel good about how much time they spend at home, and attend to their personal well-being.

Often couples come to the conclusion that one or both of them needs to spend less time at work and more time at home. Doing this in a gender-balanced way means both spouses need to retreat into lower-paying, less demanding occupations or, alternatively, work part-time. Most families can't afford to have two incomes compromised by low wages or limited hours; they may, though, be able to afford one compromised income. This might push a family to specialize. Features of the economy, then, make it difficult for both parents to pull back at work and spend more time at home.

Even if a family could theoretically afford two compromised incomes, marriage and employment law can make this situation challenging in practice. Of the families that have health insurance, most access it through a parent's employer, but this benefit typically only accrues to employees who work a forty-hour workweek. Families either need at least one adult with a full-time job or they need to pay for health insurance themselves, which can be prohibitively expensive.[35] (Of course, individuals who live in countries with nationalized health care don't face this problem, and the Affordable Care Act may change the situation in the United States.)

Time is another resource that strains families. The placement of homes, child care centers, workplaces, and doctors' offices in different parts of town is an institutional barrier to sharing paid and unpaid work. Long commutes add to the work day, making it even more difficult for income earners to participate in home life. Commutes aren't inevitable but a consequence of zoning laws that separate residential and commercial districts. If we zoned differently, it might be easier for families to share at home.

Among high-income earners, the tax code further rewards breadwinner/housewife families over those that share these duties; the income of a couple in which one earns $140,000 a year and the other earns nothing is taxed at a lower rate than that of a couple in which both partners earn $70,000.[36] This is a tax incentive for the couple to specialize.

These are just a few examples of how institutional policies push families to divide paid and unpaid work in uneven ways. Studies have shown that these forces impact same-sex as well as heterosexual couples. Three-quarters of gay and lesbian couples with two working parents specialize.[37] Institutional pressures are part of why we might see such divisions of labor in gay and lesbian households, where sex isn't a factor.

GENDERED DECISIONS ABOUT SPECIALIZATION These institutional pressures to specialize might explain asymmetry in divisions of labor, but they don't explain why women typically take on the heavier domestic roles. The answer has partly to do with ideologies, but institutional forces play a role here as well. Most couples, for example, consider their finances when deciding who should focus on work and who should focus on the house and kids. Often the smartest thing to do is rely on the career of the partner who has a higher salary and greater opportunity for advancement.[38] Since men typically earn more money than women, heterosexual couples may choose to prioritize the man's career for purely economic reasons.

When a child arrives, it may make sense, above and beyond any biological or ideological reasons, for the mother to take time off from work. Many moms relish this opportunity and many dads are jealous. Still, there is a price to pay: Each month that a woman stays out of the workforce is a month in which her partner is building a career. By the time she's ready to work full-time again, he's "ahead" of her. He may have gotten a promotion or a raise; in any case, his

FIGURE 11.2 | AVERAGE NUMBER OF PAID WORK HOURS PER WEEK, BY NUMBER OF CHILDREN

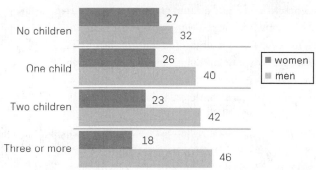

Source: Pew Research Center, "On Pay Gap, Millennial Women Near Parity—For Now," Dec. 11, 2013, pewsocialtrends.org/2013/12/11/on-pay-gap-millenial-women-near-parity-for-now/

greater experience now makes him more employable. Now it makes even *more* economic sense for the couple to prioritize his career instead of hers. Instead of deciding to let her take a turn—so that she can prioritize work for a while and he can enjoy the pleasures of family life—she may get a part-time job or switch to a less demanding occupation. This may be the best option for the pair, but it also strengthens his advantage over her in the workplace and motivates continued specialization. The more they specialize, the more economic sense it will make to continue doing so.

Gender dynamics outside the family also explain why gender asymmetry in the division of labor isn't static but increases as relationships get more serious. At the beginning of relationships, men and women tend to use their time in similar ways. The differences grow larger as relationships become more serious: from boyfriend/girlfriend to a couple that lives together, from cohabitation to marriage, and from married to married with kids.[39] New mothers tend to cut back on their work hours, while new fathers tend to ramp up at work instead of down.[40] As you can see in Figure 11.2, additional children exacerbate this trend. As a result of their longer work days, men often do less housework.[41] In response, wives often work even less, citing their husbands' hours and the new housework demands as a reason why.[42]

In sum, institutional forces that make sharing difficult resonate with ideological commitments: men's inclination toward neo-traditional families and women's acceptance of the ideology of intensive motherhood. In the face of these pressures, families make choices and sacrifices. Some manage to carve out sharing relationships, others do not, and still other couples break apart.

DIVISIONS OF LABOR IN FAMILIES

So far we've discussed how ideological and institutional forces press families to make gendered choices that align with a neo-traditional ideology. Still, families are diverse. In this section, we review seven ways of arranging family life: two solutions involving specialization, two sharing solutions, two types of self-reliant parenting, and the choice of childlessness.

Neo-traditionalist Divisions of Labor

As the averages reveal, the most common type of family is one in which each spouse specializes. Some of these families resemble the idealized 1950s bread-winner/housewife model, others are a modified version. We'll start with the latter.

THE SUPERMOM AND THE NEO-TRADITIONAL DAD When faced with neo-traditionalist men who resist sharing housework and child care, the desire to do right by their children, and a need or wish to work, many employed mothers work full time and still take on the lion's share of the second shift. Juggling work, the logistics of day care, and the needs of a spouse and children can be difficult. Deb, a factory worker, explains how she arranges child care for her two children so that both she and her husband, Mario, can work full time:

> When I work the 7 A.M. to 3 P.M. shift we start the day about a quarter to five. I can't bring the children to the sitter until 6:30 A.M., but I have to punch in at the plant by 6:45, so I race. On weekdays, I have two sitters because Melody, our main babysitter, can't take all three kids. On the weekends, I take them to my mom, to Mario's cousin, or to my mother-in-law. Usually, I bring one child to each house, because when Gina and Hunter are together, they're monsters. When Mario and I both work the same hours, the kids get to spend the night at their grandparents' for the whole week.[43]

Supermoms may not be neo-traditionalists themselves but, because they are working full-time jobs, they will struggle to manage the second shift. In fact, the average mom spends fifty-three hours a week on paid and unpaid work combined, but this includes housewives with zero time spent on paid work. Excluding them, the average *employed* mother spends seventy-one hours a week on paid and unpaid work.[44] They have half the leisure time of men and spend ten more hours per week multitasking.[45] As a result, partners married to neo-traditionalists often wear themselves out trying to bring home a paycheck and do the majority of the second shift. Without enough hours in the day to play all their roles, moms can feel like they're falling short in every part of life: as a mother, as a spouse, and as an employee. "[I felt like] I was doing everything wrong," admitted one mother.[46]

Their husbands may be happy to help if they're asked: "She'll always give [the baby] a bath, or if she can't, she'll tell me to do it because I won't do it unless she tells me, but if she asks me to do it I'll do it," says one dad.[47] But even neo-traditionalist men who are good "helpers" typically don't take responsibility for child care and housework. This is why when dads do housework and child care, it is often described as "stepping in," giving mommy a "break," "babysitting," "pitching in," and "helping out."[48] This can create ugly interpersonal dynamics. Their partners, who have to ask for help, often feel like "nags." Anyone who works full-time and takes responsibility for domestic work may find themselves acting and feeling similarly. Consider Don, who had this to say about his same-sex partner, Gill, who resists equal participation in housework:

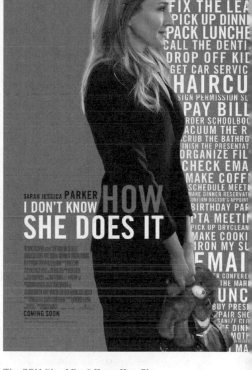

The 2011 film *I Don't Know How She Does It*, starring Sarah Jessica Parker, relies on and affirms the stereotype of the supermom who does everything.

I have to prod him; "bitch at him" is what he would say. I have found it difficult to figure out ways to bring up the condition of the house without creating too much of a fight. I sort of have learned that there are certain times to bring it up. I especially try to avoid bringing things up when he just gets home from work. I find he is more willing to help, or at least to hear it, later at night. Of course, he doesn't see any of this—it's annoying—nor does he recognize what an effort it is to get him to help.[49]

When partnered with a neo-traditional person, being a househusband can feel just as disempowering as being a housewife. Likewise, women can take on the masculine role in a neo-traditionalist household. Ruth, in a relationship with Cindy for nearly a decade, comments:

I have learned how to read Cindy for moods and I know when I can get her to do stuff and when I can't. It's sort of a subtle negotiation. I don't know if she realizes that I am scanning the moments waiting to ask her to clean out the fireplace or hose out the garage, but that's what I do. I sort of get in tune with the rhythm of her life now and it seems to work.[50]

In neo-traditional households the domestic partner does more of the work involved in the second shift as well as more of the cognitive work of family life (planning and delegating chores), even though he or she is also often working full-time. This can cause resentment to build up on both sides.

THE MODERN BREADWINNER/HOUSEWIFE   Most supermom/neo-traditionalist families are solidly in the middle class: wealthy enough to be economically secure but not secure enough to live on one salary. In contrast, women at both high and low income levels may find themselves pushed out of the workforce entirely. Highly paid men who make the elusive "family wage" can afford for one parent to stay home.[51] Among the wealthiest 5 percent of families, 42 percent include a stay-at-home parent.

Interestingly, we also see a disproportionate number of breadwinner/housewife arrangements at the bottom of the economic hierarchy.[52] Over half of families with incomes in the bottom 20 percent of households have a person who stays home full-time.[53] It might be tempting to think that low-income breadwinner/housewife families struggle financially because they've chosen to sacrifice a paycheck in order to avoid putting their child in day care, but that's not usually the case. In low-income households, wives overwhelmingly stay home because day care costs more money than they are able to earn at the low-wage jobs to which they have access. In most states the average cost of child care exceeds tuition at a public college. In the state where child care is cheapest, Mississippi, day care for an infant absorbs a third of the income of a full-time worker earning minimum wage; in Massachusetts, where it's the most expensive, it *exceeds* the entire income of that same worker by over $2,000 a month.[54] Accordingly, some low-income families leave one person at home because it actually saves them money. It also pushes them into specialization.

The modern breadwinner/housewife arrangement may seem ideal compared with the overworked supermom and nagged husband. At least one person can dedicate themselves full-time to the second shift. Studies show, however, that stay-at-home mothers are decidedly less happy than moms who work, even if they really *wanted* to be a stay-at-home wife.[55] Partly for this reason, these marriages end in divorce more often than any other kind.[56]

Sharing Solutions

If breadwinner/housewife marriages are the most likely to end in divorce, ones in which there is sharing are the least likely. In fact, all things being equal, spouses and cohabitators with fair divisions of labor have sex more frequently, are less likely to go to relationship counseling, divorce less, and are more happily married.[57] Sociologists generally consider duties shared if the division of labor is between 50/50 and 60/40. There are two ways to build a sharing relationship: outsourcing and turning inwards.

OUTSOURCERS While highly educated men with high-paying careers may be in the best position to support a housewife, they are also among the most likely to marry a woman who has a similar level of education and ambition. Their wives may choose to stay home, but they may also decide to keep a strong focus on work. Most of these families will need to hire a substantial amount of help to allow both parents to remain on accelerated career tracks. This is **domestic outsourcing**, paying non-family members to do family-related tasks.

To a certain extent, outsourcing is now the rule for families. Most children are placed in some form of day care. Higher-income families can even hire live-in nannies who are present and available nearly twenty-four hours a day. We also see the outsourcing of meals (eating in restaurants, getting take-out, ordering delivery, or buying prepared meals from the grocery store), work around the house (hiring housekeepers, gardeners, a "handyman" to fix things, a neighbor kid to shovel the sidewalk after it snows), chores and errands (accountants, tailors, dry cleaners, dog groomers, drivers, or mechanics), and direct child care and instruction (babysitters, of course, but also tutors, swimming instructors, and camp counselors).

Depending on their resources, families can buy a great deal of help from non-family members, enabling them to balance the competing demands on their time. Elena, a vice president of public relations, gives us a hint as to how many family-related tasks some in-home day-care workers handle:

> We have a nanny who comes in. . . . She's actually great at cleaning and she's really good at, well, she's not really good at doing the laundry, but she does my laundry, and so that's just great in itself. . . . I mean it's not like paying her to do that because she's paid to do something else [child care], but she is awesome, and she takes our library books back and she takes our movies back and she'll go to the cleaners. Yeah, she's the best! And she'll go to the grocery store for me.[58]

Nannies and other forms of outsourcing are one way that class-privileged couples can build and maintain relationships where they do similar amounts of child care and housework. This is a form of sharing, but it has an ugly underbelly. As one *New York Times* editorialist asked: "Are we achieving more egalitarian marriages [for the middle and upper classes] at the cost of a more egalitarian society?[59] We answer this question later in the chapter. First, we'll discuss another approach to equal sharing.

TURNING AWAY FROM WORK TOGETHER While domestic outsourcing allows both parents to be career-oriented, some couples choose to point their energies in the opposite direction. Sometimes both members of a couple decide to de-emphasize work and focus on raising a child.[60] One such couple was able to arrange it so that both could work part-time—the husband was an editor and the wife an accountant—and someone could always be home during the day. Another couple both quit high-paying jobs and became teachers when they had their first child. Dual-nurturer couples are often relatively affluent but non-materialistic. They make economic sacrifices when they disinvest at work but are able to do so because of financial advantage. That is, only people who make high salaries can afford to work part-time.

Sharing relationships are happier and more stable than relationships with specialization, but some are stronger than others. Dual-nurturer couples consisting of a woman who does 60 percent of the domestic work and a man who does 60 percent of the breadwinning are the most stable.[61] Half-and-half arrangements are less stable and gender-swapped relationships—in which the man does 60 percent of the homemaking and the woman does 60 percent of the breadwinning—are less stable still. This suggests that we're more comfortable with *almost* sharing than we are with sharing, and that when the script gets flipped it can strain relationships.

Self-Reliance as a Solution

While people tend to have strong feelings about sharing versus specializing, some won't have the opportunity to negotiate a division of household labor with another person. By choice or circumstance, they simply won't end up with someone. Others will find that their negotiations go sour and they divorce.

DIVORCED PARENTS Conflict over household responsibilities is among the top reasons why between a third and half of all marriages will end in divorce.[62] As we've already established, both men and women overwhelmingly want egalitarian relationships, but men turn neo-traditional when asked about their backup plan. Unfortunately, as illustrated in Figure 11.3, men's typical fallback position clashes spectacularly with what most women want.

Faced with a husband who wants them to be a housewife or work part-time, almost three-quarters of women would rather divorce and raise their kids alone. Danisha, for example, took her mother's advice to heart:

> She taught me your marriage is not who you are. It's one thing to want to live with your husband and all that good stuff, but don't get to the point where you can't do things on your own. Because a lot of women, friends of hers, regret that life has passed them by and they're stuck.[63]

FIGURE 11.3 | MEN AND WOMEN'S FALLBACK PLANS

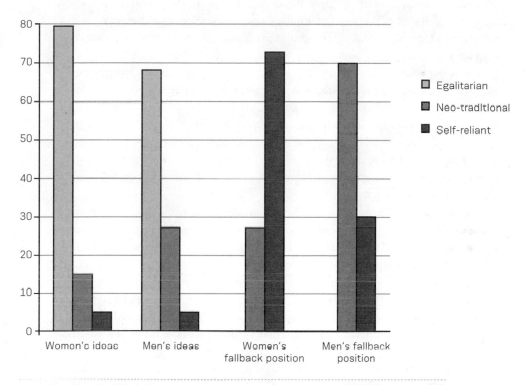

Source: Kathleen Gerson, *The Unfinished Revolution: Coming of Age in a New Era of Gender, Work and Family* (New York: Oxford University Press, 2010), 129

Patricia's mother's life also offered her a cautionary tale:

> My mother's such a leftover from the fifties and did everything for my father. I'm not planning to fall into that trap. I'm really not willing to take that from any guy at all.[64]

Some women, like Monique, learn to fear a breadwinner/housewife model the hard way:

> I was dependent on my kids' father, and I never want to be dependent on a man ever again. . . . I have the kids now, and I want the job, the career. When I have all that, I can add a man if he's a good guy, and if he's not, let him go.[65]

Young women's desire for independence contrasts sharply with the neo-traditionalist fallback positions of the majority of men. A recent study resonates with Gerson's results: 66 percent of women between the ages of eighteen and thirty-four say that "being successful in a high-paying career" is "very important" or, even, "one of the most important things" in their lives.[66] Women also strongly value parenting: Over half (59 percent) report that "being a good parent" is a top priority.[67] A much smaller percentage (37 percent) say the same about marriage.

These are some pretty stunning findings. What appears to be a happy convergence between men's and women's ideals—both are egalitarians—can turn into an intractable situation. When their ideals bump up against an institutional context that makes sharing difficult, many couples feel betrayed and resentful. Some of these couples will divorce. And, when couples separate, custody is granted to the mother the majority of the time: 83 percent of single, divorced custodial parents are mothers and almost half of all mothers will spend at least some time as a single parent.[68]

How happy are divorced parents? It depends. As we know, while divorced men are less happy, on average, than their married counterparts, divorced women are happier. The second shift helps explain why. Women without husbands spend fewer hours on household chores because some husbands create more housework than they provide. So divorce may offer women the opportunity to live a more enjoyable life that conforms to their own ideologies. In contrast, men lose the domestic support of women that they enjoyed during marriage, the same support that pressed many women to leave in the first place.

GOING IT ALONE Another route to self-reliance is to begin that way. Sociologists Kathryn Edin and Maria Kefalas spent five years getting to know 162 racially diverse low-income single mothers in Philadelphia.[69] Many of them had children while they were young and unmarried, something that many Americans believe to be self-defeating. Why did these women make this choice? Why didn't they work hard in school, go to college, find a job and a husband, and *then* have a child?

The answer to this question is counterintuitive. While the U.S. government has argued that the answer to unmarried mothers in poverty is to convince them to value marriage, these young women *already* value marriage very much. The marriages in their neighborhoods are all too often torn apart by poverty and men's imprisonment. With these relationships in mind, young women are hopeful yet skeptical about the possibility of finding a man with whom they can build a stable lifelong relationship. Aiming to be careful, poor women often wait five or ten years before marrying a man they're dating. They want to be as sure as possible that their marriage will last. In contrast, middle-class women tend to feel confident that they can make a marriage work, so they wait only one or two years. In other words, it is exactly because low-income women take marriage so seriously, and understand its fragility, that they are less likely to marry before having a child.

Delaying marriage isn't only about a dearth of available men and testing a relationship, however. Edin and Kefalas discovered that many low-income young women conflate marriage with a middle-class lifestyle. One of their interviewees, Jen, dropped out of school in the tenth grade after getting pregnant at fifteen. She described what she thought marriage was like:

> If I was gonna get married, I would want to be married like my Aunt Nancy and Uncle Pat. They live in the mountains. She has a job. My Uncle Pat is a state trooper; he has lots of money. They live in the [Poconos]. It's real nice out there. Her kids go to Catholic school. . . . If I get married, I would have a life like [theirs].[70]

This lifestyle, however, is a long way off, perhaps even unreachable for Jen, given that she lives in a neglected urban neighborhood with limited economic opportunities. For Jen, marriage means being able to move out of her parents' house, rent or buy a humble home, pay for a car and car insurance, and build up a bit of savings—and that was going to have to wait.

In the meantime, when young low-income women get pregnant, they may have little reason not to keep the child. Middle- and upper-class women in high school see a child as interfering with their plans for college and a career. Poor youth don't often imagine that these things are on the horizon for them (and they're probably right). They consider an early pregnancy less than ideal, but something they can embrace. Moreover, children help make a difficult life feel meaningful.[71] Parenting is one of the few truly important and rewarding activities that isn't systematically made unavailable to them.

For child care, young mothers often turn to extended families: grandparents, aunts, cousins, and even older siblings. The insistent individualism behind the ideology of intensive motherhood—in which one mother tends devotedly to her own children only—is less common. Poor women rely on **othermothers**, women in the neighborhood who act as substitute mothers out of inclination or kindness.[72] In turn, they are othermothers to other women's children. Fatherhood, as well, is often less closely connected to biology; in poor and working-class African American communities, a number of men often take a fatherly interest in children such that paternal attention comes from many different sources.[73]

On the other end of the class spectrum, some middle- and upper-class women are making the same choice at an older age.[74] While rates of unmarried births among low-income women of color are actually dropping, those among white educated women are going up.[75] Few people anticipate that they will be alone during their prime childbearing years, but about one-third of people will be.[76] As having a child out of wedlock has become less stigmatized, voluntary unmarried motherhood has increased. It more than doubled among white women during the 1980s and has tripled among women with high-status white-collar

occupations.[77] These are women who went to college and established themselves in careers but never met a person with whom to have a child.

Like low-income teenagers, they would prefer to conceive a child while in a
stable relationship, but this has been elusive for them. So, they, too, decide to
have children on their own. Anna, a forty-year-old "single mother by choice,"
explains how she came to her decision:

> I really believe that children are made from two people that love each other and
> want to create a family. But if that is not an option, you just have to draw a way
> around really. Because if you are running out of time, you just have to see what
> option you have to have a child. And then have a father [later].[78]

Many women today have the economic resources, access to technology, and
enough social support to make a family without a husband. They can do this,
in part, because domestic outsourcing has made it possible. For high-income
single mothers, this might mean hiring a nanny; for those with middle incomes,
it might involve buying prepared food from the supermarket. In both cases,
though, they are able to trade economic resources for goods and services that
mothers have traditionally provided.

Childlessness

Everyone has a second shift—household chores and errands are a part of all our
lives—but children intensify this work. Accordingly, some people are managing
the burden of the second shift by forgoing parenting altogether.

In 2012, the birthrate was the lowest recorded in American history.[79] One
out of five American women over forty is currently childless (Figure 11.4).[80] As
many as one in three women in generations X and Y is likely to exit her childbearing years without reproducing.[81] While traditionally it has been women
with higher levels of education who have remained childless, women with less
education are increasingly following suit.

This rise in childlessness is partly a response to the demands of the ideology
of intensive mothering. Kay, a twenty-four-year-old accountant-in-training, explained why she didn't want to become a mother:

> To be honest, the biggest thing that comes to mind is sacrifice. And it just seems
> sacrifice of your own personal identity and all of your own wishes or desires, you
> have to give those up for someone else. It just seems a terrible, terrible burden.[82]

Janie, a forty-year-old secretary, was watching her sister parent and felt
similarly:

*Whenever I go around there she talks about the children; they're the focal point
of her life. She doesn't seem to be a woman in her own right. She is either a wife
to Graham or a mother to her kids and I go away thinking, oh no, I wouldn't swap
my life with hers.*[83]

Especially for middle- and upper-class women and men, childlessness may be
attractive because it offers them the opportunity to do other interesting things.
This concept is still rather new for women. Highly effective birth control options
and abortion became legal and accessible only during the late '60s and '70s,
and only since then have women had the opportunity to excel in challenging,
respected, and high-paying careers. For women who have access to these occupations, childlessness is a tempting choice precisely because having children
is no longer the only way for women to feel like they're doing something valuable with their lives. Samantha, a thirty-four-year-old professional, is one such
woman. She wasn't interested in the daily demands of parenting—"the little
baby voices, and the screaming, and the tantrums, and the constant questions."[84] She wanted to continue to excel in her career, travel, enjoy delicious
meals, and bask in quiet afternoons.

Other people are choosing voluntary childlessness out of ambivalence. Callie, also a thirty-four-year-old professional, is not 100 percent against the idea of
having kids; she's just not sure:

*I'm married and in a long-term, stable, very happy relationship and the ques-
tion is, is it the intention that we go on together, [have a child], and see what
happens . . . or is my life so full and happy the way it is that I don't want to do*

FIGURE 11.4 | CHILDLESSNESS IN THE UNITED STATES

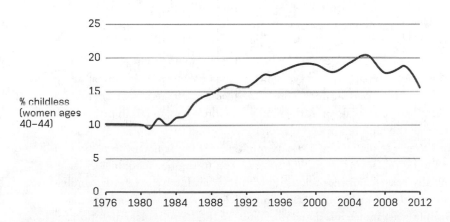

% childless
(women ages
40–44)

Source: U.S. Census Bureau, Current Population Survey, June 1976–2010

anything that could jeopardize that? I really do think that it's gotten to a point where I'm going to be happy either way.[85]

Unlike Callie, who believes she will be happy either way, thirty-two-year-old Joanne is ambivalent about having children out of concern for her future. Her husband lost his job twice in two years. "So every time we get everything set up," she says, "we get knocked back down."[86]

I'm not comfortable enough to risk the difficulty of having a child in a situation like this when I don't feel confident that I can provide the things that they would need. . . . Everything is so uncertain and unstable; I can't see a clear solid ground ahead of me. Until I have that, it makes me very hesitant to move forward.[87]

Joanne wonders if things will stabilize before she feels too old to have kids. "Do I push it up to thirty-seven?" she asks. "Or do I just say this isn't something that is going to happen for me?" When asked how she feels about the possibility of lifelong childlessness, she's "unhappy but not devastated."

Many people, then, are daunted by the ideology of intensive motherhood, unsure about their finances, or worried about keeping up with the pressures at work. Their own childhoods may serve as cautionary tales. The children of housewives are familiar with the sacrifice of women's own aspirations and financial stability. The children of working wives recognize that being a supermom can be overwhelming and are often disappointed in their fathers. The children of single mothers know firsthand that having another person to help and support you is not guaranteed. Children raised by high-achieving women who were able to hire nannies and other types of household help may resent their mothers' ambition and absence. Given these factors—whether out of resolve (like Samantha), optimism (like Callie), or pessimism (like Joanne)—many women today aren't sure they can or wish to make the sacrifices they believe parenting would require.

There are many different ways to divide paid and unpaid labor; all of them are gendered. When one partner stays home or goes part-time, it is almost always the woman. If one partner does more of the second shift, it's a good bet that it's the wife. When couples divorce, the mother is more likely to retain primary legal custody of the children or end up doing more child care in practice. And when families turn to maids and day care or nannies, they are often implicitly understood to be replacements for *her* contribution to the household, not his. Wives typically have a closer relationship with their children's caretakers and are more involved with instructing and communicating with them. Even among sharers, a slightly asymmetrical division of labor, in the stereotypical direction, is associated with the greatest stability. All of this contributes to women's disadvantage within both families and society.

HOUSEWORK, PARENTING, AND POWER

Women's disproportionate responsibility for housework and child care disadvantages women as a whole, exacerbates inequality among women, and places them at odds with one another. While we think of families as places where love and care take center stage, they are also places in which both gender difference and inequality are reproduced, and these inequalities intersect with other social hierarchies as well. Below, we discuss how responsibility for housework and child care is about both gender and power.

The Loss of Status and Interpersonal Power

Victorian women introduced the ideology of intensive motherhood as a way to resist the androcentric devaluation of the domestic sphere when it became separate from work during the Industrial Revolution. These efforts were not wholly successful. Housework and child care are still low-status activities. When journalist Ann Crittenden had her first child she was a foreign correspondent for *Newsweek,* a financial reporter for *The New York Times,* and a Pulitzer Prize nominee. None of this seemed to matter, she said, once she became a mother. Whereas once she'd been "*The* Ann Crittenden" at fancy New York cocktail parties, now she was "just a mom." She wrote that she felt like she'd "shed status like the skin off a snake."[88] A woman she interviewed about this phenomenon explained how it felt to go from being a young professional to a young mother:

> *We are the very women who were successful in what the women's revolution was all about, which was to be able to get out there and be the equal of the guys.... And suddenly [you have a baby and] you're back in the female world. It's a shock.... Raising children is still part of a relatively low-status world. Everything was gone once I started to stay home. In my new job as a mother, I had no salary and no professional contacts.... No more dinners out. No work clothes.... It was as if everything were being taken away from me.*[89]

When we ask our students what their parents would think if they decided to have a child right after graduation and become a stay-at-home caregiver, both men and women often suggest that their mothers and fathers would be disappointed, or even horrified. Among other possible responses, students imagine their parents would ask, "What did we spend all that money on college for!?" or exclaim, "That would be a waste of your intelligence!" It is as if people think parenting requires zero knowledge and even less brain power. Accordingly, people sometimes say that a woman who stays at home "doesn't *do* anything." "Oh, so you don't work?" a housewife might be asked, as she quickly mops the kitchen floor so she can have time to run by the dry cleaner before picking up her child from preschool, feeding him a snack, and finding something for him to do so she can begin preparing dinner for her husband and ten-year-old. Even housewives sometimes refer to their work as *"just* staying home," doing nothing important, in other words.

No wonder men aren't interested in doing it. In fact, many men express just these sentiments when asked how they would feel if *they* specialized in domestic labor. Josh, for instance, explains:

> *I would never stay home. I have a friend who's like that, and I strongly disapprove. The father just stays home. I think it's wrong because his wife's out there working seven days a week, and he's doing* nothing *except staying home.*[90]

Often, gay men view housework similarly. Rich, for example, asked, "What about one's self-respect?" when he contemplated being a househusband. "I don't see how one could live with oneself by not doing *something* for a living."[91] Note how Matthew and Josh's language—"doing nothing" vs. "doing something"—betrays their belief that feminized household labor isn't really anything.

In interpersonal relationships, those who specialize in domestic work can sometimes feel that their partners don't value their contribution to the household, and they might be right. In an interview, a husband let slip how little regard he had for the last twelve years of his wife Kuae's life, during which time she'd been a stay-at-home mom:

> *Being the kind of person I am, Type A . . . always going after something, I wonder what I could have done, having twelve years to sort of think about what I want to do. I sometimes think, Wow, I could have been an astronaut in twelve years, or I could have been something different that I'd really enjoy. . . . What could I have been in twelve years of self-discovery?*[92]

His comments reveal that part of him wondered what Kuae had been doing, as if taking care of a home and three children took no time at all. To him, she had done nothing. For her part, Kuae was well aware that her husband devalued her work at home: "I think he has struggled with assigning value," she said stonily.

Cliff, a stay-at-home dad, also felt underappreciated and taken advantage of by his wife:

When she has a day off, she wants to relax, but sometimes I find it frustrating that while I'm finishing up the load of laundry or putting [clothes] away, she's lounging on the couch, watching some movie or reading a book. So there certainly have been times that I resent the fact that I do so much of the cleaning. . . . I wish she'd appreciate what I'm doing.[93]

In addition to losing status, people who specialize in the unpaid labor of the household might also feel that they have less ability to negotiate for what they want. One wife who quit her job to stay home with her children gave an example of how she'd lost bargaining power:

It's funny now because he is the breadwinner so there have been . . . opportunities to relocate and get a better position and the money was better. You're just put in a position where you have to just follow. Before when we were both working we would talk it out. I'd say, "No, I want to stay here." And now you really can't.[94]

This disempowerment can extend to decisions about purchases, divisions of labor, and child care. Indeed, studies of decision making between spouses show that couples are more likely to follow men's preferences when a wife and husband disagree.[95] We generally see power differences in all couples where one person specializes in domestic work: among heterosexual neo-traditionalists, gender-swapped heterosexual couples, gays and lesbians, and even polyamorous relationships involving three or more people.[96]

The vulnerability that comes with taking disproportionate responsibility for domestic work is not just about status and interpersonal dynamics, though; it's also about money.

The Economic Vulnerability of Caregivers

As we've discussed, though men and women are both working hard to sustain their families, women are more likely than men to take time out of the workforce and de-prioritize their careers. This harms women's short- and long-term financial security. In fact, moms make significantly less money than dads in almost all developed countries.[97]

Crittenden has a name for the lost wages, benefits, and Social Security contributions that come with taking time out of the workforce to raise small children and then re-entering it with less momentum: the mommy tax. Among full-time working women, mothers earn $0.66 for every dollar men make, whereas women without children earn $0.90.[98] In contrast, fathers actually make *more* money than men without kids, almost 20 percent more.[99] So it's the intersection of gender and parenting—being a mother, specifically—that creates disadvantage.

Crittenden calculated that a college-educated American woman was likely to sacrifice $1.31 million over the course of her lifetime for the pleasures of having children. Other research confirms the trend. Economist Sylvia Ann Hewlett compared the incomes of mothers who took time out of the workforce with those who didn't. She found an 11 percent decrease in income for women who took less than a year off and a 37 percent decrease for those who were out for three years or more.[100]

Divorce exacerbates the vulnerability. Nearly half (42 percent) of single mothers will find themselves below the poverty line; they are almost six times more likely to be in poverty than married women.[101] Some of these single moms are poor because they aren't working. This is partly because it's structurally impossible: Being simultaneously the breadwinner and the caretaker means being able to arrange and pay for child care during her working hours. If a woman is low income, she simply may not be able to afford it. Government subsidies for low-income single mothers help some women out of this bind, but these programs are woefully underfunded and don't reach a large proportion of the people in need. Even if they are able to access these programs, women are only allowed to use them for two years, after which they are ineligible. Twenty-two American states have children on waiting lists for subsidized child care; the families are eligible, but the state has nowhere to place them.[102] In California, about 280,000 children are waiting.

When women can't afford to work because of the cost of child care, it contributes to their short- and long-term financial fragility. However, many working single mothers are also in poverty. Two-thirds of single moms work for wages, but this doesn't necessarily insulate them from the vulnerability that parenting brings.[103] The federal minimum wage is $7.25 an hour. A full-time employee earning minimum wage who doesn't miss a single day of work for a year earns $290 a week; that's $15,080 a year. According to how the government measures poverty, that's enough to support a single adult but, for a single adult with a child, it's officially below the poverty line.[104] Consequently, many single mothers fall into the population of the **working poor**, individuals who work but still live in poverty.

The economic vulnerability that comes with being a mother—both for those who divorce their husbands and for those who stay married and de-prioritize their careers—has led scholars to assert that we are seeing a **feminization of poverty**, a trend in which the poor are increasingly female. Because there is no "daddy tax," but instead a daddy benefit, a single mother is almost twice as likely to be in poverty as a single father.[105] One out of seven single mothers goes to food banks, 20 percent receive food stamps, and 10 percent are on welfare; many more qualify but don't apply.[106] Stunningly, motherhood is the single strongest predictor of bankruptcy in middle age and poverty in old age.[107]

These numbers reveal that one of the functions of marriage is still to transfer economic resources from men to women. Women as a group do not enjoy the same level of economic security as men. As long as they remain married to a man who is willing to share his income and wealth, this may not be very noticeable, but if he rescinds his support or she chooses divorce, a woman's economic vulnerability can become painfully obvious. The asymmetric focuses of married men and women, with women spending more time with the house and the children and men spending more time at work, may look fair on the face of it—they both put in approximately the same number of hours on their shared lives—but because we reward only one of those jobs with money, this asymmetry hurts women more than men in the long run.

Because of androcentrism, we devalue the feminized domestic sphere relative to the masculinized work sphere. And because of sexism, we feel comfortable expecting women to bear the brunt of this trivialized, unpaid, and sometimes disparaged activity. Men and women get pressed into these roles, even when they don't want them, by both ideological and institutional forces. In this way, family life is a form of systematic gender subordination not unlike the relationships between doctors and nurses or bosses and secretaries: It brings men and women into different and unequal relationships. The fact that this occurs through heterosexual coupling instead of occupational choices doesn't mean it's not a form of inequality; it's just a particularly intimate one.

Family and Inequality among Women: The Downside of Outsourcing

Outsourcing may help women mediate some of the loss of status, power, and economic well-being that we've outlined, but it also intensifies inequality among different kinds of women. When families outsource housework and child care, the people they hire are almost always female and more disadvantaged than the family members who are buying their services: 95 percent of domestic workers are women, 54 percent are a racial or ethnic minority, 32 percent have less than a high school education, 46 percent are foreign-born, and 35 percent are noncitizens.[108] While employment is a good thing, domestic jobs are generally considered "bad jobs" with long hours, low pay, inflexibility, insecurity, little chance for advancement, and few (if any) benefits. And, while some nannies enjoy highly paid, glamorous jobs in extravagantly rich locations, the average wage for a live-in nanny is $6.76 an hour; two-thirds are paid below the minimum wage.[109] Many domestic workers are not covered by either minimum wage or Social Security laws and the Supreme Court has just denied them the right to unionize.

Importantly, many of the women who perform housework and child care for pay also have children of their own. Because their wages are low, they purchase the even lower-wage services of even poorer women. These women, in turn, leave their own children with family members or friends. Sociologist Rhacel Parrenas calls this a **care chain**, a series of nurturing relationships in which the care of children, the disabled, or the elderly is displaced onto increasingly disadvantaged paid or unpaid carers.[110] She explains:

> *An older daughter from a poor family in a third world country cares for her siblings (the first link in the chain) while her mother works as a nanny caring for the children of a nanny migrating to a first world country (the second link) who, in turn, cares for the child of a family in a rich country (the final link).*[111]

Caring brings in decreasing financial returns as you go down the chain. A nanny working for a wealthy family in the United States might earn $400 a week. She, in turn, may pay a live-in domestic worker in her country of origin $40 a week. That worker may leave her children to be taken care of by their grandmother for free.

These care chains are not only economic; they displace love and its benefits by pushing it up the chain.[112] Nannies who are also mothers find their love and attention displaced onto their employers' children.[113] They spend weekdays organizing and chaperoning character- and skill-building activities with the children they are paid to care for; meanwhile, on weekends and evenings they have to fit in their own errands, house cleaning, and other routine activities for their families. A nanny may be with her own children during this time, but her *primary* attention is overwhelmingly focused on the children of her employer.

This displacement is especially extreme for migrants. Vicky, a thirty-four-year-old mother who left the Philippines to work for a family in Beverly Hills, explains how she misses her five children: "[It's] very depressing," she sighed. She finds solace in loving the child for whom she nannies: "In my absence from my children, the most I could do with my situation is give all my love to that child."

So the child in Beverly Hills benefits from Vicky's love as well as the love of both his or her own parents. Vicky's time and attention are diverted from her own children, whom she can love only from afar. That absence is partially filled by attention from their lower-paid nanny in the Philippines, who likely has her own child or children in an even less secure arrangement, where they are deprived of a certain amount of love and attention from their own mother. In

This photo features an example of the top of the care chain, in which the caretaking of middle- or upper-class children becomes the responsibility of poorer women, often women of color, whose own children receive less care as a result.

other words, the excess love that the child in Beverly Hills receives comes at the expense of another, less fortunate child.

Many employers feel *entitled* to this displacement: They *prefer* that their nannies leave their own children with someone else when they come to work. One such employer explained:

> I wanted someone whose primary purpose here was to take care of [my child,] Jennifer. . . . I felt that if they brought their own child . . . [they would] be watching him as he was crawling into everything, and maybe neglect Jennifer.[114]

Another explained that she prefers to employ women who have immigrated because she doesn't want her nanny to be distracted by his or her own loved ones: "I needed the person here in the house and have our family as their priority and not their family as their priority."[115] Some employees expect their nannies to neglect their own families as a condition of employment.

Class-privileged women can join men in the workplace by replacing themselves. They may avoid (some of) the mommy tax and gain esteem in the workplace, thereby avoiding the consequences that come with being "just a mom." This practice doesn't liberate women as a group, though, because *another woman* comes in to do that work. In other words, outsourcing is a patriarchal bargain.

It doesn't eliminate the cultural and economic costs that come with mothering, it just pushes them off onto women with less status. That is, the primary thing that has allowed wealthy women to work is the disadvantage of other women.

Revisiting the Question

If marriage is better for women than ever, why do married women report lower levels of happiness than married men and single women?

Marriage contracts are no longer explicitly gendered, but gender continues to be an organizing principle of family life. The idea that household chores and child care are the woman's responsibility persists. This is reflected in both how we think about child care and household chores and who actually performs these duties. Even when both partners want a balance between home and work, institutional forces often make sharing difficult.

The continued feminization of housework and child care contributes to ongoing inequality. Doing domestic work translates into a loss of status, bargaining power, and financial security. This situation harms everyone who specializes in this work: housewives and househusbands, single parents, working parents married to neo-traditionalists, dual-nurturers who turn away from work, and the poorly paid domestic workers who take up some of the extra burden. Overwhelmingly, these people are female. Women are less happy than men in marriage, then, because it is an institution that systematically presses them into doing the low-status domestic work of our society.

Next . . .

Since 1964 the federal government has strengthened gender equality in the workplace. Today women make up 47 percent of the workforce, and they can be found in every occupation.[116] Still, men reap more rewards at work. Women are less likely than men to be in well-paid, high-prestige jobs that are considered skilled and involve managing employees. Our question for the next chapter is:

If women now have equal protection in the workplace, why aren't they as successful as men at work?

Let's find out.

FOR FURTHER READING

Ball, Carlos. *The Right to be Parents: LGBT Families and the Transformation of Parenthood*. New York: New York University Press, 2012.

Blackstone, Amy. "Doing Family without Having Kids." *Sociology Compass* 8, no. 1 (2014): 52–62.

Ehrenreich, Barbara, and Arlie Hochschild. *Global Woman: Nannies, Maids, and Sex Workers in the New Economy*. New York: Henry Holt and Company, 2004.

Sutherland, Jean-Anne. "Mothering, Guilt and Shame." *Sociology Compass* 4, no. 5 (2010): 310–21.

Wall, Glenda, and Stephanie Arnold. "How Involved is Involved Fathering?: An Exploration of the Contemporary Culture of Fatherhood." *Gender & Society* 21, no. 4 (2007): 508–27.

WE'RE HERE TO SAVE YOUR
ASS, NOT KISS IT!

—YOUR FRIENDLY FLIGHT ATTENDANT[1]

Work

Today's women are giving men a run for their money. Two-thirds say that a high-paying job is important to them, compared with 56 percent of men.[2] And yet, women are not as financially successful as men. In the first year out of college, male graduates earn, on average, $8,000 more a year than female graduates.[3] We see this phenomenon even among the most high-achieving young people. A study of Harvard grads found that men entering the finance industry were four times more likely than women to report a starting salary of more than $110,000.[4] Likewise, among Harvard grads going into technology and engineering jobs, 79 percent of men reported a salary of more than $90,000, compared with 44 percent of women. This gap in pay only gets wider over time: Women earn $0.82 for every dollar earned by men in the first year after graduation; just ten years later, it drops all the way down to $0.69.[5]

This difference in male and female earnings persists despite federal laws designed to guarantee equality, which led us to ask:

Q+A   **If women now have equal protection in the workplace, why aren't they as successful as men at work?**

In this chapter we'll get up close and personal with occupations and earnings. Drawing on data from the U.S. Bureau of Labor Statistics, we'll explain how paid work is gendered in ways that affirm difference and entrench inequality. Along the way, we'll address the main reasons why women are less successful at work than men. Some of the disadvantage, we'll see, is due to simple discrimination against women. But the story also involves the tendency for jobs to be predominantly male or female, the different value attributed to men's and women's work, the challenges of being both a good parent and a good worker, and employers' beliefs about mothers and fathers.

So buckle up, put your seat backs and tray tables in their full upright and locked position, and direct your attention to the flight attendant.

THE CHANGING WORKPLACE

In the 1960s and '70s, airlines sexualized their stewardesses to attract a mostly male customer base. As part of this effort, Southwest Airlines flight attendants were required to wear hot pants and leather go-go boots.

"Next to being a Hollywood movie star, nothing was more glamorous," said a starry-eyed stewardess in 1945.[6] World War II was over and women were being pushed out of the workforce, but flight attendants were embarking on a new adventure. Only about 10 percent of Americans had ever flown in an airplane and most were afraid to do so.[7] Stewardesses were certifiably adventurous. They took risks to see parts of the world that their sisters would probably never see. Along the way, they would rub elbows with the world's elite: their passengers. As historian Kathleen Barry contends: "Few women journeyed as regularly or as far from home, or came into contact with the rich and famous as often, as a typical stewardess did."[8]

Airlines hired women whom they believed represented ideal femininity. Chosen for their beauty and poise, and almost exclusively from among the white, educated, and slender, they were as much of an icon as Miss

America. The promise of a fresh-faced, kind, and accommodating stewardess was a staple of airline advertising. As one of America's sweethearts, she also appeared in commercials for products from soft drinks to cigarettes.

By the 1960s, airlines were in the "business of female spectacle," unabashedly selling women's attractiveness to customers.[9] Sexual innuendo was the rule. Perhaps most famous was the National Airlines' campaign in which stewardesses invited passengers to "Fly Me."[10] Their advertising included the guarantee "We'll Fly You Like You've Never Been Flown Before." Feminists later replied "Go Fly Yourself, National!" Their saucy substitution of "fly" for another f-word was lost on no one.

The strategy of sexual objectification was industry wide: Continental stewardesses pledged, "We Really Move Our Tails for You"; Air Jamaica promised, "We Make You Feel Good All Over"; Air France replied, "Have You Ever Done It the French Way?"; Braniff Airlines asked their male passengers, "Does Your Wife Know You're Flying

I'm Cheryl. Fly me to the Sunshine States of America.

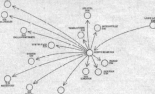

You think I'm just another pretty face? I'm not.

I'm a fresh attitude towards air travel to the States. A refreshingly honest definition of who we are, why we're special, and what we're doing to be even better.

Here's who we are: We're Cheryl (me), and Margie and Linda and Laura and Jo. And a lot of people behind the scenes, like Bob and Tom and Ron and Lee. (They're not just pretty faces either.)

And here's what we're doing (and why we're special): We're helping nice people (hopefully you) go to nice places in the Sunshine States of America, like Miami and other warm places in Florida and the Caribbean and Latin America, plus New Orleans and Houston and Los Angeles and San Francisco. We're helping nice people have fun en route, too: with movies* and stereo* and delicious meals, and just being left alone, if that's what you want.

The way we figure it: the more we like you, the more you'll like us. It's that simple.

So we're not just a bunch of people. We're an airline. And you can call us by our first name: National.

Fly Cheryl. Fly National Airlines.

For reservations call your travel agent or National Airlines, 81 Piccadilly, London, W.1. (01 629 8272).

*Movies and stereo by In-Flight Motion Pictures, Inc. Available at nominal charge. National honours American Express, Barclaycard, Carte Blanche, Diners Club, UATP, our own card and cash.

In this ad for National Airlines of London from the 1960s, Cheryl's inviting gaze is presented alongside the airline's invitation to "fly" her.

with Us?"; TWA offered flights with stewardesses of exotic nationalities; and Pacific Southwest Airlines riffed on their acronym, having flight attendants wear buttons that said "Pure, Sober, and Available."[11] Uniforms followed suit. The knee-length skirts and suit jackets of earlier days were pushed aside in favor of mini-skirts, short shorts, and go-go boots.

Still, it wasn't all fun and hot pants. Standards of appearance were strict.[12] Disqualifications and pink slips were issued for big feet, chubby legs, poor posture, the wrong haircut, glasses, acne, short nails, imperfect teeth, not wearing makeup, or any supposed flaw the recruiters identified. They claimed that their objections to broad noses, coarse hair, and full lips was race-neutral but, of course, they were not.[13] When first hired in the 1970s after multiple court battles, African American flight attendants were required to straighten their hair. A ban on "hook noses" was used to exclude Jewish women.

Women were required to wear girdles and submit to routine weigh-ins and measurement of their busts, waists, hips, and thighs. They were fired if they

The first African American flight attendant in the United States, Ruth Carol Taylor, began working in the sky in 1958.

gained weight. "You run a $1.5 billion business," said a United Airlines official, "and it boils down to whether some chicks look good in their uniforms. If you have fat stewardesses, people aren't going to fly with you."[14] Airlines also terminated the employment of women who got married, became pregnant, or reached their early thirties. A manager once told a group of flight attendants: "If you haven't found a man to keep you by the time you're twenty-eight, then TWA won't want you either."[15]

Stewardesses also faced routine sexual harassment. Airlines marketed them as available sex partners and then instructed them that the customer was always right.[16] African American flight attendants faced their own unique version; some of the overwhelmingly white customers were hostile racists, but others would proposition them for a "black experience."[17]

Meanwhile, female flight attendants were among the most poorly paid employees in the airline industry. They were paid a third of what pilots earned and two-thirds the wages of the mostly male ground workers. They were also paid significantly less than the few male flight attendants; at Pan Am men earned 140 percent of a female flight attendant's salary. Men also enjoyed promotions, more responsibility, nicer accommodations on layovers, larger pensions, greater scheduling flexibility, and more sick leave. Plus, they didn't face weigh-ins or forced retirements.

Then 1964 happened. Stewardesses filed a case against the airline industry on the first day the government began considering violations of the new Civil Rights Act.[18] Flight attendants would initiate over 100 lawsuits in eighteen months. Over the next sixty years, women across the occupational spectrum would use the act to gain access to essentially all occupations. Companies no longer had the right to pay women less, deny them promotion, or otherwise discriminate based on gender. As companies faced potential lawsuits, their overtly discriminatory practices slowly eroded.

Yet, men—especially white men—still have substantial advantages in the workplace. They are more likely to engage in paid work than women and work more hours per week and more weeks per year. They get better benefits and are more likely to get on-the-job training. They are more likely to have jobs considered "skilled" and are more likely to be in management. They unquestionably dominate the highest rungs of corporate ladders. As of 2013, 96 percent of CEOs, 86 percent of executive officers, and 84 percent of corporate officers in Fortune 500 companies were men.[19]

Perhaps the most succinct measure of men's advantage in the workplace is the **gender pay gap**, the difference between the incomes of the average man and woman who work full-time. As of 2013, the median earnings of American men working full-time were $860 per week.[20] Comparably, full-time working women earn $706, or 82 percent of men's wages. To put it another way, among workers employed full-time, women earn $0.82 for every dollar a man makes.

The size of the pay gap varies in response to policies and practice but is persistent across race, education level, geographic location, age, and 200 years of history. Figure 12.1 summarizes some of this variation. Notice that the gap has

FIGURE 12.1 | VARIATION IN WOMEN'S EARNINGS FOR EVERY DOLLAR OF MEN'S FOR FULL-TIME WORKERS, SELECTED COMPARISONS

Comparison	Cents/Dollar	Comparison	Cents/Dollar
By state in the U.S.:		*By education (U.S.):*	
California	83¢	Less than high school	80¢
Florida	82¢	High school graduate	76¢
New Jersey	76¢	College graduate	77¢
Texas	80¢	Master's degree	76¢
Washington, D.C.	88¢	Professional degree	72¢
Wyoming	66¢	Doctoral degree	80¢
By country:		*By race or ethnicity (U.S.):*	
Germany	78¢	Black women, men	93¢
Ireland	86¢	Black women, white men	70¢
Italy	94¢	Asian women, men	73¢
Slovenia	98¢	Asian women, white men	91¢
United Kingdom	80¢	Hispanic women, men	88¢
		Hispanic women, white men	60¢
By year (U.S.):		White women, men	81¢
1820	35¢		
1890	46¢	*By age (U.S.):*	
1930	56¢		
1960	61¢	16–24 years old	86¢
1970	60¢	25–34 years old	89¢
1990	72¢	35–44 years old	80¢
2000	74¢	45–54 years old	75¢
2010	81¢	55–64 years old	78¢
		65 and older	73¢

Source: European Commission 2012; Institute for Women's Policy Research 2011; AAUW 2013; Goldin 1990; Bureau of Labor Statistics 2013; Getz 2010[21]

been slowly shrinking over time and that it varies both among American states and among different countries. Women of all races make less money than men of the same race, but the size of the gap differs. It's smaller among groups that have overall lower wages, mostly because racial minority men, with the exception of some Asian groups, earn especially low incomes. Perhaps surprisingly, the gap is largest among men and women who earn professional degrees in fields such as law and medicine. The wage gap also increases, if unevenly, across the life cycle.

Because of the gender wage gap, over a lifetime the average woman will make $434,000 less in income than the average man.[22] Women with college degrees stand to lose about $713,000.[23] This harms women's economic stability in old age directly (it helps to have an extra half-million upon retirement) and also indirectly (women's average Social Security retirement benefit is about 75 percent that of men).[24] According to the American Association of Retired Persons, two-thirds of the disparity between men's and women's retirement income is caused by the wage gap.[25]

The rest of this chapter is devoted to exploring the forces that produce inequality at work: job segregation, discrimination against women, and the practice and ideology of parenting. We'll discuss each of these in depth.

JOB SEGREGATION

Ellen Church could have become the first female commercial pilot when she was hired by Boeing Air Transport in 1930, but Boeing didn't allow women in the cockpit.[26] So despite being a licensed pilot, she became the first female flight attendant. A different woman, Helen Richey, would be hired as a pilot by Central Airlines a few years later, but she would be the exception that proved the rule.[27] It would be four decades before we would see another. In 1978, when the International Society of Women Airline Pilots was founded, it boasted only twenty-one members.[28]

Since the inception of aviation, young women and men attracted to the excitement of air travel have largely pursued their dreams through two very different avenues: Men became pilots and women became flight attendants. It's not that different today. Flight attendants are 78 percent female and pilots are 96 percent male.[29] This is **gendered job segregation**, the practice of filling occupations with mostly male or mostly female workers. Just as we gender all kinds of things, we gender jobs. Collectively, we understand certain jobs as somehow for women (like nursing and teaching) and others as for men (construction work and computer programming), even if we don't like the labeling or think the labels fit.

Jobs aren't *inherently* masculine or feminine, of course, nor is it natural to fill certain jobs with one sex and not the other. Instead, jobs are socially constructed in ways that suggest they are best suited for stereotypical women or men, while other features that would undermine that idea are ignored.[30] For example, male insurance agents describe successful colleagues as men who love competition and possess a "killer instinct."[31] In fact, an insurance salesperson also very likely has great interpersonal skills and can communicate trustworthiness, quickly forge bonds with strangers, and read emotions. If the job were gendered female, we would probably see more emphasis on interpersonal skills and less on the predatory nature of the job.

The social construction of jobs is about actively making work meaningful in gendered ways. Not surprisingly, then, we find great variation in how jobs are gendered across cultures. Medicine is a female job in Russia and Finland; in Latvia and Lithuania dentistry is, too.[32] In Iran, Uzbekistan, Azerbaijan, and Saudi Arabia, women earn the majority of science degrees.[33] In Armenia, half of computer science college professors are women.[34] Women also dominate computer science in Malaysia, where abstract office work is seen as feminine compared to more "physical" labor.[35] Likewise, they see chemical engineering as feminine because it involves working in a lab, but civil engineering as masculine because it involves going to worksites and thinking about construction. In contrast, in

A female laborer in the Indian state of Gujarat carries bricks needed for a construction site. Construction is gendered female in India and male in the United States.

India women make up a large share of the construction industry; it makes sense to them because Indian society holds women responsible for the home.[36]

How Much Job Segregation Is There?

Internationally, the amount of gender segregation in jobs varies.[37] If we wanted perfect integration in, say, the United Kingdom, 37 percent of workers would have to switch to a differently gendered job. Among developed countries, the percentage of people who would have to switch jobs varies from 23 percent in Japan to 45 percent in Luxembourg. Canada and Australia would need 38 percent of their workers to switch jobs; Italy would need 29 percent and Israel 41 percent.

To achieve integration in the United States, 34 percent of workers would have to switch to a differently gendered job. Four in ten women work in jobs that are at least 75 percent female; men work in even more gender-segregated environments.[38] Figure 12.2 presents data for some of the most gender-segregated occupations in the United States.

We see gender segregation not just between occupations—between nursing and construction work, for example—but within them. Even apparently gender-neutral occupations are often gender segregated if you look closely. Consider that there are lots of both waitresses and waiters, suggesting that the job of servers is an integrated one, but men and women tend to work at different types of restaurants: Servers at very expensive restaurants are more likely to be male, while lower-priced restaurants tend to employ women.[39] Among doctors, gender correlates with specialty: Women make up 55 percent of pediatricians but only 15 percent of surgeons.[40] Likewise, customer service representatives hired to work in department stores are often assigned to different parts of the store depending on their sex: men in the large appliance or shoe sections, women in cosmetics, children's clothing, or housewares.[41] We're committed to gendering work even when men and women are doing more or less the same job. The skills and responsibilities of barbers and hairdressers, for instance, are more alike than different, but men and women tend to get different job titles and work in different establishments serving different customers.

Gender intersects with other characteristics to stratify the workforce. Only 700 of the approximately 71,000 American pilots are black (that's 0.98 percent) and only 20 of those 700 are female.[42] Depending on what part of the United States you're in, the (likely female) housekeeper at your local motel will be white, Latina, or African American.[43] The janitor or maintenance worker will probably be the same race but the other gender. African American women make up only 6 percent of the general population but represent a third of active-duty enlisted women in the military.[44] A full 45,830 of the 46,000 taxi drivers in New York City are male; 84 percent of them are immigrants. Jobs are even segregated by sexual

FIGURE 12.2 | SOME OF THE MOST GENDER-SEGREGATED OCCUPATIONS

Female-dominated occupations	How female is it?
Dental hygienist	98%
Preschool and kindergarten teacher	98%
Medical transcriptionist	98%
Hairdresser/cosmetologist	95%
Child care worker	95%
Secretaries and administrative assistants	94%
Medical assistant	94%
Speech-language pathologist	93%
Receptionist	92%
Registered nurse	90%
Dietician and nutritionist	90%
Nursing, psychiatric, and home-health aide	89%

Male-dominated occupations	How male is it?
Crane/tower operator	99%
Highway maintenance worker	99%
Mechanic	98%
Carpenter	98%
Firefighter	97%
Pest control worker	97%
Construction laborer	96%
Maintenance and repair worker	96%
Welder	95%
Truck driver	95%
Railroad conductor	94%
Mechanical engineer	93%

Source: Bureau of Labor Statistics, "Labor Force Statistics from the Current Population Survey: Table 11: Employed persons by detailed occupation, sex, race, and Hispanic or Latino ethnicity," retrieved 7/7/14: http://www.bls.gov/cps/cpsaat11.htm

orientation. Lesbian and bisexual women are ten times more likely than heterosexual women to work as police officers.[45] And, while not all male flight attendants are gay, gay men are overrepresented compared to the overall population.[46]

What causes this divvying up of men and women into different kinds of jobs?

Causes of Job Segregation

Men and women usually end up in gender-stereotypical jobs through a complicated congruence of socialization, networking, employer selection, and employee desertion.

The **socialization hypothesis** suggests that men and women respond to gender stereotypes when planning, training, and applying for jobs.[47] In one

Coding and other computer-related positions are one of the few fields in which the share of women has actually declined in the past few decades.

study, psychologists invited students into a classroom and asked them to fill out a questionnaire regarding their interest and perceived ability in computer science.[48] One set of people entered a room that was covered in "computer geeky" things: a *Star Trek* poster, comic books, video game boxes, empty soda cans and junk food, and technical magazines. The other group entered a room without these objects. Men were unfazed by the geekery, but women who encountered the geeked-up room were significantly less likely to say they were considering a computer science major. So, to a degree, men and women self-select into jobs socially constructed as "for" their sex.

Another factor relates to how people hear about and get jobs. This is the **network hypothesis**: Hiring often occurs through personal networks, which are themselves gendered, so hiring is gendered in turn.[49] When a job opens up, existing employees are often the first to know. They tell their friends, who tend to be of the same sex (as well as class, race, sexual orientation, etc.). Applications are then gendered and, since employers tend to like referrals from current employees, hiring is even more so.

The **employer selection hypothesis** proposes that employers tend to prefer men for masculine jobs and women for feminine jobs, slotting applicants into gender-consistent roles during hiring and promotion. Certain kinds of factory work, for instance, are heavily female because employers prefer to hire women.

As one manager at a high-tech manufacturing company told a researcher: "Just three things I look for in hiring: small, foreign, and female."[50]

Finally, when individuals enter a job dominated by the other sex, they are more likely than other workers to leave that occupation in favor of a new one. This is the **desertion hypothesis**: Workers tend to abandon counter-stereotypical occupations at a higher rate than stereotypical ones. One study found that at the end of ten years, 61 percent of women in male-dominated occupations had left their job, compared with less than 30 percent of their male colleagues; half of these women switched to a female-dominated occupation.[51]

All four of these factors—socialization, networks, selection, and desertion—are at play, with selection and desertion likely the most substantial contributors. As a result, men and women tend to find themselves in jobs that are stereotyped for their own gender. This *in itself*, however, doesn't contribute to the pay gap. Gendered job segregation is only the beginning.

Different and Unequal

Celio Diaz was the first man to use the Civil Rights Act to sue for gender discrimination.[52] In the 1960s, only 4 percent of flight attendants were men; most airlines refused to hire them. Diaz had been rejected by Pan Am, which argued that men simply couldn't "convey the charm, the tact, the grace, the liveliness that young girls can."[53] Or, if they could, Pan Am claimed, it might "arouse feelings" in a male passenger "that he would rather not have aroused."[54] Pan Am appealed all the way to the U.S. Supreme Court, but they lost. Beginning in 1971, airlines were forced to begin hiring men alongside women. The media had a field day. The *Miami Herald* ran a story with a picture of a stocky, hairy-legged man in a miniskirt and knee-high socks, a purse hanging from his cocked arm. It read: "Here's the worst thing that could happen to commercial airlines."[55]

It's funny that the American media thought the idea of a "he-stewardess" was funny because the first "stewardess" was actually a "steward."[56] His name was Jack Sanderson and he was fourteen when he was hired by Daimler Airway (later British Airways) in 1922.[57] The job was almost exclusively male for some time. Pan Am, the largest international carrier in the United States at the time, maintained an all-male steward workforce for sixteen years. It integrated in 1944, as did many other airlines, because of the shortage of male laborers during World War II. By 1958, Pan Am had entirely reversed its policy: The airline now hired only female flight attendants. Soon American flight attendants were almost all female. One advertising executive in 1967 explained: "When a tired businessman gets on an airplane, we think he ought to be allowed to look at a pretty girl."[58]

The occupation's "sex change" is a great example of the social construction of work; it also reveals how prestige and pay tend to follow sex. Early airlines

Think of her as your mother.

She only wants what's best for you.
A cool drink. A good dinner. A soft pillow and a warm blanket.
This is not just maternal instinct. It's the result of the longest
Stewardess training in the industry.
Training in service, not just a beauty course.
Service, after all, is what makes professional travellers prefer American.
And makes new travellers want to keep on flying with us.
So we see that every passenger gets the same professional treatment.
That's the American Way.

Fly the American Way
American Airlines

Although the text of this ad for American Airlines presents its flight attendants as both motherly and professional, the picture tells a very different story of women's service work.

hired white male flight attendants in order to assure passengers that they were in good hands. Ocean liners and train cars, the models on which airlines built their businesses, largely employed black porters, but airlines believed that their overwhelmingly white passengers would not feel comfortable placing their lives in the hands of black men. So they hired white men to ensure that the occupation carried a degree of gravitas. Stewards embodied professionalism and dignity, wearing military-inspired uniforms and changing into white sport coats and gloves to serve dinner. They were chaperones of the sky but also capable crews. They assured passengers that "the white men in the cabin as well as the cockpit were competent and in control."[59]

When the aisle was turned over to women, the role was reimagined. As the occupation was feminized, the importance of the job was downplayed and the subordinate role of supportive and sometimes sexually playful service was played up. As one flight attendant described it, the job became "part mother, part servant, and part tart."[60]

Just like with cheerleading, there was a decline in status when the steward was replaced by the stewardess. We have seen such changes in response to the feminization or masculinization of many different occupations. Clerical work in the United States, for example, was almost exclusively male until the late 1800s. Typing was considered "too strenuous for women."[61] Later, as it became associated with women, the necessary qualification would be shifted from "arduous labor" to "dexterity."[62] Today most people don't think much of "secretaries," but they were respected enough at one time that we still use the term to refer to high-level government positions like secretary of state.

Because women dominated the ranks of typists in the 1900s, women's support work translated into mathematical analysis, early computer programming, and map-making during World War II. Women were employed by the U.S. government in top secret positions as mathematicians and "compute-ers," workers who operated and supervised computing machines.[63] Women also held 60 percent of the jobs in statistical analysis at the CIA.[64] They were preferred because it was believed that the work required patience, something women supposedly had, thanks to "maternal instinct."

In the '60s, women would dominate computing.[65] "It's just like planning a dinner," explained a female programmer to *Cosmopolitan* magazine in 1967; it "requires patience and the ability to handle detail. Women are 'naturals' at computer programming."[66] Of course, since then the occupation has become associated with men and has risen in both prestige and pay.

More recently, both pharmacy and veterinary science have become feminized; over the last forty years, they have become 54 percent and 51 percent female, respectively. Wages have correspondingly stagnated compared to similar occupations like medicine and law, which have seen less feminization (today at 34 percent and 31 percent female, respectively).[67]

In the 1960s, Melba Roy was assistant chief of research programs at NASA's Trajectory and Geodynamics Division. She also led a collective of NASA mathematicians known as "computers," or people who used machines to compute.

The data are clear: As women enter an occupation, status goes down; as men enter it, status goes up. Because status is connected to the gender of a job, we also find an **androcentric pay scale**, a strong correlation between wages and the gender composition of the job.[68] In fact, according to a study by the Bureau of Labor Statistics, the gender composition of a job is the *single largest contributor* to the gender wage gap.[69] It is more important than level of unionization, marital status, industry, supply and demand, the safety or comfort of the work, and workers' education and experience. Even controlling for all these things, "women's work" pays, on average, anywhere between 5 percent and 21 percent less than "men's work."[70] The effect grows larger as occupations become increasingly male or female dominated.

If there is an androcentric pay scale, then we should expect male-dominated jobs to be among the highest paying. They are. Consider Figure 12.3, which lists all American occupations (for which there is reliable demographic

These IBM computers look unusual and outdated to our modern eyes, but the female technicians may also seem surprising given our myth of progress on all fronts for women. The rising
status of computer sciences is associated with a falling share of women in this field.

data) that pay, on average, over $100,000 a year.[71] In the rightmost columns, we
include the gender and race composition of these high-paying jobs, from most to
least male-dominated. Since men make up 53 percent of the workforce, any job
that is more than 53 percent male is disproportionately so, or more male than
we would expect by chance alone. Likewise, since 68 percent of the workforce
identifies as white, any job that is more than 68 percent white is disproportionately so.

Figure 12.3 shows that twenty of the twenty-five highest-paying occupations
are more than 53 percent male and ten are more than 75 percent male. All but
three of these occupations—computer hardware engineer, software developer,
and medical/health professor—are disproportionately white. The five jobs that
are dominated by women are all dominated by white women. In the last chapter
we introduced the idea of the feminization of poverty; we might call the concentration of men in high-earning occupations a **masculinization of wealth**.[72]

Importantly, instead of reflecting a reality about the value of work done by
men and women, the androcentric pay scale reflects a deep-seated cultural belief that the things men do are more valuable and deserve higher pay than the
things women do.[73] That is, the pay scale is not gendered because these occupations just happen to be ones that require more education, skill, or experience.

FIGURE 12.3 | GENDER AND RACE COMPOSITION OF THE HIGHEST-PAYING JOBS IN THE UNITED STATES

Occupation	Avg Annual Wage	% Male	% White
Aircraft pilot	$111,960	96%	90%
Aerospace engineer	$104,810	91%	80%
Engineering professor	$100,100	90%	74%
Architect/engineering manager	$133,240	89%	86%
Computer hardware engineer	$103,980	85%	64%
Chief executive	$176,840	83%	87%
Chemical engineer	$102,270	82%	78%
Mathematician	$101,280	82%	80%
Software developer	$102,550	80%	61%
Dentist	$166,910	76%	86%
Geoscientist	$106,780	74%	90%
Computer/IT manager	$129,130	73%	74%
Financial services sales agent	$100,910	72%	79%
General and operations manager	$114,850	71%	80%
Lawyer	$130,880	69%	87%
Physician/surgeon	$190,060	66%	69%
Law professor	$115,500	62%	85%
Judge or magistrate	$102,470	61%	82%
Political scientist	$104,600	60%	87%
Medical/health professor	$100,370	58%	49%
Advertising/promotions manager	$121,150	51%	79%
Purchasing manager	$106,200	49%	77%
Financial manager	$123,260	46%	75%
Pharmacist	$114,950	46%	70%
Human resources manager	$109,590	28%	77%

Source: Bureau of Labor Statistics 2013; APSA 2011; AALS 2009; AAMC 2012; AMS 2009; Blue et al. 2005[74]

On the contrary, even when we hold these things constant, the gender composition of a job plays an important role in determining wages.

The Value of Gendered Work

Do flight attendants have skills?

Most people seriously underestimate what flight attendants are trained to do. Flight attendants learn hundreds of regulations and the safety features of multiple types of airplanes. They know how to evacuate a plane on land or sea within ninety seconds; fight fires 35,000 feet in the air; keep a heart attack or stroke victim alive; calm or restrain an anxious, aggressive, or mentally ill passenger; respond to hijackings and terrorist attacks; communicate effectively with people who are frozen in fear; and survive in the case of a crash landing in the jungle, sea, desert, or arctic. As one flight attendant said: "I don't think of myself as a sex symbol or a servant. I think of myself as somebody who knows how to open the door of a 747 in the dark, upside down, and in the water."[75]

Flight attendants are doing a job that is supposed to remain invisible unless needed. One flight attendant described it like this:

> I have an outer appearance of calm and reserve. I look relaxed, professional and ready to serve the passengers' needs.... But what they don't see are my antennae, which are always raised for something out of the ordinary. You always have to be ready for an emergency—something with another crew member, passenger has an epileptic attack, emergency landing. I could go on and on.[76]

In 2013 an Asiana flight crash-landed at San Francisco International Airport. While the survival of all but two of the 307 passengers was called a "miracle," the survival rate was in no small part thanks to the flight attendants on board. They successfully enacted the protocol for a ninety-second evacuation, despite two slides that didn't correctly deploy. As passengers were fleeing the wreckage, some flight attendants fought the rising flames while others hacked trapped passengers out of their seatbelts with knives. They carried injured passengers out on their backs. "I wasn't really thinking, but my body started carrying out the steps needed for an evacuation," explained Lee Yoon Hye, one of the flight attendants. "I was only thinking about rescuing the next passenger."[77] Later she learned that she had sustained a broken tailbone.

Even when survival is unlikely, many flight attendants take their job gravely seriously. As one flight attendant said:

> If we were going to make a ditching in water, the chances of our surviving are slim, even though we know exactly what to do. But I think I would probably—and I think I can say this for most of my fellow flight attendants—be able to keep [the passengers] from being too worried about it. I mean my voice might quiver a little during the announcements, but somehow I feel we could get them to believe ... the best.[78]

Many lives have been saved, and many final moments have been less filled with sheer terror, thanks to well-trained and effective flight attendants who are committed to doing their job well—if necessary, until the bitter end.

Airlines, though, are loath to reveal the intense and ongoing emergency, security, first-aid, combat, and survival training that flight attendants receive. Talking about the "live fire pit" and "ditching pool" used for training might remind passengers of the potential dangers of air travel.[79] It's much better for airlines if we think that flight attendants are just "sky waitresses" and, if we're lucky, we will never be in a situation in which their skills and knowledge become suddenly and terrifyingly apparent.

So, many of the skills that flight attendants have are invisible to most of us most of the time, both by circumstance and design. Meanwhile, we tend to dismiss the work we see as unskilled. Early airlines hired women for their extraordinary beauty, grace, and charm. They were to have a "modest but friendly smile," be "alert, attentive, not overly aggressive, but not reticent either," "outgoing but not effusive," "enthusiastic with calm and poise," and "vivacious but not effervescent."[80] No problem, right? All women *don't* naturally have these skills; that's why flight attendants were valorized as the perfect women.

The job isn't as glamorous as it used to be, but this just means that flight attendants have to work even harder to soothe passengers, who also notice that air travel isn't as glamorous as it used to be. Contemporary flight attendants increasingly interact with tired, frustrated, and uncomfortable passengers, some of whom are nasty or abusive. We call this part of the job **emotion work**, the act of controlling one's own emotions and managing the emotions of others. Flight attendants are tasked with seamlessly performing the proper emotions in interaction with an impossibly wide range of people who bring their own, often negative emotions to the moment. And, thousands of feet up in the air, there is no manager to ask for help or call for backup. Trying to summarize the job, one flight attendant said:

> *[It] requires judgment, ingenuity, skill, and independence in an area of the most difficult sort—not handling inanimate and usually predictable machinery—but large numbers of human beings of all ages, walks of life, varied national and racial backgrounds, under panic conditions.*[81]

And one has to be nice about it. One stewardess described having to "force a drunk passenger in the back of the cabin to sit down and stop throwing cigarette butts on the floor *with gentleness*."[82] Another explained how she managed the problem of sexual harassment without offending her customer: "[I]t is better to avoid confrontation. If someone puts their hand on your bottom, you should say, 'Excuse me, sir, but my bottom accidentally fell into your hand.'"[83]

These are impressive interpersonal talents. "Even when people are paid to be nice," wrote one scholar studying this kind of emotion work, "it is hard for them to be nice at all times, and when their efforts succeed, it is a remarkable accomplishment."[84] Or, as one flight attendant put it: "We, basically, are the best actors and actresses in the world. We should get Academy Awards every month."[85]

Undeniably, these skills are also *valuable* resources for the airlines. Yet airlines have historically framed their flight attendants' performances in the cabin as "natural." As historian Kathleen Barry explains:

> *[A]irlines' favorite metaphor for stewardesses' work was that they were playing gracious hostess to guests in one's own home, which suggested their efforts were a natural, voluntary expression of female domesticity and of social rather than economic value.*[86]

The work of flight attendants, in other words, was defined as *outside the realm of work*. If being nice just comes naturally, then the flight attendants are just being themselves. And we don't pay people just to be themselves, right? To say that because women are naturally good at something, they needn't be compensated for it, is a great example of benevolent sexism, something we'll discuss in more detail later in the chapter.

Being a flight attendant is considered "women's work," and work that women disproportionately do is often framed as natural to the female sex, understood to be "part of what women *are* rather than what women *do*."[87] In contrast, "men's work" is considered skilled work almost by definition. Stereotypes of men include being good with their hands, talented at understanding how things work, and steadfast behind the wheel. If we were inclined to devalue these skills, we could argue that it was only natural that men would become surgeons, engineers, and truck drivers. Given the opportunity, the logic would go, they would do these things anyway because that's just how they *are*; we'll pay them for their time, but it's ridiculous to argue that these are *skills*.

That is, in fact, exactly how "women's work" is frequently understood. Soothing an autistic child, organizing twenty kindergarteners, making middle-school kids care about literature, ensuring that a boss's day runs smoothly, and carefully monitoring the health of an elderly patient at their home all require knowledge, skill, concentration, effort, creativity, problem solving, and emotion work. But we have learned to think of these activities as unworthy of compensation as skilled labor.

If jobs filled by women are devalued in part because of their association with women, then we should expect these jobs to pay less than jobs associated with men. They do. Consider Figure 12.4, which lists all American occupations (for which there is reliable demographic data) that pay, on average, under $22,000 a year.[88] In the right-most columns, we include the gender and race composition of these low-paying jobs. Since women make up 47 percent of the workforce, any job that is more than 47 percent female is disproportionately so. Likewise, since 32 percent of the workforce identifies as a racial minority, any job that is more than 32 percent minority is more so than we would expect by chance alone.

More than two-thirds of the (sixteen of twenty-three) lowest-paying occupations are disproportionately female; six are more than three-fourths female. The remainder of the jobs—the ones not disproportionately held by women—are filled by men, but not white men. With the exception of automotive service workers (the guys at Jiffy Lube, for instance), all of the lowest-paying jobs in America are disproportionately staffed by racial minority women (in twelve occupations) or, barring that, mostly women or racial minorities (in three and six occupations, respectively).

The devaluation of feminized occupations is especially acute for **care work**, work that involves face-to-face caretaking of the physical, emotional, and edu-

FIGURE 12.4 | GENDER AND RACE COMPOSITION OF THE LOWEST-PAYING JOBS IN THE UNITED STATES

Occupation	Avg Yearly Wage	% Female	% Minority
Child care worker	$21,310	95%	39%
Manicurist/pedicurist	$21,440	93%	35%
Maid and housekeeping	$21,820	88%	61%
Home health aide	$21,830	88%	53%
Restaurant host/hostess	$19,570	82%	30%
Personal care aide	$20,830	78%	51%
Cashier	$20,370	72%	34%
Food concession/cafeteria worker	$19,430	71%	32%
Waiter/waitress	$20,710	71%	35%
Fast food preparation and service	$18,720	65%	35%
Hotel/motel desk clerk	$21,960	65%	43%
Bartender	$21,630	60%	22%
Food preparation worker	$20,910	58%	45%
Garment and textile worker	$20,730	54%	68%
Laundry/dry cleaning worker	$21,540	54%	67%
Lifeguards/ski patrol	$20,720	53%	18%
Amusement park attendant	$20,020	46%	37%
Bartender helper	$19,690	44%	47%
Cook	$21,240	38%	54%
Farmworkers and laborer	$19,990	20%	53%
Dishwasher	$18,930	19%	59%
Parking lot attendant	$21,540	12%	64%
Automotive service workers	$21,600	9%	31%

Source: Bureau of Labor Statistics, "Labor Force Statistics from the Current Population Survey: Table 11: Employed persons by detailed occupation, sex, race, and Hispanic or Latino ethnicity," retrieved 7/13/13: http://www.bls.gov/cps/cpsaat11.htm; Bureau of Labor Statistics, "Occupational Employment Statistics: May 2013 National Occupational Employment and Wage Estimates: United States," April 1, 2014, http://www.bls.gov/oes/current/oes_nat.htm

cational needs of others: children, the elderly, the sick, and the disabled. These jobs are paid *even less* than other feminized jobs, holding education and skill constant.[89] Consider the job of child care. In 2012, the average yearly income for child care workers was $21,310. Only twenty-two of the 800 jobs listed by the Bureau of Labor Statistics had lower annual wages; 99.5 percent of jobs in America pay better.[90] You know who's paid more than the people who are taking care of children? People who take care of coats in the coat check, parked cars, broken bicycles, dry cleaning, motel reservations, and road kill.

We tend to think that masculine work is, literally, more valuable. This is not because men simply have more valuable skill sets; it's because skill itself is an abstract good that must be socially constructed. When jobs are filled by members of groups that occupy the tops of hierarchies, their social status will rub off on the work they do. This has been tested empirically.[91] Psychologist Lynn Liben and two colleagues asked ten- and eleven-year-olds to rate the status of fake jobs like "cilpster" (a person who tests batteries) and "heigist" (a person who ensures water quality).[92] The children who were told that these jobs were performed by men gave them higher status rankings than the children who were told they were done primarily by women. In other studies, college students asked to rank the prestige of jobs will rank them lower if they are told that the occupation is feminizing and higher if they're told it's masculinizing.[93] As Paul Attewell explains, "the social standing and perceived skill of an occupation stems in large part from the power of those workers rather than from the intrinsic complexity of the work itself."[94]

This phenomenon is androcentric, not purely sexist, so both men and women can lose prestige and income when they enter a feminine occupation. Women working in predominantly female occupations earn 26 percent less than women working in mostly male ones; men pay a similar price.[95] It also explains the pay gaps between heterosexual and homosexual women and men.[96] Openly gay and bisexual men are more likely to go into feminized occupations and openly gay and bisexual women into masculinized ones. Gay and bisexual men earn about 30 percent less than heterosexual men, whereas gay and bisexual women earn about 20 percent more than their heterosexual sisters.

Job segregation contributes to the gender pay gap because both men and women—whether they're employers or workers—tend to attribute more value to "men's work" than "women's work." An occupation disproportionately filled

Elise Ross, a clinical nurse in Washington, DC, is part of a profession that is believed to come naturally to women, thus justifying the perception of the occupation as less skilled than equally difficult but masculinized jobs.

by women is seen as *legitimately* lower paid than an occupation dominated by men. Because of this, job segregation doesn't just create a differentiated workforce, it creates an unequal one. Feminized occupations filled by women are generally lower paid than masculinized occupations filled by men, especially if these jobs involve caring for others.

Job segregation explains a large part of the pay gap, but not all of it. Women are not just paid less than men overall, they are also paid less than men *in the same occupations*. This discrepancy suggests that other factors are at play, notably sexism and facts and fictions about parenting.

DISCRIMINATION AND PREFERENTIAL TREATMENT

Thanks to the Civil Rights Act of 1964, it's no longer *legal* to discriminate based on gender, but discrimination didn't simply vanish. Enforcing the new law meant going to court, proving the existence of discrimination and the intent to discriminate, and creating consequences. It took decades for the hundreds of cases filed by flight attendants, for example, to make their way through the courts. The last marriage ban was struck down in 1970; routine weigh-ins for female (but not male) members of the cabin crew were standard as late as the 1990s.[97]

Today, flight attendants still deal with sexual objectification from coworkers and passengers as well as bosses who police their bodies.[98] Sexual harassment from passengers is just a "hazard of the job," according to one flight attendant.[99] Some pilots also continue to see flight attendants as a source of sexual titillation and pleasure to which they're entitled. In 2011 a pilot hoping to "get lucky" on his layover was caught on tape complaining to his co-pilot that the flight attendants assigned to his flight were "[e]leven fucking over-the-top fucking, ass-fucking homosexuals and a granny."[100] And, yes, there is a pay gap in this profession: Female flight attendants make $0.89 for every dollar made by their male counterparts.[101]

Today's female flight attendants are paid less *even when doing the same job*. This is true for almost every occupation in the United States. Figure 12.5 shows the wage gap in the most common occupations for men and women, ranked from smallest difference in pay (among customer service representatives) to the largest (among retail salespersons).

Gender discrimination certainly accounts for some of the wage gap within occupations. If this sounds implausible, consider the stories of people who have been both a man and a woman in the workplace. Sociologist Kristen Schilt interviewed twenty-nine transmen, people who had transitioned from

FIGURE 12.5 | WOMEN'S EARNINGS FOR EVERY DOLLAR OF MEN'S IN THE 10 MOST COMMON OCCUPATIONS FOR WOMEN AND MEN*

Occupation	Cents/Men's Dollar
Customer service representative	95¢
Registered nurse	95¢
Administrative assistant	93¢
Cook	93¢
Cashier	86¢
Teacher, elementary and middle school	86¢
Manager, administrative assistants	84¢
Home health care aide	83¢
Laborers, freight, stock, and material movers	82¢
Janitor	81¢
Manager, other	80¢
Manager, retail sales	78¢
Salesperson, wholesale and manufacturing	75¢
Truck driver	74¢
Salesperson, retail	71¢

* Some of the most common occupations for men are also the most common for women, so the total number of occupations is less than 20.

Source: Ariane Hegewisch, Claudia Williams, and Amber Henderson. 2011. "Fact Sheet: The Gender Wage Gap: 2010." Institute for Women's Policy Research. http://www.iwpr.org/publications/pubs/the-gender-wage-gap-by-occupation-updated-april-2011.

female to male. Two-thirds—especially those who were white and tall— reported that they received a post-transition advantage at work. Trevor, for instance, found that his ideas were taken more seriously: "[A] woman would make a comment or observation and be overlooked. . . . I would raise my hand and make the same point. . . . and it would be like, 'That's an excellent point!'"[102] Crispin, who worked at Home Depot, said that customers would dismiss his expertise when he was a she, but he now found that his advice was heartily welcomed. Henry said that he was suddenly "right a lot more" than he had been before.[103]

As a result of being perceived as more competent and productive, transmen said they could do less work and still get more credit than they did when they were female. If they wanted, they could be less nice and suffer no consequences. Keith said that behavior that was perceived as overly "assertive" when he was a woman was seen as "take charge."[104] Preston explained that before his transition, his bosses and coworkers often dragged their feet when it came to getting him what he needed to do his job. Since his transition, things have changed: "I swear it was like from one day to the next of me transitioning [to male], I need this, this is what I want and [snaps his fingers]. I have not had to fight about anything."[105] Thomas told a story that sums it up: After his transition, a client commended his boss for firing "Susan" and hiring the "new guy" who was "just delightful!" Of course, Thomas *was* Susan.[106]

Because of discrimination of this sort, women and men continue to turn to the courts for justice. Many private companies and public service sectors have lost or settled gender-based class action lawsuits in the last ten years, including Abercrombie & Fitch, Albertson's, Bell Canada, Best Buy, Boeing, Coca-Cola, Goodyear, Heald College, Hewlett-Packard, Home Depot, the International Longshoremen's Union, Los Alamos National Laboratory, Merrill Lynch, Metropolitan Life Insurance Company, Mitsubishi Motors, Morgan Stanley, Novartis Pharmaceuticals, Outback Steakhouse, Publix Supermarkets, Smith Barney/Citigroup, State Farm Insurance, Wachovia, Wal-Mart, Wells Fargo, United Airlines, Union Pacific Railroad, the Federal Bureau of Investigation, and the Mint. Clearly, sexism is still prevalent in the workplace.

Scholars have identified three forms that sexism takes in the workplace: hostile and benevolent sexism, a double bind for women, and preferences for men.

Hostile and Benevolent Sexism

Discrimination against women sometimes takes the form of hostile sexism. Some men feel like women should stay in the home or shouldn't be doing men's work. A female electrician, Kay, faced hostile sexism from one of her coworkers:

> [He] told me that in other countries the women know their place and that I was taking a good paying job away from a man and that I should be at home taking care of my kids. . . . He said maybe I should move to another cunt'ry.[107]

Sometimes hostile sexism takes the form of isolation or deliberate carelessness that puts women at physical risk. Female construction workers report being put in dangerous positions, such as being forced to do "two-man" jobs all by themselves just to prove they can do it.[108] Such women are in lose-lose situations: If they try to prove they can "work like a man," they end up doing the dirtiest work or getting hurt. If they refuse to do that kind of work, they get accused of demanding "special treatment."

In other cases, women are seen as interrupting the boys-will-be-boys collegiality that makes working in male-dominated occupations fun for some men. The Los Angeles Fire Department is currently facing a class-action lawsuit brought by the 3 percent of their firefighters who are female—more than 80 percent of whom have allegedly experienced or observed sexual harassment.[109] A male captain explained that when women were on duty, the firefighters couldn't do "locker room stuff" like look at pornography or ogle attractive women from the fire truck. Their resentment sometimes manifests as hostile sexism.

In extreme cases women are targeted sexually.[110] One of the female firefighters suing the city of Los Angeles refused to have sex with a coworker who crept into her bed while she was asleep on an overnight shift at the station. She reported that he "taunted her for weeks" for refusing his advances. Other women are retaliated against or fired when they refuse to engage in sexual contact. Some women become victims of sexual violence. Women who don't perform the feminine apologetic by balancing their appropriation of masculinity with a performance of femininity are even more likely to be targeted than women who do. This suggests that sexual harassment is a way for men to reassert their dominance, rather than just a harmless show of attraction.[111]

In these instances, women are a **symbolic threat**; their presence potentially degrades the identity of the dominant group. Female construction workers, firefighters, and other women in masculinized occupations present a symbolic threat to men in their trades insofar as the men's self-esteem comes, in part, from being a man doing men's work. This fear is not without justification. We know that pay does in fact go down when women enter a profession in significant numbers and that men in those jobs are not protected from the drop in status that comes with feminization.

Not all discrimination is hostile; discrimination in the workforce can also take a more benevolent form. In this case, men who believe they're being chivalrous try to protect women from unpleasant, dirty, confrontational, dangerous, or otherwise unfeminine activities and, in doing so, end up undermining women's career trajectories. Cynthia, a construction worker, described how her coworker behaved toward her at work and what she did about it:

> One journeyman treated me more like his wife because he pampers his wife. [He would say:] "Don't carry this and don't carry that." I started getting in this rut of standing at the bottom of the ladder handing him tools. So one day, I said this is such crap, I've got to do something. I just started doing everything before he had a chance. I'd grab the ladder and make him do the light work. I said, "Let me do some work, I'm an electrician."[112]

Jenny had a similar experience: "They just don't want me to do the work because they're afraid I'm going to get hurt," she explained.[113] Benevolent sexists hurt female employees when their "protection" gets in the way of them learning their job or demonstrating their skills.

Of course, not all men exhibit sexist behavior at work and, even among those who do, some are more aggressive or persistent than others.[114] On average, men with housewives at home are more likely to be discriminatory. Unfortunately for women, it is these men who are also disproportionately the bosses, officers, and managers who have the power to shape careers. A few particularly sexist superiors—whether they're the benevolent or the hostile type—can significantly harm a woman's career, even if she is generally surrounded by supportive colleagues of both sexes. The composition of the workplace matters, too. Employees of companies that employ a higher proportion of women are generally more likely to believe that their female colleagues are just as capable as their male ones.[115] The presence of high-status female managers also makes a difference, bringing down the pay gap between men and women in their companies.[116]

In male-dominated occupations, women not only have to deal with hostile and benevolent sexism; they also have to contend with the idea that women just aren't as suited as men for these occupations, a sentiment often shared by men and women alike.

The Double Bind

Women in masculine occupations often suffer from the perception that they're just not quite right for the job. Traits seen as ideal in male-dominated occupations are seen as inherently male. Some attorneys, for example, will describe litigators in gendered terms. Being a lawyer is a "male thing," they say; it's "men beating each other up."[117] Ineffective attorneys are described as "impotent" or, simply, as "having no balls." If we use male terms to describe competent employees, then it shouldn't be a surprise that descriptions of a successful business leader overlap more with descriptions of the typical man than the typical woman.[118] Indeed, both men and women report preferring male bosses and respond more negatively when female superiors offer feedback.[119]

This isn't just about androcentrism (preferring masculine traits and choosing men because they are believed to be more likely to possess them), it's about sexism: Men are seen as better leaders and supervisors no matter what qualities are considered ideal for the job. In one study, participants rated two hypothetical candidates for the job of police chief: one named Michael and the other Michelle.[120] When Michael was described as "streetwise" and Michelle as "formally educated," participants recommended hiring Michael on the basis that he was tough, a risk taker, and physically fit. When Michelle was described as streetwise, however, they *still* recommended Michael, this time on the basis that he was well-educated, able to communicate with the media, and politically connected. In other words, participants moved the goalposts in order to ensure that, whatever the qualifications, Michael was seen as more qualified than Michelle. Both men and women exhibited this bias, but men more so than women.

If a job is associated with men, then women will face a contrast between the normative worker in that occupation and who they are. This is the double bind discussed in our chapter about inequality: To be successful at her job, a woman needs to do masculinity, but to be accepted by her boss, colleagues, and clients, she needs to do femininity.[121] Each undermines the other. Feminine women are seen as likeable but incompetent, while women who do masculinity are seen as competent but not likeable.

Accordingly, studies show that women who act confident in their abilities, ask for raises and promotions, and negotiate with their bosses are evaluated less positively than women who don't and men who do.[122] One study examined how people responded to hypothetical men and women who expressed anger (considered an appropriate emotion for men) or sadness (appropriate for women) after losing a client because a colleague was late to a meeting.[123] The angry male was evaluated most favorably, followed by the sad female, the sad male and, lastly and least, the angry female. They saw the angry woman as "out of control," but considered the angry man to be legitimately upset. Asked to attribute a salary to each, participants offered the angry woman $0.62 on the angry man's dollar. Likewise, whereas men who negotiate their salary or make a case for a raise are sometimes evaluated negatively, studies find that women who do the same are evaluated far more negatively. One study found that women were penalized 5.5 times more than men and it didn't matter if they demanded or asked nicely.[124] So women are damned if they do and damned if they don't.

Invisible Obstructions

Together, these findings—the presence of hostile and benevolent sexism and the double bind—are behind the **glass ceiling** concept, the idea that there is an invisible barrier between women and top positions in masculine occupations. Women simply don't get tapped for training, mentorship, or promotions as often as men. One study of 4,143 graduates from international business schools found a pay gap of $31,258 per year, with men twice as likely to be at the senior executive level.[125] The gender difference emerged right away. Men, on average, entered the workforce at a higher rank with a better salary. Men advanced and saw their pay rise more quickly. These findings were true even when researchers accounted for the number of years in the workforce, the industry they worked in, their geographical location, whether they had children, the strategies they used for advancement, whether they aspired to be CEO, and whether they worked in a nonprofit, government, or educational setting. Even very successful businesswomen feel the strain: Nearly three-quarters of successful female executives at Fortune 1000 companies agree that gender stereotypes are a barrier to women's success.[126]

When women do break through the glass ceiling, they often encounter a **glass cliff**, a heightened risk of failing, compared with similar men.[127] This is not because women are unsuited for leadership; rather, it's because women tend to be promoted during times of company crisis and given jobs that have a higher risk of failure. This phenomenon has been shown in both experiments and in real life contexts as wide-ranging as funeral homes, music festivals, political elections, and law. Because of the glass cliff, the average tenure of a female CEO is 4.8 years, about 60 percent as long as that of the 8.2-year tenure of the average male CEO.[128]

The glass cliff phenomenon probably sounds strange: If women are seen as less capable than men, why would companies promote women in times of crisis? The answer has less to do with how managers feel about women than it does with how they feel about their male coworkers. When decision makers are predominantly male, they may make efforts to ensure that men with whom they feel chummy get the cushier, easier, and more secure positions. The bad jobs are then given to whoever is left over: typically women and racial minorities of both sexes.[129] This was the experience of one female Marine Corps officer: "It's the good old boys network. The guys helping each other out and we don't have the women helping each other out because there are not enough of us around. The good old boys network put the guys they want to get promoted in certain jobs to make them stand out, look good."[130]

When women succeed in precarious positions, and they often do, their reward is often to be put in charge of another fragile project. Many women, faced with a revolving door of failing assignments, eventually do fail. Or they burn out from stress and leave the occupation. In fact, while we often hear the claim that women "opt out" of high-pressure jobs because they want to spend more time with their families, in real life women cite this as the reason for leaving their jobs only 2 to 3 percent of the time (that is, no more often than men). Dissatisfaction, feelings of underappreciation, blocked opportunities, discrimination, and harassment are much more significant factors for women.[131] If women seem to be less ambitious than men, then, this trait is at least partly explained by the fact that they face barriers at work that men, all things being equal, do not.

This explanation resonates with research on work more generally: Studies show that both women and men in low- or no-mobility positions tend to "limit their aspirations, seek satisfaction in activities outside of work, dream of escape, and create sociable peer groups in which interpersonal relationships take precedence over other aspects of work."[132] People who work in occupations like secretary with little to no chance of promotion often place a higher value on other things in life than their jobs. It is also true of some factory workers, who typically have no chance of promotion especially after age thirty-five; they tend to "work for the weekend," finding pleasure and meaning elsewhere. In contrast, both women and men in high-mobility positions with a significant chance of promotion are "highly motivated and aspire to top management positions."[133]

Preferential Treatment for Men in Female-Dominated Occupations

If women face a double bind when they are integrating a male occupation, then men may face a similar double bind. Likewise, men in female-dominated occupations may suffer from being cut out of the "old girls' club." Perhaps the problem isn't sexism, but being a token or minority in an occupation. If that were the case, we might expect men to face the same struggles as women. It turns out, they do not.

Men in female-dominated occupations are disadvantaged relative to men in male-dominated occupations. Men doing "women's work" often face a great deal of policing from friends and family. Men also suffer from the same depressed wages as women in feminized occupations, but they are not disadvantaged in these occupations relative to their female coworkers. Instead of facing glass ceilings or cliffs, they often face a **glass escalator**: an invisible ride to the top offered to men in female-dominated occupations.[134] In a study of 5,734 secondary and elementary school teachers, all else being equal, men were three times more likely than women to be promoted to administrative positions over a two-year period.[135] A series of studies have found that men in female-dominated occupations are advantaged in terms of pay, promotions, and support from colleagues and supervisors.[136] That is, if they're white; men of color do not appear to ride the glass escalator alongside white men.[137]

Being on a glass escalator isn't always a blessing. Sociologist Christine Williams, who coined the phrase, explained that men often "face invisible pressures to move up in their professions" such that they have to "work to stay in place." She explained how a male librarian, six months after starting his first job, was criticized by his supervisors for "not shooting high enough."[138] "Seriously," he said, "They assumed that because I was a male—and they told me this . . . that somehow I wasn't doing the kind of management-oriented work that they thought I should be doing." He worked in the children's collection for ten years and had to fight the whole time to avoid being promoted; he enjoyed the job he had.

Gender stereotypes are at work here—not only positive ones, like the idea that men are stronger leaders and, therefore, better suited to management and supervisory positions, but negative ones as well, like men aren't *really* good at child care or "we're a little nervous about why a man wants to teach kindergarten, so let's get him into administration."

Men who pursue feminized occupations, then, may face policing from their peers and bring home a lower salary than they would if they were in a male-dominated occupation but, relative to their female colleagues, they will be promoted more quickly and earn more money.[139] This isn't necessarily what all men want, but it does translate into advantages at work and the persistence of the pay gap.

The glass ceiling and the glass cliff conspire to keep men at the top. Women are often good at knowing when to be more masculine and when to be more feminine so as to influence others to see them in a positive light.[140] But this delicate dance is a burden and not all women are equally good at it. Men don't have to do it at all, unless they're marginalized in some other way; then they have their own tightrope to walk. Instead, they benefit from preferential treatment in both male-dominated and female-dominated occupations.[141]

Discrimination against women and preferential treatment for men help explain why women make less money than men even when they're working the same number of hours in the same occupation. This means that job integration would help close the gender pay gap, but it wouldn't close it completely. Expectations surrounding parenthood create an additional set of problems for women and privileges for men.

PARENTHOOD: THE FACTS AND THE FICTION

Before the mid-1960s, stewardesses were contractually required to quit if they got married. The rule reflected the belief that women's primary occupation in life was to tend to their husbands. United Airlines, for example, claimed that married women couldn't possibly continue on as flight attendants because "the irregularity and uncertainty inherent in stewardesses' work schedules were in conflict with the woman's role in married life."[142]

This supposed conflict between work and marriage lives on today in the form of the debate over "work/life balance," a problem that is almost always considered to be a "women's issue." The conflict rests on the incompatibility of two hegemonic cultural ideologies: intensive motherhood, which we discussed in the last chapter, and the **ideal worker norm**, the idea that an employee should have the ability to devote themselves to their job without the distraction of family responsibilities.[143] According to this logic, workers are less than ideal to the extent that they sometimes need time off to do family-related tasks (attend parent-teacher meetings, care for sick children or ailing grandparents, step in when daycare arrangements fall through) or are hindered in their ability to go above and beyond stated job responsibilities (to work late and on weekends, work on short notice, or relocate for the company). Employment, in other words, continues to "operate as if workers have domestic wives" and those who can't work as if they do are lesser workers.[144]

All individuals with family responsibilities (and many without) often find themselves straining to live up to this ideal, but women bear the brunt of the clash between the ideology of intensive motherhood and the ideal worker norm.[145] Because of this, women who have children face a **motherhood penalty**, a loss in wages associated with becoming a mother. In fact, the pay gap between mothers and non-mothers is larger than the one between men and women.[146] One study found that thirty-year-old women without children earn $0.90 for every dollar earned by men, while mothers of the same age earn $0.73.[147] Women who become mothers will experience, on average, a 7 percent decline in their wages for each child.[148] Married women, poor women, and white women face the largest penalties. In contrast, dads receive a **fatherhood premium**, a wage increase that accrues to married men who become fathers.[149] Married fathers earn 4 to 7 percent more than married men without children. Stepfathers, fathers without custody of their kids, racial minorities, and less educated men see a smaller fatherhood premium or none at all.

The motherhood penalty and fatherhood premium are a result of both *how* we divide up the labor of households and employers' *beliefs* about how we do so.

Work and the Division of Household Labor

If a woman has two children three years apart and takes a break from work that lasts from the birth of the first child until the second child enters pre-school, she'll have been out of the workforce for seven years. Those are unpaid years and, when she returns to work, she will be less experienced on the job than a comparable person who didn't take time off. Most women do not take this much time out of the workforce, but women take more than men. One analysis of college graduates ten years post-graduation (that is, women's prime childbearing years) found that 17 percent of women were working part-time and 23 percent were taking a break from the workforce, compared with 2 percent and 1 percent of men, respectively.[150] As discussed in the last chapter, these years leave women at a disadvantage at work.

What happens when a woman goes back to work after having a child also plays a role. Recall that married mothers and fathers have a tendency to specialize: Men do about two-thirds of the paid work and women do about two-thirds of the housework and child care.[151] The burden of the second shift may push some women to disinvest at work. In this case, they may embrace being put on a **mommy track**, a workplace euphemism that refers to expecting less from mothers, with the understanding that they are sacrificing the right to expect equal pay, regular raises, or promotions. So, mothers may put in fewer hours or exert less effort at work than men and non-mothers. They may do so because it's the best division of labor for their family, or the only one their spouse will tolerate, or they may do so because they value time with family more than time at work.

In contrast, fathers often increase their effort at work because they take seriously the idea that they should be breadwinners. This choice likely resonates with their employers' gender ideology. Employers sometimes accept that a woman needs to respond to her children's schedule and take care of emergencies, even if they begrudge them this flexibility. Those same employers often do not accept that men have to do the same. "That's what a wife is for," they might say, or some other woman in his life such as a grandmother or a nanny.[152]

Domestic demands on women's time and men's greater freedom to invest at work are plausible causes of mothers' economic disadvantage compared to fathers and non-mothers. But employers' beliefs about mothers and fathers are likely the most significant contributors to the motherhood penalty/fatherhood premium problem.[153]

Beliefs about Moms and Dads

Even women who maintain high levels of productivity at work may find themselves put on the mommy track. Many employers see mothers as less-than-ideal employees and fathers as especially ideal ones, regardless of how much talent and effort men and women display at work.[154] In fact, mothers *do* put in great amounts of effort at work.[155] Their hard work, however, often goes unrecognized not only because they're women, but because they're moms.

"Men in my office were putting money on the table that I would never show up at work again when the baby was born," said Denise, an assistant marketing director at a technology firm. "I had to prove that when I came back, I was as good as I was when I left. Men were waiting to say, 'I *told* you so.'"[156] Denise's experience reflects a well documented problem faced by many working mothers: Their supervisors and coworkers don't take them seriously as employees.[157] In surveys, mothers' value as workers is ranked as about equivalent to other stigmatized identities: elderly persons and people receiving welfare. And the more motherly they are, the more we devalue them. One study found that respondents judged breastfeeding mothers to be less competent workers than mothers who bottle-feed.[158]

The bias against mothers is reinforced by one in favor of fathers. Sociologist Shelley Correll and her colleagues studied whether individuals reviewing applications for a marketing job would evaluate female and male parents and non-parents differently.[159] They did. Figure 12.6 shows that mothers were considered to be the least hirable and, if hired, worth $11,000 less per year than non-mothers. Mothers were rated as the least competent, committed, promotable, and suited for management training. In contrast, fathers were rated *more* favorably than non-fathers: They were seen as more committed and more likely to be promoted. They were also considered to be worth $6,000 more a year than non-fathers and $13,000 more than mothers.

These are striking findings. Do they hold up in the real world? Yes. Following up, Correll and her colleagues sent 1,276 résumés to 638 employers. Mothers received fewer than half as many callbacks as non-mothers. Fathers were called back at a slightly higher rate than non-fathers. Non-mothers were the most preferred, revealing that a preference for men is not what's driving the data.

FIGURE 12.6 | LIKELIHOOD OF HIRE AND PROPOSED SALARY BY GENDER AND PARENTHOOD STATUS

	% Recommended for Hire	Proposed Salary
Non-Mothers	84%	$148,000
Fathers	73%	$150,000
Non-Fathers	62%	$144,000
Mothers	47%	$137,000

Source: Correll, Shelley, Stephen Benard, and In Paik, "Getting a Job: Is There a Motherhood Penalty?" *American Journal of Sociology* 112, 5 (2007): 1297–1339.

Talking about women's disadvantage relative to men in the workforce, then, threatens to take us somewhat off course; it obscures the fact that women's disadvantage is not rooted in gender alone but is strongly related to the intersection of gender and parenthood. The different career paths of moms and dads are influenced by both gendered practice—how we actually divide up labor—and gender stereotypes related to parenthood.

Revisiting the Question

 If women now have equal protection in the workplace, why aren't they as successful as men at work?

Women are less successful for a complex set of reasons: About 10 percent of the pay gap is explained by differences in job experience due to time spent in and out of the workforce, largely for the purposes of caregiving.[160] Almost half (49 percent) is explained by job segregation and the devaluation of women's work. The remaining 41 percent is likely due to discrimination against women and mothers.

Not all of these factors are present to the same degree in every workplace. Discrimination against women is a larger factor in blue-collar occupations than discrimination against mothers, while the opposite appears to be true in white-collar workplaces.[161] Many supervisors, both male and female, go out of their way to ensure women can compete on equal footing with men. Many women are talented and dedicated enough to overcome at least some of the gendered disadvantages. Still, despite many individual and organizational examples to the contrary, women as a group still face barriers to success at work that men do not.

As a result, women who work full-time earn $0.82 for every dollar earned by comparable men. For the typical woman, that means earning $8,008 less each year. This isn't just problematic *in principle*. For poor women and their families, economic disadvantage translates into *real* deprivation: an inability to pay rent, keep food on the table, or buy their children back-to-school clothes. For more financially secure women, it translates into fewer opportunities and pleasures. With an extra $8,008 a year, a woman could pay the majority of the tuition and fees at her local state college, get a massage every two and a half days for a year, or learn how to fly an airplane.[162] If she invested it, experts predict it'd be worth $43,463 twenty-five years later. If she saved for ten years, $80,080 would be enough to start a small business or put a hefty down payment on a house. Maybe she's not interested in buying a home and settling down. She could use that money to take an entire year off work, maybe two. It's easy to think about the wage gap in purely theoretical terms, but money buys everything but happiness. It matters.

Next . . .

The last few chapters have established that gender inequality is not just a theoretical exercise but a lived experience. Sexism, androcentrism, and subordination play a role in how we understand and express our sexualities, organize and experience our home lives, and pursue our careers and plan for retirement. Gendered ideas, interactions, and institutions structure our lives at every turn, creating both difference and inequality. Gender inequality is clearly not good for women, but it's not ideal for most men either. This is what motivates many people to get involved in changing or conserving the social constructions, interpersonal interactions, and institutions that organize our societies. In the next chapter, we'll ask:

 How do people change societies?

This is politics.

FOR FURTHER READING

Cooper, Marianne. "Being the Go-to Guy: Fatherhood, Work and Masculinity in Silicon Valley." *Qualitative Sociology* 23, no. 4 (2000): 379–405.

Kang, Miliann. "The Managed Hand: The Commercialization of Bodies and Emotions in Korean Immigrant-Owned Nail Salons." *Gender & Society* 17, no. 6 (2003): 820–39.

Kessler-Harris, Alice. "The Wage Conceived: Value and Need as Measures of a Woman's Worth." Pp. 6–32 in *A Woman's Wage: Historical Meanings and Social Consequences.* Lexington: The University of Kentucky Press, 1990.

Stone, Pamela. "The Rhetoric and Reality of 'Opting Out.'" *Contexts* 6, no. 4 (2007): 14–19.

Vendantam, Shankar. "Salary, Gender, and the Social Cost of Haggling." *Washington Post*, July 30, 2007.

FEMINISM IS THE RADICAL NOTION THAT WOMEN ARE PEOPLE.

—MARIE SHEAR[1]

13

Politics

In 1848 a small group of American women made the decision to seek **suffrage**, the right to vote. For most of modern history, governments did not allow women this right, nor the other rights and responsibilities of citizenship—to serve on juries, give legal testimony, or hold public office—and American women were no exception. Many thought the idea was impossible, dangerous, even laughable. Opponents mocked suffragists, suggesting that giving women the vote was as ridiculous as giving it to housecats.

The fight for suffrage was not won quickly or easily, and many suffragists died of old age before they could see their efforts realized. In addition to ridicule, suffragists faced government repression and violence. Most suffragists were peaceful, but some weren't above aggression themselves. One group in the United Kingdom set buildings on fire and learned jujitsu to defend themselves from the police.[2] Over 1,000 suffragists would be imprisoned in the United Kingdom and United States. There they endured brutal force-feeding after initiating hunger strikes that endangered their lives.[3] Their governments were not going to allow them to become martyrs.

The fight for suffrage involved both inspiring coalitions and ugly divides. Many suffragists were **abolitionists** first, activists in the fight against human slavery. White and black men and women

This pro-suffrage cat from around 1908 may look cute, but don't be fooled—it was used to suggest that giving women the vote would be as absurd as extending the right to felines.

worked side by side for this hard-won victory. After slavery was abolished in 1865 and black men were granted suffrage in 1869, black women continued to fight valiantly for their own vote. As abolitionist Sojourner Truth observed: "If colored men get their rights, and colored women not theirs, the colored men will be masters over the women, and it will be just as bad as it was before."[4]

White suffragists often disagreed on whether their efforts should benefit all women or only white women.[5] Anti-suffrage activists tapped into widespread animosity toward black people, reminding a racist public that women's suffrage would not only put women into the voting booth, it would double the black vote. Some suffragist groups were themselves racist, excluding black women from their organizations, activities, or platforms. Many black women started suffrage organizations of their own.

In the 1880s, suffragists around the world were forming alliances and collectively strategizing on how best to win their campaigns. By the early 1900s, this international women's organizing had begun to shift public opinion in their favor. Finland and New Zealand were the first to grant women the right to vote in the 1910s. The United States came around in 1920, giving suffrage to both black and white women together. By then the movement was rolling across the globe. In less than thirty years, women's suffrage became a global norm.[6] As we write this book, only one nation, Saudi Arabia, has not extended the vote to women, though the king has promised female suffrage by 2015.[7]

Today **universal suffrage**, the right of all citizens to vote, is the very definition of democracy. This right is taken for granted, so much so that many people don't even know the word anymore. In the 1800s, however, universal suffrage was a wholly **radical claim**, or an idea that doesn't (yet) resonate with most members of a population.[8] In fact, it was a massively important

The suffragists of Cleveland in 1916 were trying hard to get men to support their cause.

step toward dismantling political systems that recognized some people as full citizens but not others. The concept of universal suffrage was also extraordinarily disruptive to the social order and the distribution of power. It is a testament to the fact that, even when social conditions are stubbornly entrenched and defended by powerful people, change—even radical change—is possible. Our final question, then, is:

 Q+A   How do people change societies?

This chapter is about the politics of gender: how people change and resist change to the gender order. Feminist politics involve efforts to make societies more gender equal. Feminists wrestle with governments and other organizations to this end, but they also struggle with one another. They have always and continue to disagree about what a **feminist utopia**—or a perfectly gender-egalitarian society—might look like and how we should get there. We'll offer an introduction to these topics, but first we'll discuss why feminists are concerned with what governments are doing at all. What is the state and why should we care?

THE STATE

States are institutions entrusted with the power to regulate everyday life on behalf of the group. They are what we, in more ordinary language, refer to as countries or nations. States are important because they wield a greater power than almost any other social entity on earth, second only, perhaps, to global alliances like the United Nations and multinational bodies like the International Monetary Fund. They have vast resources and the exclusive right to pass laws, collect taxes, and detain and imprison citizens. States can even legally wage war according to a set of international rules.

They have not always existed, but today states are the hegemonic way of organizing decision making about group welfare. **Governance** is the process of making decisions for the nation, ensuring the state's accountability to its citizens and enforcing the laws of the land. There are two ways to think about gender and governance.[9] The first involves the **governance of gender**: how gender shapes the way that residents of states are regulated. The second is the **gender of governance**: who holds political office and whether it matters. In this section, we talk about both.

The Governance of Gender

In Japan the birthrate has fallen to 1.4 children per woman, far below the number required to maintain the population. Japanese authorities are in a panic to figure out why. Scholars point to a failure to protect working mothers (70 percent of women quit their job when they become pregnant) and the prohibitive cost of childrearing (2.5 times more expensive than in the United States).[10] There are so few babies that, as one commentator put it, "Sales of adult diapers will soon surpass those of baby diapers."[11] The country is scrambling to institute policies that will encourage families to have more children.

This is very serious business. Population demographics—the numbers of births, balanced by deaths and migration—influence whether a country can feed and educate its citizens, fill its jobs, support its elderly, or fight a war. So we count on states to make decisions that increase the likelihood that just the right number of babies are born.

One such decision involves how enthusiastically to support parenting. Table 13.1 shows the parental leave policies of a sample of states. The far right column is the total number of weeks the state guarantees new parents can take off from their jobs; in most cases, either their employers or the government subsidizes their wages so that parents lose little or no income. The second column from the right shows that states vary in whether their benefits extend to nearly all parents or only those who meet certain employment qualifications.

TABLE 13.1 | NUMBER OF WEEKS OF PARENTAL LEAVE AND PERCENT OF WORKERS COVERED IN SELECT COUNTRIES

Country	Moms only # wks (% of pay)	Dads only # wks (% of pay)	Either or both # wks (% of pay)	Coverage % of pop.	Total # wks
United States	-	-	12 (0)	10–32	12
Philippines	9 (100)	1 (100)	-	68–89	10
India	12 (100)	-	-	<10	12
Nigeria	12 (50)	-	-	<10	12
China	14 (100)	-	-	10–32	14
Kenya	13 (100)	2 (100)	-	10–32	15
S. Africa	17 (80)	<1 (000)	-	33–65	17+
Brazil	17 (100)	1 (100)	-	33–65	18
Mexico	18 (100)	-	-	10–32	18
Chile	18 (100)	1 (100)	6 (100)	66–89	25
Denmark	18 (100)	2 (100)	32 (100)	90–100	52
Australia	-	2 (**)	18 (**) + 34 (0)	66–89	54
Canada	15 (55)* + 2 (0)	-	35 (55)* + 2 (0)	66–89	54
S. Korea	13 (100)	<1 (0)	52 (40)	10–32	65+
Sweden	14 (80)	2 (80)	65 (**) + 15 (0)	90–100	96
Israel	14 (100)*	-	104 (0)	90–100	118
Japan	14 (67)	-	104 (50)*	33–65	128
Germany	14 (100)	-	52 (67) + 104 (**)	66–89	157
France	16 (100)*	2 (100)	26 (**) + 130 (0)	66–89	174
Poland	26 (100)	2 (100)	26 (60) + 130 (**)	90–100	184

*But only to a certain income level.
**Pay isn't a percent of income but is instead based on a flat rate or the minimum wage.
Source: International Labour Organization. 2014. Maternity and Paternity at Work: Law and Practice across the World. ilo.org/publns, accessed July 31, 2014.

The United States is on the low end, guaranteeing that new parents can take twelve weeks off work, if they can afford to do so without pay, and that benefit is available to less than a third of citizens (those who work part-time, for example, or for small companies are excluded).

States do other things to encourage parenthood, too. Finland, for example, gives each new mother a "baby box" worth about $700, filled with diapers, baby

This government-sponsored billboard in the capital city of Qinghai province in western China exalts the country's one-child policy, suggesting that a family with a mother, a father, and a single child leads to happiness and prosperity.

clothes, crib sheets, and other goods. France offers an incentive by providing day care at virtually no cost.

China had the opposite problem, inspiring the government to implement the infamous "one-child policy." Though the policy has been loosened recently, a significant proportion of China's urban population is still allowed only one child by the government.[12] Other countries facing overpopulation use incentives instead of legal penalties and coercion. India distributes material encouraging couples to have just one child and offers money in return for undergoing sterilization.

It matters whether people have babies, but states need people to work, too. A productive economy needs workers so states can collect taxes to fund everything from space exploration to Social Security. They try to both promote and limit participation in the workforce. They may limit the workweek, specify overtime rates, enforce retirement ages, and safeguard unionization (or not). States can also protect corporate profits by setting a low minimum wage, then subsidizing family incomes when wages are too low to meet basic costs. Social services like Medicaid, low-income housing, child-care waivers, and supplemental nutrition programs, or "food stamps," keep employees afloat when their wages are too low to do so.

States govern in gendered ways. Today they typically do so with a balance of incentives and disincentives that don't *specifically* apply differently to men and women but have gendered *effects* because we live in a gendered society.

The race and gender of these demonstrators, who are protesting their low wages on the corporate campus of McDonald's, reflect the composition of the working poor today. The minimum wage has lost so much purchasing power that even a full-time job won't keep families with children out of poverty.

In other words, these policies support some visions of the gender order but not others. As we discussed previously, tax laws allow upper-class families with a single breadwinner to keep more of their money than families with dual breadwinners. This tax break, which offers an incentive for parents to specialize in paid or unpaid work rather than share in both, thus promotes the breadwinner/housewife model of marriage.

In contrast, current welfare policy in the United States discourages poor single mothers from staying home, requiring them to work to remain eligible for benefits. This means that state policy encourages high-income women to choose stay-at-home motherhood, but discourages it among low-income mothers. Regardless of whether you think poor mothers should work, it might be surprising that state policy encourages one kind of mothering for poor kids and another for wealthier ones. Simultaneously, the state strongly associates fatherhood with economic support, facilitating breadwinning among high-income men with tax incentives and aggressively pursuing "child support"—defined only as money—from low-income men.[13]

Family and work represent two vital policy arenas, but the state intervenes in gendered ways in essentially every area of life. Accordingly, feminists are interested in using the state to enhance equality between men and women and ensure that it doesn't make inequality worse. Feminists press the state to commit to gender equality with explicit policies, like the Civil Rights Act prohibiting

FIGURE 13.1 | MINIMUM-WAGE WORKERS, 2013

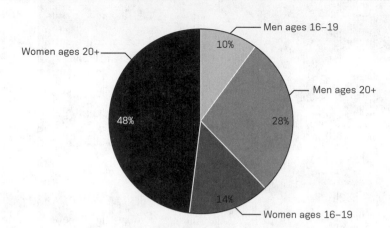

Source: Bureau of Labor Statistics. 2013. "Characteristics of Minimum Wage Workers, 2013."
http://www.bls.gov/cps/minwage2013.pdf, accessed 6/13/14.

discrimination, but they are also concerned with the *unintended* gendered effects of policies. In other words, they are interested in things that are obviously about gender (like sexual assault laws and access to birth control), but also things that are less obviously so. The minimum wage, for instance, is unmistakably a class issue, but because nearly two-thirds of minimum-wage workers are women, it's also a feminist one. Leaving the minimum wage low contributes to the feminization of poverty, while raising it would disproportionately improve women's financial situations and reduce economic inequality between women and men.

Ideally, most feminists want politicians to commit to **gender-aware policymaking** in which consideration of the effects on both men and women—and different kinds of men and women—is a required part of the policymaking process. Vienna offers a successful example of this practice. City planners considered gender when reorganizing their public transit system and discovered that it was organized around the needs of male commuters.[14] The typical woman had more diverse transit needs that included shopping, taking children to school and doctor appointments, and getting to work and back again at more irregular times. To make the transit system friendlier to the typical woman, the city instituted zoning rules to minimize distances among housing, stores, and medical clinics, and scheduled more trains and busses during the day.

These changes not only reduced the isolation and stress of mothers, but also addressed the needs of "atypical" men: single or stay-at-home dads or men who are retired, disabled, or unemployed. They helped men because the system wasn't *really* organized around men to begin with; it was organized around the *stereotype* of a privileged man.

Decisions made to help women often also make life a little easier for other people who don't meet the hegemonic ideal. Curb cuts in sidewalks, for instance, the tiny "driveways" at crosswalks, help people pushing strollers, disproportionately women, but also help people in wheelchairs, those riding bikes, and people who need to pull rolling carts or suitcases instead of carrying bags or backpacks.

Gender continues to be an afterthought in U.S. policy, but it has become less so elsewhere. The European Union adopted gender-aware policymaking, which they call gender mainstreaming, almost twenty years ago. The programs of the United Nations—from peacekeeping operations to refugee support—now give attention to gender as a matter of official policy.[15]

States intervene in gender relations both on purpose and by accident. The choices made by our political representatives affect the extent to which we must conform to the gender binary, live gendered lives, and struggle with inequality. This is why early American women wanted the right to vote, and it continues to motivate women to get involved in politics today.

The Gender of Governance

More women hold political office than ever before. Across the world, the percentage of women in **legislatures**—bodies elected to represent their constituents in regulating the affairs of the country—ranges from 0 to 50 percent. Table 13.2 shows the rise in the number of female politicians over time. The countries most inclusive of women are those with highly egalitarian approaches to gender (such as the Scandinavian countries) and states where wars have

TABLE 13.2 | HISTORICAL COMPARISON OF THE PERCENTAGE OF WOMEN IN POLITICS ACROSS REGIONS

Region	Percent Women in Legislatures						
	1955	1965	1975	1985	1995	2005	2013
United States	3%	2%	4%	5%	11%	15%	18%
Scandinavia	10%	9%	16%	28%	34%	38%	41%
Western Industrial*	4%	4%	6%	9%	13%	23%	27%
Latin America	3%	3%	5%	8%	10%	17%	20%
Africa	1%	3%	5%	8%	10%	16%	21%
Eastern Europe	17%	18%	25%	27%	8%	16%	20%
Asia	5%	5%	3%	6%	9%	15%	18%
Middle East	1%	1%	3%	4%	4%	8%	13%

Includes the United States; does not include Scandinavian countries.
Source: Paxton, P., Kunovich, S., and M. Hughes. "Gender in Politics," *Annual Review of Sociology* 33 (263–284), 2007.[16]

left many men dead and discredited their leadership (as in Rwanda and Sierra Leone). In these types of countries, women represent about 40 percent of members of legislatures.[17]

The United States has not been a global leader in this regard.[18] As of 2013, the U.S. Congress was about 18 percent female.[19] Internationally, this level of representation is the middle of the pack.[20] Still, the rapid rise of women in American politics is remarkable; of all the women who have *ever* been elected to Congress in its 224-year history, a third (98 of 293) are holding seats at the time we are writing this book.[21] Thirty of these are women of color.

As of 2014, no woman has yet been elected president of the United States, but the idea no longer seems as unnatural as it once did. The percent of Americans who say they are willing to vote for a "qualified woman" for president has grown substantially since 1958, when 55 percent of people said they would.[22] Today 90 percent or more would support a female candidate, at least in theory. Female heads of state are nothing new, though. The first woman to lead a modern country was Sirimavo Bandaranaike of Sri Lanka, who was elected in 1960. Since then, more than fifty women have led their countries. These leaders have been found disproportionately in Europe, but every region on earth has seen at least one female leader.

These gains have come through two complementary mechanisms. First, women fought to be recognized.[23] Second, men had to change how they thought about women as well, and decide that including them was the right thing to do. It took both men *and* women, then, and both voters and candidates, to change the face of government.

Women's presence in politics disrupts all three types of inequality: the classic patriarchal rule that women cannot hold power (sexism), the modified patriarchal belief that power is inherently masculine (androcentrism), and men's prerogative to make decisions on behalf of women (subordination). But does it make a difference? In other words, does **symbolic representation**—women's presence in government—translate into **substantive representation**—policies important and helpful to women?

SYMBOLIC TO SUBSTANTIVE REPRESENTATION Some people think it does. In 1991 an African American law professor, Anita Hill, testified before the Senate Judiciary Committee that she had been sexually harassed by a nominee to the Supreme Court, Clarence Thomas. This was a scandalous accusation, then even more than now. The public was transfixed. What they saw was an all-white, all-male panel of fourteen senators deliver an "aggressive, gloves-off" attack on Hill's character.[24] Many women saw this as a sign that men did not understand women's experiences. They brought their frustration to the ballot box.[25] The increased numbers of female candidates elected that year persuaded the media to define it "Year of the Woman."

Pictured here is the Senate Judiciary Committee for the Clarence Thomas confirmation hearings (1991), in which Anita Hill, Thomas's former assistant at the U.S. Equal Employment Opportunity Commission, accused the future Supreme Court justice of sexual harassment.

More recently, in the 2012 election Democratic Senate candidate Claire McCaskill of Missouri was considered a likely loser. The race turned in her favor when her opponent, Republican Todd Akin, argued against allowing abortion in the case of rape. "Legitimate rape," he said, couldn't lead to conception because "the female body has ways to try to shut that whole thing down."[26] The suggestion that women who became pregnant after an assault were not "legitimately" raped, not to mention general dismay at his biological illiteracy, caused an outcry. McCaskill won in a veritable landslide.

Both these stories suggest that at least some voters believe that female politicians are good for women. Is this how it works? Yes and no.

On many issues—such as the economy, religion, and the highly partisan issue of abortion—gender makes little difference.[27] Diversity among women means that there are many ways in which they are different from one another. Moreover, both men and women belong to political parties with concrete policy agendas. Once you take party membership into account, male and female politicians tend to vote similarly on legislation they are asked to consider.[28]

That said, female politicians do tend to vote differently than men on issues that obviously affect female constituents.[29] They show strong support for social welfare, women's health, and family-friendly workplaces, and for reducing inequality of all kinds.[30] Moreover, all things being equal, women are more likely than men to introduce bills that address women's needs.[31] So, sometimes men and women vote similarly, and sometimes differently, but having female politicians changes what they're voting *on*. Many male politicians support the initiatives of female politicians, reminding us that it's not just that women vote "like men." Men also vote "like women" when they have the opportunity to do so.

Consider as an example the issue of men's violence against women. Until at least the 1960s, domestic violence, sexual harassment, stalking, sexual assault, and rape went largely unregulated by the government. Sexual harassment was so normalized that there was literally no name for it.[32] Violence between intimate partners was seen as part of men's legitimate right to "govern" their own homes. And sexual assault and rape—especially when perpetrated by a friend or acquaintance—were often seen as just "boys being boys." Between spouses, rape was impossible; husbands were legally allowed to force sex on unwilling wives.[33]

Just as they had with suffrage, women started a movement; they raised money, recruited volunteers, opened domestic violence shelters, and staffed rape crisis lines. They redefined men's violence against women as a crime, collected data to demonstrate its prevalence, and argued that state involvement was essential to protecting women's freedom. This work outside of legislatures enabled female politicians to justify putting the issue on the public agenda. And they did, asking their governments to fund programs and pass laws intended to protect women's safety.[34]

Getting women elected is one step toward ensuring that politicians remember that women are part of the population they are governing. If women weren't in legislatures, we would be less likely to see issues of importance to female constituents raised at all. When these issues are raised, the presence of female politicians improves the chances of them being addressed. Feminist activists on the outside of formal politics can use government commitments to equality to press for implementation and real change. Likewise, they can work to change public opinion in ways that help politicians on the inside, enabling further change. The best-case scenario is cooperation between feminists on the inside with those on the outside.[35]

Of course, all this assumes that it's rather easy to know what's best for women. In fact, we've yet to discuss what gender equality might actually look like. The truth is that even feminists don't agree.

Theorizing Gender Equality

It's tough to do justice to the diversity of opinions on this issue, but we can give you an idea of some ways that feminists think about how to reach a feminist utopia. We'll discuss three approaches to gender equality that correspond, roughly, to the three types of inequality. Most countries incorporate at least some policies that reflect each.

Equal access aims to end sexism by dismantling legal barriers and reducing sex discrimination. The United States is a good example of a society that enjoys many of the benefits of equal access. Examples of this approach include laws that make it illegal to discriminate in the workplace, guarantee equal access to education, and allow women to enlist in the military.

Such policies significantly reduce sexism, but they can exist quite comfortably alongside androcentrism and subordination. They don't do anything to encourage people to value femininity, nor do they ensure that women will be able, in practice, to enter the masculine arenas to which these policies promise access. Equal access works well, then, for women who aim to be in the same places that men already are, whether in a coal mine or a boardroom, but it doesn't do anything to widen men's opportunities (most will likely continue hugging the masculine side of the binary) and may not appeal to women who prefer the feminized spheres of life.

An **equal value** model is designed to tackle the problem of androcentrism by raising the value of the feminine to match the value of the masculine. This strategy is compatible with gendered divisions of labor, but resists the idea that different is unequal. A society characterized by equal value, for example, would reward reproductive labor (pregnancy, breastfeeding, and child care responsibilities) so that it didn't result in economic insecurity for women. The policies adopted by some of the countries featured in Table 13.1, for example, promote the equal value of child care when they pay either or both parents for the work involved with taking care of a new baby.

For women as well as men who embrace femininity, equal value is a more promising model than equal access. It would destigmatize the feminine side of the binary, giving men the opportunity to balance femininity and masculinity, much as women already do. It would also raise the prestige and pay of both women and men who work in feminized jobs or specialize in the domestic sphere.

Some countries put more emphasis on equal value than equal access. Compared to the United States, for instance, Germany has relatively weak antidiscrimination laws but generous social services for parents. Mothers are guaranteed fourteen weeks of leave at full pay. In addition, either parent can draw up to 67 percent of their salary for additional months of child care (varying depending on who takes it), and there is the option of two additional years of low-wage child-care time, which in practice mostly mothers take. Moreover, part-time workers, often mothers, enjoy wage protection and pro-rated benefits. As a result of these opportunities, German mothers often work quite a bit less than American mothers.[36] This means that American women have more opportunities than German women to compete in the workplace, but German women who have children often enjoy greater emotional and financial well-being, whether or not they have a partner.

Some feminists are enthusiastic about the potential of the equal value model. In their view, gender difference is a significant source of pleasure, and could be even more so.[37] If gender was no longer a metaphor for power, men wouldn't feel the need to be masculine to feel powerful, and neither would women. New femininities and masculinities might emerge. Meanwhile, if the binary was no longer an ideological infrastructure for inequality, its importance might fade, making more room for people who don't identify as male or female.

Other feminists, however, are concerned that equal value strategies will lead to coercive enforcement of gender-binary arrangements. Both the Vatican and the Arab states of the Middle East use the idea of equal value to resist equal access claims. They believe that the gender binary is God given, so gender-specific rights and responsibilities are holy. In this scenario, women and men would enjoy equal status, but they would be penalized if they strayed from their expected roles. This is OK with some feminists, but not others.

If equal access tackles sexism and equal value androcentrism, then the **equal sharing** approach targets subordination by attempting to ensure that men and women participate equally in masculine and feminine spheres. Unlike the equal access approach, this model presses for dramatic shifts in how men spend their time. It does so by indirectly addressing the devaluation of femininity by providing incentives for men and women to take proportionate responsibility for the less valued parts of life. In this way, costs and advantages would be spread around more equitably.

Some countries have instituted equal sharing policies. Studies have shown, for example, that when fathers get involved in infant care, it reduces family conflict and shifts men's participation in housework and child care long-term, increasing the number of hours men spend on both.[38] To encourage this, some states have added gender-neutral parental leave, as shown in Table 13.1. Canada gives new moms fifteen weeks off at 55 percent pay but also includes thirty-five weeks at the same rate that can be used by either parent or shared between them. States that value sharing also tend to encourage parents of both sexes to work. Sweden and Denmark, for example, offer well-paid leaves covering nearly all parents, but they don't encourage either parent to stay out of the labor force too long.

Because of social norms, mothers are still more likely than fathers to take advantage of gender-neutral benefits, so some countries are trying to push families even harder to share. In Iceland, for example, parents get nine months of paid leave, but three months of these can only be used by the father. If he doesn't take them, the family forfeits the paid time off. Eleven of the countries featured in Table 13.1 offer dads-only benefits and a few, including Sweden, Denmark, and Germany, have additional "share it or lose it" rules for some of their otherwise gender-neutral benefits.

The sharing approach appeals greatly to those who believe that we should be working to establish societies in which gender all but disappears as a meaningful category.[39] A gender-free world may seem impossible, but many things that were impossibly strange to people just a century or two ago are common sense today.

Beyond the ideas of equal access, value, and sharing, there are different ways of thinking about what a feminist utopia looks like, leading many to speak in terms of feminisms, plural.[40] There are socialist feminists who worry most about the intersection of gender with class; libertarian and anarchist feminists who focus on freeing women and men from state control; eco-feminists who draw connections between men's treatment of women and their treatment of nature; feminists who think that women and men are essentially the same and ones who think we are inherently different; there are black, Chicana, and postcolonial feminisms; separatist feminists who want nothing to do with men, feminists who are men, and feminists who make understanding masculinity their primary concern; feminist reformers who try to achieve incremental gains; and radical feminists who specialize in asking societies for things that seem impossible.

As this list suggests, people who call themselves "feminist" often have very different ideas about how to solve the problem of gender inequality. This plurality of opinion can cause disagreement, but it can also spark productive conversations about what feminist activism should look like. Let's turn to that topic next.

FEMINIST ACTIVISM

The suffragist Elizabeth Cady Stanton understood that the vote was the first step toward women's full emancipation. "The grant of this right," she declared, "will secure all the others." In fact, founding documents of many countries around the world were amended in the latter half of the 1900s to grant equal political rights to women, but the U.S. Constitution was not one of them. Instead, the Supreme Court first held that women were a "new class of citizens" who could vote but who did not automatically have other rights.

American feminists have introduced an Equal Rights Amendment every year since 1923. It would amend the Constitution to include the following: "Equality of rights under the law shall not be denied or abridged by the United States or by any state on account of sex." Feminists are still waiting to see it passed and ratified. As a result, the Constitution still does not require that men and women be given equal political or social rights. Instead, feminists have had to fight for each right individually.

Because there is no constitutional requirement that women be treated equally, Congress can pass gender-equality laws, but it doesn't have to, nor does it have to renew the ones now on the books. Women's right to credit cards, jury duty, and equal education—in fact, all women's rights—are contingent on the

Senator Robert Menendez is flanked by representatives of women's groups at a 2012 rally to mark the fortieth anniversary of the Equal Rights Amendment's passage by Congress. The legislation, which was first proposed in 1923 and pledged an end to discrimination against women, did not receive enough state ratifications to be added to the U.S. Constitution. Activists and politicians continue to organize for its adoption.

whims of legislators and the will of their constituents. It might sound impossible to you that such rights could disappear, but there's no rule that radical changes can't involve a return to somewhere we've already been, or a place you think is even worse.

The Equal Rights Amendment would make gender equality a matter of constitutional guarantee instead of legislative gains and losses, so feminists continue to fight for it, and to protect and extend the rights they've already won. They do this both through "regular" politics—voting, supporting legislation, and lobbying—and also "irregular" politics like protest campaigns and public marches and demonstrations. The remainder of this chapter is about how women and their allies have used these tactics to secure rights for women, and continue to do so.

Feminist Politics

Social movements are collective, non-governmental efforts to change societies. Their efforts often—but do not exclusively—target the state. **Women's (social) movements** are ones in which women attempt to determine what kinds of policies will improve their lives. Sometimes they aim, at least in theory, to

This young man is an embedded feminist—someone who tries to accomplish feminist goals in spaces (such as the Occupy movement) that are not explicitly feminist.

improve the circumstances of *all* women; other times they are meant to consider the needs of certain kinds of women specifically.[41] White women have often been insensitive to the needs of women of color, for example, and so women of color have often formed feminist groups for themselves. By definition, women's movements are **autonomous** in that they can function independently of men's participation and approval.[42] This was how suffragist Alice Duer Miller described feminism in 1915:

> *A Feminist, my daughter,*
> *Is any woman now who cares*
> *To think about her own affairs*
> *As men don't think she oughter.*

Autonomous feminism says it doesn't matter if "men don't think she oughter" have certain ideas or make certain demands on the state; women have their own organizations, their own affairs, and the freedom to set their own agenda.

While autonomous women's movements have disproportionately been led by and focused on the needs of privileged women, mixed-sex movements and organizations—ones that are not exclusively concerned with the lives of women—have typically attracted feminists who face multiple disadvantages: working-class or poor women, immigrant women or women of color, sexual minorities, and older and disabled women. Feminists are found in all types of social movements, in important social organizations (like the military and the Catholic Church), and, of course, in political parties.[43] We call them **embedded feminists**, people who try to do feminist work in not explicitly feminist spaces.

Feminism itself has become more sensitive to diversity than many autonomous women's movements have been in the past, thanks to debates among feminist activists.

The Politics of Feminism

Feminists who are socially disadvantaged in multiple ways have worked hard to ensure that the women's movement is inclusive. They have prodded otherwise privileged feminists, who don't always apply an intersectional lens, to see that different kinds of women may need different things and, all too often, women are complicit in the oppression of other kinds of women. Thanks to their hard work, feminists have learned to be more thoughtful about their own privileges.[44] This self-awareness has added texture and depth to feminist politics by widening the scope of their attention to many of the inequalities that women live with that have nothing to do with gender.

It hasn't always been easy to get white, class-privileged, and otherwise advantaged women to attend to the needs of other women, and it can be challenging to do justice inclusively, given the wide diversity of men and women. For example, when feminists succeeded in criminalizing men's violence against women, as we discussed earlier, they were dismayed to discover that the new laws were enforced with more rigor against black- and brown-skinned men. Even today, these men are more likely than white men to be put on trial for sexual assault, have higher rates of conviction, and receive harsher sentences.[45]

The data suggest, also, that white women still enjoy special status in the eyes of judges and juries: Black men who are accused of sexually assaulting white women are more likely to be convicted and serve longer prison sentences than black men who are accused of assaulting black women. Meanwhile, African American and Native American women, especially, continue to encounter these forms of violence with little protection.[46] Feminists today are fighting to extend protection from men's violence to women of color and change the racial bias in how laws are used to control men.

The timeline in Table 13.3 lists just some of the victories of American feminists in the last 100 years. All of these rights were, at one time or another, considered absurd. Yet, through serious struggles waged over many decades, politics turned radical ideas into the status quo. These American feminist victories were part of a global shift; women in every country on earth have fought for their rights, sometimes with even greater success.[47]

Transnational feminist activism involves efforts by feminists to change gender relations outside their own states and collaboration among feminists in different countries. Feminists doing this kind of work also struggle with the challenges posed by the diversity of women and men in these countries as well as differences among countries. Just as national politics tends to reflect the

TABLE 13.3 | 100 YEARS OF FEMINIST VICTORIES IN THE U.S.

1920: Women win the right to vote.

1922: Women married to non-citizen men are able to retain their own citizenship.

1924: Native American men and women win suffrage.

1928: Puerto Rican women win suffrage.

1936: The federal government legalizes the dissemination of information about birth control.

1963: The Equal Pay Act makes it illegal to pay men and women different wages for the same work.

1964: The Civil Rights Act outlaws discrimination on the basis of racial, ethnic, or national origin, religion, and sex.

1965: *Griswold v. Connecticut* decriminalizes the use of birth control by married people.

1967: Executive Order 11375 expands affirmative action policies to include women.

1968: Gender segregation of "Help Wanted" ads is ruled illegal.

1970: The last "marriage ban" keeping married women from paid employment is struck down.

1971: The first man wins a lawsuit claiming gender discrimination.

1972: *Eisenstadt v. Baird* extends the right to use contraceptives to single people.
Title IX bans sex discrimination in schools receiving federal funding.

1973: *Roe v. Wade* grants women the right to legal abortion in the first and second trimesters.

1974: The Equal Credit Opportunity Act establishes married women's right to have a credit card in their own name and, thus, have a credit history and score.

1975: Women are granted equal rights and responsibilities for jury duty alongside men.
In Connecticut, the first woman is elected governor in her own right.

1976: Military academies are ordered to admit women.
Nebraska becomes the first state to make marital rape illegal.

1978: The Pregnancy Discrimination Act protects pregnant women from being fired, overruling a Supreme Court decision that this was not discrimination against women.

1981: Women are allowed to enlist in all military branches.
The Supreme Court overturns state laws giving a husband sole power to control property jointly owned with his wife.
The first woman is appointed to the Supreme Court.

1986: Sexual harassment is acknowledged by the Supreme Court to be sex discrimination.

1987: The Civil Rights Restoration Act overrules a Supreme Court decision that Title IX only applies to education programs directly funded by federal government.

1992: In the "Year of the Woman" women are elected to Congress in unprecedented numbers.

1993: The Family and Medical Leave Act guarantees some employees unpaid leave for family care needs.
The last state (North Carolina) criminalizes marital rape.

1994: The Violence Against Women Act increases criminal penalties and funds special sexual assault units.

TABLE 13.3 | *continued*

1998: Same-sex sexual harassment is recognized by the Supreme Court.

2004: Massachusetts becomes the first state to legalize same-sex marriage.

2005: The Supreme Court rules that it is illegal to retaliate against people who report sex discrimination.

2007: The House of Representatives selects its first female speaker of the house.

2009: The Lily Ledbetter Fair Pay Restoration Act overturns a Supreme Court decision that prevented women from challenging past pay discrimination that they have newly discovered.

2010: The Navy ban on women serving on submarines is overturned.

2012: Contraception becomes required part of insurance coverage under the Affordable Care Act.

2013: The military ban on women in combat positions is overturned.
The renewal of the Violence Against Women Act extends protection for immigrant and Native American women.

needs and interests of already privileged groups, international politics tends to be dominated by the most powerful countries. Reflecting this bias, Western feminists often try to export their own version of women's liberation to other countries, where it fails to resonate. Efforts to "help" women in other countries often meet with resistance. Ultimately, Western feminists have to come to terms with a troublesome tendency to think they are more *advanced* than women in other countries. Over time, Western feminists have become better at recognizing that their culturally specific version of feminism is not universal.

The debate over the head scarf is a good example of this type of back and forth. Some have claimed that new immigrants to Europe bring oppressive practices that threaten to undermine gender equality. In response, states began taking measures meant to protect immigrant women from immigrant men. When France banned all public symbols of religion in 2003, including the head scarf, feminists disagreed about whether this was good for women.[48] Some argued that the head scarf symbolized women's subordination to men and that Muslim women were essentially being forced to cover their hair in public. This notion was rejected, however, by some women from cultural and religious backgrounds where head covering was the norm. They didn't like the requirement to *not* wear a head scarf any more than they liked the requirement to wear one. They wanted to make their own choices, not the ones that their supposedly more advanced Western sisters would make.

Politics is never simple. It isn't easy to figure out how to effectively represent the interests of a varied populace. Sometimes policies have harmful effects that are unintended. Moreover, feminists can't keep others from manipulating their message and agenda. Ultimately, however, these tensions have strengthened feminist ideas, broadened the scope of activism, and made women's issues part

This cartoon by Malcolm Evans draws attention to the fact that definitions of women's oppression and liberation can vary quite tremendously.

of other types of political activism. Alongside these growing pains, feminists have made extraordinary changes to societies.

Feminism Today

There remains a great deal to accomplish in future generations, but today's feminists face serious obstacles: backlash against feminism, the co-optation of feminist language, and the rise of individualism. Still, there are reasons to be optimistic. We'll tackle the bad news first and end with the good.

BACKLASH One obstacle to feminist activism is an active **anti-feminist countermovement**, individuals and groups who organize to oppose feminist social change. They push to stop or overturn feminist goals. Perhaps the greatest anti feminist victory was the campaign against the Equal Rights Amendment. Congress passed it in 1972, but amendments to the Constitution also require ratification by three-quarters of the states. Anti-feminists stirred up anxieties about what it would mean to guarantee women's equal rights (fear of women's inclusion in the military was a major concern; so, too, was the specter of restrooms not segregated by gender), and they blocked ratification in fifteen states, leaving the amendment three states short.

Today women's right to control their own reproduction is being targeted by opponents who seek to limit access to both abortion and contraception. In 2013,

A protester outside the French embassy in London is dressed in a niqab, one of the full-face veils traditionally worn by Muslim women in public that France outlawed in 2010. The price for noncompliance? One hundred and fifty euros and classes in French citizenship.

twenty-two American states passed a whopping seventy laws aimed at restricting women's access to abortion, including mandatory counseling and waiting periods, required parental consent or notification, and new regulations on abortion clinics, many of which were forced to close.[49] Eighty-seven percent of counties in America do not have an abortion provider.[50] Data shows that these laws don't reduce the incidence of abortion, but they do make it much more difficult for women to exercise their right to one.[51]

A different type of backlash is the spread of negative stereotypes about feminists. Television evangelist Pat Robertson is a colorful example. He once described feminism as "a socialist, anti-family, political movement that encourages women to leave their husbands, kill their children, practice witchcraft, destroy capitalism, and become lesbians." Most people wouldn't go *that* far, but a surprising number of people believe that feminists are ugly, uptight, angry, aggressive, harsh, strident, demanding, dogmatic, man-hating lesbians.[52] Only 26 percent of people say that *feminist* is a positive term.[53]

Consider Google search results: A person can type in two words—such as "feminists are"—and see how the search engine auto-completes the phrase. At least eleven of the fifteen phrases are negative, suggesting that feminists are crazy, wrong, and annoying; should be ashamed of themselves; need to shut up, get laid, and learn to take a joke; or should be shot, killed, and die. People think some pretty ugly things about feminists. Or, at least, we think that's what *other people* think.

This may be why, compared to previous generations, not as many young people today use the word *feminist* to describe themselves.[54] About 16 percent of men and 23 percent of women identify as feminists.[55] Most people aren't anti-feminists; they're ambivalent. In one study, 60 percent of twenty-three- to twenty-four-year-old women were "fence-sitters" or used phrases like "I'm (not) a feminist, but . . . ."[56] Another 26 percent had never thought about it. Pop star Beyoncé sounded ambivalent when she explained to *Vogue*: "That word can be very extreme. . . . I guess I am a modern-day feminist. I do believe in equality. . . . But I'm happily married. I love my husband."[57] Her comment reflects the worry among some people that feminists are women who don't like men. Lady Gaga said so explicitly: "I'm not a feminist," she once said. "I love men."[58] Lana Del Rey just called it boring: "For me, the issue of feminism is just not an interesting concept."[59]

Being a feminist is also sometimes associated with being angry or hurt. "Nothing has happened to me that I would have to be that way," explained one woman interviewed about whether she identified as a feminist.[60] She seemed to think that feminism was like post-traumatic stress disorder, the result of a terrible experience that damages you for life. Marissa Mayer, CEO of Yahoo, captured a similar stereotype when she said that she wasn't a feminist because she didn't have a "chip on the shoulder."[61]

Ironically, despite rejection of and ambivalence about the term, 83 percent of young people think that there is feminist work left to be done. In light of this fact, negative stereotypes about feminists—and people's discomfort with the label—suggest that *actual* feminists have lost control over its meaning. After all, it would be counterproductive for feminists to portray *themselves* as unlikeable. Since the mid '80s, though, when 30 to 40 percent of women identified as feminists, people sympathetic to the movement have lost ground to Pat Robertson and others who wish to portray feminism in a negative light.[62]

CO-OPTATION Another force that undermines women's movements is the **corporate co-optation of feminism,** or the use of feminist-sounding language and imagery for marketing purposes.[63] One of the earliest manifestations of such advertising occurred in 1929, during the first wave of the feminist movement. That year, the American Tobacco Company paid a handful of women to walk in the New York Easter parade and smoke cigarettes.[64] At the time, it was against gender rules for women to smoke in public, which limited the profits of cigarette makers. For their stunt, they re-branded cigarettes as "torches of freedom."

Almost forty years later, during the second wave, Virginia Slims debuted one of the most famous ad slogans of all time, "You've come a long way, baby," again equating smoking with feminist progress. It was quickly followed by another memorable slogan, "Because you're worth it."[65] This was L'Oréal's effort to co-opt feminism to sell beauty products. They still use a version of the slogan—"Because we're worth it"—today.[66]

As the long life of the L'Oréal slogan suggests, co-optation remains a popular strategy. Companies now try to get consumers involved. Both makeup company CoverGirl and feminine hygiene product brand Always have recently taken this approach with hashtags #GirlsCan and #LikeaGirl, each accompanying the companies' ad campaigns. CoverGirl promises that girls can do anything they want, including "make the world a little more easy, breezy, and beautiful."

Most of this marketing reduces feminism to individual empowerment, implicitly promising to improve the lives of women who buy their products, often with no rationale whatsoever. The hair care company Pantene, for example, has recently been running ads that explicitly address gender inequality in the workplace, followed up with the slogan: "Be strong and shine." Shine through gender bias, the ad instructs, by tossing your glowing mane.

There is a more explicit embrace of feminist concerns in Dove's decision to brand itself as a company that contests standards of beauty harmful to American women. It successfully created what was, as of the spring of 2013, the most viral ad of all time, Real Beauty Sketches.[67] In the ad, a sketch artist draws women as they describe themselves and as another describes them, then reveals both sketches to the participants. The message is that others see their beauty more clearly than they do. One participant responded: "I should be more grateful of my natural beauty. It impacts the choices and friends that we make, the jobs we apply for, how we treat our children. It impacts everything. It couldn't be more critical to our happiness." In other words, it's empowering just to feel more beautiful.

Fair enough. But, at best, the message is that each individual woman can choose to feel better about how she looks. But since Dove's #realbeauty and #redefiningbeauty campaigns never suggest that looks are irrelevant to a woman's value, the challenge to looks-ism is reduced to a reflection of an individual woman's psychology rather than a challenge to socially supported gender norms. Urging women to feel better about their looks can also be a tactic to make them more interested in working on realizing the promise their appearance holds.

Challenging the social power of appearance norms in actual interactions, after all, would disrupt Dove's bottom line: Women would spend a lot less money on skin and hair care products if they were less worried about being judged on their looks. It's important to never lose sight of the fact that even marketing with feminist content is, first and foremost, an advertisement made to entice people to buy things. Companies can rarely fairly be called feminist. Dove, for example, is owned by Unilever, which also owns Axe, a brand that is famous for its unusually sexist advertising.

The frequency with which feminist themes appear in advertising has made "girl power" a cliché, as marketers use the idea to sell everything from tampons to toys. The preponderance of such rhetoric makes it conceptually difficult to distinguish between feminism and self-concern. At its worst, it's simply egotistical, telling girls and women that they are awesome just by virtue of being female and so deserve to be and have anything they want. Marketers stroke the egos of women with slogans like "Every day is women's day" (Banif Bank) and "Because every woman is a queen" (CoverGirl) that encourage women to think of themselves as entitled to special treatment. Being a feminist is not the same thing as having a diva complex. Likewise, advertising that tells girls and women they should be self-centered does not empower women to work for gender justice for anyone but themselves.

A DECLINE IN COLLECTIVIST THINKING Rising levels of **individualism** among Americans, especially millennials (typically described as individuals born from the early 1980s to the early 2000s), reflect a new focus on the individual over the group.[68] There has been a marked increase in the frequency with which words and phrases indicating an individualist orientation appear in American music and books in English and a corresponding growth in individualist thinking.[69]

Along with marketer-induced self-centeredness, individualism makes it easy to conflate personal achievement with feminist progress. The book *Lean In*, which spent most of 2013 on the *New York Times* bestseller list, illustrates some of these tendencies. In it Sheryl Sandberg, the chief operating officer of Facebook, offers women tips for career advancement, focusing on things they do to hold themselves back from success. A billionaire herself, her advice applies primarily to women who are poised to compete with men at the top of powerful American companies. *You, too, can be a winner in this system*, she whispers encouragingly.

However, ambitious and competitive women, no matter how successful, are not automatically feminist heroes if making it to "the top" reinforces the disadvantages of the women who work "below" them. This is not women's empowerment, it's a patriarchal bargain; it tells women to accept the system as it is—patriarchal and winner-take-all—in exchange for success within it.[70] To paraphrase activist and writer Linda Burnham, Sandberg is telling women to go along to get ahead.[71]

This leaves lots of women behind. Women who are not poised to rise to the top of a company, as most women and men are not, don't benefit from this type of thinking. They don't need to lean in; they need child care and a living wage. When feminism meets individualism, it's all too common for activists to forget that what benefits them personally may not benefit women as a group.

If this generation of feminists is going to make continued progress toward gender equality, they're going to have to fight anti-feminist backlash, the materialist orientation of marketing, the rising levels of individualism and the conflation of feminist progress with patriarchal bargains. But there are exciting reasons to expect feminists to be successful in the coming years.

NEW OPPORTUNITIES FOR FEMINISTS Of all generations alive today, millennials show the strongest support for gender equality and are more likely than members of generation X (born in the early 1960s to mid-1970s) to be actively involved in feminist organizing.[72] Young feminists today are also more diverse than previous generations: They are more likely to identify as queer, nonwhite, or multiracial, and are more politicized around disability.[73] As a result, today's feminists better understand that differences among women need to inform their politics. This hasn't eliminated discrimination and ethnocentrism in feminist organizing, but intersectionality is undeniably a central part of the conversation.[74]

Young feminists are likely to be successful in pressing for future changes, thanks in part to the feminists who came before them. One of the most enduring legacies of the women's movement of the 1970s is the wide range of feminist organizations and services that have become part of the ordinary political landscape. Talking about gender and advocating on behalf of women no longer seems radical at all. A substantial majority of people today believe that men and women are inherently equal and should be treated as such.[75] People are nervous about identifying as a feminist, but feminism still has a lot of support.

Some of that support will come from inside legislatures. There are many reasons why the majority of American politicians are still men, but sexism isn't one of them. In fact, the average man in the United States seems rather indifferent toward a candidate's sex, whereas the average woman tends to prefer females.[76] As a result, when women in Western countries run for office today, they raise just as much money as men, get as many votes, and are equally likely to win.[77] If we can make it possible for more women to run, we will see continued shifts in both symbolic and substantive representation. And, since men often support measures to enhance gender equality when given the opportunity, this is an exciting route for change.

Feminist activism has made strides within individual countries, but it is also increasingly global. Today's feminists inherit a series of global networks and transnational organizations that have mainstreamed concern with gender equality.[78] Beginning in 1975, the United Nations began organizing international conferences focused on the well-being of women worldwide. The symbolic statement in support of gender equality, the Convention on the Elimination of All Forms of Discrimination Against Women, was adopted in 1979. Sixteen years later, 183 countries agreed to a global Platform for Action driven by the belief that "women's rights are human rights."[79] These statements have helped to legitimate an international norm of gender equality, an accepted standard to which countries can now be pressed to conform.[80] International development projects are increasingly gender-aware and equitable in their effects.

Meanwhile, technology is making a difference. The rise of new social media has made it easier for feminists of this generation to find information and social support for political activism. Feminists today use social networks and websites to find one another and share ideas. Websites and Twitter feeds are less costly, more efficient, and wider-reaching than the mimeographs and newsprint used by women's groups of the 1970s.[81]

The Internet and its tools enable anyone with access to them the opportunity to produce content for others to consume. Before the Internet, media gatekeepers strongly controlled what could be mass-produced and disseminated through print, radio, and television. But today, anyone with access to the Internet can contribute to the international conversation. This has been democratizing—it has given a much wider proportion of the population the ability to produce, not just consume, media content—and has disproportionately helped those who have been and continue to be excluded from formal media production, including people of color, queer activists, and those struggling for disability rights. For anyone with an Internet connection, an amazing array of feminists is just a search away. Regardless of whether this vast global network brings activists into the streets, it supports a sense of community built around norms of gender equality.

New frontiers for activism are less limited by geography than ever before and encompass a wide range of opportunities for engagement, from formal politics to informal encouragement for taking gender risks.

Revisiting the Question

 How do people change societies?

With passion, commitment, and cooperation. In every society there is tension between the gender order—entrenched and often unquestioned ideas about gender, interactions that reproduce it, and gendered institutions—and the power of individuals to resist and transform it. Every individual has at least a little bit of power and, when individuals join together, that power accumulates. In other words, the system is bigger than any one of us, but *we're in it together*. If enough of us decide we want to change it, we can.

And people have. States have changed dramatically over just the last 100 years. In turn, they have changed the way states govern gender and even the face of governance. Feminists can take a great deal of credit for these changes.

They have changed each other as well, setting up a new generation of activists to imagine an even more radical future.

Next . . .

A farewell and some advice!

FOR FURTHER READING

Crenshaw, Kimberle. "Demarginalizing the Intersection of Race and Sex: A Black Feminist Critique of Antidiscrimination Doctrine, Feminist Theory and Anti-racist Politics." *University of Chicago Legal Forum* 140 (1989): 139–67.

Ferree, Myra Marx, and Christina Ewig. "Global Feminist Organizing: Identifying Patterns of Activism. Pp. 148–62 in *The Women's Movement in Protest, Institutions and the Internet: Australia in Transnational Perspective*, edited by Sarah Maddison and Marian Sawer. New York: Routledge, 2013.

Gengler, Amanda. "Selling Feminism, Consuming Femininity." *Contexts* 10, no. 2 (2011): 68–69.

Hooks, Bell. "Dig Deep: Beyond Lean In." *The Feminist Wire*, October 28, 2013.

Mernissi, Fatema. "Size 6: The Western Woman's Harem." Pp. 208–219 in *Scheherazade Goes West: Different Cultures, Different Harems*. New York: Washington Square Press, 2001.

Reger, Jo. *Everywhere and Nowhere. Contemporary Feminism in the United States.* New York: Oxford University Press, 2012.

Rothman, Barbara. "Now You Can Choose! Issues in Parenting and Procreation." In *Revisioning Gender*, edited by Myra Marx Ferree, Judith Lorber, and Beth Hess, 399–415. Walnut Creek, CA: Altamira Press, 2000.

Wade, Lisa. "Defining Gendered Oppression." *Gender & Society* 23, no. 3 (2009): 293–314.

> IN MANY WAYS IT IS A TERRIBLE
> LESSON; IN MANY WAYS A
> MAGNIFICENT ONE.
>
> —C. WRIGHT MILLS, ON SOCIOLOGY[1]

Onward

Gender is a powerful idea that shapes our experience of ourselves, each other, and the institutions with which we interact. It's pervasive and unavoidable. And while it's fun sometimes—more for some of us than others—it's also unfair. Our ideas about gender support a hierarchical system, one that intersects with other hierarchies in ways that ensure that some men have more power than other men and most women.

Everyone pays a price.

Men as well as women must contend with forces that narrow the options for the type of person they're allowed to be. It may not feel like oppression—men are constantly told that masculinity is better than femininity and many have internalized an aversion to the feminine that has come to feel natural—but masculinity, even for men who take to it easily, is not the same thing as freedom. It's a set of rules that threatens to undermine men's value in their own eyes and those of others. Still, many men—even those who find themselves near the bottom of the masculine hierarchy—embrace the gender order because it offers a psychological wage: the idea that they're superior to women and at least to some other men.

Some women, in turn, might feel like gender isn't the oppressive force it used to be. Their daily lives may feel freer than those of the men around them, and they may be right. But the cultural permission to perform masculinity isn't liberation; it's an "homage to patriarchy."[2] It affirms the superiority of men and masculinity, just as men's avoidance of femininity is a sign that they think less of it. Women are allowed a taste of the privileges that come with being male—and if they are otherwise advantaged in society, they may enjoy other privileges as well—but ultimately the requirement to do femininity translates into a social system in which women as a group will be seen as less valuable than men and will do a disproportionate amount of the least rewarded work.

For young people in college, this might sound absurd. The average woman outperforms her male peers throughout school: She gets better grades, runs the clubs, dominates student government, and outnumbers men in higher education. But privilege is, by definition, unearned. The advantages that come with being male are more acutely noticeable in heterosexual interaction (where women enjoy fewer orgasms and face greater danger) and will be more obvious in the workplace (where the average male college graduate will earn more than his female counterpart from day one) in families (where the responsibility for unpaid housework and child care falls disproportionately on women), and in the power centers of our societies (where men overwhelmingly are positioned to make the big decisions).

Those are the facts. The gender binary isn't real, it isn't fair, and we can't pretend it doesn't affect us.

We understand that this is an unpleasant reality. This is why we began this chapter with C. Wright Mills's observation that sociology is in many ways a terrible lesson. But Mills also points out that thinking sociologically is *magnificent*, because understanding the systems in which we live enables us to make more informed decisions for ourselves, treat others with more empathy, and maybe even change society for the better. So, before we end, we want to offer some suggestions about how to put the lessons of this book to work in your daily life.

Consider tossing your gender binary glasses.

With your glasses off, you can now see the gender binary for what it really is—a social construction—but you'll still encounter the idea that men and women are opposite sexes every day. Try to be skeptical. Don't forget the basics: All differences are average differences with a great deal of overlap; men are not all alike and neither are women; and all differences and similarities are caused by the intersection of nature and nurture, not one or the other.

This applies to *you*, too, of course. If you're a person who sometimes worries about whether you fit into the binary, know that it's perfectly normal to wonder.

The binary isn't real, so, to a greater or lesser degree, we're all square pegs being hammered into round holes. Don't blame yourself for how uncomfortable it is. And, even if you personally feel quite comfortable, try to be understanding toward people who aren't and give them space for finding their own comfort zone.

Think about how you want to interact with others.

You already break gender rules all the time, but now you probably do so more consciously. When you're policed, remember that there are three options: obey and refrain from breaking the rule, break the rule but offer an account that affirms it, or renounce the rule as arbitrary and unnecessary. The last option has the most potential for destabilizing the rules and the gender binary they protect. Think about if and when you might want to do this. It would be exhausting to do it all the time and, in some cases, the price you could pay might be too high. Sometimes, though, the rewards outweigh the costs.

You can also choose to police the policers by pointing out other people's efforts to enforce gender rules. Challenging the entitlement of others to demand obedience to gender rules can provoke both mild and severe negative reactions: irritated parents, alienated friends, angry bosses, or retaliation from peers. Pay attention to when other people are likely to get your point and then balance the harm of their policing with the penalties you might face. Sometimes it will feel like the right thing to do.

Another possibility is to personally opt out of gender policing. This will take practice, since most of us police gender out of habit. Don't forget that policing people away from gender stereotypes (like pushing a little sister to be less concerned with her appearance) is not the *opposite* of policing, it's just enforcing a different set of gender rules. Opting out means not reacting to gender performances *at all*, refraining from comments or reactions aimed at endorsing, questioning, or attacking someone's choices based on whether they're a man or woman. If you choose to do this, you'll be quietly contributing to a freer and less judgmental space for your friends, family, and coworkers.

Reflect on your relationship with the institutions around you.

Gendered institutions push us to make decisions consistent with the gender order at the same time that their hegemony can make these choices seem natural and inevitable. Now you know that the gender order is an illusion and you can use this knowledge to wrest some autonomy from the institutions that bear down on you.

You may want to do this in order to satisfy your individual preferences. Resisting institutional pressures can mean living a life more in tune with who you are. Or, you may choose to resist these pressures because of the way that institutions place you into unequal relationships with others. Because institutions reflect not only gender inequality but all social inequities, our participation often means being advantaged by virtue of someone else's disadvantage. We hope you keep sight of this fact and make it a practice to ask how institutions are tying you to both visible and invisible others in ways you may not like.

Some institutions are in real flux, making it easier to get around them. At this point in history, for example, the way we institutionalize family life is undergoing rapid and dramatic change. When so many people are making unconventional choices, it becomes easier for others to do so. Neither marriage, nor heterosexuality, nor parenthood is mandatory anymore. Consider all your options.

Other institutions are much more deeply entrenched, but even in these cases there are some things we can do. The institutions that function to produce, transport, and sell the vast majority of goods and services that we consume are incredibly hard to avoid, for instance, but there are some choices you can make. Buying clothes second hand is a way to avoid supporting a garment industry that exploits mostly female labor. Buying gender-neutral products over gendered ones—from deodorant, to exercise equipment, to cell phone covers—can discourage companies from exploiting gender stereotypes to get your money. Think about how you can opt out, even in small ways, of institutions that you feel have harmful effects on people's lives.

Some of you may have more freedom than others to make choices that oppose institutionalized norms; it depends on your particular mix of advantages and disadvantages. If you *can* make counter-institutional choices, and you choose to do so, know that you'll be slowly helping to dismantle ideologies and practices that others have less freedom to resist. You'll be using your privilege, in other words, to help others with less of it.

Remember that the mechanisms that produce inequality aren't simple.

Compared to the average person, you have a much more sophisticated understanding of how gender inequality is maintained. Most people are familiar with the idea of sexism and object to the idea that one sex should receive preferential treatment, but androcentrism and subordination are less well understood and less obviously problematic. But *you* understand. You're tuned into the hierarchy of men and the way that gender inequality places men in competition for the rewards that accrue to masculinity; you are also aware that not all men benefit equally from gender inequality.

You see that that intersectionality complicates the notion that anyone is subordinated or elevated by virtue of their sex alone. You're more likely to notice how women, too, enjoy certain privileges and enter into relationships of exploitation. You are aware of how much is going on when individual men or women make patriarchal bargains, and you can be both more critical of and sympathetic to these choices. Relatedly, you have a more nuanced sense of the attitude, behavior, and policy changes required to challenge gender inequality, as well as a healthy appreciation for just how intensely feminists debate the issue.

Use this knowledge to resist the common misperceptions about feminist progress, like the idea that equality is simply a matter of ensuring equal access and that we can proclaim "mission accomplished" once we get a few privileged women into corner offices. Or the notion that men have nothing to gain from reducing gender inequality, as if they, too, aren't in many ways constrained by the gender binary. Question the suggestion that feminists are driven by anger instead of empathy; feminists are in it not because they hate men, but because they care about both men and women and the struggles they face. Recognize, too, that because most feminists are concerned with racism, poverty, and other -isms and injustices, their goal is not to point fingers; since there is always some dimension on which any given person has some privilege, it would be self-destructive to think about activism as a matter of assigning guilt and claiming innocence. Finally, be suspicious of anyone who tells you that liberation can be found in the right purchase, a good slogan, or sheer narcissism.

All this may leave you with more questions than answers, which is a really good place to be. Keep asking those questions, trying out answers, listening to others' perspectives, and forming your own theory of how the world works. No one has the last word on truth. So, continue to puzzle over the ideas we've shared, add them to the bank of information you've learned from others, see if they explain your own experiences, and let your understanding of the world evolve.

Know that change is always possible.

Sometimes problems seem overwhelmingly large and entrenched, but now you know that gender relations change, sometimes dramatically and surprisingly quickly. At the core of these changes are people. Social change is about power and everybody has some. Individuals work—alone or together—to imagine, enact, and share new ways of doing things.

Some of you may be passionate about reducing gender inequality and may decide to make activism a central part of your life. There are lots of ways to do this. You can write and speak about injustice, donate time or money to feminist organizations, or be an activist in your workplace, church, or political campaign.

Others of you may not be interested in activism, but that doesn't mean that your choices aren't political ones. We're all political whether we like it or not: We either accept the status quo—whether enthusiastically or reluctantly—or try to change things. Doing nothing *is* doing something. That's OK, but know that this is a political choice, too.

Even if you're not a passionate activist, there are probably *some* things you'd like to see change. Go ahead and pick a battle or two. That's how most of us do it.[3] Maybe you decide to be the person in your social circle who stops everyone else from telling rape jokes or using *gay* as an insult; you might give relief to an assault survivor or gay friend you didn't know you had. Or maybe you're a woman who decides to quit wearing makeup every day because you hate it; suddenly you're an inspiration for a friend who wasn't as brave or deeply motivated.

If you're a student, you can question the local gender order. Maybe you'll be the one to start an organization on campus dedicated to exploring what it means to be a man, the one who ensures that the college provides unisex bathrooms for gender queer and transitioning students, or the one who does the research to find out whether your school's sexual assault policy is in compliance with federal law (most aren't).[4] It might be intimidating, and it's impossible to know if you'll succeed, but these are all things you could do *today*. Think about what inspires you.

Once you leave school, you'll have even more opportunities to re-make the world. As a police officer, parent, teacher, or religious leader you will be a part of the institutions that maintain order, raise and educate young people, nurture spirituality, and promote social responsibility. You may be an employee of a corporation with a hand in making key decisions about how its goods are designed, produced, or marketed; its profits allocated; or its impact on the environment managed. You might see ways to improve these institutions from the inside or you might take your critique outside and try to press for change from there. Make like-minded friends and see what you can do. As the anthropologist Margaret Mead famously said: "Never doubt that a small group of thoughtful, committed citizens can change the world; indeed, it's the only thing that ever has."[5]

Ultimately, no matter how passionate you are, aim for balance. As legal scholar Joan Williams reminds us, "Equality is not everything, even for feminists themselves."[6] Maybe another political issue is more important to you: campaign finance reform, global warming, or the HIV epidemic. All of these issues are important and, as you already likely suspect, gendered. It's also OK to want peace at the holiday dinner table, even if your grandfather still thinks it's strange that women today wear pants. It's OK to want to look beautiful in an evening gown or dashing in a tuxedo. That craft beer with the sexist ad campaign is *delicious*; we get it. Even the most dedicated feminists make trade-offs.

They balance a desire for social justice with the need for happy, productive, meaningful lives. Feminist principles win out sometimes and not others. And that's life.

Enjoy the vertigo.

For better or worse, gender offers us a clear path through life; it helps us make decisions, from the minor to the momentous. Without gender to push some options off to the side and place others in front of us, we are left to make these decisions with fewer guidelines.

This can be incredibly disorienting. Sociologist Barbara Risman uses the word "vertigo" to capture how dizzying letting go of gendered logic can be.[7] Standing at a precipice, looking out at a vast expanse of possibility, you are no longer protected by familiar boundaries. It is both exhilarating and frightening. Enjoy the magnificent lessons you've learned: the way that understanding that gender is a social construction makes life a little more fun, a little more interesting, and a little freer.

It's pretty great, actually.

But know, also, that the terrible part never fully goes away. At times it will be upsetting. Feel free to be annoyed and share your frustrations. This might make people a little annoyed at *you*, but there are worse things. Sometimes the terrible part will be deeply personal, as you struggle with your own fears. Other times you will be angry with what you see around you and feel small and powerless to change things. We all do from time to time. And, of course, sometimes you can only laugh.

In the mix of frustration, disorientation, and hope, though, is the magic. It's what frees our minds and gives us the motivation to think up alternate realities. So go ahead and imagine the unimaginable.

GLOSSARY

abolitionists activists in the fight against human slavery

account an explanation for why a person broke the rule that then excused his or her behavior

ageism prejudice based on a preference for the young and the equating of signs of aging with decreased social value

agrarian societies in which the invention of agriculture—the cultivation of domesticated crops—allows groups to put down roots

androcentric pay scale a strong correlation between wages and the gender composition of a job

androcentrism the granting of higher status, respect, value, reward, and power to the masculine compared to the feminine

anti-feminist countermovement individuals and groups who organize to oppose feminist social change

associative memory a phenomenon in which cells in our brains that process and transmit information make literal connections between concepts, such that some ideas are associated with other ideas

autonomous functioning independently of men's participation and approval

benevolent sexism the attribution of positive traits to women that, nonetheless, justify women's subordination to men

binary a system with two and only two separate and distinct parts, like binary code (the 1s and 0s used in computing) or a binary star system (in which two stars orbit around each other)

biological differences differences caused by hormones, brain morphology, or genetics

brain organization theory the idea that male and female brains may have different strengths and weaknesses

brain plasticity our brain's ability to respond to the environment

breadwinner/housewife marriage a model of marriage that did not legally subordinate wives to husbands, but continued to define the rights and responsibilities of husbands and wives differently; women owed men domestic services and men were legally required to support their wives financially

brotherhood the distribution of power to a certain class of men

bystander intervention programs programs that educate students about sexual assault and teach them how to spot likely incidents and safely intervene

care chain a series of nurturing relationships in which the care of children, the disabled, or the elderly is displaced onto increasingly disadvantaged paid or unpaid carers

care work work that involves face-to-face caretaking of the physical, emotional, and educational needs of others

colorism a racist preference for light skin

commodification the process by which goods transition from something a family provided for itself into something bought with a wage

commodity a thing that can be bought and sold

compulsory heterosexuality a rule that all men be attracted to women and all women to men

corporate co-optation of feminism the use of feminist-sounding language and imagery for marketing purposes

cult of domesticity the notion that women could and should wholeheartedly embrace the work of making a loving home

cultural competence a familiarity and facility with how the members of a society typically think and behave

cultural traveling moving from one cultural or subcultural context to another and sometimes back

culturalism the idea that we are "blank slates" that become who we are purely through learning and socialization

culturally unintelligible to be so outside the symbolic meaning system that people will not know how to interact with you

daddy benefit a name for the phenomenon in which fathers actually make more money than men without kids

desertion hypothesis a theory that suggests workers tend to abandon counter-stereotypical occupations at a higher rate than stereotypical ones

distinction efforts to distinguish one's own group from others

doing gender a phrase used to describe the ways in which we actively obey and break gender rules

domestic outsourcing paying non-family members to do family-related tasks

double bind a situation in which cultural expectations are contradictory

downward mobility a decline in one's socioeconomic position

drag queens and kings conventionally gendered and often heterosexual men and women who dress up and behave like members of the opposite sex, usually for fun or pay

egalitarians people who prefer relationships in which both partners do their fair share of breadwinning, housekeeping, and child-rearing

embedded feminists people who try to do feminist work in not explicitly feminist spaces

emotion work the act of controlling one's own emotions and managing the emotions of others

emphasized femininity an exaggerated form of femininity "oriented to accommodating the interests and desires of men"

emphatic sameness strategy by which women try to be "just one of the guys"

employer selection hypothesis a theory that proposes that employers tend to prefer men for masculine jobs and women for feminine jobs, slotting applicants into gender-consistent roles during hiring and promotion

equal access a model of creating egalitarianism by dismantling legal barriers and reducing sex discrimination

equal sharing a model of creating egalitarianism that targets subordination by attempting to ensure that men and women participate equally in masculine and feminine spheres

equal value a model of creating egalitarianism designed to tackle the problem of androcentrism by raising the value of the feminine to match the value of the masculine

erotic marketplace the ways in which people are organized and ordered according to their perceived sexual desirability

extended adolescence a significant period of time during which young people (who are no longer kids) prepare for a future (when they'll finally be "real" adults)

family wage an income paid to one male earner that was large enough to support a home, a wife, and children

fatherhood premium a wage increase that accrues to married men who become fathers

female a type of sex

female-bodied used to specify that sex refers to the body and may not extend to how a person feels or acts

feminine apologetic a requirement that women balance their appropriation of masculine interests, traits, and activities with feminine performance

feminine things we associate with women

feminism the belief that all men and women should have equal rights and opportunities

feminist utopia a perfectly gender-egalitarian society

feminization of poverty trend in which the poor are increasingly female

formal gender equality the legal requirement that men and women be treated more or less the same

gender the symbolism of masculinity and femininity that we connect to being male-bodied or female-bodied

gender-aware policymaking policymaking in which consideration of the effects on both men and women—and different kinds of men and women—is a required part of the policymaking process

gender binary glasses a pair of lenses that separate everything we see into masculine and feminine categories

gender binary the idea that there are only two types of people—male-bodied people who are masculine and female-bodied people who are feminine

gender dysphoria the sense that one is a man trapped in a woman's body, or vice versa

gender equivocation the use of both emphasized femininity and emphatic sameness when they're useful and culturally expected

gender identity a sense of oneself as male or female

gender of governance who holds political office and whether it matters

gender order the social organization of gender relations in a society

gender pay gap the difference between the incomes of the average man and woman who work full-time

gender policing responses to the violation of gender rules aimed at promoting conformity

gender rules instructions for how to appear and behave as a man or woman

gender salience the relevance of gender across contexts, activities, and spaces

gender strategy finding a way of doing gender that works for us as unique individuals who are also shaped by other parts of our identity and the realities of our lives

gendered institution one in which gender is used as an organizing principle

gendered job segregation the practice of filling occupations with mostly male or mostly female workers

gendered love/sex binary a projection of the gender binary onto the ideas of love and sex

gene-environment interaction the fact that a gene can express itself in many, sometimes thousands of different ways and the environment is an important determining factor, telling our genes what to do and when

genes a set of instructions for building and maintaining our bodies

genotype a unique set of genes

glass ceiling the idea that there is an invisible barrier between women and top positions in masculine occupations

glass cliff a heightened risk of failing that often follows the glass ceiling

glass escalator an invisible ride to the top offered to men in female-dominated occupations

going steady practice of an often short-lived, but still exclusive, public pairing off

good girl/bad girl dichotomy the idea that women who behave themselves sexually are worthy of respect and women who don't are not

governance of gender how gender shapes the way that residents of states are regulated

governance the process of making decisions for the nation, ensuring the state's accountability to its citizens and enforcing the laws of the land

hegemonic masculinity a type of man, idealized by men and women alike, who functions to justify and naturalize gender inequality

hegemony a state of collective consent to inequality that is secured by the idea that it is inevitable, natural, or desirable

heteronormative the assumption that everyone is heterosexual unless there are signs indicating otherwise

heterosexual male gaze a way of looking at society from the perspective of a hypothetical heterosexual man

hierarchy of men a rough ranking of men from most to least masculine, with the assumption that more masculine is better

homonormativity a term used to describe sexual minorities who try to be as "normal" as possible

homophobia the fear and hatred of sexual minorities

hookup culture a new norm on college campuses in which casual sexual contact in the absence of romantic intentions is held up by many as an ideal

hormone feedback loops the fact that hormone levels don't just influence us to do things; the things we do also influence our hormone levels

hormones messengers in a chemical communication system

hostile sexism the condemnation of women with negative instead of positive stereotypes and the use of threats and violence to enforce women's subservience to men

hunter-gatherer societies that migrate seasonally, following crops and game across the landscape

hypermasculinity extreme conformity to the more aggressive rules of masculinity

ideal worker norm the idea that an employee should have the ability to devote themselves to their job without the distraction of family responsibilities

ideology a set of ideas widely shared by members of a society that guides identities, behaviors, and institutions

ideology of intensive motherhood the idea that (1) mothers should be the primary caretaker of their children, (2) child-rearing should include "copious amounts of time, energy, and material resources," and (3) giving children these things takes priority over all other interests, desires, and demands

individualism an attitude that reflects a new focus on the individual over the group

injection model of socialization a model in which genderless children are "dosed" with a gender role in their childhood

institutions persistent patterns of social interaction aimed at meeting the needs of a society that can't easily be met by individuals alone

intersectionality the fact that gender is not an isolated social fact about us, but instead intersects with our other identities

intersex bodies that are not clearly male or female

learned differences differences that are a result of how we're raised (for example, religion or parent-ing) or our socio-cultural environment (for example, education or media consumption)

learning model of socialization a model that suggests that socialization is a lifelong process of learning and re-learning gendered expectations and how to negotiate them

legislatures bodies elected to represent their constituents in regulating the affairs of the country

lynching murder carried out by citizens in the absence of due process, most notoriously by hanging

male a type of sex

male flight a phenomenon in which men abandon feminizing arenas of life

male-bodied used to specify that sex refers to the body and may not extend to how a person feels or acts

marriage bans policies against employing married women

masculine things we associate with men

masculinization of wealth the concentration of men in high-earning occupations

matrix of domination a structure in which multiple hierarchies intersect to create a pyramid of privilege, leaving on top only those people who are advantaged in every hierarchy

mental rotation the ability to imagine an object rotating in your mind

modified patriarchy patriarchy in which power is symbolically, but not legally, linked to men and masculinity

mommy tax a name for the lost wages, benefits, and Social Security contributions that come with taking time out of the workforce to raise small children and then re-entering it with less momentum

mommy track a workplace euphemism that refers to expecting less from mothers, with the understanding that they are sacrificing the right to expect equal pay, regular raises, or promotions

motherhood penalty a loss in wages associated with becoming a mother

mutable responsive to efforts to shift or disrupt

naturalism the idea that biology affects our behavior independently of our environment

nature/nurture debate argument between people who believe that observed differences between men and women are biological and those who believe that these differences are acquired through socialization

neo-traditionalists people who embrace a modified version of traditionalism: they think that a woman should be able to work if she desires, but only if it doesn't interfere with her "real" duty to take care of her husband and children

network hypothesis a theory that hiring often occurs through personal networks, which are themselves gendered, so hiring is gendered in turn

norms beliefs and practices that, by being institutionalized, are well known, widely followed, and culturally approved

observed differences the results of surveys, experiments, and other ways of collecting information

orgasm gap a phenomenon in which women involved in heterosexual relationships report fewer orgasms than men

othermothers women in the neighborhood who act as substitute mothers out of inclination or kindness

partnership marriage a model of marriage based on love and companionship between two equals who negotiate a division of labor unique to their relationship

patriarch/property marriage a model of marriage in which a woman was entered into a marriage by her father, who owned her until he "gave her away" at the wedding

patriarchal bargain a deal in which an individual or group accepts or even legitimates some of the costs of patriarchy in exchange for receiving some of its rewards

patriarchy literally, the rule of the father; it refers to the control of female and younger male family members by select adult men, or patriarchs

personal exception theory of gender a theory that allows us to reconcile our own complex identity with what we think we know about men and women by assuming that we're unusually unique

phenotype an observable set of physical and behavioral traits

policies explicit and codified expectations, often with stated consequences for deviance

politics of responsibility a form of resistance to negative racial stereotypes that involves being "good" and following conservative norms of appearance and behavior

priming trick in which study subjects are reminded of a stereotype right before a test

production the making of goods for sale

protective legislation policies designed to protect women from exploitation by restricting their workplace participation

push-and-resist dynamic a situation in which it is normal for men to press sexual activity consistently in the direction of increasing intimacy (whether he wants to or not) and for women to stop or slow down the accelerating intimacy when he's going "too far" (whether she wants to or not)

radical claim an idea that doesn't (yet) resonate with most members of a population

rape culture an environment that justifies, naturalizes, and even glorifies sexual pressure, coercion, and violence

reproduction the making and nurturing of human beings

second shift work that greets us when we come home from work

self-objectify the process by which people internalize the idea that their value is heavily dependent on their physical attractiveness

separate spheres the idea of a masculinized work world and a feminized home life

service and information economy an economy dependent on jobs focused on providing services for others or working with ideas

sex physical differences in primary sexual characteristics (the presence of organs directly involved in reproduction) and secondary sexual characteristics (such as patterns of hair growth, the amount of breast tissue, and distribution of body fat)

sex-influenced genes that do different things in male and female bodies

sexism prejudice against people based on their biological sex

sex-limited genes only expressed if they are in a male or female body

sex-linked traits tied to whether a person is a genetic female (XX) or genetic male (XY)

sexual dimorphism differences between males and females in appearance and behavior

sexual double standard different rules for the sexual behavior of men and women

sexual minorities gay, lesbian, and bisexual people

sexual objectification the reduction of a person to his or her sex appeal

sexual script the rules that guide sexual interaction

sexual subjectification the process by which people are told what their internal thoughts and feelings should be

sharing doing more or less symmetrical amounts of paid and unpaid work

smashing a term used to describe having a same-sex crush

social construction a process by which we make reality meaningful through shared interpretation

social movements collective, non-governmental efforts to change societies

social structure the entire set of institutions within which we live our lives

socialization hypothesis a theory that suggests that men and women respond to gender stereotypes when planning, training, and applying for jobs

specialization splitting unpaid and paid work so that each partner does more of one than the other

spectating watching one's sexual performance from the outside

stalled revolution a sweeping change in gender relations that is stuck halfway through

states institutions entrusted with the power to regulate everyday life on behalf of the group

subjectivity internal thoughts and feelings

subordination the placing of women into positions that make them subservient to or dependent on men

substantive representation policies important and helpful to women

suffrage the right to vote

symbolic representation women's presence in government

symbolic threat a presence that potentially degrades the identity of the dominant group

traditionalists people who ascribe to the values of the breadwinner/housewife marriage that emerged with industrialization and came to be seen as "traditional" and who believe that men should be responsible for earning income and women should be responsible for housework and child care

transnational feminist activism activism that involves efforts by feminists to change gender relations outside their own states and collaboration between and among feminists in different countries

transsexual a person who experiences gender dysphoria

treating a practice in which a man funds a woman's night on the town

universal suffrage the right of all citizens to vote

wage money gained from working in places like factories, mines, and shops that belong to others

women's (social) movements ones in which women attempt to determine what kinds of policies will improve their lives

working poor individuals who work but still live in poverty

NOTES

Chapter 1: Introduction

1. Elizabeth Semmelhack, *Heights of Fashion: A History of the Elevated Shoe* (Penzanze, UK: Periscope, 2008).

2. Nancy E. Rexford, *Women's Shoes in America, 1795–1930* (Kent, OH: Kent State University Press, 2000).

3. Shari Benstock and Suzanne Ferriss, "Introduction," in *Footnotes on Shoes*, ed. Shari Benstock and Suzanne Ferriss (New Brunswick, New Jersey: Rutgers University Press, 1993).

Chapter 2: Ideas

1. Carol Martin and Diane Ruble, "Children's Search for Gender Cues," *Current Directions in Psychological Science* 13, no. 2 (2004): 67.

2. Thomas Laqueur, *Making Sex: Body and Gender from the Greeks to Freud* (Cambridge: Harvard University Press, 1990).

3. Quoted in Laqueur, note 11, p. 4.

4. Gilbert Herdt, *Same Sex, Different Cultures: Exploring Gay and Lesbian Lives* (Boulder, CO: Westview Press, 1997).

5. Niko Besnier, "Polynesian Gender Liminality Through Time and Space," in *Third Sex, Third Gender: Beyond Sexual Dimorphism in Culture and History*, ed. Gilbert Herdt (New York: Zone, 1994), 285–328; Serena Nanda, *Gender Diversity: Cross-Cultural Variations* (Long Grove, IL: Waveland Press Inc., 2000).

6. Marc Lacey, "A Lifestyle Distinct: The Muxe of Mexico," *New York Times*, December 6, 2008.

7. Don Kulick, *Travesti: Sex, Gender, and Culture Among Brazilian Transgendered Prostitutes* (Chicago: The University of Chicago Press, 1998).

8. Christine Helliwell, "'It's Only a Penis': Rape, Feminism, and Difference," *Signs* 25, no. 3 (2000): 806–807.

9. Christine Gailey, "Evolutionary Perspectives on Gender Hierarchy," in *Analyzing Gender: A Handbook of Social Science Research*, ed. Beth Hess and Myra Marx Ferree (Newbury Park, CA: Sage Publications Inc., 1987).

10. Ifi Amadiume, *Male Daughters, Female Husbands: Gender and Sex in an African Society* (London: Zed Books, 1987).

11. Nelly Oudshoorn, *Beyond the Natural Body: An Archeology of Sex Hormones* (New York: Routledge, 1994).

12. Ross Nehm and Rebecca Young, "'Sex Hormones' in Secondary School Biology Textbooks," *Science and Educucation* 17 (2008): 1175–90.

13. Jenny Nordberg, "Afghan Boys Are Prized, So Girls Live the Part," *New York Times*, September 20, 2010.

14. René Grémaux, "Woman Becomes Man in the Balkans," in *Third Sex, Third Gender: Beyond Sexual Dimorphism in Culture and History*, ed. Gilbert Herdt (New York: Zone, 1996); Antonia Young,

Women Who Become Men: Albanian Sworn Virgins (New York: Berg, 2000); and Serena Nanda, *Gender Diversity: Cross-Cultural Variations* (Long Grove, IL: Waveland Press Inc., 2000).

15. Nicola Smith, "Sworn virgins dying out as Albanian girls reject manly role," *Times of London*, January 6, 2008, http://www.timesonline.co.uk/tol/news/world/europe/article3137518.ece.

16. Stanley B. Alpern, *Amazons of Black Sparta: The Women Warriors of Dahomey* (New York: New York University Press, 1998).

17. Interface Project, http://www.interfaceproject.org; "Androgen insensitivity syndrome," *PubMed Health*, July 19, 2012, http://www.ncbi.nlm.nih.gov/pubmedhealth/PMH0002163/.

18. Natalie Angier, *Woman: An Intimate Geography* (New York: Houghton Mifflin, 1999).

19. Intersex Society of North America. "How common is intersex?" n.d., http://www.isna.org/drupal/node/view/91; see also http://www.researchgate.net/publication/11812321_How_sexually_dimorphic_are_we_Review_and_synthesis/file/d912f505c59821d339.pdf; Gary Gates, "How many people are lesbian, gay, bisexual, and transgender?" The Williams Institute, 2011, http://williamsinstitute.law.ucla.edu/wp-content/uploads/Gates-How-Many-People-LGBT-Apr-2011.pdf.

20. National Institutes of Health, "What is Klinefelter Syndrome?" 2007, http://rarediseases.info.nih.gov/gard/8705/klinefelter-syndrome/case/22820/case-questions.

21. Mayo Clinic Staff, "Triple X Syndrome," *Mayo Clinic*, November 8, 2012, http://www.mayoclinic.com/health/triple-x-syndrome/DS01090.

22. Medline Plus, "Turner Syndrome," *National Institutes of Health*, January 4, 2014, http://www.nlm.nih.gov/medlineplus/turnersyndrome.html.

23. Margaret McDowell et al., Anthropometric Reference Data for Children and Adults: United States, 2003–2006, *National Health Statistics Reports* 10 (2008): 1–48.

24. Melissa Whitworth, "Victoria's Secret show: What does it take to be a Victoria's Secret Angel?" *Telegraph*, November 7, 2011, http://fashion.telegraph.co.uk/news-features/TMG8872623/Victorias-Secret-show-What-does-it-take-to-be-a-Victorias-Secret-Angel.html.

25. American Society of Plastic Surgeons; Alex Kuczynski, "A Sense of Anxiety a Shirt Won't Cover," *New York Times*, June 14, 2007.

26. Peter Berger and Thomas Luckmann, *The Social Construction of Reality: A Treatise in the Sociology of Knowledge* (New York: Doubleday, 1966).

27. Bem Banerji and Sandra Lipsitz, "Androgyny and gender schema theory: A conceptual and empirical integration," in *Nebraska Symposium on Motivation 1984: Psychology and Gender*, ed. T. B. Sonderegger (Lincoln: University of Nebraska Press, 1985).

28. Daniel Schacter and Elaine Scarry, *Memory Brain and Belief* (Cambridge: Harvard University Press, 2001); Steven B. Most, Anne Verbeck Sorber, and Joseph G. Cunningham, "Auditory Stroop reveals implicit gender associations in adults and children," *Journal of Experimental Social Psychology* 43, no. 2 (2007): 287–94.

29. Bem Banerji and Sandra Lipsitz, "Androgyny and gender schema theory: A conceptual and empirical integration," in *Nebraska Symposium on Motivation 1984: Psychology and Gender*, ed. T. B. Sonderegger (Lincoln: University of Nebraska Press, 1985).

30. Bem Banerji and Sandra Lipsitz, "Gender Schema Theory: A Cognitive Account of Sex Typing," *Psychological Review* 88, no. 4 (1981): 354–64.

31. Alison P. Lenton, Irene V. Blair, and Reid Hastie, "Illusions of Gender: Stereotypes Evoke False Memories," *Journal of Experimental Social Psychology* 37, no. 1 (2001): 3–14; L. S. Liben and M. L. Signorella, "Gender-Related Schemata and Constructive Memory in Children," *Child Development* 51, no. 1 (1980): 11–18.

32. Carol L. Martin and Charles F. Halverson, Jr., "The Effects of Sex-Typing Schemas on Young Children's Memory," *Child Development* 54, no. 3 (1983): 563–74.

33. Carol Martin and Diane Ruble, "Children's Search for Gender Cues," *Current Directions in Psychological Science* 13, no. 2 (2004): 67–70; Timothy J. Frawley, "Gender Schema and Prejudicial Recall: How Children Misremember, Fabricate, and Distort Gendered Picture Book Information," *Journal of Research in Childhood Education* 22, no. 3 (2008): 291–303; A. Cann and S. R. Newbern, "Sex stereotype effects in children's picture recognition," *Child Development* 55, no. 3 (1984): 1085–90; Carol L. Martin and Charles F. Halverson, Jr., "The Effects of Sex-Typing Schemas on Young Children's Memory," *Child Development* 54, no. 3 (1983): 563–74; J. Susskind, "Children's Perception of Gender-Based Illusory Correlations: Enhancing Preexisting Relationships Between Gender and Behavior," *Sex Roles*

48, no. 11 (2003): 483–94; Lea Conkright, Dorothy Flannagan, and James Dykes, "Effects of pronoun type and gender role consistency on children's recall and interpretation of stories," *Sex Roles* 43, no. 7/8 (2000): 481–97.

34. Heather M. Kleider et al., "Schema-driven source misattribution errors: remembering the expected from a witnessed event," *Applied Cognitive Psychology* 22, no. 1 (2008): 1–20.

35. Lauren R. Shapiro, "Eyewitness testimony for a simulated juvenile crime by male and female criminals with consistent or inconsistent gender-role characteristics," *Journal of Applied Developmental Psychology* 30, no. 6 (2009): 649–66.

36. Ibid., 651.

37. Armand Chatard, Serge Guimond, and Leila Selimbegovic, "'How good are you in math?' The effect of gender stereotypes on students' recollection of their school marks," *Journal of Experimental Social Psychology* 43, no. 6 (2007): 1017–24.

Chapter 3: Bodies

1. Kathryn Dindia, "Men are from North Dakota, Women are from South Dakota," in *Sex Differences and Similarities in Communication*, 2nd ed., ed. Kathryn Dindia and Daniel J. Canary (Mahwah, NJ: Erlbaum, 2006), 3–18.

2. Dorothy Sayers, "The Human-Not-Quite-Human," in *On the Contrary: Essays by Men and Women*, ed. Martha Rainbolt and Janet Fleetwood (New York: SUNY Press, 1983), 10.

3. Janet Hyde, "The Gender Similarities Hypothesis," *American Psychologist* 60, no. 6 (2005): 581–92.

4. University of Medicine and Dentistry of New Jersey, "Effect Size and Clinical/Practical Significance," n.d. (As a result of the New Jersey Medical and Health Sciences Education Restructuring Act, on July 1, 2013, most schools and units of the University of Medicine and Dentistry of New Jersey (UMDNJ), transferred to Rutgers, The State University of New Jersey. This study may have been removed from the internet in the process.)

5. Janet Hyde, "The Gender Similarities Hypothesis," *American Psychologist* 60, no. 6 (2005): 581–92.

6. Mary Beth Oliver and Janet S. Hyde, "Gender differences in sexuality: A meta-analysis," *Psychological Bulletin* 114 (1993): 29–51.

7. Reviewed in Janet Hyde, "The Gender Similarities Hypothesis," *American Psychologist* 60, no. 6 (2005): 581–92.

8. M. H. Davies and L. A. Kraus, "Personality and empathic accuracy," in *Empathic Accuracy*, ed. William J. Ickes (New York: The Guilford Press, 1997), 144–68; Nancy Briton and Judith Hall, "Beliefs about Female and Male Non-Verbal Communication," *Sex Roles* 32 (1995): 79–90.

9. D. M. Marx and D. A. Stapel, "It depends on your perspective: The role of self-relevance in stereotype-based underperformance," *Journal of Experimental Social Psychology* 42 (2006): 768–75.

10. K. J. K. Klein and S. D. Hodges, "Gender Differences, Motivation, and Empathic Accuracy: When it Pays to Understand," *Personality and Social Psychology Bulletin* 27, no. 6 (2001): 720–30.

11. G. Thomas and G. R. Maio, "Man, I Feel Like a Woman: When and How Gender-Role Motivation Helps Mind-Reading," *Journal of Personality and Social Psychology* 95, no. 5 (2008): 1165–79.

12. Joan Chrisler and Donald McCreary, eds., *Handbook of Gender Research in Psychology* (New York: Springer, 2010),

13. Brian Nosek, Mahzarin Banaji, and Anthony Greenwald, "Math = Male, Me = Female, Therefore Math ≠ Me," *Journal of Personality and Social Psychology* 83, no. 1 (2002): 44–59.

14. Natalie Angier and Kenneth Chang, "Gray Matter and Sexes: A Gray Area Scientifically," *New York Times*, January 24, 2005, http://www.nytimes.com/2005/01/24/science/24women.html?_r=1.

15. Janet S. Hyde et al., "Gender similarities characterize math performance," *Science* 321 (2008): 494–95; Sara M. Lindberg et al., "New trends in gender and mathematics performance: A meta-analysis," *Psychological Bulletin* 136 (2010): 1123–35.

16. Natalie Angier and Kenneth Chang, "Gray Matter and Sexes: A Gray Area Scientifically," *New York Times*, January 24, 2005, http://www.nytimes.com/2005/01/24/science/24women.html?_r=1.

17. Ibid.

18. Brian A. Nosek et al., "National differences in gender-science stereotypes predict national sex differences in science and math achievement," *Proceedings of the National Academy of Sciences* 106, no. 26 (2009):10593–97.

19. Luigi Guiso et al., "Culture, gender, and math," *Science* 320, no. 5880 (2008): 1164–65; Nicole Else-Quest, Janet Hyde, and Marcia Linn, "Cross-National Patterns of Gender Differences in Mathematics: A Meta-Analysis," *Psychological Bulletin* 136, no. 1 (2010): 103–127.

20. Natalie Angier and Kenneth Chang, "Gray Matter and Sexes: A Gray Area Scientifically," *New York Times*, January 24, 2005, http://www.nytimes.com/2005/01/24/science/24women.html?_r=1.

21. Janet S. Hyde et al., "Gender similarities characterize math performance," *Science* 321 (2008): 494–95; Sara M. Lindberg et al., "New trends in gender and mathematics performance: A meta-analysis," *Psychological Bulletin* 136 (2010): 1123–35.

22. Diane Halpern et al., "The Science of Sex Differences in Science and Mathematics." *Psychological Science in the Public Interest* 8, no. 1 (2007): 1–51.

23. Elizabeth Spelke, "Sex Differences in Intrinsic Aptitude for Mathematics and Science? A Critical Review," *American Psychologist* 60, no. 9 (2005): 950–58.

24. Joan Burrelli, *Thirty-Three Years of Women in S&E Faculty Positions*, InfoBrief. Science Resources Statistics, NSF 08-308, National Science Foundation Directorate for Social, Behavioral, and Economic Sciences, 2008, http://www.nsf.gov/statistics/infbrief/nsf08308/nsf08308.pdf; see also Robert J. Daverman (AMS Secretary), "Statistics on women mathematicians compiled by the AMS," *Notices of the AMS* 58 (2011): 1310.

25. Ian Craig, Emma Harper, and Caroline Loat, "The Genetic Basis for Sex Differences in Human Behaviour: Role of the Sex Chromosomes," *Annals of Human Genetics* 68 (2004): 269–84.

26. Ibid.

27. R. Scott Hawley, and Catherine A. Mori, *The Human Genome: A User's Guide* (San Diego, CA: Academic Press, 1999).

28. E. Turkheimer and D. F. Halpern, "Sex differences in variability for cognitive measures: Do the ends justify the genes?" *Perspectives on Psychological Science* 4 (2009): 612–14.

29. Wendy Johnson, Andrew Carothers, and Ian J. Deary, "A Role for the X Chromosome in Sex Differences in Variability in General Intelligence?" *Perspectives on Psychological Science* 4, no. 6 (2009): 598–611.

30. Angela Book, Katherine Starzyk, and Vernon Quinsey, "The Relationship Between Testosterone and Aggression: A Meta-Analysis," *Aggression and Violent Behavior* 6 (2001): 579–99; Allan Mazur and Alan Booth, "Testosterone and Dominance in Men," *Behavioral and Brain Sciences* 21 (1998): 353–97; Melissa Hines, *Brain Gender* (New York: Oxford University Press, 2004).

31. Roy Baumeister, Kathleen Catanese, and Kathleen Vohs, "Is There a Gender Difference in Strength of Sex Drive? Theoretical Views, Conceptual Distinctions, and a Review of Relevant Evidence," *Personality and Social Psychology Review* 5, no. 3 (2001): 242–73.

32. Robert Sapolsky, *The Trouble with Testosterone and Other Essays on the Biology of the Human Predicament* (New York: Simon and Schuster, 1997), 154; William Yates et al., "Psychosexual Effects of Three Doses of Testosterone Cycling in Normal Men," *Biological Psychiatry* 45, no. 3 (1999): 254–60.

33. Diane Halpern, *Sex Differences in Cognitive Abilities*, 4th ed. (New York: Psychology Press, 2012); E. G. Oinonen, Kirsten Mazmanian, and Dwight Mazmanian, "Effects of oral contraceptives on daily self-ratings of positive and negative affect," *Journal of Psychosomatic Research* 51 (2001): 647–58.

34. Annette Stanton et al., "Psychosocial Aspects of Selected Issues in Women's Reproductive Health: Current Status and Future Directions," *Journal of Consulting and Clinical Psychology* 66 (2002): 313–22; Sharon Golub, *Periods: From Menarche to Menopause* (Newbury Park, CA: Sage, 1992).

35. Jessica McFarlane, Carol Martin, and Tannis Williams, "Mood Fluctuations: Women versus men and menstrual versus other cycles," *Psychology of Women Quarterly* 12 (1988): 201–24; Jessica McFarlane and Tannis Williams, "Placing Premenstrual Syndrome in Perspective," *Psychology of Women Quarterly* 18 (1994): 339–74.

36. Anne Fausto-Sterling, *Myths of Gender: Biological Theories about Women and Men* (New York: Basic Books, 1992).

37. Diane Halpern, *Sex Differences in Cognitive Abilities*, 4th ed. (New York: Psychology Press, 2012).

38. Anthony Esgate and David Groome, *An Introduction to Applied Cognitive Psychology* (Hove: Psychology Press, 2004).

39. Diane Halpern, *Sex Differences in Cognitive Abilities*, 4th ed. (New York: Psychology Press, 2012).

40. Ibid.

41. Melissa Hines, *Brain Gender* (New York: Oxford University Press, 2004); Kristina A. Pfannkuche, Anke Bouma, and Ton G. G. Groothuis, "Does testosterone affect lateralization of brain and behaviour? A meta-analysis in humans and other animal species," *Philosophical Transactions of the*

Royal Society 364 (2009): 929–42; Iris E. Sommer et al., "Sex differences in handedness, asymmetry of the Planum Temporale and functional language lateralization," *Brain Research* 1206 (2008): 76–88.

42. Diane Halpern, *Sex Differences in Cognitive Abilities*, 4th ed. (New York: Psychology Press, 2012); Melissa Hines, *Brain Gender* (New York: Oxford University Press, 2004).

43. Rebecca Jordan-Young, *Brain Storm: The Flaws in the Science of Sex Differences* (Cambridge: Harvard University Press, 2010); Diane Halpern, *Sex Differences in Cognitive Abilities*, 4th ed. (New York: Psychology Press, 2012).

44. Geert J. De Vries, "Sex Differences in Adult and Developing Brains: Compensation, compensation, compensation," *Endocrinology* 145, no. 3 (2004): 1063–68.

45. Melissa S. Terlecki, Nora S. Newcombe, and Michelle Little, "Durable and generalized effects of spatial experience on mental rotation: Gender differences in growth patterns," *Applied Cognitive Psychology* 22 (2007): 996–1013.

46. Jing Feng, Ian Spence, and Jay Pratt, "Playing an action video game reduces gender differences in spatial cognition," *Psychological Science* 18 (2007): 850–55.

47. Richard De Lisi, and Jennifer Wolford, "Improving Children's Mental Rotation Accuracy with Computer Game Playing," *The Journal of Genetic Psychology* 163, no. 3 (2002): 272–82.

48. I. D. Cherney et al., "Experiential factors on sex differences in mental rotation." *Perceptual and Motor Skills* 96 (2003): 1062–70.

49. For a summary, see Isabelle D. Cherney, "Mom, Let Me Play More Computer Games: They Improve My Mental Rotation Skills," *Sex Roles* 59 (2008): 776–86.

50. Nora Newcombe, "Science Seriously: Straight Thinking About Spatial Sex Differences," in *Why Aren't More Women in Science? Top Researchers Debate the Evidence*, ed. Stephen Ceci and Wendy Williams (Washington, DC: American Psychological Association, 2007).

51. Lise Eliot, *Pink Brain, Blue Brain* (New York: Houghton Mifflin Harcourt Publishing Company, 2009); I. D. Cherney and K. L. London, "Gender-linked differences in the toys, television shows, computer games, and outdoor activities of 5-to 13-year-old children," *Sex Roles* 54 (2006): 717–26; Joanne Kersh, Beth M. Casey, and Jessica Mercer Young, "Research on spatial skills and block building in girls and boys: The relationship to later mathematics learning," in *Mathematics, science and technology in early childhood education: Contemporary perspectives on mathematics in early childhood education*, ed. B. Spodak and O. N. Saracho (Charlotte, NC: Information Age, 2008), 233–53.

52. Susan C. Levine et al., "Socioeconomic status modifies the sex difference in spatial skill," *Psychological Science* 16 (2005): 841–45; K. G. Noble, M. F. Norman, and M. J. Farah, "Neurocognitive correlates of socioeconomic status in kindergarten children." *Developmental Science* 8 (2005): 74–87.

53. Maryann Baenninger and Nora Newcombe, "Environmental input to the development of sex-related differences in spatial and mathematical ability," *Learning and Individual Differences* 7, no. 4 (1995): 363–79.

54. Lise Eliot, *Pink Brain, Blue Brain* (New York: Houghton Mifflin Harcourt Publishing Company, 2009), 6.

55. Thomas Pynchon, *Gravity's Rainbow* (New York: Penguin, 1974), 251.

56. Anne Fausto-Sterling, "The Bare Bones of Sex: Part I–Sex and Gender," *Signs* 30, no. 2 (2005): 1510.

57. Described in Michael J. Meaney, "The nature of nurture: maternal effects and chromatin remodelling," in *Essays in Social Neuroscience*, ed. John T. Cacioppo and Gary G. Berntson (Cambridge: Massachusetts Institute of Technology Press, 2004).

58. Judith Lorber, *Paradoxes of Gender* (New Haven: Yale University Press, 1993), x.

59. Cecil R. Reynolds and Elaine Fletcher-Janzen, *Concise Encyclopedia of Special Education: A Reference for the Education of the Handicapped and Other Exceptional Children and Adults* (New York: John Wiley and Sons, 2004).

60. Ibid., 428.

61. See also Bruce Perry and Maia Szalavitz, *The Boy Who Was Raised as a Dog and Other Stories from a Child Psychiatrist's Notebook* (New York: Basic Books, 2008).

62. Peter Berger and Thomas Luckmann, 1966. *The Social Construction of Reality: A Treatise in the Sociology of Knowledge* (New York: Doubleday, 1966).

63. Rebecca Jordan-Young, *Brain Storm: The Flaws in the Science of Sex Differences* (Cambridge: Harvard University Press, 2010), 271; Michael Meaney, "Nature, Nurture, and the Disunity of Knowledge," *Annals New York Academy of Sciences* 935 (2001): 50–61.

64. Genetic Science Learning Center, "Insights from Identical Twins," *Learn.Genetics*, January 5, 2014, http://learn.genetics.utah.edu/content/epigenetics/twins/.

65. Barbara Bradley Hagerty, "A Neuroscientist Uncovers a Dark Secret," *NPR*, June 29, 2010, http://www.npr.org/templates/story/story.php?storyId=127888976 .

66. Kristen Jacobson, "Considering Interactions between Genes, Environments, Biology, and Social Context," *American Psychological Association* (April 2009), http://www.apa.org/science/about/psa/2009/04/sci-brief.aspx.

67. R. J. Cadoret et al., "Genetic-environmental interaction in the genesis of aggressivity and conduct disorders," *Archives of General Psychiatry* 52 (1995): 916–24.

68. Allan Mazur, Elizabeth Susman, and Sandy Edelbrock, "Sex Difference in Testosterone Response to a Video Game Contest," *Evolution and Human Behavior* 18, no. 5 (1997): 317–26; Richard E. Nisbett and Dov Cohen, *Culture of Honor: The Psychology of Violence in the South* (Boulder, CO: Westview, 1996); A. G. Booth et al., "Testosterone, and winning and losing in human competition," *Hormones and Behavior* 23 (1989): 556–71; A. Booth, D. R. Johnson, and D. A. Granger, "Testosterone and men's depression: the role of social behavior," *Journal of Health and Social Behavior* 40 (1999): 130–40; Robert Sapolsky, *The Trouble with Testosterone and Other Essays on the Biology of the Human Predicament* (New York: Simon and Schuster, 1997).

69. Allan Mazur, Alan Booth, and James Dabbs, Jr., "Testosterone and Chess Competition," *Social Psychology Quarterly* 55, no. 1 (1992): 70–77.

70. Paul C. Bernhardt et al., "Testosterone Changes During Vicarious Experiences of Winning and Losing Among Fans at Sporting Events," *Physiology and Behavior* 65, no. 1 (1998): 59–62.

71. Gad Saad and John Vongas, "The Effect of Conspicuous Consumption on Men's Testosterone Levels," *Organizational Behavior and Human Decision Processes* 110, no. 2 (2009): 80–92.

72. Alicia Salvador, "Coping with Competitive Situations in Humans," *Neuroscience and Biobehavioral Reviews* 29, no.1 (2005): 195–205.

73. Leander Van der Meij et al., "The Presence of a Woman Increases Testosterone in Aggressive Dominant Men," *Hormones and Behavior* 54, no. 5 (2008): 640–44.

74. David Edwards, "Competition and Testosterone," *Hormones and Behavior* 50 (2006): 682.

75. National Science Foundation, "Men Also Wired for Childcare," *National Science* Foundation, September 13, 2011, http://www.nsf.gov/news/news_summ.jsp?cntn_id=121658.

76. Christopher Kuzawa et al., "Fatherhood, pair-bonding, and testosterone in the Philippines," *Hormones and Behavior* 56, no. 4 (2009): 429–35.

77. Martin N. Muller et al., "Testosterone and paternal care in East African foragers and pastoralists," *Proceedings of the Royal Society: Biological Sciences* 276 (2009): 347–54.

78. Anne Fausto-Sterling, "The Bare Bones of Sex: Part I–Sex and Gender," *Signs* 30, no. 2 (2005): 1491–1528.

79. Quoted in Anne Fausto-Sterling, *Myths of Gender: Biological Theories about Women and Men* (New York: Basic Books, 1992), 217.

80. Charlie Lovett, *Olympic Marathon: A Centennial History of the Games' Most Storied Race* (Westport, CT: Praeger Publishers, 1997).

81. Anne Fausto-Sterling, "The Bare Bones of Sex: Part I–Sex and Gender," *Signs* 30, no. 2 (2005).

82. Phys.org., "Annual Bone Fracture Rate Almost 4 Percent and Double Previous Estimates," *Phys.org*, January 17, 2008, http://phys.org/news119786629.html.

83. Rebecca Jordan-Young, *Brain Storm: The Flaws in the Science of Sex Differences* (Cambridge: Harvard University Press, 2010), 285.

84. Diane Halpern, *Sex Differences in Cognitive Abilities*, 4th ed. (New York: Psychology Press, 2012); Rebecca Jordan-Young, *Brain Storm: The Flaws in the Science of Sex Differences* (Cambridge: Harvard University Press, 2010).

85. David R. Moore and Robert V. Shannon, "Beyond cochlear implants: awakening the deafened brain," *Nature Neuroscience* 12 (2009): 686–91.

86. Alex Tresniowski and Ron Arias, "The Boy Who Sees with Sound," *People*, July 14, 2006, http://www.people.com/people/article/0,26334,1212568,00.html.

87. Richard J. Haier et al., "MRI Assessment of Cortical Thickness and Functional Activity Changes in Adolescent Girls Following Three Months of Practice on a Visual-Spatial Task," *BioMed Central Research Notes* 2 (2009): 174.

88. Marco Taubert et al., "Dynamic Properties of Human Brain Structure: Learning-Related Changes

in Cortical Areas and Associated Fiber Connections," *The Journal of Neuroscience* 30 (2010): 11670–77.

89. James Flynn, "The Mean IQ of Americans: Massive Gains 1932 to 1978," *Psychological Bulletin* 95 (1984): 29–51; Ulric Neisser, ed., *The Rising Curve: Long-Term Gains in IQ and Related Measures* (Washington, DC: American Psychological Association, 1998).

90. H. L. Mencken, "The Divine Afflatus" *New York Evening Mail*, November 16, 1917.

91. Edward O. Wilson, "On Human Nature," in William Andrew Rottschaefer. *The Biology and Psychology of Moral Agency* (Cambridge: Cambridge University Press, 1998). 58.

Chapter 4: Performances

1. Digest of Education Statistics, Table 290. Bachelor's, master's, and doctor's degrees conferred by degree-granting institutions, by sex of student and discipline division: 2009–10, http://nces.ed.gov /programs/digest/d11/tables/dt11_290.asp.

2. Sandra L. Bem, *The Lenses of Gender: Transforming the Debate on Sexual Inequality* (New Haven: Yale University Press, 1993), 149.

3. Margo DeMello, *Encyclopedia of Body Adornment* (Westport, CT: Greenwood Press, 2007).

4. Amy Wilkins, *Wannabes, Goths, and Christians: The Boundaries of Sex, Style, and Status* (Chicago: The University of Chicago Press, 2008), 35.

5. For a review, see Carol Martin and Diane Ruble, "Children's Search for Gender Cues," *Current Directions in Psychological Science* 13, no. 2 (2004): 69.

6. Joan Roughgarden, *Evolution's Rainbow: Diversity, Gender and Sexuality in Nature and People* (Berkeley: University of California Press, 2004), 27.

7. Michael Messner, "Barbie Girls versus Sea Monsters: Children Constructing Gender," *Gender and Society* 14, no. 6 (2000): 765–84; Barrie Thorne, *Gender Play* (New Brunswick, NJ: Rutgers, 1995).

8. Carol Martin and Diane Ruble, "Children's Search for Gender Cues." *Current Directions in Psychological Science* 13, no. 2 (4002): 67.

9. Ibid., 67.

10. David F. Bjorklund, *Children's thinking: Developmental function and individual differences* (Belmont, CA: Wadsworth, 2000).

11. Carol Martin and Diane Ruble, "Children's Search for Gender Cues." *Current Directions in Psychological Science* 13, no. 2 (4002): 67–70.

12. Hanns Trautner et al., "Rigidity and flexibility of gender stereotypes in childhood: Developmental or differential?" *Infant and Child Development* 14, no. 4 (2005): 365–81.

13. Michael Kimmel, *The Gendered Society* (New York: Oxford University Press, 2004), 94.

14. United States Federal Bureau of Investigation, Hate Crime Statistics 2011, http://www.fbi.gov /about-us/cjis/ucr/hate-crime/2011/narratives /incidents-and-offenses.

15. Betsy Lucal, "What it Means to be Gendered Me: Life on the Boundaries of a Dichotomous Gender System," *Gender & Society* 13, no. 6 (1999): 781–797.

Chapter 5: Intersections

1. Fem Korsten, "Grappling with My Sexuality Now That I'm in a Wheelchair," *xoJane UK* (blog), September 19, 2012, http://www.xojane.co.uk/issues /disability-sexuality-street-harassment.

2. Gloria Anzaldua, *Borderlands/La Frontera: The New Mestiza* (San Francisco: Aunt Lute Books, 1987); Kimberlé W. Crenshaw, "Mapping the Margins: Intersectionality, Identity Politics, and Violence against Women of Color," *Stanford Law Review* 43, no. 6 (1991): 1241–99; Patricia Hill Collins, *Black Feminist Thought: Knowledge, Consciousness, and the Politics of Empowerment* (New York: Routledge, 1991).

3. Arlie Hochschild, *The Second Shift* (New York: Viking, 1989).

4. Arlie Hochschild, "Giving at the Office," in *Men and Masculinity: A Text-Reader*, ed. Theodore Cohen (Belmont, CA: Wadsworth, 2001), 282–89.

5. Kathleen Gerson, *No man's land: Men's changing commitments to family and work* (New York: Basic Books, 1993).

6. Theodore Cohen and John Durst, "Leaving Work and Staying Home: The Impact on Men of Terminating the Male Economic-Provider Role," in *Men and Masculinity: A Text-Reader*, ed. Theodore Cohen (Belmont, CA: Wadsworth, 2001), 302–19.

7. Arlie Hochschild, *The Second Shift* (New York: Viking, 1989).

8. Carla Shows and Naomi Gerstel, "Fathering, Class, and Gender: A Comparison of Physicians and EMTs," *Gender & Society* 23, no. 2 (2009): 161–87.

9. Ibid., 179.

10. Karen D. Pyke, "Class-Based Masculinities: The Interdependence of Gender, Class, and Interpersonal Power," *Gender & Society* 10, no. 5 (1996): 531.

11. Kris Paap, *Working Construction: Why White Working-Class Men Put Themselves—and the Labor Movement—in Harm's Way* (Ithaca and London: IRL Press, 2006), 137.

12. Matthew Desmond, *On the Fireline: Living and Dying with Wildland Firefighters* (Chicago: The University of Chicago Press, 2007).

13. Joane Nagel, *Race, ethnicity, and sexuality: Intimate intersections, forbidden frontiers* (New York: Oxford University Press, 2003).

14. Ibid.

15. Yolanda Niemman et al., "Use of Free Responses and Cluster Analysis to Determine Stereotypes of Eight Groups," *Personality and Social Psychology Bulletin* 20 (1994): 379–90.

16. Ann Ferguson, *Bad Boys: Public Schools in the Making of Black Masculinity* (Ann Arbor, MI: The University of Michigan Press, 2001).

17. Ibid.

18. Ibid., 87.

19. Brent Staples, "Just Walk on By: A Black Man Ponders His Power to Alter Public Space," in *Reconstructing Gender: A Multicultural Anthology*, ed. Estelle Disch (New York: McGraw Hill, 1997), 168.

20. Joe R. Feagin, "The Continuing Significance of Race: Antiblack discrimination in public places," in *Rethinking the Color Line: Readings in Race and Ethnicity*, ed. Charles A. Gallagher (New York: McGraw Hill, 1999), 101–116.

21. Sarah Childress, "Is There Racial Bias in 'Stand Your Ground' Laws?" *Frontline*, PBS, July 31, 2012, http://www.pbs.org/wgbh/pages/frontline/criminal-justice/is-there-racial-bias-in-stand-your-ground-laws/.

22. Tushar Kansal, *Racial Disparity in Sentencing: A Review of the Literature* (Washington, DC: The Sentencing Project, 2005), https://docs.google.com/viewer?url=http%3A%2F%2Fwww.prisonpolicy.org%2Fscans%2Fsp%2Fdisparity.pdf; Christopher Maxwell, "The Impact of Race on the Adjudication of Sexual Assault and Other Violent Crimes," *Journal of Criminal Justice* 31 (2003): 523–38.

23. Robert Fogel, *Without Consent or Contract: The Rise and Fall of American Slavery* (New York and London: W.W. Norton and Company, 1989).

24. Drucilla Cornell, "Las Grenudas: Recollections on Consciousness-Raising," *Signs* 25, no. 4 (2000): 1033–39; Patricia Hill Collins, *Black Sexual Politics: African Americans, Gender, and the New Racism* (New York: Routledge, 2004).

25. Rose Weitz, "Women and their Hair: Seeking Power through Resistance and Accommodation," *Gender & Society* 15, no. 5 (2001): 680.

26. Yolanda Niemman et al., "Use of Free Responses and Cluster Analysis to Determine Stereotypes of Eight Groups," *Personality and Social Psychology Bulletin* 20 (1994): 379–90.

27. Robert Lee, *Orientals: Asian Americans in Popular Culture* (Philadelphia: Temple University Press, 1999).

28. Anthony Chen, "Lives at the Center of the Periphery, Lives at the Periphery of the Center: Chinese American Masculinities and Bargaining with Hegemony," *Gender & Society* 13, no. 5 (1999): 584–607.

29. Yen L. Espiritu, *Asian American women and men* (Thousand Oaks, CA: Sage, 1997); Renee E. Tajima, "Lotus blossoms don't bleed: Images of Asian women," in *Making Waves*, ed. Asian Women United of California (Boston: Beacon Press, 1989), 308–317.

30. Karen Eng, "The Yellow Fever Pages," *Bitch* 12, Summer 2000, 69.

31. Ibid., 70.

32. Karen D. Pyke and Denise L. Johnson, "Asian American Women and Racialized Femininities: 'Doing' Gender across Cultural Worlds," *Gender & Society* 17, no. 1 (2003): 46.

33. Ibid., 45.

34. Amy Wilkins, *Wannabes, Goths, and Christians: The Boundaries of Sex, Style, and Status* (Chicago: The University of Chicago Press, 2008), 52.

35. Ibid.

36. Ibid., 151.

37. Ibid., 198.

38. Gerard Wright, "Gay Grief in Cowboy Country," *Guardian*, March 27, 1999, http://www.guardian.co.uk/books/1999/mar/27/books.guardianreview7?INTCMP=SRCH.

39. Laura Hamilton, "Trading on Heterosexuality: College Women's Gender Strategies and Homophobia," *Gender & Society* 21, no. 2 (2007): 156.

40. Kirsten Dellinger and Christine Williams, "Makeup at Work: Negotiating Appearance Rules in the Workplace," *Gender & Society* 11, no. 2 (1997): 162.

41. Michael Price, "Rugby as a gay men's game" (Ph.D. diss., University of Warwick, Coventry, UK, 2000).

42. Jennifer Taub, "Bisexual Women and Beauty Norms: A Qualitative Examination," in *Lesbians, Levis and Lipstick: The Meaning of Beauty in Our Lives*, ed. Joanie Erickson and Jeanine Cogan, Haworth Gay and Lesbian Studies (New York: Routledge, 1999), 27–36.

43. Lisa Duggan, *The Twilight of Equality? Neoliberalism, Cultural Politics, and the Attack On Democracy* (Boston: Beacon Press, 2003).

44. Jennifer Taub, "Bisexual Women and Beauty Norms: A Qualitative Examination," in *Lesbians, Levis and Lipstick: The Meaning of Beauty in Our Lives*, ed. Joanie Erickson and Jeanine Cogan, Haworth Gay and Lesbian Studies (New York: Routledge, 1999), 31.

45. JeeYeun Lee, "Why Suzie Wong is not a Lesbian: Asian and Asian American Lesbian and Bisexual Women and Femme/Butch/Gender Identities," in *Queer Studies: A Lesbian, Gay, Bisexual and Transgender Anthology*, ed. Brett Beemyn and Mickey Eliason (New York: New York University Press, 1996), 123.

46. Patricia Hill Collins, *Black Feminist Thought: Knowledge, Consciousness, and the Politics of Empowerment* (New York: Routledge, 1991).

47. Lisa Rofel, "Qualities of Desire: Imagining Gay Identities in China," *GLQ* 5, no. 4 (1999): 451–74; Raymond Hibbins, "Sexuality and Constructions of Gender Identity among Chinese Male Migrants in Australia," *Asian Studies Review* 30 (2006): 289–303.

48. Michael Stambolis-Ruhstorfer, "Labels of Love: How Migrants Negotiate (or Not) the Culture of Sexual Identity," *American Journal of Cultural Sociology* 1, no.3 (2013): 321–345.

49. Mignon R. Moore, "'Black and Gay in L.A.': The Relationships Black Lesbians and Gay Men have with their Racial and Religious Communities," in *Black Los Angeles: American Dreams and Racial Realities*, ed. Darnell Hunt and Ana-Christina Ramon (New York: New York University Press, 2010), 188–212.

50. Jane Ward, "Straight Dude Seeks Same: Mapping the Relationships between Sexual Identities, Practices, and Cultures," in *Sex Matters: The Sexuality and Society Reader*, ed. Mindy Stombler, et al. (New York: W. W. Norton, 2008), 29–35.

51. For a review of this phenomenon among Asian immigrants, see Yen Le Espiritu, "Asian American Panethnicity: Bridging Institutions and Identities," in *Rethinking the Color Line: Readings in Race and Ethnicity*, ed. Charles A. Gallagher (New York: McGraw Hill, 1999).

52. Cecilia Menjivar, "The Intersection of Work and Gender: Central American Immigrant Women and Employment in California," *American Behavioral Scientist* 42, no. 4 (1999): 609.

53. Ibid., 616.

54. Ibid., 611.

55. Michael Stambolis-Ruhstorfer, "Labels of Love: How Migrants Negotiate (or Not) the Culture of Sexual Identity," *American Journal of Cultural Sociology* (forthcoming).

56. Lesley Doyal, Sara Paparini, and Jane Anderson, "'Elvis Died and I Was Born': Black African Men Negotiating Same-Sex Desire in London," *Sexualities* 11, no. 1–2 (2008): 171–92.

57. Ibid., 179–80.

58. Thomas J. Gerschick, "Toward a Theory of Disability and Gender," *Signs: Journal of Women in Culture and Society* 25, no. 4 (2000): 1264.

59. R. Noam Ostrander, "When Identities Collide: Masculinity, Disability, and Race," *Disability & Society* 23, no. 6 (2008): 585–97.

60. Ibid., 594.

61. Ingunn Moser, "Sociotechnical Practices and Difference: On the Interferences between Disability, Gender, and Class," *Science, Technology, and Human Values* 31, no. 5 (2006): 537–64.

62. Ibid., 538.

63. Ibid., 548.

64. Thomas Gerschick and Adam Miller, "Coming to Terms: Masculinity and Physical Disability," in *Men's Health and Illness: Gender, Power, and the Body*, ed. Donald Sabo and David Frederick Gordon (Thousand Oaks: Sage Publications, 1995). 187–88.

65. R. Noam Ostrander, "When Identities Collide: Masculinity, Disability, and Race," *Disability & Society* 23, no. 6 (2008): 592.

66. Tom Shakespeare, Kath Gillespie-Sells, and Dominic Davies, *The Sexual Politics of Disability: Untold Desires* (London, UK: Cassell, 1996).

67. Ibid, 10.

68. Michelle Fine and Adrienne Asch, *Women with Disabilities: Essays in Psychology, Culture and Politics* (Philadelphia: Temple University Press, 1988), 29.

69. Harilyn Rousso, "Daughters with Disabilities: Defective Women or Minority Women?" in *Women*

with *Disabilities: Essays in Psychology, Culture and Politics*, ed. Michelle Fine and Adrienne Asch (Philadelphia: Temple University Press, 1988), 139–171.

70. Nasa Begum, "Disabled Women and the Feminist Agenda," *Feminist Review* 40 (1992): 70–84.

71. Deborah Lisi, "Found voices: Women, disability and cultural transformation," *Women & Therapy* 14, no. 3/4 (1994): 195–209.

72. Ibid.

73. Ingunn Moser, "Sociotechnical Practices and Difference: On the Interferences between Disability, Gender, and Class," *Science, Technology, and Human Values* 31, no. 5 (2006): 553.

74. Ibid., 554.

75. Cheryl Laz, "Act Your Age," *Sociological Forum* 13, no. 1 (1998): 85–113.

76. Ibid., 86.

77. Barbro Johanssen, "Doing Age and Gender through Fashion," in *INTER: A European Cultural Studies Conference in Sweden, 11–13 June 2007*, ed. Johan Fornäs, Martin Fredriksson, conference proceedings (2007): 285, http://www.ep.liu.se/ecp/025/029/ecp072529.pdf.

78. Duncan Kennedy, *Sexy Dressing, Etc.: Essays on the Power and Politics of Cultural Identity* (Cambridge: Harvard University Press, 1993), 164.

79. R. N. Butler, "Age-ism: another form of bigotry," *Gerontologist* 9 (1969): 243–46.

80. Susan Sontag, "The Double Standard of Aging," *The Saturday Review*, September 23, 1972, 29–38.

81. Ibid.

82. Ibid.

Chapter 6: Inequality: Men and Masculinities

1. Quoted in Natalie Adams and Pamela Bettis. "Commanding the Room in Short Skirts: Cheering as the Embodiment of Ideal Girlhood," *Gender & Society* 17, no. 1 (2003): 76.

2. Rebecca Boyce, "Cheerleading in the Context of Title IX and Gendering in Sport," *The Sports Journal* 11, no. 3: (2008).

3. Quoted in Laurel Davis, "A Postmodern Paradox? Cheerleaders at Women's Sporting Events," in *Women, Sport, and Culture*, ed. Susan Birrell and Cheryl Cole (Champaign: Human Kinetics Press, 1994), 153.

4. James McElroy, *We've got spirit: The life and times of America's greatest cheerleading team* (New York: Simon & Schuster, 1999), 15.

5. Pamela Paxton, Sheri Kunovich, and Melanie Hughes. "Gender in Politics," *Annual Review of Sociology* 33 (2007): 263–84; Law Library of Congress, State Suffrage Laws, http://memory.loc.gov/ammem/awhhtml/awlaw3/suffrage.html.

6. Mykol Hamilton, "Masculine Bias in the Attribution of Personhood: People = Male, Male = People," *Psychology of Women Quarterly* 15, no. 3 (1991): 393–402.

7. *Thesaurus.com* s.v. "power," http://www.thesaurus.com/browse/power?s=t, accessed September 9, 2014.

8. *Thesaurus.com* s.v. "femininity," http://www.thesaurus.com/browse/femininity?s=t, accessed September 9, 2014.

9. Joan Wallace Scott, *Gender and the Politics of History* (New York: Columbia University Press, 1999), 44.

10. Janet Swim, et al., "Joan McKay Versus John McKay: Do Gender Stereotypes Bias Evaluations?" *Psychological Bulletin* 105, no. 3 (1989): 409–29; Pamela Paxton, Sheri Kunovich, and Melanie Hughes. "Gender in Politics," *Annual Review of Sociology* 33 (2007): 263–84.

11. Corinne Moss-Racusin, et al., "Science Faculty's Subtle Gender Biases Favor Male Students," *Proceedings of the National Academy of Sciences* 109, no. 41 (2012): 16474–479.

12. Janet Swim, et al., "Joan McKay Versus John McKay: Do Gender Stereotypes Bias Evaluations?" *Psychological Bulletin* 105, no. 3 (1989): 409–29.

13. Bureau of Labor Standards, Employed Persons by Detailed Occupation and Sex, 2007 Annual Averages, 2008, http://www.bls.gov/cps/wlf-table11-2008.pdf.

14. Bureau of Labor Standards, Employed Persons by Detailed Occupation and Sex, 2007 Annual Averages, 2008, http://www.bls.gov/cps/wlf-table11-2008.pdf; General Aviation Manufacturers Association, General Aviation: Statistical Databook & Industry Outlook, 2010, http://www.gama.aero/files/GAMA_DATABOOK_2011_web.pdf.

15. Emily Kane, "'No Way My Boys Are Going to be Like That!' Parents' Responses to Children's Gender Nonconformity," *Gender & Society* 20, no. 2 (2006): 149–76.

16. Ibid., 159.

17. Ibid., 159.

18. Michael Kimmel, "Masculinity as Homophobia: Fear, Shame and Silence in the Construction of Gender Identity," in *Theorizing Masculinities*, ed.

Harry Brod and Michael Kaufman, SAGE Series on Men and Masculinity (Newbury Park: Sage Publications, 1994), 119–142.

19. Eric Anderson, "Open Gay Athletes: Contesting Hegemonic Masculinity in a Homophobic Environment," *Gender & Society* 16, no. 6 (2002): 860–77; C. J. Pascoe, "'Dude, You're a Fag': Adolescent Masculinity and the Fag Discourse," *Sexualities* 8, no. 3 (2005): 329–46.

20. Eric Anderson, "Open Gay Athletes: Contesting Hegemonic Masculinity in a Homophobic Environment," *Gender & Society* 16, no. 6 (2002): 860–77; C. J. Pascoe, "'Dude, You're a Fag': Adolescent Masculinity and the Fag Discourse," *Sexualities* 8, no. 3 (2005): 329–46.

21. Eric Anderson, "Open Gay Athletes: Contesting Hegemonic Masculinity in a Homophobic Environment," *Gender & Society* 16, no. 6 (2002): 872.

22. Ibid., 872.

23. Gwen Sharp, "Policing Masculinity in Slim Jim's 'Spice Loss' Ads," *Sociological Images* (blog), August 21, 2012, http://thesocietypages.org/socimages/2012/08/21/policing-masculinity-in-slim-jims-spice-loss-ads/.

24. "Top 10: Drinks Real Men Don't Order," *AskMen*, http://www.askmen.com/top_10/entertainment/top-10-drinks-real-men-dont-order_10.html; "Girl Drinks—A List of Drinks Men Should Never Order," *CampusSqueeze*, http://www.campussqueeze.com/post/Girl-Drinks—A-List-of-Drinks-Men-Should-Never-Order.aspx.

25. Paula England and Su Li, "Desegregation Stalled: The Changing Gender Composition of College Majors, 1971–2002," *Gender & Society* 20, no. 5 (2006): 657–77.

26. Anne Lincoln, "The Shifting Supply of Men and Women to Occupation: Feminization in Veterinary Education," *Social Forces* 88, no. 5 (2010): 1969–98.

27. R. Stillwell and J. Sable, Public School Graduates and Dropouts from the Common Core of Data: School Year 2009–10: First Look (Provisional Data) (NCES 2013-309rev). U.S. Department of Education. Washington, DC: National Center for Education Statistics, 2013, http://nces.ed.gov/pubsearch; Office for Civil Rights. Gender Equity in Education: A Data Snapshot. Office for Civil Rights, 2012, http://www2.ed.gov/about/offices/list/ocr/docs/gender-equity-in-education.pdf.

28. U.S. Department of Education, National Center for Education Statistics, *The Condition of Education 2012* (NCES 2012-045), Table A-47-2, 2012; Office for Civil Rights, Gender Equity in Education: A Data Snapshot. Office for Civil Rights, 2012, http://www2.ed.gov/about/offices/list/ocr/docs/gender-equity-in-education.pdf.

29. Tamar Lewin, "At Colleges, Women are Leaving Men in the Dust," *New York Times*, July 9, 2006, http://www.nytimes.com/2006/07/09/education/09college.html?pagewanted=all.

30. Jack Kahn, Benjamin Brett, and Jessica Holmes, "Concerns with Men's Academic Motivation in Higher Education: An Exploratory Investigation of the Role of Masculinity," *Journal of Men's Studies* 19, no. 1 (2011): 65–82; Paul Willis, *Learning to Labor: How Working Class Kids Get Working Class Jobs* (New York: Columbia University Press, 1977); D. Epstein, "Real boys don't work: 'underachievement', masculinity, and the harassment of 'sissies'," in *Failing Boys? Issues in Gender and Achievement*, ed. D. Epstein et al. (Buckingham: Open University Press, 1998), 96–108.

31. Jack Kahn, Benjamin Brett, and Jessica Holmes, "Concerns with Men's Academic Motivation in Higher Education: An Exploratory Investigation of the Role of Masculinity," *Journal of Men's Studies* 19, no. 1 (2011): 65–82.

32. Ibid.

33. "Poverty in the United States: Frequently Asked Questions," *National Poverty Center*, http://www.npc.umich.edu/poverty/; "The Lost Decade of the Middle Class: Fewer, Poorer, Gloomier," *Pew Research: Social & Demographic Trends*, August 22, 2012, http://www.pewsocialtrends.org/2012/08/22/the-lost-decade-of-the-middle-class/.

34. R. W. Connell, *Gender and Power: Society, the Person, and Sexual Politics* (Stanford: Stanford University Press, 1987); R. W. Connell and James Messerschmidt, "Hegemonic Masculinity: Rethinking the Concept," *Gender & Society* 19, no. 6 (2005): 829–59.

35. Erving Goffman, *Stigma* (Englewood Cliffs, NJ: Prentice Hall, 1963).

36. Michael Kaufman, "Men, Feminism, and Men's Contradictory Experiences of Power," in *Theorizing Masculinities*, ed. Harry Brod and Michael Kaufman, SAGE Series on Men and Masculinity (Newbury Park: Sage Publications, 1994), 142–165.

37. Ibid., 148.

38. Keith Edwards and Susan Jones, "'Putting My Man Face On': A Grounded Theory of College Men's Gender Identity Development," *Journal of College Student Development* 50 (2009): 216.

39. Ibid., 219.

40. Ibid., 218.

41. Michael Kaufman, "Men, Feminism, and Men's Contradictory Experiences of Power," in *Theorizing Masculinities*, ed. Harry Brod and Michael Kaufman, SAGE Series on Men and Masculinity (Newbury Park: Sage Publications, 1994), 142–165.

42. Judith Kegan Gardiner, "Masculinity, the Teening of America, and Empathic Targeting," *Signs: Journal of Women in Culture and Society*, 25, no. 4 (2000): 1257–61.

43. Douglas Schrock and Michael Schwalbe, "Men, Masculinity, and Manhood Acts," *Annual Review of Sociology* 35 (2009): 277–95.

44. Federal Bureau of Investigation, Crime in the U.S., 2012, http://www.fbi.gov/about-us/cjis/ucr/crime-in-the-u.s/2012/crime-in-the-u.s.-2012/tables/42tabledatadecoverviewpdf, accessed May 6, 2014.

45. Douglas Schrock and Michael Schwalbe, "Men, Masculinity, and Manhood Acts," *Annual Review of Sociology* 35 (2009): 277–95; Jen'nan Ghazal Read and Bridget K. Gorman, "Gender and Health Inequality." *Annual Review of Sociology* 36 (2010): 371–86; U.S. Federal Bureau of Investigation, Crime in the United States, 2012, http://www.fbi.gov/about-us/cjis/ucr/crime-in-the-u.s/2012/crime-in-the-u.s.-2012; James Byrnes, David Miller, and William Schafer, "Gender Differences in Risk Taking: A Meta-Analysis," *Psychological Bulletin* 125, no. 3 (1999): 367–83; Bryan Denham, "Masculinities in Hardcore Bodybuilding," *Men and Masculinities* 11, no. 2 (2008): 234–42.

46. World Health Organization, "Gender and Road Traffic Injuries," *Gender and Health* (2002), http://whqlibdoc.who.int/gender/2002/a85576.pdf.

47. For a review, see Will Courtenay, "Constructions of Masculinity and their Influence on Men's Well-Being: A Theory of Gender and Health," *Social Science & Medicine* 50 (2000): 1385–401.

48. Ibid.; American Cancer Society, Skin Cancer, 2007, http://www.cancer.org/acs/groups/content/@nho/documents/document/skincancerpdf.pdf.

49. Will Courtenay, "Constructions of Masculinity and their Influence on Men's Well-Being: A Theory of Gender and Health," *Social Science & Medicine* 50 (2000): 1385–401.

50. Zed Nelson, *Love Me* (Rome: Contrasto, 2009), http://www.zednelson.com/?LoveMe:31.

51. Douglas Schrock and Michael Schwalbe, "Men, Masculinity, and Manhood Acts," *Annual Review of Sociology* 35 (2009): 289.

52. Beverly Fehr, *Friendship Processes*, SAGE series on close relationships (Newbury Park, Sage Publications, 1996); Jeffrey Hall, "Sex Differences in Friendship Expectations: A Meta-Analysis," *Journal of Social and Personal Relationships* 28, no. 6 (2011): 723–47; Geoffrey Greif, *Buddy System: Understanding Male Friendships*, (New York, Oxford University Press, 2008).

53. Niobe Way, *Deep Secrets* (Cambridge: Harvard University Press, 2011), 2.

54. Miller McPherson, Lynn Smith-Lovin, and Matthew Brashears, "Social Isolation in America: Changes in Core Discussion Networks over Two Decades," *American Sociological Review* 71, no. 3 (2006): 353–75.

55. Lillian Rubin, *Just Friends: The Role of Friendship in Our Lives* (New York: Harper & Row, 1985); Gale Berkowitz, "UCLA Study On Friendship Among Women: An alternative to fight or flight," *Melissa Kaplan's Chronic Neuroimmune Diseases*, 2002, http://www.anapsid.org/cnd/gender/tendfend.html; Natasha Raymond, "The Hug Drug," *Psychology Today*, November 1, 1999, http://www.psychologytoday.com/articles/199911/the-hug-drug; Tara Parker-Pope, "What Are Friends For? A Longer Life," *New York Times*, April 20, 2009, http://www.nytimes.com/2009/04/21/health/21well.html?_r=4&.

56. Matthew Desmond, *On the Fireline: Living and Dying with Wildland Firefighters* (Chicago: The University of Chicago Press, 2007), 96.

57. Ibid., 103.

58. P. Tjaden and N. Thoennes, Full Report on the Prevalence, Incidence and Consequences of Violence Against Women. Washington, DC: U.S. Department of Justice, National Institute of Justice, 2011; Centers for Disease Control and Prevention National Intimate Partner and Sexual Violence Survey, 2010, http://www.cdc.gov/violenceprevention/pdf/nisvs_executive_summary-a.pdf; U.S. Department of Justice. 2011. Criminal Victimization, 2005. Bureau of Justice Statistics.

59. Deniz Kandiyoti, "Bargaining with Patriarchy," *Gender & Society* 2, no. 3 (1988): 274–90.

60. Michael Messner, "Becoming 100 Percent Straight," in *Privilege*, ed. Michael Kimmel and Abby Ferber (Boulder, CO: Westview Press, 2003), 184.

61. Yeung King-To, Mindy Stombler, and Renee Wharton, "Making Men in Gay Fraternities: Resisting and Reproducing Multiple Dimensions of Hegemonic Masculinity," *Gender & Society* 20, no. 1 (2006): 5–31.

62. Ibid., 22.

63. Lori Kendall, "'Oh no! I'm a nerd!': Hegemonic masculinity on an online forum," *Gender & Society*, 14, no. 2 (2000): 256–74.

64. Jackson Katz, "8 Reasons Why Eminem's Popularity is a Disaster for Women," 2002, http://www.jacksonkatz.com/pub_eminem2.html.

Chapter 7: Inequality: Women and Femininities

1. Natalie Adams and Pamela Bettis, "Commanding the Room in Short Skirts: Cheering as the Embodiment of Ideal Girlhood," *Gender & Society* 17, no. 1 (2003): 73–91.

2. Laura Grindstaff and Emily West, "Cheerleading and the Gendered Politics of Sport." *Social Problems* 53, no. 4 (2006): 500.

3. Ibid., 509–10.

4. Ibid., 510.

5. Bill Pennington, "Pompoms, Pyramids and Peril," *New York Times* March 30, 2007.

6. Frederick Mueller, "Cheerleading Injuries and Safety," *Journal of Athletic Training* 44, no. 6 (2009): 565–66.

7. Emily Kane, "'No Way My Boys Are Going to be Like That!' Parents' Responses to Children's Gender Nonconformity," *Gender & Society* 20, no. 2 (2006): 149–76.

8. Ibid., 156–57.

9. Tom Vanden Brook, "Pentagon Opening Front-Line Combat Roles to Women." *USA Today*, June 18, 2013.

10. Allison Glock, "The Selling of Candace Parker," *ESPN*, March 10, 2009.

11. Ibid.

12. Ibid.

13. Ibid.

14. Pepper Schwartz, "Marissa Mayer, the Geek as Babe." *CNN*, August 21, 2013.

15. Sandra Lee Bartky, "Foucault, Femininity, and the Modernization of Patriarchal Power," in *Writing on the Body: Female Embodiment and Feminist Theory*, ed. Katie Conboy, Nadia Medina, and Sarah Stanbury (New York: Columbia University Press, 1997), 141.

16. Ibid., 132.

17. D. R. Carney, A. J. C. Cuddy, and A. J. Yap, "Power Posing: Brief Nonverbal Displays Affect Neuroendocrine Levels and Risk Tolerance," *Psychological Science*, 21 (2010): 1363–68; J. Fischer et al., "Empower my decisions: The effects of power gestures on confirmatory information processing," *Journal of Experimental Social Psychology*, 47 (2011): 1146–54; L. Huang et al., "Powerful Postures Versus Powerful Roles: Which Is the Proximate Correlate of Thought and Behavior?" *Psychological Science*, 22 (2011): 95–102.

18. Sandra Lee Bartky, "Foucault, Femininity, and the Modernization of Patriarchal Power," in *Writing on the Body: Female Embodiment and Feminist Theory*, ed. Katie Conboy, Nadia Medina, and Sarah Stanbury (New York: Columbia University Press, 1997), 141.

19. Ibid, 141.

20. Deborah Rhode, 1997. *Speaking of Sex: The Denial of Gender Inequality* (Cambridge, MA: Harvard University Press, 1997), 15.

21. ABC News, "George Sodini's Blog: Full Text By Alleged Gym Shooter," August 5, 2009, http://abcnews.go.com/US/story?id=8258001&page=1&singlePage=true.

22. Valerie Jenness, "Engendering Hate Crime Police: Gender, the 'Dilemma' of Difference, and the Creation of Legal Subjects," *Journal of Hate Studies* 2, no. 1 (2003): 74.

23. Megan Garvey, "Transcript of the disturbing video 'Elliot Rodger's Retribution,'" *Los Angeles Times*, May 24, 2014, http://www.latimes.com/local/lanow/la-me-ln-transcript-ucsb-shootings-video-20140524-story.html.

24. P. Tjaden and N. Thoennes, *Full Report on the Prevalence, Incidence and Consequences of Violence against Women*. Washington, DC: U.S. Department of Justice, National Institute of Justice, 2011.

25. P. Tjaden and N. Thoennes, *Full Report of the Prevalence, Incidence, and Consequences of Violence against Women: Findings From the National Violence Against Women Survey Research Report*. Washington, DC, and Atlanta, GA: U.S. Department of Justice, National Institute of Justice, and U.S. Department of Health and Human Services, Centers for Disease Control and Prevention, NCJ 183781, 2000.

26. J. A. Fox and M. W. Zawitz, *Homicide Trends in the U.S.: Intimate Homicide*, Washington, DC: Bureau of Justice Statistics, U.S. Department of Justice, 2007.

27. Peter Glick et al., "Beyond Prejudice as Simple Antipathy: Hostile and Benevolent Sexism Across

Cultures," *Journal of Personality and Social Psychology* 79, no. 5 (2000): 765.

28. J. Berdahl, "The Sexual Harassment of Uppity Women," *Journal of Applied Psychology* 92 (2007): 42-37.

29. Kelly Dedel, "Sexual Assault of Women by Strangers," *Problem-Oriented Guides for Police: Problem-Specific Guides Series* 62 (2011), http://www.cops.usdoj.gov/files/RIC/Publications/e081115390_POPSexualAssault-508.pdf.

30. R. W. Connell, *Gender and Power: Society, the Person, and Sexual Politics*, (Stanford: Stanford University Press, 1987), 183.

31. Michael Kimmel, "Saving the Males: The Sociological Implications of the Virginia Military Institute and the Citadel," *Gender & Society* 14, no. 4 (2000): 494–516.

32. Ju-min Park, "Is South Korea Ready for 'Madame President'?" *Chicago Tribune*, December 11, 2012.

33. Ermine Saner, "Top 10 sexist moments in politics: Julia Gillard, Hillary Clinton and more," *Guardian*, June 14, 2013.

34. Gina Serignese Woodall and Kim L. Fridkin, "Shaping Women's Chances: Stereotypes and the Media," in *Rethinking Madam President: Are We Ready for a Woman in the White House?* ed. Lori Cox Han and Caroline Heldman (Boulder, CO: Lynne Rienner Publishers, 2007), 1–16.

35. "Top 10 sexist moments in politics." *Hindustani Times* (New Delhi), June 16, 2013, http://www.hindustantimes.com/StoryPage/Print/1077050.aspx.

36. Ibid.

37. Tina Fey, *Bossypants* (New York: Little, Brown and Company, 2011), 216.

38. Nathan Heflick and Jamie Goldenberg, "Sarah Palin, a Nation Object(ifie)s," *Sex Roles* 65 (2011): 156–64.

39. Patricia Hill Collins, *Black Feminist Thought: Knowledge, Consciousness, and the Politics of Empowerment* (Boston: Unwin Hyman, 1990). bell hooks, *Feminist Theory: From Margin to Center* (Cambridge, MA: South End Press, 1984). Gloria Anzaldua, *Borderlands/La Frontera: The New Mestiza* (San Francisco, CA: Aunt Lute Books, 1987). Trinh T. Minh-ha, *Woman, Native, Other: Writing Postcoloniality and Feminism* (Bloomington, IN: Indiana University Press, 1989).

40. Patricia Hill Collins, *Black Feminist Thought: Knowledge, Consciousness, and the Politics of Empowerment* (New York: Routledge, 1990).

41. "Pro-Feminist Men's Groups Links," *Feminist.com*, http://www.feminist.com/resources/links/links_men.html .

42. *White Ribbon*, http://www.whiteribbon.ca/; Michael Kaufman, "White Ribbon Campaign: 20 Years Working to End Violence Against Women," *Michael Kaufman* (blog), November 24, 2011, http://www.michaelkaufman.com/2011/white-ribbon-campaign-20-years-working-to-end-violence-against-women/.

43. *National Organization for Men Against Sexism*, http://site.nomas.org/principles/.

44. Floyd Dell, "Feminism for Men," in *Against the Tide: Profeminist Men in the United States, 1776–1990, a Documentary History*, ed. Michael Kimmel and Thomas Mosmiller (Boston: Beacon Press, 1992 [1917]).

45. Jean Twenge, "Status and Gender: The Paradox of Progress in an Age of Narcissism," *Sex Roles* 61 (2009): 338–40.

46. Philip Cohen, "How Can We Jump-Start the Struggle for Gender Equality?" *New York Times*, November 23, 2013.

Chapter 8: Institutions

1. Bruno Latour and Steve Woolgar, *Laboratory Life: The Social Construction of Scientific Facts* (New Jersey: Princeton University Press, 1986), 260.

2. Juliet Lapidos, "Do Kids Need a Summer Vacation?" *Slate*, July 11, 2007, http://www.slate.com/articles/news_and_politics/explainer/2007/07/do_kids_need_a_summer_vacation.html.

3. Barrie Thorne, *Gender Play: Girls and Boy in School* (New Brunswick, NJ: Rutgers University Press, 1993), 44.

4. Ibid, 44.

5. Ibid, 84.

6. Terry Kogan, "Sex Separation: The Cure-All for Victorian Social Anxiety," in *Toilet: Public Restrooms and the Politics of Sharing*, ed. Harvey Molotch and Laura Norén (New York: New York University Press, 2010), quoted on p. 157.

7. Ibid, quoted on p. 157.

8. Ibid, 145–64.

9. Harvey Molotch and Laura Norén, *Toilet: Public Restrooms and the Politics of Sharing* (New York: New York University Press, 2010).

10. Betsy Lucal, "What it Means to be Gendered Me: Life on the Boundaries of a Dichotomous Gender System," *Gender & Society* 13, no. 6 (1999): 787.

11. Ibid, 787.

12. "Sports Industry Overview," Plunkett Research, Ltd., 2013, http://www.plunkettresearch.com/sports%20recreation%20leisure%20market%20research/industry%20statistics.

13. Jean Twenge, "Mapping Gender: The Multifactorial Approach and the Organization of Gender-Related Attributes," *Psychology of Women Quarterly* 23, no. 3 (1999): 405–502.

14. R. Miles, *The Rites of Man: Love, Sex, and Death in the Making of the Male* (Hammersmith, UK: Paladin, 1992); Michael Messner, *Power at Play: Sports and the Problem of Masculinity* (Boston: Beacon Press, 1992), 24.

15. R. W. Connell, *Which Way is Up?* (North Sydney: George Unwin and Allen, 1983), 18.

16. Michael Messner, "Becoming 100% Straight," in *Privilege: A Reader*, ed. Michael Kimmel and Abby Ferber (Philadelphia: Westview Press, 2010), 87.

17. Michael Messner, *Power at Play: Sports and the Problem of Masculinity* (Boston: Beacon Press, 1992), 33.

18. Messner quoted in Jennifer Hargreaves, *Sporting Females: Critical Issues in the History and Sociology of Women's Sports* (New York: Routledge, 1994), 38.

19. Barrie Thorne, *Gender Play: Girls and Boy in School* (New Brunswick, NJ: Rutgers University Press, 1993), 95.

20. Todd W. Crosset, *Outsiders in the Clubhouse: The World of Women's Professional Golf* (Albany: State University of New York Press, 1995), 223–24.

21. Michael Messner, "Boys and Girls Together: The Promise and Limitations of Equal Opportunity in Sports," in *Sex, Violence, and Power in Sports: Rethinking Masculinity*, ed. Michael Messner and Donald Sabo (Freedom, CA: The Crossing Press, 1994), 200.

22. Mariah Nelson, *The Stronger Women Get, the More Men Love Football: Sexism and the American Culture of Sports* (New York: Avon Books, 1995).

23. Jane English, "Sex Equality in Sports," in *Femininity, Masculinity, and Androgyny*, ed. Mary Vetterling-Braggin (Boston: Littlefield, Adams, 1982).

24. Michael Messner, 1994. "Sports and Male Domination: The Female Athlete as Contested Ideological Terrain," in *Women, Sport and Culture*, ed. Susan Birrell and Cheryl L. Cole (Champaign, IL: Human Kinetics, 1994), 65–80.

25. Ibid, 71.

26. Ibid, 71.

27. Abigail Feder, 1995. "'A Radiant Smile from the Lovely Lady': Overdetermined Femininity in 'Ladies' Figure Skating," in *Women on Ice*, ed. Cynthia Baughman (New York: Routledge, 1995), 24.

28. International Federation of Body Building and Fitness, *IFBB Rules: Men and Women Bodybuilding, Men Classic Bodybuilding, Women Fitness, Men Fitness, Women Bodyfitness*. IFBB International Congress, 2008.

29. Susan Mitchell and Ken Dyer, *Winning Women: Challenging the Norms in Australian Sport* (Ringwood, Victoria: Penguin, 1985).

30. Lex Boyle, "Flexing the Tensions of Female Muscularity: How Female Bodybuilders Negotiate Normative Femininity in Competitive Bodybuilding," *Women's Studies Quarterly* 33, no. 1/2 (2005): 134–49; see also Anne Bolin, "Vandalized Vanity: Feminine Physiques Betrayed and Portrayed," in *Tattoo, Torture, Mutilation, and Adornment: The Denaturalization of the Body in Culture and Text*, ed. Frances Mascia-Lees and Patricia Sharpe (New York: State University of New York Press, 1992), 79–99.

31. Michael Messner, *Power at Play: Sports and the Problem of Masculinity* (Boston: Beacon Press, 1992), 1.

32. Jonathan Wall, "Girl Football Player Sits Out Game After Foe Threatens Forfeit," *Yahoo Sports*, October 13, 2011.

33. Colleen O'Connor, "Girls Going to the Mat," *Denver Post*, December 23, 2007.

34. Eileen McDonagh and Laura Pappano, *Playing with the Boys: Why Separate Is Not Equal in Sports* (New York: Oxford University Press, 2008).

35. Staff, "Vision Quest: Alaskan Girl Wins State H.S. Wrestling Title Over Boys," *Sports Illustrated*, February 6, 2006.

36. "The World's Highest-Paid Athletes," *Forbes*, June 2013, http://www.forbes.com/athletes/list/.

37. Todd W. Crosset, *Outsiders in the Clubhouse: The World of Women's Professional Golf* (Albany: State University of New York Press, 1995), 224.

38. Laura La Bella, *Women in Sports* (New York: The Rosen Publishing Group, 2013).

39. Todd W. Crosset, *Outsiders in the Clubhouse: The World of Women's Professional Golf* (Albany: State University of New York Press, 1995), 225.

40. Harvey Molotch, "On Not Making History: What NYU Did with the Toilet and What it Means for the World," in *Toilet: Public Restrooms and the Politics of Sharing*, ed. Harvey Molotch and Laura Norén (New York: New York University Press, 2010), 255–72.

41. Ibid, 258.

42. Ibid, 261.

43. Jon Entine, "The 'Scheming, Flashy Trickiness' of Basketball's Media Darlings, The Philadelphia 'Hebrews'–Err . . . Sixers," *Jewish Magazine*, July 2001, http://www.jewishmag.com/45mag/basketball/basketball.htm.

44. Len Canter, "Basketball: The Jewish Game . . . A to Z," *Chutzpah*, Winter 2010, 47.

45. U.S. Code Title 20, Chapter 38, Section 1681: Sex, *Legal Information Institute*, http://www.law.cornell.edu/uscode/20/1681.html.

46. National Coalition for Women and Girls in Education, "Title IX at 40: Working to Ensure Gender Equity in Education," Washington, DC: 2012.

47. Raewyn Connell, *Gender and Power: Society, the Person, and Sexual Politics* (Stanford: Stanford University Press, 1987), 139.

48. Bruno Latour and Steve Woolgar, *Laboratory Life: The Social Construction of Scientific Facts* (Princeton: Princeton University Press, 1986), 260.

Chapter 9: Change

1. Jaclyn Geller, *Here Comes the Bride: Women, Weddings, and the Marriage Mystique* (New York: Four Walls Eight Windows, 2001).

2. John D'Emilio and Estelle Freedman, *Intimate Matters: A History of Sexuality in America* (Chicago: University of Chicago Press, 1997).

3. Quoted in Claude Levi-Strauss, *The Elementary Structures of Kinship* (Boston: Beacon Press, [1949], 1969), 481.

4. Francis J Bremer and Tom Webster, *Puritans and Puritanism in Europe and America: A Comprehensive Encyclopedia*, vol. 2 (Santa Barbara: ABC-CLIO, Inc., 2006), 152.

5. Alan Taylor, *American Colonies* (New York: Viking, 2001).

6. Robert Fogel, *Without Consent or Contract: The Rise and Fall of American Slavery* (New York: W. W. Norton and Company, 1989); Shirley Hill, "Class, Race, and Gender Dimensions of Child Rearing in African American Families," *Journal of Black Studies* 31, no. 4 (2001): 494–508.

7. Quoted in Robert Fogel, *Without Consent or Contract: The Rise and Fall of American Slavery* (New York: W. W. Norton and Company, 1989), 163.

8. Estelle Freeman, "Sexuality in Nineteenth-Century America: Behavior, Ideology, and Politics," *Reviews in American History* 10, no. 4 (1982): 196–215.

9. Ibid.; see also Robert Woods, *The Demography of Victorian England and Wales* (Cambridge: Cambridge University Press, 2000).

10. Estelle Freeman, "Sexuality in Nineteenth-Century America: Behavior, Ideology, and Politics," *Reviews in American History* 10, no. 4 (1982): 196–215.

11. Ibid; see also Steven Seidman, "The Power of Desire and the Danger of Pleasure: Victorian Sexuality Reconsidered," *Journal of Social History* 24, no. 1 (1990): 47–67.

12. Francesca Cancian, "The Feminization of Love," *Signs* 11, no. 4 (1986): 692–709; Steven Seidman, "The Power of Desire and the Danger of Pleasure: Victorian Sexuality Reconsidered," *Journal of Social History* 24, no. 1 (1990): 47–67.

13. John D'Emilio and Estelle Freedman, *Intimate Matters: A History of Sexuality in America* (Chicago: University of Chicago Press, 1997), 28.

14. Steven Seidman, "The Power of Desire and the Danger of Pleasure: Victorian Sexuality Reconsidered," *Journal of Social History* 24, no. 1 (1990): 47–67; Estelle Freeman, "Sexuality in Nineteenth-Century America: Behavior, Ideology, and Politics," *Reviews in American History* 10, no. 4 (1982): 196–215.

15. Ibid.

16. Robert Long, "Sexuality in the Victorian Era." Lecture Presented to Innominate Society, http://www.innominatesociety.com/Articles/Sexuality%20In%20The%20Victorian%20Era.htm.

17. Ibid.

18. William Acton, *Prostitution, Considered in its Moral, Social, and Sanitary Aspects* (1870), http://archive.org/details/prostitutioncons00acto; Stephanie Coontz, "Blame affairs on evolution of sex roles," *CNN Opinion*, November 18, 2012, http://www.cnn.com/2012/11/17/opinion/coontz-powerful-men-affairs/index.html.

19. Estelle Freeman, "Sexuality in Nineteenth-Century America: Behavior, Ideology, and Politics," *Reviews in American History* 10, no. 4 (1982): 196–215; Joane Nagel, *Race, Ethnicity, and Sexuality:*

Intimate Intersections, Forbidden Frontiers (New York: Oxford University Press, 2003).

20. Joy Hakim, *War, Peace, and All That Jazz* (New York: Oxford University Press, 1995).

21. Douglas Harper, *Online Etymology Dictionary*, 2014, http://www.etymonline.com/index.php?allowed _in_frame=0&search=sexy&searchmode=none.

22. John D'Emilio and Estelle Freedman, *Intimate Matters: A History of Sexuality in America* (Chicago: University of Chicago Press, 1997), 279.

23. Quoted in D'Emilio and Freedman, 226–27.

24. Beth Bailey, *From Front Porch to Back Seat* (Baltimore: Johns Hopkins University, 1988).

25. Ibid., 14.

26. Ibid., 20.

27. Ibid., 20.

28. Kathy Peiss, "'Charity Girls' and City Pleasures: Historical Notes on Working-Class Sexuality, 1880–1920," in *Passion and Power: Sexuality in History*, ed. Kathy Peiss and Christina Simmons, with Robert A. Padgug (Philadelphia: Temple University Press, 1989), 63.

29. Ibid., 61.

30. Lynn Peril, *College Girls: Bluestockings, Sex Kittens, and Coeds, Then and Now* (New York: W. W. Norton and Company, 2006).

31. John M. Murrin et al., *Liberty, Equality, Power: A History of the American People* (Boston: Thomson Wadsworth, 2008).

32. Ibid.

33. John D'Emilio and Estelle Freedman, *Intimate Matters: A History of Sexuality in America* (Chicago: University of Chicago Press, 1997), 279.

34. Ibid., 199.

35. National Abortion Federation, "History of Abortion," http://www.prochoice.org/about_abortion /history_abortion.html.

36. B. E. Wells and J. M. Twenge, "Changes in young people's sexual behavior and attitudes, 1943–1999: A cross-temporal meta-analysis," *Review of General Psychology* 9 (2005): 249–61; Jennifer L. Petersen and Janet Shilbey Hyde, "A Meta-Analytic Review of Research on Gender Differences in Sexuality, 1993–2007," *Psychological Bulletin* 136, no. 1 (2010): 21–38.

37. Stephanie Coontz, "The World Historical Transformation of Marriage," *Journal of Marriage and Family* 66, no. 4 (2004): 974–79, 977.

38. Ibid.

39. Linda Gordon, *Social Insurance and Public Assistance: The Influence of Gender in Welfare Thought in the United States, 1890–1935* (Madison: University of Wisconsin Press, 1992).

40. Stephanie Coontz, *The Way We Never Were: American Families and the Nostalgia Trap* (New York: Basic Books, 1992), 58.

41. Estelle Freeman, "Sexuality in Nineteenth Century America: Behavior, Ideology, and Politics," *Reviews in American History* 10, no. 4 (1982): 196–215.

42. Stephanie Coontz, *The Way We Never Were: American Families and the Nostalgia Trap* (New York: Basic Books, 1992).

43. Ibid., 25, 27.

44. John D'Emilio and Estelle Freedman, *Intimate Matters: A History of Sexuality in America* (Chicago: University of Chicago Press, 1997), 283.

45. K. A. Cuordileone, "'Politics in an Age of Anxiety': Cold War Political Culture and the Crisis in American Masculinity, 1949–1960," *The Journal of American History* 87, no. 2 (2000): 515–45.

46. Francis J. Bremer and Tom Webster. 2006. *Puritans and Puritanism in Europe and America: A Comprehensive Encyclopedia*, vol. 2 (Santa Barbara: ABC-CLIO, Inc., 2008), 152.

47. Carroll Smith-Rosenberg, *Disorderly Conduct: Visions of Gender in Victorian America* (New York: Oxford University Press, 1985), 55–56.

48. Beth Bailey, *From Front Porch to Back Seat* (Baltimore: Johns Hopkins University, 1988); Lynn Peril, *College Girls: Bluestockings, Sex Kittens, and Coeds, Then and Now* (New York: W. W. Norton and Company, 2006).

49. John D'Emilio and Estelle Freedman, *Intimate Matters: A History of Sexuality in America* (Chicago: University of Chicago Press, 1997), citing a study by Katharine Davis, p. 193.

50. Ibid., 289.

51. U.S. Selective Service and Victory (Washington DC: Government Printing Office, 1948), 91.

52. John D'Emilio and Estelle Freedman, *Intimate Matters: A History of Sexuality in America* (Chicago: University of Chicago Press, 1997), 290.

53. For historical context, see the documentary *Before Stonewall*, dir. Greta Schiller and Robert Rosenberg (1984), http://www.imdb.com/title /tt0088782/.

54. K. A. Cuordileone, "'Politics in an Age of Anxiety': Cold War Political Culture and the Crisis in

American Masculinity, 1949–1960," *The Journal of American History* 87, no. 2 (2000): 515–45.

55. Fred Fejes, "Murder, Perversion, and Moral Panic: The 1954 Media Campaign against Miami's Homosexuals and the Discourse of Civic Betterment," *Journal of the History of Sexuality* 9, no. 3 (2000): 305–47.

56. K. A. Cuordileone, "'Politics in an Age of Anxiety': Cold War Political Culture and the Crisis in American Masculinity, 1949–1960," *The Journal of American History* 87, no. 2 (2000): 532.

57. Ibid., 515–45.

58. Beth Bailey, *From Front Porch to Back Seat* (Baltimore: Johns Hopkins University Press, 1988).

59. Ibid., 53.

60. John D'Emilio and Estelle Freedman, *Intimate Matters: A History of Sexuality in America* (Chicago: University of Chicago Press, 1997), 261.

61. Cited in Beth Bailey, *From Front Porch to Back Seat* (Baltimore: Johns Hopkins University Press, 1988), 81.

62. Stephanie Coontz, *The Way We Never Were: American Families and the Nostalgia Trap* (New York: Basic Books, 2002), 202.

63. United States Census Bureau, *Estimated Median Age of First Marriage, by Sex: 1890 to Present* (2004), http://www.census.gov/population/socdemo/hh-fam/tabMS-2.pdf.

64. Alfred Kinsey, *Sexual Behavior of the Human Male* (Bloomington: Indiana University Press, 1948).

65. Betty Friedan, *The Feminine Mystique* (New York: W. W. Norton and Company, 1963), 15.

66. Louis Menand, "Books as Bombs: Why the Women's Movement Needed *The Feminine Mystique*," *New Yorker*, January 24, 2011, http://www.newyorker.com/arts/critics/books/2011/01/24/110124crbo_books_menand.

67. Stephanie Coontz, *A Strange Stirring: The Feminine Mystique and American Women at the Dawn of the 1960s* (Philadelphia: Basic Books, 2011).

68. Stephanie Coontz, *The Way We Never Were: American Families and the Nostalgia Trap* (New York: Basic Books, 1992).

69. Ibid., 31.

70. Carol Warren, *Madwives: Schizophrenic Women in the 1950s* (New Brunswick, NJ: Rutgers University Press, 1987).

71. Stephanie Coontz, *The Way We Never Were: American Families and the Nostalgia Trap* (New York: Basic Books, 1992), 37.

72. Quoted in ibid., 37.

73. Jennifer L. Reimer, "Psychiatric Drugs: A History in Ads," *Practical Madness*, March 2010, http://www.practiceofmadness.com/2010/03/psychiatric-drugs-a-history-in-ads/.

74. Stephanie Coontz, *The Way We Never Were: American Families and the Nostalgia Trap* (New York: Basic Books, 1992), 36.

75. S. Straussner and P. Attia, "Women's Addiction and Treatment through a Historical Lens," in *The Handbook of Addiction Treatment for Women*, ed. S. Straussner and S. Brown (San Francisco: Jossey-Bass, 2002), 3–25.

76. Betty Friedan, *The Feminine Mystique* (New York: W. W. Norton and Company, 1963), 15.

77. Barbara Ehrenreich, *The Hearts of Men: American Dreams and the Flight from Commitment* (New York: Anchor Books, 1987).

78. Ibid, 50.

79. Ibid, 50.

80. Claudia Goldin, *Understanding the Gender Gap: An Economic History of American Women* (New York: Oxford University Press, 1990).

81. Judith Warner, *Perfect Madness: Motherhood in the Age of Anxiety* (New York: Riverhead Books, 2005), 138; D. A. Cotter, J. M. Hermsen, and P. England, "Moms and jobs: Trends in mothers' employment and which mothers stay home," in *American families: A multicultural reader*, ed. S. Coontz, M. Parson, and G. Raley, 2nd. ed. (New York: Routledge, 2008), 379–86.

82. Claudia Goldin, *Understanding the Gender Gap: An Economic History of American Women* (New York: Oxford University Press, 1990); Stephanie Coontz, *The Way We Never Were: American Families and the Nostalgia Trap* (New York: Basic Books, 1992).

83. Beth Bailey, *From Front Porch to Back Seat* (Baltimore: Johns Hopkins University Press, 1988).

84. Claudia Goldin, *Understanding the Gender Gap: An Economic History of American Women* (New York: Oxford University Press, 1990).

85. Ibid.

86. Ibid.

87. Ibid.

88. Ibid.

89. Cynthia Deitch, "Gender, Race, and Class Politics and the Inclusion of Women in the Title VII of the 1964 Civil Rights Act," *Gender & Society* 7, no. 2 (1993): 183–203.

90. Jo Freeman, *We Will Be Heard: Women's Struggles for Political Power in the United States* (New York: Rowman & Littlefield Publishers, 2008).

91. James Dobson, "Dr. James Dobson's Newsletter: Marriage on the Ropes?" *Focus on the Family Newsletter*, September 2003, http://www.catholicfamily catalog.com/dr-james-dobson-on-marriage.htm.

92. Myra Marx Ferree, "The Gay Wedding Backlash," *Newsday*, May 23, 2004

93. Ibid.

94. Stephanie Coontz, "The World Historical Transformation of Marriage." *Journal of Marriage and Family* 66, no. 4 (2004): 974.

95. Pew Research Social & Demographic Trends Project, "The Decline of Marriage and Rise of New Families," *Pew Research Center*, November 18, 2010, http://www.pewsocialtrends.org/2010/11/18/the -decline-of-marriage-and-rise-of-new-families/.

96. United States Census Bureau, "Profile America: Facts for Features: Unmarried and Single Americans Week, Sept. 16–22, 2012," *United States Census Bureau*, July 31, 2012, http://www.census.gov /newsroom/releases/archives/facts_for_features _special_editions/cb12-ff18.html; Dave Gilson, "The Myth of the Lonely American," *Mother Jones*, February 23, 2012, http://www.motherjones.com /media/2012/02/eric-klinenberg-going-solo-singles.

97. Pew Research Social & Demographic Trends Project, "The Decline of Marriage and Rise of New Families," *Pew Research Center*, November 18, 2010, http://www.pewsocialtrends.org/2010/11/18/the -decline-of-marriage-and-rise of new-families/.

98. D'Vera Cohn et al., "Barely Half of U.S. Adults are Married – A Record Low." *Pew Research Center*, December 14, 2011, http://www.pewsocialtrends.org /2011/12/14/barely-half-of-u-s-adults-are-married -a-record-low/.

99. Pew Research Social & Demographic Trends Project, "The Decline of Marriage and Rise of New Families," *Pew Research Center*, November 18, 2010, http://www.pewsocialtrends.org/2010/11/18/the -decline-of-marriage-and-rise-of-new-families/.

100. Stephanie Coontz, "The World Historical Transformation of Marriage." *Journal of Marriage and Family* 66, no. 4 (2004): 978.

101. Pew Research Social & Demographic Trends Project, "A Portrait of Stepfamilies," *Pew Research Center*, January 13, 2011, http://www.pewsocial trends.org/2011/01/13/a-portrait-of-stepfamilies/.

102. Nate Silver, "Opinion on Same-Sex Marriage Appears to Shift at Accelerated Pace," *FiveThirty-Eight*, August 12, 2010, http://www.fivethirtyeight .com/2010/08/opinion-on-same-sex-marriage -appears-to.html; Pew Research Social & Demographic Trends Project, "The Decline of Marriage and Rise of New Families," *Pew Research Center*, November 18, 2010, http://www.pewsocialtrends .org/2010/11/18/the-decline-of-marriage-and-rise -of-new-families/.

103. Myra Marx Ferree. "The Gay Wedding Backlash," *Newsday*, May 23, 2004.

Chapter 10: Sexualities

1. Rachel Allison and Barbara Risman, "'It Goes Hand in Hand with the Parties': Race, Class, and Residence in College Negotiations of Hooking Up," *Sociological Perspectives* 57, no. 1 (2014): 108.

2. Jess Butler, *Sexual Subjects: Hooking Up in the Age of Postfeminism* (PhD diss, University of Southern California, 2013), 74.

3. Norval Glenn and Elizabeth Marquardt, "Hooking Up, Hanging Out and Hoping for Mr. Right: College Women on Mating and Dating Today," *Institute for American Values*, 2001, http://fmmh.ycdsb .ca/teachers/f00027452/f00027453/mfhook.pdf.

4. P. England, E. F. Shafer, and A. C. K. Fogerty, (2008). "Hooking up and forming relationships on today's college campuses," in *The Gendered Society Reader*, ed. Michael Kimmel (New York: Oxford University Press, 2008), 531–93; Lisa Wade and Caroline Heldman, "Hooking Up and Opting Out: What Students Learn about Sex in their First Year of College," in *Sex for Life: From Virginity to Viagra, How Sexuality Changes Throughout our Lives*, ed. Laura Carpenter and John DeLamater (New York: New York University Press, 2012), 128–145.

5. Lisa Wade, unpublished research.

6. U. S. Census Bureau, "Live Births, Deaths, Infant Deaths, and Maternal Deaths: 1900 to 2001" (2003), http://www.census.gov/statab/hist/HS 13.pdf.

7. Angus McLaren, *Twentieth Century Sexuality: A History* (Oxford: Blackwell Publishers Ltd., 1999).

8. Tom Smith, "A Report: The Sexual Revolution?" *The Public Opinion Quarterly* 54, no. 3 (1990): 415–35; Elina Haavio-Mannila, J. P. Roos, and Osmo Kontula. "Repression, Revolution and Ambivalence: The Sexual Life of Three Generations," *Acta Sociologica* 39, no. 4 (1996): 409–30; Gerbert Kraaykamp, "Trends and Countertrends in Sexual Permissiveness: Three Decades of Attitude Change in The Netherlands 1965–1995," *Journal of Marriage and Family* 64 (2002): 225–39; George H. Gallup, Jr., "Current Views on Premarital, Extramarital Sex,"

June 24, 2003, http://www.gallup.com/poll/8704/current-views-premarital-extramarital-sex.aspx.

9. Angus McLaren, *Twentieth Century Sexuality: A History* (Oxford: Blackwell Publishers Ltd., 1999).

10. Brooke Wells and Jean Twenge, "Changes in Young People's Sexual Behavior and Attitudes, 1943–1999: A Cross-Temporal Meta-Analysis," *Review of General Psychology*, 9 (2005): 249–261; Jennifer L. Petersen and Janet Shilbey Hyde, "A Meta-Analytic Review of Research on Gender Differences in Sexuality, 1993–2007." *Psychological Bulletin* 136, no. 1 (2010): 21–38.

11. Angus McLaren, *Twentieth Century Sexuality: A History* (Oxford: Blackwell Publishers Ltd., 1999).

12. Ibid.

13. Ibid.

14. Lawrence Finer, "Trends in premarital sex in the United States, 1954–2003," *Public Health Reports* 122, no. 1 (2007): 73–78, http://www.ncbi.nlm.nih.gov/pubmed/17236611; http://kff.org/hivaids/report/national-survey-of-adolescents-and-young-adults/.

15. Laura M. Carpenter, *Virginity Lost: An Intimate Portrait of First Sexual Experiences* (New York: New York University Press, 2005).

16. Lisa Wade and Caroline Heldman, "Hooking Up and Opting Out: What Students Learn about Sex in their First Year of College," in *Sex for Life: From Virginity to Viagra, How Sexuality Changes Throughout our Lives*, ed. Laura Carpenter and John DeLamater (New York: New York University Press, 2012), 128–145.

17. Laura M. Carpenter, *Virginity Lost: An Intimate Portrait of First Sexual Experiences* (New York: New York University Press, 2005).

18. Joyce C. Abma, Gladys M. Martinez, and Casey E. Copen, "Teenagers in the United States: Sexual Activity, Contraceptive Use, and Childbearing, National Survey of Family Growth 2006–2008," *Vital and Health Statistics* Series 23, no. 30 (June 2010), http://www.ncbi.nlm.nih.gov/pubmed/17236611; http://kff.org/hivaids/report/national-survey-of-adolescents-and-young-adults/.

19. Mary Madden and Amanda Lenhart, "Online Dating," Pew Internet and American Life Project, 2006, http://www.pewinternet.org/Reports/2006/Online-Dating.aspx.

20. Michael Rosenfeld and Reuben Thomas, "Searching for a Mate: The Rise of the Internet as Social Intermediary," *American Sociological Review* 77, no. 4 (2012): 523–47.

21. Christian Rudder, "Your Looks and Your Inbox," *OkTrends*, November 17, 2009, http://blog.okcupid.com/index.php/your-looks-and-online-dating/.

22. Ibid.

23. Ibid.

24. Yen Lee Espiritu, *Asian American Women and Men: Labor, Laws, and Love* (Lanham, Maryland: Rowman & Littlefield Publishers, Inc., 2008), 110.

25. Christian Rudder, "How Your Race Affects The Messages You Get," October 5, 2009, http://blog.okcupid.com/index.php/your-race-affects-whether-people-write-you-back/.

26. Ken-Hou Lin and Jennifer Lundquist, "Mate Selection in Cyberspace: The Intersection of Race, Gender, and Education," *American Journal of Sociology* 119, no. 1 (2013): 183–215.

27. Courtney Weaver, "Tiny, flat-chested, and hairless!," *Salon*, May 6, 1998, http://www.salon.com/1998/05/06/weav_22/.

28. Ken-Hou Lin and Jennifer Lundquist, "Mate Selection in Cyberspace: The Intersection of Race, Gender, and Education," *American Journal of Sociology* 119, no. 1 (2013): 183–215.

29. See also: Ken-Hou Lin and Jennifer Lundquist, "Mate Selection in Cyberspace: The Intersection of Race, Gender, and Education," *American Journal of Sociology* 119, no. 1 (2013): 183–215; Michael Rosenfeld and Reuben Thomas, "Searching for a Mate: The Rise of the Internet as Social Intermediary," *American Sociological Review* 77, no. 4 (2012): 523–47.

30. Jerry A. Jacobs and Teresa G. Labov, "Gender Differentials in Intermarriage among Sixteen Race and Ethnic Groups," *Sociological Forum* 17 (2002): 621–46; U.S. Census Bureau, America's Families and Living Arrangements. Table FG-4, 2010, http://www.census.gov/population/www/socdemo/hh-fam/cps2010.html.

31. Zhenchao Qian and Daniel T. Lichter, "Social Boundaries and Marital Assimilation: Interpreting Trends in Racial and Ethnic Intermarriage," *American Sociological Review* 72, no. 1 (2007): 68–94; Zhenchao Qian and Daniel T. Lichter. "Changing Patterns of Interracial Marriage in a Multiracial Society," *Journal of Marriage and Family* 73, no. 5 (2011): 1065–84.

32. Zhenchao Qian, 2005. "Breaking the Last Taboo: Interracial Marriage in America," *Contexts* 4, no. 4 (2005): 33–37.

33. Ariel Levy, *Female Chauvinist Pigs: Women and the Rise of Raunch Culture* (New York: Simon and Schuster, 2006).

34. Lisa Wade and Gwen Sharp, "Selling Sex," in *Images that Injure: Pictorial Stereotypes in the Media*, ed. Lester Paul and Susan Ross (Westport, CT: Praeger, 2011), 165.

35. Sinikka Elliot, *Not My Kid: What Parents Believe about the Sex Lives of Their Teenagers* (New York: New York University Press, 2012).

36. Laura Mulvey, "Visual Pleasure and Narrative Cinema," *Screen* 16, no. 3 (1975): 6–18.

37. J. K. Swim, L. L. Hyers, L. L. Cohen, and M. J. Ferguson, "Everyday sexism: Evidence for its incidence, nature, and psychological impact from three daily diary studies," *Journal of Social Issues* 57 (2001): 31–53; M. J. Thompson, "Gender in Magazine Advertising: Skin Sells Best," *Clothing and Textiles Research Journal* 18 (2000): 178–81; Erin Hatton and Mary Nell Trautner, "Equal Opportunity Objectification? The Sexualization of Men and Women on the Cover of *Rolling Stone*," *Sexuality & Culture* 15, no. 3 (2011): 256–78, http://www.acsu .buffalo.edu/~trautner/Hatton_Trautner_Sexuality _and_Culture.pdf.

38. Marika Tiggemann and Julia K. Kuring, "The role of body objectification in disordered eating and depressed mood," *British Journal of Clinical Psychology* 43, no. 3 (2004): 299–311; N. M. McKinley, "Gender differences in undergraduates' body esteem: The mediating effect of objectified body consciousness and actual/ideal weight discrepancy," *Sex Roles* 39 (1998): 113–23; N. M. McKinley, "Longitudinal gender differences in objectified body consciousness and weight-related attitudes and behaviors: Cultural and developmental contexts in the transition from college." *Sex Roles* 54 (2006a): 159–73; S. M. Lindberg, J. S. Hyde, and N. M. McKinley, "A measure of objectified body consciousness for preadolescent and adolescent youth," *Psychology of Women Quarterly* 30 (2006): 65–76; M. R. Hebl, E. B. King, and J. Lin, "The swimsuit becomes us all: Ethnicity, gender, and vulnerability to self-objectification," *Personality and Social Psychology Bulletin* 30 (2004): 1322–31; S. E. Lowery et al., "Body image, self-esteem, and health-related behaviors among male and female first year college students," *Journal of College Student Development* 46, (2005): 612–23; Shelly Grabe, Janet Shibley Hyde, "Body Objectification, MTV, and Psychological Outcomes Among Female Adolescents," *Journal of Applied Psychology*, 39, no. 12 (2009): 2840–858; Shelly Grabe, Janet Shibley Hyde, and Sara M. Lindberg, "Body Objectification and Depression in Adolescents: The Role of Gender, Shame, and Rumination," *Psychology of Women Quarterly* 31, no. 2 (2007): 164–75.

39. B. L. Fredrickson and T. A. Roberts, "Objectification Theory: Toward Understanding Women's Lived Experiences and Mental Health Risks," *Psychology of Women Quarterly* 21, no. 2 (1997): 173–206.

40. Rachel M. Calogero and J. Kevin Thompson, "Potential implications of the objectification of women's bodies and sexual satisfaction," *Body Image* 6, no. 2 (2009): 145–48; Amy Steer and Marika Tiggemann, "The Role of Self-Objectification in Women's Sexual Functioning," *Journal of Social and Clinical Psychology* 27, no. 3 (2008): 205–25.

41. Y. Martins, M. Tiggemann, and A. Kirkbride, "Those speedos become them: The role of self-objectification in gay and heterosexual men's body image," *Personality and Social Psychology Bulletin* 33 (2007): 634–47.

42. David Whittier and Rita Melendez, "Intersubjectivity in the Intrapsychic Sexual Scripting of Gay Men," *Culture, Health & Society* 6, no. 2 (2004): 131–43.

43. John Gagnon and William Simon, *Sexual Conduct: The Social Sources of Human Sexuality* (Chicago: Aldine, 1973).

44. W. F. Flack, Jr. et al., "Risk factors and consequences of unwanted sex among university students," *Journal of Interpersonal Violence* 22, no. 2 (2007): 139–57; H. Littleton et al., "Risky situation or harmless fun? A qualitative examination of college women's bad hook-up and rape scripts," *Sex Roles* 60, no. 11/12 (2009): 793–804; E. Paul, "Beer goggles, catching feelings, and the walk of shame: Myths and realities of the hookup experience," in *Relating difficulty: The processes of constructing and managing difficult interaction*, ed. D. C. Kirkpatrick, S. Duck, and M. K. Foley (Mahwah: Lawrence Erlbaum, 2006), 141–60.

45. David Lisak and Paul Miller. "Repeat Rape and Multiple Offending Among Undetected Rapists," *Violence and Victims* 17, no. 1 (2002): 73–84.

46. Stephanie McWhorter et al., "Reports of Rape Reperpetration by Newly Enlisted Male Navy Personnel," *Violence and Victims* 24, no. 2 (2009): 204–18.

47. Jocelyn Hollander, "The Roots of Resistance to Women's Self-Defense," *Violence Against Women* 15, no. 5 (2009): 574–94.

48. J. Clay-Warner, "Avoiding rape: The effects of protective actions and situational factors on rape outcome," *Violence and Victims* 17 (2002): 691–705; S. E. Ullman, "Does offender violence escalate when women fight back?" *Journal of Interpersonal Violence* 13 (1998): 179–92; S. E. Ullman, "A 10-year

update of 'Review and critique of empirical studies of rape avoidance,'" *Criminal Justice and Behavior* 34 (2007): 1–19.

49. UK Center for Research on Violence Against Women, "Top Ten Things Advocates Need to Know: 7. What Percentage of Rape Cases Gets Prosecuted? What Are the Rates of Conviction?" December 2011, http://www.uky.edu/CRVAW/files/TopTen/07 _Rape_Prosecution.pdf.

50. E. O. Laumann er al., *The social organization of sexuality: Sexual practices in the United States* (Chicago: The University of Chicago Press, 1994).

51. M. Douglass and L. Douglass, *Are We Having Fun Yet?* (New York: Hyperion, 1997); Alfred Kinsey et al., *Sexual Behavior in the Human Female* (Philadelphia: Saunders, 1953); see also S. Thompson, "Search for tomorrow: On feminism and the reconstruction of teen romance," in *Pleasure and danger: Exploring female sexuality*, ed. C. S. Vance (London: Pandora, 1989).

52. Emily Coleman, Peter Hoon, and Emily Hoon, "Arousability and Sexual Satisfaction in Lesbian and Heterosexual Women," *The Journal of Sex Research* 19, no. 1 (1983): 58–73; John Harvey, Amy Wenzel, and Susan Sprecher, *The Handbook of Sexuality in Close Relationships* (New York: Routledge, 2004); Shere Hite, *The Hite Report: A Nationwide Study of Female Sexuality* (New York: Seven Stories Press, 1977).

53. Anne Bolin, "French Polynesia," *The International Encyclopedia of Sexuality Volume I–IV*, ed. Robert T. Francoeur (New York: The Continuum Publishing Company, 1997–2001), http://www2.hu -berlin.de/sexology/IES/frenchpolynesia.html.

54. Elisabeth Anne Lloyd, *The Case of the Female Orgasm: Bias in the Science of Evolution* (Boston: Harvard University Press, 2005); Shere Hite, *The Hite Report: A Nationwide Study of Female Sexuality* (New York: Seven Stories Press, 1977).

55. Lisa Wade, Emily Kremer, and Jessica Brown, "The Incidental Orgasm: The Presence of Clitoral Knowledge and the Absence of Orgasm for Women," *Women and Health* 42, no. 1 (2005): 117–38; Diana Sanchez, Jennifer Crocker, and Karlee Boike, "Doing Gender in the Bedroom: Investing in Gender Norms and the Sexual Experience," *Personality and Social Psychology Bulletin* 31, no. 10 (2005): 1445–55.

56. P. England, E. F. Shafer, and A. C. K. Fogerty, (2008). "Hooking up and forming relationships on today's college campuses," in *The Gendered Society Reader*, ed. Michael Kimmel (New York: Oxford University Press, 2008), 531–93.

57. K. A. Bogle, *Hooking up: Sex, dating, and relationships on campus* (New York: New York University Press, 2008); E. Paul, "Beer goggles, catching feelings, and the walk of shame: Myths and realities of the hookup experience," in *Relating difficulty: The processes of constructing and managing difficult interaction*, ed. D. C. Kirkpatrick, S. Duck, and M. K. Foley (Mahwah: Lawrence Erlbaum, 2006), 141–60; T. A. Lambert, A. S. Kahn, and K. J. Applie, (2003). "Pluralistic ignorance and hooking up," *Journal of Sex Research* 40 (2003): 129–33.

58. P. England, E. F. Shafer, and A. C. K. Fogerty, (2008). "Hooking up and forming relationships on today's college campuses," in *The Gendered Society Reader*, ed. Michael Kimmel (New York: Oxford University Press, 2008), 531–93; Lisa Wade and Caroline Heldman, "Hooking Up and Opting Out: What Students Learn about Sex in their First Year of College," in *Sex for Life: From Virginity to Viagra, How Sexuality Changes Throughout our Lives*, ed. Laura Carpenter and John DeLamater (New York: New York University Press, 2012), 128–145.

59. E. T. Pascerella and P. T. Terezini, *How college affects students: A third decade of research* (San Francisco: Jossey-Bass, 2005); B. J. Willoughby et al., "The decline of in loco parentis and the shift to coed housing on college campuses," *Journal of Adolescent Research* 24, no. 1 (2009): 21–36; J. P. Earle, "Acquaintance rape workshops: Their effectiveness in changing the attitudes of first year college men," *NASPA Journal* 46, no. 3 (2009): 417–33.

60. L. Hamilton and E. A. Armstrong. "Gendered Sexuality in Young Adulthood: Double Binds and Flawed Options," *Gender & Society* 23, no. 5 (2009): 589–616.

61. L. Hamilton and E. A. Armstrong. "Gendered Sexuality in Young Adulthood: Double Binds and Flawed Options," *Gender & Society* 23, no. 5 (2009): 589–616.

62. K. A. Bogle, *Hooking up: Sex, dating, and relationships on campus* (New York: New York University Press, 2008); Donna Freitas, *Sex and the Soul: Juggling Sexuality, Spirituality, Romance, and Religion on America's College Campuses* (New York: Oxford University Press, 2008); J. J.Owen et al., "'Hooking Up' among College Students: Demographic and Psychosocial Correlates," *Archives of Sexual Behavior* 39, no. 3 (2010): 653–63.

63. Laura Hamilton, "Trading on Heterosexuality: College Women's Gender Strategies and Homophobia," *Gender & Society* 21, no. 2 (2007): 145–72; Leila Rupp et al., "Queer Women in the Hookup Scene: Beyond the Closet?" *Gender & Society*, forthcoming.

64. Laura Hamilton, "Trading on Heterosexuality: College Women's Gender Strategies and Homophobia," *Gender & Society* 21, no. 2 (2007): 145–72.

65. Evelyn Brooks Higginbotham, *Righteous Discontent: The Women's Movement in the Black Baptist Church, 1880-1920* (Cambridge: Harvard University Press, 1993); Rashawn Ray and Jason A. Rosow, "Getting Off and Getting Intimate: How Normative Institutional Arrangements Structure Black and White Fraternity Men's Approaches toward Women," *Men and Masculinities* 12, no. 5 (2010): 523–46.

66. Personal communication: Paula England; Rachel Allison and Barbara Risman, "'It Goes Hand in Hand with the Parties': Race, Class, and Residence in College Negotiations of Hooking Up," *Sociological Perspectives* 57, no. 1 (2014): 102–23.

67. Personal communication: Paula England; Rachel Allison and Barbara Risman, "'It Goes Hand in Hand with the Parties': Race, Class, and Residence in College Negotiations of Hooking Up," *Sociological Perspectives* 57, no. 1 (2014): 102–23; L. Hamilton and E. A. Armstrong, "Gendered Sexuality in Young Adulthood: Double Binds and Flawed Options," *Gender & Society* 23, no. 5 (2009): 589–616; Laura Hamilton, "Trading on Heterosexuality: College Women's Gender Strategies and Homophobia," *Gender & Society* 21, no. 2 (2007): 145–72; Elizabeth Armstrong and Laura Hamilton, *Paying for the Party: How College Maintains Inequality* (Boston: Harvard University Press, 2013).

68. L. Hamilton and E. A. Armstrong, "Gendered Sexuality in Young Adulthood: Double Binds and Flawed Options," *Gender & Society* 23, no. 5 (2009): 589–616.

69. Rachel Allison and Barbara Risman, "'It Goes Hand in Hand with the Parties': Race, Class, and Residence in College Negotiations of Hooking Up," *Sociological Perspectives* 57, no. 1 (2014): 102–23.

70. Rachel Allison and Barbara Risman, "'It Goes Hand in Hand with the Parties': Race, Class, and Residence in College Negotiations of Hooking Up," *Sociological Perspectives* 57, no. 1 (2014): 111.

71. Angus McLaren, *Twentieth Century Sexuality: A History* (Oxford: Blackwell Publishers Ltd., 1999).

72. American Association of University Women, SAAM: Sexual assault on campus, 2009, www.aauw.org, accessed June 11, 2009; H. M. Karjane, B. S. Fisher, and F. T. Cullen, *Sexual assault on campus: What colleges and universities are doing about it.* United States Department of Justice, December 2002.

73. American Association of University Women, SAAM: Sexual assault on campus, 2009, www.aauw.org, accessed April 5, 2014.

74. Victoria Banyard, Elizabethe Plante, and Mary Moynihan. "Bystander education: Bringing a broader community perspective to sexual violence prevention," *Journal of Community Psychology* 32, no. 1 (2004): 61–79; Victoria Banyard, Mary Moynihan, and Elizabethe Plante, "Sexual violence prevention through bystander education: An experimental evaluation." *Journal of Community Psychology* 35, no. 4 (2007): 463–81; Ann Coker et al., "Evaluation of Green Dot: An Active Bystander Intervention to Reduce Sexual Violence on College Campuses," *Violence Against Women* 17, no. 6 (2011): 777–96.

75. E. A. Armstrong, P. England, and A. C. K. Fogarty, "Orgasm in college hook-ups and relationships," in *Families as They Really Are*, ed. Barbara Risman (New York: W.W. Norton and Company, 2009).

76. J. J. Owen et al., "'Hooking Up' among College Students: Demographic and Psychosocial Correlates," *Archives of Sexual Behavior* 39, no. 3 (2010): 653–63.

77. E. A. Armstrong, P. England, and A. C. K. Fogarty, "Orgasm in college hook-ups and relationships," in *Families as They Really Are*, ed. Barbara Risman (New York: W.W. Norton and Company, 2009).

78. E. Armstrong, P. England, and A. Fogarty, "Accounting for Women's Orgasm and Sexual Enjoyment in College Hook-ups and Relationships," *American Sociological Review* 77, no. 3 (2012): 435–62.

79. Lisa Wade and Caroline Heldman, "Hooking Up and Opting Out: What Students Learn about Sex in their First Year of College," in *Sex for Life: From Virginity to Viagra, How Sexuality Changes Throughout our Lives*, ed. Laura Carpenter and John DeLamater (New York: New York University Press, 2012), 128–145.

80. P. England, E. F. Shafer, and A. C. K. Fogerty, "Hooking up and forming relationships on today's college campuses," in *The Gendered Society Reader*,

ed. Michael Kimmel (New York: Oxford University Press, 2008), 531–93.

81. E. Armstrong, P. England, and A. Fogarty, "Accounting for Women's Orgasm and Sexual Enjoyment in College Hook-ups and Relationships," *American Sociological Review* 77, no. 3 (2012): 435–62.

82. E. O. Laumann et al., *The social organization of sexuality: Sexual practices in the United States* (Chicago: The University of Chicago Press, 1994).

83. Richard Fry, "The Reversal of the College Marriage Gap," *Pew Research: Social & Demographic Trends*, October 7, 2010, http://www.pewsocial trends.org/2010/10/07/the-reversal-of-the-college -marriage-gap/.

84. Betsey Stevenson and Justin Wolfers, "The Paradox of Declining Female Happiness, 2009, http://clalit2oplus.co.il/NR/rdonlyres/08586B39 -9E87-4A86-ACDA-BB50CD52F1EB/0/The _Paradox_of_Declining_Female_Happiness.pdf; Sampson Lee Blair and Michael P. Johnson, "Wives' Perceptions of the Fairness of the Division of Household Labor: The Intersection of Housework and Ideology," *Journal of Marriage and the Family* 54, no. 3 (1992): 570–81; Theodore N.Greenstein, "Gender Ideology and the Perceptions of the Fairness of the Division of Household Labor: Effects on Marital Quality," *Social Forces* 74, 3 (1996): 1029–42; Arlie Hochschild, *The Second Shift* (New York: Penguin Group, 1989); Michelle Frisco and Kristi Williams, "Perceived Housework Equity, Marital Happiness, and Divorce in Dual-Earner Households," *Journal of Family Issues* 24, no. 1 (2003): 51–73; Mamadi Corra et al., "Trends in Marital Happiness by Gender and Race, 1973 to 2006," *Journal of Family Issues* 30, no. 10 (2009): 1379–1404; P. R. Amato et al., "Continuity and change in marital quality between 1980 and 2000," *Journal of Marriage and Family* 65, no. 1 (2003): 1–22; R. A. Faulkner, M. Davey, and A. Davey, "Gender-related predictors of change in marital satisfaction and marital conflict," *American Journal of Family Therapy* 33, no. 1 (2005): 61–83; R. G. Henry, R. B. Miller, and R. Giarrusso, "Difficulties, disagreements, and disappointments in late-life marriages," *International Journal of Aging & Human Development* 61, no. 3 (2005): 243–65; G. Kaufman and H. Taniguchi, "Gender and marital happiness in later life," *Journal of Family Issues* 27, no. 6 (2006): 735–57; L. L. W. Tsang et al., "The effects of children, dual earner status, sex role traditionalism, and marital structure on marital happiness over time," *Journal of Family and Economic Issues* 24, no. 1 (2003): 5–26.

Chapter 11: Families

1. Arlie Hochschild, *The Second Shift* (New York: Penguin Group, 1989), 7.

2. Betsey Stevenson and Justin Wolfers, "The Paradox of Declining Female Happiness," Bonn, Germany: IZA, May 2009, http://clalit2oplus.co.il/NR /rdonlyres/08586B39-9E87-4A86-ACDA-BB50CD 52F1EB/0/The_Paradox_of_Declining_Female _Happiness.pdf; Sampson Lee Blair and Michael P. Johnson, "Wives' Perceptions of the Fairness of the Division of Household Labor: The Intersection of Housework and Ideology," *Journal of Marriage and the Family* 54 (1992): 570–81; Theodore N. Greenstein, "Gender Ideology and the Perceptions of the Fairness of the Division of Household Labor: Effects on Marital Quality," *Social Forces* 74 (1996): 1029–42; Arlie Hochschild, *The Second Shift* (New York: Penguin Group, 1989); Michelle Frisco and Kristi Williams, "Perceived Housework Equity, Marital Happiness, and Divorce in Dual-Earner Households," *Journal of Family Issues* 24, no. 1 (2003): 51–73; Mamadi Corra et al., "Trends in Marital Happiness by Gender and Race, 1973–2006," *Journal of Family Issues* 30, no. 10 (2009): 1379–404; P. R. Amato et al., "Continuity and change in marital quality between 1980 and 2000," *Journal of Marriage and Family*, 65 (2003): 1–22; R. A. Faulkner, M. Davey, and A. Davey, "Gender-related predictors of change in marital satisfaction and marital conflict," *American Journal of Family Therapy*, 33 (2005): 61–83; R. G. Henry, R. B. Miller, and R. Giarrusso, "Difficulties, disagreements, and disappointments in late-life marriages," *International Journal of Aging & Human Development*, 61 (2005): 243–65; G. Kaufman and H. Taniguchi, "Gender and marital happiness in later life," *Journal of Family Issues*, 27 (2006): 735–57; L. L. W. Tsang et al., "The effects of children, dual earner status, sex role traditionalism, and marital structure on marital happiness over time," *Journal of Family and Economic Issues*, 24, no. 1 (2003): 5–26; Betsey Stevenson and Justin Wolfers, "The Paradox of Declining Female Happiness," Bonn, Germany: IZA, May 2009, http://clalit2oplus.co .il/NR/rdonlyres/08586B39-9E87-4A86-ACDA -BB50CD52F1EB/0/The_Paradox_of_Declining _Female_Happiness.pdf.

3. Calculated using these three sources: Daphne Lofquist, Terry Lugaila, Martin O'Connell, and Sarah Feliz, "Households and Families: 2010," United States Census Bureau, April 2012, http:// www.census.gov/prod/cen2010/briefs/c2010br-14 .pdf; Bureau of Labor Statistics, "Table 6. Employment status of mothers with own children under

3 years old by single year of age of youngest child and marital status, 2011–2012 annual averages," (last modified April 26, 2013), http://www.bls.gov /news.release/famee.t06.htm; U.S. Congress Joint Economic Committee, "Women and the Economy 2010: 25 Years of Progress but Challenges Remain," August 2010, http://www.jec.senate.gov/public /?a=Files.Serve&File_id=8be22cb0-8ed0-4a1a-841b -aa91dc55fa81.

4. David Cotter, Paula England, and Joan Hermsen, "Moms and Jobs: Trends in Mothers' Employment and Which Mothers Stay Home," in *American Families: A Multicultural Reader*, ed. Stephanie Coontz (New York: Routledge, 2008).

5. Arlie Hochschild, *The Second Shift* (New York: Penguin Group, 1989).

6. Suzanne Bianchi, John Robinson, and Melissa Milkie, *Changing Rhythms of American Family Life* (New York: Russell Sage Foundation, 2007).

7. Gornick and Meyers 2003 in Suzanne Bianchi, John Robinson, and Melissa Milkie, *Changing Rhythms of American Family Life* (New York: Russell Sage Foundation, 2007).

8. Kimberley Fisher et al., "Gender Convergence in the American Heritage Time Use Study," *Social Indicators Research* 82 (2006): 1–33; David Cotter, Paula England, and Joan Hermsen, "Moms and Jobs: Trends in Mothers' Employment and Which Mothers Stay Home," in *American Families: A Multicultural Reader*, ed. Stephanie Coontz (New York: Routledge, 2008); Nicholas Townsend, *The Package Deal: Marriage, Work, and Fatherhood in Men's Lives* (Philadelphia, PA: Temple University Press, 2002); United States Department of Labor, "Women in the Labor Force in 2010," http://www.dol.gov/wb /factsheets/Qf-laborforce-10.htm#.UNzcVuQ72Ag.

9. J. Sunderland, "Baby entertainer, bumbling assistant and line manager: Discourses of fatherhood in parent craft texts," *Discourse and Society* 11, no. 2 (2000): 249–74; J. Sunderland, "'Parenting' or 'mothering'? The case of modern child care magazines," *Discourse and Society* 17, no. 4 (2006): 503–27; Glenda Wall and Stephanie Arnold, "How Involved is Involved Fathering?: An Exploration of the Contemporary Culture of Fatherhood," *Gender & Society* 21, no. 4 (2007): 508–527; Jennifer Krafchick et al., "Best Selling Books Advising Parents about Gender: A Feminist Analysis," *Family Relations* 54 (2005): 84–100.

10. J. Sunderland, "'Parenting' or 'mothering'? The case of modern child care magazines," *Discourse and Society* 17, no. 4 (2006): 512.

11. Lisa Rashely, "'Work it Out with Your Wife': Gendered Expectations and Parenting Rhetoric Online," *Feminist Formations* 17, no. 1 (2005): 58–92.

12. Amazon Mom sign-up page, *Amazon*, http:// www.amazon.com/gp/mom/signup http://www .amazon.com/gp/mom/signup/welcome, accessed September 10, 2014.

13. Gayle Kaufman, "The portrayal of men's family roles in television commercials," *Sex Roles* 41, no. 5/6 (1999): 439–58.

14. Kristin Natalier, "'I'm Not His Wife': Doing Gender and Doing Housework in the Absence of Women," *Journal of Sociology* 39, no. 3 (2003): 253–69.

15. Ibid.

16. Ibid., 260.

17. D. Berkowitz, "Maternal Instincts, Biological Clocks, and Soccer Moms: Gay Men's Parenting and Family Narratives," *Symbolic Interaction* 34, no. 4 (2011): 514–35.

18. Ibid., 518.

19. Kathleen Gerson, *The Unfinished Revolution: Coming of Age in a New Era of Gender, Work, and Family* (New York: Oxford University Press, 2010).

20. Ibid., 105–107.

21. Suzanne Bianchi, John Robinson, and Melissa Milkie, *Changing Rhythms of American Family Life* (New York: Russell Sage Foundation, 2007).

22. Kim Parker and Wendy Wang, "Modern Parenthood: Roles of Moms and Dads Converge as They Balance Work and Family," *Pew Research: Social & Demographic Trends*, March 14, 2013, http://www .pewsocialtrends.org/2013/03/14/modern-parent hood-roles-of-moms-and-dads-converge-as-they -balance-work-and-family/?src=rss_main; Kimberley Fisher et al., "Gender Convergence in the American Heritage Time Use Study," *Social Indicators Research* 82 (2006): 1–33.

23. Jane Riblett Wilkie, Myra Marx Ferree, and Kathryn Stother Ratcliff, "Gender and Fairness: Marital Satisfaction in Two-Earner Couples," *Journal of Marriage and Family* 60 (1998): 577–94.

24. Arlie Hochschild, *The Second Shift* (New York: Penguin Group, 1989), 62, 68.

25. Ibid., 62, 68.

26. Kathleen Gerson, *The Unfinished Revolution: Coming of Age in a New Era of Gender, Work, and Family* (New York: Oxford University Press, 2010), 176.

27. Ibid., 162.

28. Ibid., 167.

29. D. Feder, "Feminists to Women: Shut Up and Do as You're Told," *Human Events* (March 2006): 15.

30. Sharon Hays, *The Cultural Contradictions of Motherhood* (New Haven: Yale University Press, 1996), 8.

31. Thomas Weisner and Ronald Gallimore, "My Brother's Keeper: Child and Sibling Caretaking," *Current Anthropology* 18 (1977): 169–89; Elinor Ochs and Carolina Izquierdo. "Responsibility in Childhood: Three Developmental Trajectories," *Ethos* 37, no. 4 (2009): 394.

32. Peter Stearns, *Anxious Parents: A History of Modern Childrearing in America* (New York: New York University Press, 2004), 3.

33. Sharon Hays, *The Cultural Contradictions of Motherhood* (New Haven: Yale University Press, 1996), 159.

34. Nicholas Townsend, *The Package Deal: Marriage, Work, and Fatherhood in Men's Lives* (Philadelphia: Temple University Press, 2002).

35. The Henry J. Kaiser Family Foundation, "Average Per Person Monthly Premiums in the Individual Market, 2010," http://kff.org/other/state-indicator/individual-premiums/.

36. This doesn't apply to the *highest* income earners because social security taxation is capped.

37. Christopher Carrington, *No place like home: Relationships and family life among lesbians and gay men* (Chicago: The University of Chicago Press, 1999), 187.

38. Ibid.

39. Jane Riblett Wilkie, Myra Marx Ferree, and Kathryn Ratcliff, "Gender and Fairness: Marital Satisfaction in Two-Earner Couples," *Journal of Marriage and the Family* 60 (1998): 577–94; J. Baxter, B. Hewitt, and M. Haynes, "Life course transitions and housework: Marriage, parenthood, and time on housework," *Journal of Marriage and Family* 70 (2008): 259–72; Gupta 1999 and Robinson and Godbey 1999 in Suzanne Bianchi, John Robinson, and Melissa Milkie, *Changing Rhythms of American Family Life* (New York: Russell Sage Foundation, 2007); Jane Riblett Wilkie, Myra Marx Ferree, and Kathryn Ratcliff, "Gender and Fairness: Marital Satisfaction in Two-Earner Couples," *Journal of Marriage and the Family* 60 (1998): 577–94.

40. Shelly Lundberg and Elaina Rose, "Parenthood and the Earnings of Married Men and Women," *Labour Economics* 7, no. 6 (2000): 689–710.

41. Bianchi 2000; Peterson and Gerson 1992; Crouter and McHale 2005; all in Suzanne Bianchi, John Robinson, and Melissa Milkie, *Changing Rhythms of American Family Life* (New York: Russell Sage Foundation, 2007).

42. Mary Blair-Loy, *Competing Devotions: Career and Family among Women Executives* (Cambridge: Harvard University Press, 2003).

43. Arlie Hochschild, *The Time Bind: When Work Becomes Home and Home Becomes Work* (New York: Henry Holt and Company, 2001), 177.

44. Suzanne Bianchi, John Robinson, and Melissa Milkie, *Changing Rhythms of American Family Life* (New York: Russell Sage Foundation, 2007).

45. Shira Offer and Barbara Schneider, "Revisiting the Gender Gap in Time-Use Patterns: Multitasking and Well-Being among Mothers and Fathers in Dual-Earner Families," *American Sociological Review* 76, no. 6: 809–33; John Robinson and Geoffrey Godbey, *Time for Life: The Surprising Ways Americans Use Their Time*, 2nd ed. (University Park: Penn State University Press, 1999); Kimberley Fisher et al., "Gender Convergence in the American Heritage Time Use Study," *Social Indicators Research* 82 (2006): 1–33; OECD, Society at a Glance, "Key Findings on Chapter 1: Unpaid Work," December 4, 2011, http://www.oecd.org/social/soc/47573400.pdf; Janeen Baxter, 1997. "Gender Equality and Participation in housework: A Cross-National Perspective," *Journal of Comparative Family Studies* 28 (1997): 220–47; Mary Dorinda Allard et al., "Comparing Child care Measures in the ATUS and Earlier Time-Diary Studies," *Monthly Labor Review* 130, 5 (2007): 27–36.

46. Judith Warner, *Perfect Madness: Motherhood in the Age of Anxiety* (New York: Riverhead Books, 2005), 26.

47. Susan Walzer, "Thinking About the Baby: Gender and the Division of Infant Care," *Social Problems* 43, no. 2 (1996): 199.

48. J. Sunderland, "'Parenting'or 'mothering'? The case of modern child care magazines," *Discourse and Society* 17, no. 4 (2006): 521.

49. Christopher Carrington, *No place like home: Relationships and family life among lesbians and gay men* (Chicago: University of Chicago Press, 1999), 79–80.

50. Ibid., 79.

51. David Cotter, Paula England, and Joan Hermsen. "Moms and Jobs: Trends in Mothers' Employment and Which Mothers Stay Home," in *American*

Families: A Multicultural Reader, ed. Stephanie Coontz (New York: Routledge, 2008).

52. David Cotter, Paula England, and Joan Hermsen. "Moms and Jobs: Trends in Mothers' Employment and Which Mothers Stay Home," in *American Families: A Multicultural Reader*, ed. Stephanie Coontz (New York: Routledge, 2008).

53. Ibid.

54. Child Care Aware of America, "Parents and the High Cost of Child Care: 2012 Report" (Arlington, VA: 2012), http://www.naccrra.org/sites/default/files/default_site_pages/2012/cost_report_2012_final_081012_0.pdf.

55. Glenna Spitze, "Women's Employment and Family Relations: A Review," *Journal of Marriage and the Family* 50 (1988): 595-18.

56. Lynn Cooke, "'Traditional' Marriages Now Less Stable Than Ones Where Couples Share Work and Household Chores," in *Families as they Really Are*, ed. Barbara Risman (New York: W. W. Norton and Company, 2010).

57. Neil Chethik, *VoiceMale: What Husbands Really Think About their Marriages, their Wives, Sex, Housework, and Commitment* (New York: Simon & Schuster, 2006), 116.

58. Carolyn Stuenkel, "A Strategy for Working Families: High-Level Commodification of Household Services," in *Being Together, Working Apart: Dual-Career Families and the Work-Life Balance*, ed. Barbara Schneider and Linda J. Waite (New York: Cambridge University Press, 2005), 260.

59. Annie Murphy Paul, "The Real Marriage Penalty," *New York Times*, November 19, 2006, http://www.nytimes.com/2006/11/19/magazine/19wwln_idealab.html.

60. Barbara Risman, *Gender Vertigo: American Families in Transition* (New Haven: Yale University Press, 1999).

61. Lynn Cooke, "'Traditional' Marriages Now Less Stable Than Ones Where Couples Share Work and Household Chores," in *Families as they Really Are*, ed. Barbara Risman (New York: W. W. Norton and Company, 2010).

62. CDC, "Marriage and Cohabitation in the United States: A Statistical Portrait Based on Cycle 6 (2002) of the National Survey of Family Growth." *Vital and Health Statistics* 23, 28 (2010).

63. Kathleen Gerson, *The Unfinished Revolution: Coming of Age in a New Era of Gender, Work, and Family* (New York: Oxford University Press, 2010), 129.

64. Ibid., 129.

65. Ibid., 134.

66. Eileen Patten and Kim Parker, "A Gender Reversal On Career Aspirations: Young Women Now Top Young Men in Valuing a High-Paying Career, *Pew Research: Social & Demographic Trends*, April 19, 2012, http://www.pewsocialtrends.org/2012/04/19/a-gender-reversal-on-career-aspirations/?src=prc-headline.

67. Ibid.

68. David M. Blau and Wilbert H. van der Klaauw, "A Demographic Analysis of the Family Structure Experiences of Children in the United States," Bonn, Germany: IZA, August 2007, http://ideas.repec.org/p/iza/izadps/dp3001.html; Timothy S. Grall, "Custodial Mothers and Fathers and Their Child Support: 2009," U.S. Census Bureau, December 2011, http://www.census.gov/prod/2011pubs/p60-240.pdf.

69. Kathryn Edin and Maria Kefalas, *Why Poor Women Put Motherhood before Marriage* (Berkeley and Los Angeles: University of California Press, 2011).

70. Kathryn Edin and Maria Kefalas, "Unmarried with Children," *Contexts* 4, no. 2 (2005): 18.

71. Ibid., 18-22.

72. Stanlie M. James, "Mothering: A possible Black feminist link to social transformation," in *Theorizing Black Feminisms: The visionary pragmatism of black women*, ed. Stanlie M. James and Abena P. A. Busia (London: Routledge, 1993), 45.

73. Lynne Haney and Miranda March, "Married Fathers and Caring Daddies: Welfare Reform and the Discursive Politics of Paternity," *Social Problems* 50, no. 4 (2003): 478.

74. Amanda Riley-Jones, "Mothers Without Men," *Guardian*, June 9, 2000, http://www.guardian.co.uk/theguardian/2000/jun/10/weekend7.weekend2.

75. Kristin Luker, *Dubious Conceptions: The Politics of Teenage Pregnancy* (Cambridge: Harvard University Press, 1996).

76. Kathleen Gerson, *No Man's Land. Men's Changing Commitments to Family and Work* (New York: Basic Books, 1993).

77. Jason DeParle, "Census Reports a sharp increase among never-married mothers: Puncturing stereotypes of out-of-wedlock births," *New York Times*, July 14, 1993.

78. Susanna Graham, "Choosing Single Motherhood? Single women negotiating the nuclear family ideal," in *Families—Beyond the Nuclear Ideal*,

ed. Daniela Cutas and Sarah Chan (London and New York: Bloomsbury Academic, 2012), http://www.bloomsburyacademic.com/view/Families-Beyond-the-Nuclear-Ideal/chapter-ba-9781780930114-chapter-007.xml.

79. Brady E. Hamilton, Joyce A. Martin, and Stephanie J. Ventura, "Births: Preliminary Data for 2012," U. S. Department of Health and Human Services, *National Vital Statistics Report* 62:3 (September 6, 2013), http://www.cdc.gov/nchs/data/nvsr/nvsr62/nvsr62_03.pdf.

80. Gretchen Livingston and D'Vera Cohn, Pew Research Center, *Childlessness Up Among All Women; Down Among Women with Advanced Degrees*, Pew Research Center's Social & Demographic Trends Project, 2010, http://www.pewsocialtrends.org/files/2010/11/758-childless.pdf.

81. Sylvia Hewlett et al., *The X Factor: Tapping into the Strengths of the 33- to 46-Year-Old Generation*, Center for Work-Life Policy, 2011.

82. R. Gillespie, "Childfree and Feminine: Understanding the Gender Identity of Voluntarily Childless Women," *Gender & Society* 17, no. 1 (2003): 131.

83. Ibid., 131.

84. Lisa Wade, Interview. Personal records.

85. Ibid.

86. Ibid.

87. Ibid.

88. Ann Crittenden, *The Price of Motherhood: Why the Most Important Job in the World Is Still the Least Valued* (New York: Henry Holt and Company, 2002), 12.

89. Ibid, 236–37.

90. Kathleen Gerson, *The Unfinished Revolution: Coming of Age in a New Era of Gender, Work, and Family* (New York: Oxford University Press, 2010), xxx.

91. Christopher Carrington, *No place like home: Relationships and family life among lesbians and gay men* (Chicago: The University of Chicago Press, 1999), 54.

92. Judith Warner, "The Opt-Out Generation Wants Back In," *New York Times*, August 7, 2013: MM25, http://www.nytimes.com/2013/08/11/magazine/the-opt-out-generation-wants-back-in.html?pagewanted=all.

93. Neil Chethik, *VoiceMale: What Husbands Really Think About their Marriages, their Wives, Sex, Housework, and Commitment* (New York: Simon & Schuster, 2006), 121.

94. Susan Walzer, "Thinking About the Baby: Gender and the Division of Infant Care," *Social Problems* 43, no. 2 (1996): 200–201.

95. Anisa Zvonkovic et al., "The Marital Construction of Gender through Work and Family Decisions: A Qualitative Analysis," *Journal of Marriage and the Family* 58, no. 1 (1996): 91–100.

96. Susan Dalton and Denise Bielby, "'That's Our Kind of Constellation': Lesbian Mothers negotiate Institutionalized Understandings of Gender within the Family," *Gender & Society* 14, no. 1 (2000): 36–61; Maureen Sullivan, "Rozzie and Harriet? Gender and Family Patterns of Lesbian Coparents," *Gender & Society* 10 (1996): 747–67; Elizabeth Sheff, *Gender, Family, and Sexuality: Exploring Polyamorous Community* (PhD diss, University of Colorado, 2005).

97. Gornick and Meyers 2003 in Suzanne Bianchi, John Robinson, and Melissa Milkie, *Changing Rhythms of American Family Life* (New York: Russell Sage Foundation, 2007).

98. Ann Crittenden, *The Price of Motherhood: Why the Most Important Job in the World is Still the Least Valued* (New York: Henry Holt and Company, 2002); Jennifer Glass, "Blessing or Curse? Work-Family Policies and Mothers' Wage Growth over Time," *Work and Occupations* 31 (2004): 367–94.

99. Renske Keizer, Pearl Dykstra, and Anne-Rigt Poortman, "Life Outcomes of Childless Men and Fathers," *European Sociological Review* 26, no. 1 (2010): 1–15; Institute for Public Policy Research, "Dads earn more while mothers earn less," December 23, 2012, http://www.ippr.org/press-releases/111/10113/dads-earn-more-while-mothers-earn-less.

100. Sylvia Ann Hewlett, *Off-Ramps and On-Ramps* (Cambridge: Harvard Business School Press, 2007), 46.

101. C. DeNavas-Walt, B. D. Proctor, and J. C. Smith, "Income, poverty, and health insurance coverage in the United States: 2010 (Current Population Report P60-239)," Washington, DC: US Census Bureau, 2011; http://www.census.gov/prod/2011pubs/p60-239.pdf; David M. Blau and Wilbert H. van der Klaauw, "A Demographic Analysis of the Family Structure Experiences of Children in the United States," Bonn, Germany: IZA, August 2007, http://ideas.repec.org/p/iza/izadps/dp3001.html; Timothy S. Grall, "Custodial Mothers and Fathers and Their Child Support: 2009," U.S. Census

Bureau, December 2011, http://www.census.gov/prod/2011pubs/p60-240.pdf.

102. http://articles.latimes.com/2002/oct/06/nation/na-children6

103. U.S. Bureau of Labor Statistics, Employment Characteristics of Families–2010, available at http://www.bls.gov/news.release/pdf/famee.pdf.

104. Jonathan Peterson, "Child-Care Issue Frames Welfare Reform Debate," *Los Angeles Times*, October 6, 2002, http://aspe.hhs.gov/poverty/12poverty.shtml/#thresholds.

105. C. DeNavas-Walt, B. D. Proctor, and J. C. Smith, "Income, poverty, and health insurance coverage in the United States: 2010 (Current Population Report P60-239)," Washington, DC: US Census Bureau, 2011.

106. U.S. Census Bureau Current Population Survey Table Creator (CPS Table Creator), available at http://www.census.gov/cps/data/cpstablecreator.html.

107. Ann Crittenden, *The Price of Motherhood: Why the Most Important Job in the World is Still the Least Valued* (New York: Henry Holt and Company, 2002); Elizabeth Warren and Amelia Tyagi, *The Two-Income Trap: Why Middle-Class Parents are Going Broke* (New York: Basic Books, 2003).

108. Linda Burnham and Nik Theodore, "Home Economics: The Invisible and Unregulated World of Domestic Work," National Domestic Workers Alliance: Center for Urban Economic Development, University of Illinois at Chicago Data Center, 2012.

109. Linda Burnham and Nik Theodore, "Home Economics: The Invisible and Unregulated World of Domestic Work," National Domestic Workers Alliance: Center for Urban Economic Development, University of Illinois at Chicago Data Center, 2012; Bureau of Labor Statistics, "May 2013 National Occupational Employment and Wage Estimates: United States," *http://www.bls.gov/oes/current/oes nat.htm#00-0000 (last modified April 1, 2014)*.

110. Rhacel S. Parreñas, *Servants of Globalization: Women, Migration and Domestic Work* (Stanford: Stanford University Press, 2001).

111. Arlie Hochschild, "The Nanny Chain," *The American Prospect*, December 19, 2001, http://prospect.org/article/nanny-chain.

112. Ibid.

113. Cameron MacDonald, *Shadow Mothers: Nannies, Au Pairs, and the Micropolitics of Mothering* (Berkeley: University of California Press, 2010).

114. Ibid., 61.

115. Ibid., 61.

116. United States Department of Labor, "Quick Stats on Women Workers, 2010," http://www.dol.gov/wb/factsheets/QS-womenwork2010.htm.

Chapter 12: Work

1. Drew Whitelegg, *Working the Skies: The Fast-Paced, Disorienting World of the Flight Attendant* (New York: New York University Press, 2007), 1.

2. Eileen Patten and Kim Parker, "A Gender Reversal on Career Aspirations: Young Women Now Top Young Men in Valuing a High-Paying Career," *Pew Research: Social & Demographic Trends*, April 19, 2012, http://www.pewsocialtrends.org/2012/04/19/a-gender-reversal-on-career-aspirations/?src=prc-headline.

3. AAUW, The Simple Truth about the Gender Pay Gap, 2013, from http://www.aauw.org/research/the-simple-truth-about-the-gender-pay-gap/; Blake Ellis, "Female Grads Earn $8,000 Less Than Men," *CNN Money*, October 23, 2012, http://money.cnn.com/2012/10/23/pf/college/women-men-pay-gap/index.html.

4. Julie Zauzmer, "Where We Stand: The Class of 2013 Senior Survey," *The Harvard Crimson*, May 28, 2013, http://www.thecrimson.com/article/2013/5/28/senior-survey-2013/?page=single.

5. AAUW, "The Simple Truth about the Gender Pay Gap," 2013, http://www.aauw.org/research/the-simple-truth-about-the-gender-pay-gap/; Blake Ellis, "Female Grads Earn $8,000 Less Than Men," *CNN Money*, October 23, 2013, http://money.cnn.com/2012/10/23/pf/college/women-men-pay-gap/index.html.

6. Kathleen Barry, "'Too Glamorous to be Considered Workers': Flight Attendants and Pink-Collar Activism in Mid-Twentieth-Century America," *Labor: Studies in Working-Class History of the Americas* 3, no. 3 (2006): 119.

7. Kathleen Barry, *Femininity in Flight: A History of Flight Attendants* (Durham: Duke University Press, 2007), 98.

8. Ibid., 62.

9. Linda Mizejewski, *Ziegfeld Girl: Image and Icon in Culture and Cinema* (Durham: Duke University Press, 1999), 12.

10. Kathleen Barry, *Femininity in Flight: A History of Flight Attendants* (Durham: Duke University Press, 2007).

11. Kathleen Barry, "'Too Glamorous to be Considered Workers': Flight Attendants and Pink-Collar Activism in Mid-Twentieth-Century America," *Labor: Studies in Working-Class History of the Americas* 3, no. 3: 135; Drew Whitelegg, *Working the Skies: The Fast-Paced, Disorienting World of the Flight Attendant* (New York: New York University Press, 2007), 47, 133.

12. Kathleen Barry, *Femininity in Flight: A History of Flight Attendants* (Durham and London: Duke University Press, 2007); Arlie Hochschild, *The Managed Heart: Commercialization of Human Feeling* (Berkeley: University of California Press, 1983); Melissa Tyler and Pamela Abbott, "Chocs Away: Weight Watching in the Contemporary Airline Industry," *Sociology* 32, no. 3 (1998): 433–50.

13. Victoria Vantoch, *The Jet Sex: Airline Stewardesses and the Making of an American Icon* (Philadelphia: University of Pennsylvania Press, 2013).

14. Drew Whitelegg, *Working the Skies: The Fast-Paced, Disorienting World of the Flight Attendant* (New York: New York University Press, 2007). 58.

15. Kathleen Barry, *Femininity in Flight: A History of Flight Attendants* (Durham: Duke University Press, 2007), 26.

16. Claire Williams, "Sky Service: The Demands of Emotional Labour in the Airline Industry," *Gender, Work and Organization* 10, no. 5 (2003): 513–50.

17. Kathleen Barry, *Femininity in Flight: A History of Flight Attendants* (Durham and London: Duke University Press, 2007), 119.

18. Ibid.

19. Catalyst, "Catalyst Quick Take: Women in U.S. Management and Labor Force" (New York: Catalyst, 2013), http://www.catalyst.org/knowledge/women-us-management-and-labor-force.

20. Bureau of Labor Statistics, "Women's Earnings, 1979–2012," 2013, http://www.bls.gov/opub/ted/2013/ted_20131104.htm.

21. European Commission, "The Situation in the E.U.," n.d., http://ec.europa.eu/justice/gender-equality/gender-pay-gap/situation-europe/index_en.htm; Ariane Hegewisch, Claudia Williams, and Amber Henderson."Fact Sheet: The Gender Wage Gap: 2010," Institute for Women's Policy Research, 2011, http://www.iwpr.org/publications/pubs/the-gender-wage-gap-by-occupation-updated-april-2011; AAUW, "The Simple Truth about the Gender Pay Gap," 2013, http://www.aauw.org/research/the-simple-truth-about-the-gender-pay-gap/; Claudia Goldin, *Understanding the Gender Gap: An Economic History of American Women* (New York: Oxford University Press, 1990); Bureau of Labor Statistics, "Median Weekly Earnings by Age, Sex, Race, and Hispanic or Latino Ethnicity, first quarter 2013," United States Department of Labor, April 19, 2013, http://www.bls.gov/opub/ted/2013/ted_20130419.htm; David Getz, "Men's and Women's Earnings for States and Metropolitan Statistical Areas: 2009," American Community Survey Briefs, September 2010, http://www.census.gov/prod/2010pubs/acsbr09-3.pdf.

22. Jessica Arons, "Lifetime Losses: The Career Wage Gap," Center for American Progress Action Fund, 2008, http://www.americanprogressaction.org/wp-content/uploads/issues/2008/pdf/equal_pay.pdf.

23. Ibid.

24. U.S. Social Security Administration, "Annual Statistical Supplement to the Social Security Bulletin, 2007: 6B: OASDI Benefits Awarded: Retired Workers," http://www.socialsecurity.gov/policy/docs/statcomps/supplement/2007/6b.pdf.

25. Jessica Arons, "Lifetime Losses: The Career Wage Gap," Center for American Progress Action Fund, 2008, http://www.americanprogressaction.org/wp-content/uploads/issues/2008/pdf/equal_pay.pdf.

26. Kathleen Barry, *Femininity in Flight: A History of Flight Attendants* (Durham: Duke University Press, 2007).

27. Henry Holden, "Women in Aviation—A Legacy of Success," *Airport Journals*, March 2003, http://www.census.gov/cps/data/cpstablecreator.html.

28. Albert Mills, "Cockpits, Hangars, Boys and Galleys: Corporate Masculinities and the Development of British Airways," *Gender, Work and Organization* 5, no. 3 (1998): 172–88.

29. Bureau of Labor Statistics, "Labor Force Statistics from the Current Population Survey: Table 11: Employed persons by detailed occupation, sex, race, and Hispanic or Latino ethnicity," http://www.bls.gov/cps/cpsaat11.htm.

30. Robin Leidner, "Selling Hamburgers and Selling Insurance: Gender, Work, and Identity in Interactive Service Jobs," *Gender & Society* 5 (1991): 174.

31. Ibid., 174; Robin Leidner, *Fast Food, Fast Talk: Service Work and the Routinization of Everyday Life* (Berkeley: University of California Press, 1993).

32. Lynn Carlisle, "The Gender Shift, the Demographics of Women in Dentistry. What Impact Will

it Have?" *In a Spirit of Caring*, n.d., http://www.spiritofcaring.com/public/488.cfm.

33. Maria Charles, "What Gender is Science?" *Contexts* 10, no. 2 (2011), http://contexts.org/articles/spring-2011/what-gender-is-science/.

34. H. Gharibyan and S. Gunsaulus, "Gender gap in computer science does not exist in one former Soviet Republic: Results of a Study," Annual Joint Conference Integrating Technology into Computer Science Education. Proceedings of the 11th annual SIGCSE conference on Innovation and Technology in computer science education. Bologna, Italy, 2006.

35. Vivian Anette Lagesen, "Extreme Make-Over? The Making of Gender and Computer Science" (PhD diss., STS report 71, Trondeim: NTNU, Department of Interdisciplinary Studies of Culture, 2005).

36. "Women in India's Construction Industry," *Women in Informal Employment: Globalizing and Organzing*, http://wiego.org/informal-economy/women-indiapercentE2percent80percent99s-construction-industry

37. Joyce Jacobsen, *The Economics of Gender* (Malden, MA: Wiley-Blackwell, 2007), data from International Labour Organization, *Yearbook of Labour Statistics* (1985–2004), 2007.

38. Ariane Hegewisch et al., "Occupational Segregation and the Gender Wage Gap in the USA," Institute for Women's Policy Research, 2012, http://www.iwpr.org/roundtable-on-women-and-economy-files/ariane-hegewisch-occupational-segregation-and-the-gender-wage-gap-in-the-usa/view.

39. Sara Rab, "Sex Discrimination in Restaurant Hiring," (master's thesis, University of Pennsylvania, 2001).

40. Association of American Medical College, "2012 Physicians Specialty Data Book," 2012, https://www.aamc.org/download/313228/data/2012physicianspecialtydatabook.pdf.

41. Barbara Reskin and Denise Bielby, "A Sociological Perspective on Gender and Career Outcomes," *Journal of Economic Perspectives* 19, no. 1 (2005): 71–86.

42. Organization of Black Aerospace Professionals (OBAP), 2010, http://www.census.gov/cps/data/cpstablecreator.html.

43. Bureau of Labor Statistics, "Labor Force Statistics from the Current Population Survey: Table 11: Employed persons by detailed occupation, sex, race, and Hispanic or Latino ethnicity," http://www.bls.gov/cps/cpsaat11.htm.

44. Eileen Patten and Kim Parker, "Women in the U. S. Military: Growing Share, Distinctive Profile," *Pew Research: Social & Demographic Trends*, http://www.pewsocialtrends.org/files/2011/12/women-in-the-military.pdf.

45. John Blandford, "The Nexus of Sexual Orientation and Gender in the Determination of Earnings," *Industrial and Labor Relations Review* 56, no. 4 (2003): 622–42.

46. Phil Tiemeyer, *Plane Queer: Labor, Sexuality, and AIDS in the History of Male Flight Attendants* (Berkeley: University of California Press, 2013).

47. Maria Charles, "A World of Difference: International Trends in Women's Economic Status," *Annual Review of Sociology* 37 (2011): 355–71; Robin Ely, "Effects of Organizational Demographics and Social Identity on Relationships among Professional Women," *Administrative Science Quarterly* 39, no. 2 (1994): 203–38.

48. Sapna Cheryan et al., "Ambient Belonging: How Stereotypical Cues Impact Gender Participation in Computer Science," *Journal of Personality and Social Psychology* 97, no. 6 (2009): 1045–60.

49. Patricia Drentea, "Consequences of Women's Formal and Informal Job Search Methods for Employment in Female-Dominated Jobs," *Gender & Society* 12, no. 3 (1998): 321–38; Roberto M. Fernandez and M. Lourdes Sosa, "Gendering the Job: Networks and Recruitment at a Call Center," *American Journal of Sociology* 111 (2005): 859–904; Roberto M. Fernandez, Emilio J. Castilla, and Paul Moore, "Social Capital at Work: Network and Employment at a Phone Center," *American Journal of Sociology* 105 (2000): 1288–356.

50. Karen Hossfield, "Hiring Immigrant Women: Silicon Valley's Simple Formula," in *Women of Color in U.S. Society*, ed. Maxine Baca Zinn and Bonnie Thornton Dill, (Philadelphia: Temple University Press, 1994), 65.

51. David J. Maume, "Occupational Segregation and the Career Mobility of White Men and Women," *Social Forces* 77, no. 4 (1999): 1449.

52. Phil Tiemeyer, *Plane Queer: Labor, Sexuality, and AIDS in the History of Male Flight Attendants* (Berkeley: University of California Press, 2013), 93.

53. Ibid., 91.

54. Ibid., 102.

55. Ibid., 113.

56. Ibid.

57. Anne Kerr, "The World's First Flight Attendant on a Conventional Aircraft," *Lady Skywriter* (blog), July 13, 2010, http://blog.ladyskywriter .com/2010/07/worlds-first-flight-attendant-on.html.

58. Kathleen Barry, *Femininity in Flight: A History of Flight Attendants* (Durham: Duke University Press, 2007), 97.

59. Kathleen Barry, Ibid.

60. Melissa Tyler and Pamela Abbott, "Chocs Away: Weight Watching in the Contemporary Airline Industry," *Sociology* 32, no. 3 (1998): 440.

61. Claudia Goldin, *Understanding the Gender Gap: An Economic History of American Women* (New York: Oxford University Press, 1990), 204.

62. Margery Davies, *Woman's Place is at the Typewriter: Office Work and Office Workers, 1870–1930* (Philadelphia: Temple University Press, 1984); Claudia Goldin, *Understanding the Gender Gap: An Economic History of American Women* (New York: Oxford University Press, 1990).

63. *Top Secret Rosies: The Female Computers of World War II.* Documentary, dir. LeAnn Erickson (2010), http://www.topsecretrosies.com/.

64. Raja Tasneem, "The Secret History of CIA Women," *Mother Jones* (November 4, 2013), http:// www.motherjones.com/politics/2013/10/women -cia-history-sexism.

65. Thomas Misa, ed., *Gender Codes: Why Women are Leaving Computing* (Hoboken, NJ: Jon Wiley and Sons, Inc., 2010).

66. Anna Lewis, "Girls Go Geek . . . Again!" *Fog Creek Software* (blog), July 26, 2011, http://blog .fogcreek.com/girls-go-geek-again/

67. Anne Lincoln, "The Shifting Supply of Men and Women to Occupation: Feminization in Veterinary Education," *Social Forces* 88, no. 5 (2010): 1969–98.

68. For a review, see Philip Cohen and Matt L. Huffman, "Individuals, Jobs, and Labor Markets: The Devaluation of Women's Work," *American Sociological Review* 68, no. 3 (2007): 443–63.

69. Stephanie Boraas and William M. Rodgers III, "How Does Gender Play a Role in the Earnings Gap? An Update," *Monthly Labor Review* (March 2003), http://www.bls.gov/opub/mlr/2003/03 /art2full.pdf; Trond Peterson and Laurie A. Morgan, 1995. "Separate and Unequal: Occupation-Establishment Sex Segregation and the Gender Wage Gap," *American Journal of Sociology* 101 (1995): 329–65; Donald J. Treiman and Heidi I. Hartman, eds., *Women, Work, and Wages: Equal Pay for Jobs of Equal Value* (Washington, DC: National Academy Press, 1981); see also: Paula England, "Gender Inequality in Labor Markets: The Role of Motherhood and Segregation," *Social Politics: International Studies in Gender, State and Society* 12, no. 2 (2005): 264–88; Philip Cohen and Matt L. Huffman, "Individuals, Jobs, and Labor Markets: The Devaluation of Women's Work," *American Sociological Review* 68, no. 3 (2007): 443–63.

70. For a review, see Philip Cohen and Matt L. Huffman, "Individuals, Jobs, and Labor Markets: The Devaluation of Women's Work," *American Sociological Review* 68, no. 3 (2007): 443–63, http://www .bls.gov/opub/mlr/2003/03/art2full.pdf.

71. Occupations with average wages over $100,000 a year for which there are not reliable demographic data include nurse anesthetist, nuclear engineer, podiatrist, natural science manager, petroleum engineer, air traffic controller, astronomer/physicist, optometrist, geological engineer, actuary, compensation/benefits manager, training/development manager, and computer/information scientist.

72. Michael S. Kimmel, "Why Men Should Support Gender Equity," *Women's Studies Review* (Fall 2005), http://www.lehman.edu/academics/inter/women -studies/documents/why-men.pdf.

73. For a review, see Philip Cohen and Matt L. Huffman, "Individuals, Jobs, and Labor Markets: The Devaluation of Women's Work," *American Sociological Review* 68, no. 3 (2007): 443–63.

74. Bureau of Labor Statistics, "Labor Force Statistics from the Current Population Survey: Table 11: Employed persons by detailed occupation, sex, race, and Hispanic or Latino ethnicity," February 26, 2014, http://www.bls.gov/cps/cpsaat11.htm; Bureau of Labor Statistics, "News Release: Occupational Employment and Wages—May 2013," April 1, 2014, http://www.bls.gov/news.release/pdf/ocwage .pdf; American Political Science Association, "Political Science in the 21st Century: Report of the Task Force on Political Science in the 21st Century," October 2011, http://www.apsanet.org /imgtest/TF_21st percent20Century_AllPages _online2.pdf; Association of American Law Schools, "2008–2009 AALS Statistical Report on Law Faculty: Gender and Age," http://www .aals.org/statistics2009dlt/gender.html; Association of American Medical Colleges, "U.S. Medical School Faculty," 2012, https://www.aamc.org/data /facultyroster/reports/325958/usmsf12.html; H. G. Grundman, "Revisiting the Question of Diversity: Faculties and Ph.D. Programs," *Notices*

of the AMS 56, no. 9: (October 2009), http://www
.ams.org/notices/200909/rtx090901115p.pdf; Blue
et al., "The Engineering Workforce: Current State,
Issues, and Recommendations" (2005), 164.

75. Quoted in Kathleen Barry, "'Too Glamorous to
be Considered Workers': Flight Attendants and
Pink-Collar Activism in Mid-Twentieth-Century
America," *Labor: Studies in Working-Class History
of the Americas* 3, no. 3 (2006): 135.

76. Drew Whitelegg, *Working the Skies: The Fast-
Paced, Disorienting World of the Flight Attendant*
(New York: New York University Press, 2007), 98.

77. Nadine Kalinauskas, "Heroic Asiana Flight Attendant Carried Passengers to Safety on Her Back,"
Yahoo! News Canada, July 13, 2013, http://ca
.news.yahoo.com/blogs/good-news/heroic-asiana
-flight-attendant-carried-passengers-safety-her
-183216700.html.

78. Arlie Hochschild, *The Managed Heart: Commercialization of Human Feeling* (Berkeley: University of California Press, 1983), 107.

79. Delta, "Flight Attendant Training," http://www
.delta.com/content/www/en_US/business-programs
/training-and-consulting-services/flight-attendant
-training.html; Drew Whitelegg, *Working the Skies:
The Fast-Paced, Disorienting World of the Flight
Attendant* (New York: New York University Press,
2007).

80. Arlie Hochschild, *The Managed Heart: Commercialization of Human Feeling* (Berkeley: University of California Press, 1983), 96.

81. Kathleen Barry, *Femininity in Flight: A History of
Flight Attendants* (Durham: Duke University Press,
2007), 78.

82. Kathleen Barry, Ibid., 108–109.

83. Drew Whitelegg, *Working the Skies: The Fast-
Paced, Disorienting World of the Flight Attendant*
(New York: New York University Press, 2007), 166.

84. Arlie Hochschild, *The Managed Heart: Commercialization of Human Feeling* (Berkeley: University of California Press, 1983), 118.

85. Drew Whitelegg, *Working the Skies: The Fast-
Paced, Disorienting World of the Flight Attendant*
(New York: New York University Press, 2007), 95.

86. Kathleen Barry, *Femininity in Flight: A History of
Flight Attendants* (Durham: Duke University Press,
2007), 27.

87. Melissa Tyler and Pamela Abbott, "Chocs Away:
Weight Watching in the Contemporary Airline Industry," *Sociology* 32, no. 3 (1998): 434.

88. Occupations with average wages under $22,000
a year for which there are not reliable demographic
data include shampooer; usher, lobby attendant,
ticket taker; coatroom attendant; and motion-
picture projectionist. Minorities include Black/
African American, Asian, and Hispanic/Latino.
The U.S. Census does not report statistics for
American Indians because their population numbers are so low. Arab and Middle Eastern Americans are considered White by the U.S. government.

89. Paula England, "Gender Inequality in Labor
Markets: The Role of Motherhood and Segregation,"
*Social Politics: International Studies in Gender,
State and Society* 12, no. 2 (2005): 264–88; Paula En-
gland, Lori L. Reid and Barbara S. Kilbourne, "The
Effect of Sex Composition on the Starting Wages
in an Organization: Findings from the NLSY," *De-
mography* 33, no. 4 (1996): 511–22.

90. Bureau of Labor Statistics, "Occupational Employment Statistics: May 2013 National Occupational Employment and Wage Estimates: United
States," April 1, 2014, http://www.bls.gov/oes
/current/oes_nat.htm#00-0000.

91. Harry Parker, Fong Chan, and Bernard Saper,
"Occupational Representativeness and Prestige
Rating: Some Observations," *Journal of Employ-
ment Counseling* 26, no. 3 (1989): 117–31; Karen
Beyard-Tyler and Marilyn Haring, "Gender-Related
Aspects of Occupational Prestige," *Vocational Be-
havior* 24, no. 2 (1984): 194–203.

92. L. S. Liben, R. S. Bigler, and H. K. Krogh, "Pink
and Blue Collar Jobs: Children's Judgments of Job
Status and Job Aspirations in Relation to Sex of
Worker," *Journal of Experimental Child Psychology*,
79 (2001): 346–63.

93. John Touhey, "Effects of Additional Men on
Prestige and Desirability of Occupations Typically
Performed by Women," *Journal of Applied Social
Psychology* 4, no. 4 (1974): 330–35; John Touhey,
"Effects of Additional Women Professionals on
Ratings of Occupational Prestige and Desirability,"
Journal of Personality and Social Psychology 29,
no. 1 (1974): 86–89.

94. Paul Attewell, "What is Skill?" *Work and Occupations* 17, no. 4 (1990): 440.

95. Stephanie Boraas and William M. Rodgers III,
"How Does Gender Play a Role in the Earnings Gap?
An Update," *Monthly Labor Review* (March 2003),
http://www.bls.gov/opub/mlr/2003/03/art2full
.pdf.

96. John Blandford, "The Nexus of Sexual Orientation and Gender in the Determination of Earnings,"

Industrial and Labor Relations Review 56, no. 4 (2003): 622–42.

97. Melissa Tyler and Pamela Abbott, "Chocs Away: Weight Watching in the Contemporary Airline Industry," *Sociology* 32, no. 3 (1998): 433–50; Claudia Goldin, *Understanding the Gender Gap: An Economic History of American Women* (New York: Oxford University Press, 1990).

98. Melissa Tyler and Steve Taylor, "The Exchange of Aesthetics: Women's Work and 'The Gift,'" *Gender, Work and Organization* 5, no. 3 (1998): 165–71; Melissa Tyler and Pamela Abbott, "Chocs Away: Weight Watching in the Contemporary Airline Industry." *Sociology* 32, no. 3 (1998): 433–50.

99. Claire Williams, "Sky Service: The Demands of Emotional Labour in the Airline Industry," *Gender, Work and Organization* 10, no. 5 (2003): 538.

100. Stephen T. Wilson, "Fly the unFriendly Skies," *SteveWilsonBlog* (blog), June 23, 2011, http://www.stevewilsonblog.com/fly-the-unfriendly-skies/.

101. "Wall Street Jobs Show Largest Gender Gap in Pay," Bloomberg TV, March 16, 2012, http://www.bloomberg.com/news/2012-03-16/shining-shoes-best-way-wall-street-women-outearn-men.html.

102. Kristen Schilt, "Just One of the Guys? How Transmen Make Gender Visible at Work," *Gender & Society* 20, no. 4 (2006): 476.

103. Ibid., 483.

104. Ibid., 477.

105. Ibid., 478.

106. Ibid., 476.

107. Vincent Roscigno, Lisette Garcia, and Donna Bobbitt-Zeher, "Social Closure and Processes of Race/Sex Employment Discrimination," *Annals of the American Academy of Political and Social Science* 609 (2007): 40.

108. Amy M. Denissen, "The Right Tools for the Job: Constructing Gender Meanings and Identities in the Male-Dominated Building Trades," *Human Relations* 63, no. 7 (2010): 1051–69.

109. Sandy Banks, "Firehouse Culture an Ordeal for Women," *Los Angeles Times*, December 3, 2006, http://www.latimes.com/news/local/la-me-fire women3dec03,0,609446.story?track=tothtml.

110. Vincent Roscigno, Lisette Garcia, and Donna Bobbitt-Zeher, "Social Closure and Processes of Race/Sex Employment Discrimination," *Annals of the American Academy of Political and Social Science* 609 (2007): 39.

111. J. Berdahl, "The Sexual Harassment of Uppity Women," *Journal of Applied Psychology* 92 (2007): 425–37.

112. Amy M. Denissen, "The Right Tools for the Job: Constructing Gender Meanings and Identities in the Male-Dominated Building Trades," *Human Relations* 63, no. 7 (2010): 1061–62.

113. Ibid., 1057.

114. Arlie Hochschild, *The Time Bind: When Work Becomes Home and Home Becomes Work* (New York: Henry Holt and Company, 2001), 108–109; Sreedhari Desai, Dolly Chugh, and Arthur Brief, "Marriage Structure and Resistance to the Gender Revolution in the Workplace," Working Paper. Social Science Research Network, 2012, http://papers.ssrn.com/sol3/papers.cfm?abstract_id=2018259.

115. Robin J. Ely, "The Power in Demography: Women's Social Constructions of Gender Identity at Work," *Academy of Management Journal* 38 (1995): 589–634.

116. Philip Cohen and Matt Huffman, "Working for the Woman? Female Managers and the Gender Wage Gap," *American Sociological Review* 72, no. 5 (2007): 681–704.

117. Jennifer L. Pierce, *Gender Trials: Emotional Lives in Contemporary Law Firms* (Berkeley: University of California Press, 1995), 68.

118. Alice Eagly and Sabine Sczesny, "Stereotypes about Women, Men, and Leaders: Have Times Changed?" in *The Glass Ceiling in the 21st Century: Understanding Barriers to Gender Equality*, ed. Manuela Barreto, Michelle Ryan, and Michael Schmitt (Washington. DC: American Psychological Association, 2009), 21–47; Virginia Schein, "A Global Look at Psychological Barriers to Women's Progress in Management," *Journal of Social Issues* 57, no. 4 (2001): 675–688.

119. Alice H. Eagly and Linda L. Carli, "Women and the Labyrinth of Leadership," *Harvard Business Review*, September 2007, http://hbr.org/2007/09/women-and-the-labyrinth-of-leadership/ar/1; A. H. Eagly, M. G. Makhijani, and B. G. Klonsky, "Gender and the Evaluation of Leaders: A Meta-Analysis," *Psychological Bulletin* 111 (1992): 3–22; O. A. O'Neill and C. A. O'Reilly, "Reducing the backlash effect: Self-monitoring and women's promotions," *Journal of Occupational and Organizational Psychology*, 84 (2011): 825–32; Leanne Atwater, James Carey, and David Waldman, "Gender and discipline in the workplace: Wait until your father gets home," *Journal of Management* 27, no. 5 (2001): 537–61;

L. Sinclair and Z. Kunda, "Motivated stereotyping of women: She's fine if she praised me but incompetent if she criticized me," *Personality and Social Psychology Bulletin* 26 (2000): 1329–42.

120. Eric Uhlmann and Geoffrey Cohen, "Constructed Criteria: Redefining Merit to Justify Discrimination," *Psychological Science* 16, no. 6 (2005): 474–80.

121. Alice H. Eagly and Linda L. Carli, "Women and the Labyrinth of Leadership," *Harvard Business Review*, September 2007, http://hbr.org/2007/09 /women-and-the-labyrinth-of-leadership/ar/1; L. A. Rudman and P. Glick, "Feminized management and backlash toward agentic women: The hidden costs to women of a kinder, gentler image of middle managers," *Journal of Personality and Social Psychology*, 77 (1999): 1004–10; A. H. Eagly, M. G. Makhijani, and B. G. Klonsky, "Gender and the evaluation of leaders: A meta-analysis," *Psychological Bulletin* 111 (1992): 3–22.

122. W. Wood and A. H. Eagly, "Biosocial construction of sex differences and similarities in behavior," in *Advances in experimental social psychology*, vol. 46, ed. J. M. Olson and M. P. Zanna (London: Elsevier, 2012).

123. Victoria Brescoll and Eric Uhlmann, "Can an Angry Woman Get Ahead? Status Conferral, Gender, and Expression of Emotion in the Workplace," *Psychological Science* 19, no. 3 (2008): 268–75.

124. Hannah Bowles, Linda Babcock, and Lei Lai, "Social Incentives for Gender Differences in the Propensity to Initiate Negotiations: Sometimes it Does Hurt to Ask," *Organizational Behavior and Human Decision Processes* 103 (2007): 84103.

125. Nancy M. Carter and Christine Silva, *Pipeline's Broken Promise* (Catalyst, 2010).

126. S.Wellington, M. Kropf, and P. Gerkovich, "What's Holding Women Back?" *Harvard Business Review* 81, no. 6 (2003): 18–19.

127. M. K. Ryan and S. A. Haslam, "The Glass Cliff: Evidence that women are over-represented in precarious leadership positions," *British Journal of Management*, 16 (2005), 81–90; Michelle Ryan and Alexander Haslam, "The Glass Cliff: Exploring the Dynamics Surrounding the Appointment of Women to Precarious Leadership Positions," *Academy of Management Review* 32, 2 (2007): 549–72.

128. K. Blanton, "Above Glass Ceiling Footing is Fragile: Factors Appear to Work Against Longer Tenures for Women CEOs," *Boston Globe*, February 18, 2005: D1.

129. Alison Cook and Christy Glass. "Glass Cliffs and Organizational Saviors: Barriers to Minority Leadership in Work Organizations," *Social Problems* 60, no. 2 (2013): 168–87.

130. Amy Nesbitt, "The Glass Ceiling Effect and its Impact on Mid-Level Female Officer Career Progression in the United States Marine Corps and Air Force" (master's thesis, Naval Postgraduate School, 2004), 78. Downloaded from http://calhoun.nps .edu/public/handle/10945/1711.

131. S. A. Hewlett and C. B. Luce, "Off-ramps and On-Ramps: Keeping Talented Women on the Road to Success," *Harvard Business Review* 83, no. 3 (2005): 43–54; Nancy M. Carter and Christine Silva, *Pipeline's Broken Promise* (Catalyst, 2010); L. K. Stroh, J. M. Brett, and A. H. Reilly, "Family Structure, Glass Ceiling, and Traditional Explanations for the Differential Rate of Turnover of Female and Male Managers," *Journal of Vocational Behavior* 49 (1996): 99–118; Nancy M. Carter and Christine Silva, *Pipeline's Broken Promise* (Catalyst, 2010).

132. Rosabeth Moss Kanter, "The Impact of Hierarchical Structures on the Work Behavior of Women and Men," *Social Problems* 23, no. 4 (1976): 415–30.

133. Ibid.

134. Christine Williams, "The Glass Escalator: Hidden Advantages for Men in the 'Female' Professions," *Social Problems* 39, no. 3 (1992): 253–67.

135. Andrew Cognard-Black, "Will They Stay, or Will They Go? Sex-Atypical Work among Token Men Who Teach," *The Sociological Quarterly* 45, no. 1 (2004): 113–39.

136. Christine Williams, *Still a Man's World: Men Who Do Women's Work* (Berkeley and Los Angeles: University of California Press, 1995); Matt Huffman, "Gender Inequality Across Wage Hierarchies," *Work and Occupations* 31, no. 3 (2004): 323–44; Mia Hultin, "Some take the glass escalator, some hit the glass ceiling: Career consequences of occupational sex segregation," *Work and Occupations* 30 (2003): 30–61; David J. Maume, "Glass ceilings and glass escalators: Occupational segregation and race and sex differences in managerial promotions," *Work and Occupations* 26, no. 4 (1999): 483–509; David J. Maume, "Is the glass ceiling a unique form of inequality? Evidence from a random-effects model of managerial attainment," *Work and Occupations* 31, no. 2 (2004): 250–74; Janice Yoder, "Rethinking tokenism: Looking beyond numbers," *Gender & Society* 5, no. 2 (1991): 178–92.

137. Adia Wingfield, "Racializing the Glass Escalator: Reconsidering Men's Experiences with Women's Work," *Gender & Society* 23, no. 1 (2009): 5–26; Ryan Smith, "Money, Benefits, and Power: A Test of the Glass Ceiling and Glass Escalator Hypotheses," *The Annals of the American Academy of Political and Social Science* 639, no. 1 (2012): 149–72.

138. Christine Williams, *Still a Man's World: Men Who Do Women's Work* (Berkeley: University of California Press, 1995), 88.

139. Mia Hultin, "Some take the glass escalator, some hit the glass ceiling: Career consequences of occupational sex segregation," *Work and Occupations* 30 (2003): 30–61; Christine Williams, "The Glass Escalator: Hidden Advantages for Men in the 'Female' Professions," *Social Problems* 39, no. 3 (1992): 253–67.

140. Victoria Brescoll and Eric Uhlmann, "Can an Angry Woman Get Ahead? Status Conferral, Gender, and Expression of Emotion in the Workplace," *Psychological Science* 19, no. 3 (2008): 268–75.

141. Michelle Budig, "Male Advantage and the Gender Composition of Jobs: Who Rides the Glass Escalator?" *Social Problems* 49, no. 2 (2002): 258–77.

142. Drew Whitelegg, *Working the Skies: The Fast-Paced, Disorienting World of the Flight Attendant* (New York: New York University Press, 2007), 55.

143. Joan Acker, "Hierarchies, Jobs, Bodies: A Theory of Gendered Organizations," *Gender & Society* 4, no. 2 (1990): 310.

144. Barbara Risman, *Gender Vertigo: American Families in Transition* (New Haven: Yale University Press, 1999), 41.

145. Arlie Hochschild, *The Second Shift* (New York: Penguin Group, 1989).

146. Ann Crittenden, *The Price of Motherhood: Why the Most Important Job in the World Is Still the Least Valued* (New York: Henry Holt and Company, 2002).

147. Jane Waldfogel, "Understanding the Family Gap in Pay for Women with Children," *The Journal of Economic Perspectives* 12, no. 1 (1998): 137–56.

148. Michelle Budig and Paula England. "The Wage Penalty for Motherhood," *American Sociological Review* 66, no. 2 (2001): 204–25; Deborah J. Anderson, Melissa Binder, and Kate Krause, "The Motherhood Wage Penalty Revisited: Experience, Heterogeneity, Work Effort and Work-Schedule Flexibility," *Industrial and Labor Relations Review* 56 (2003): 273–94.

149. Alexandra Killewald, "A Reconsideration of the Fatherhood Premium: Marriage, Coresidence, Biology, and Fathers' Wages," *American Sociological Review* 78, no. 1 (2013): 96–116; Rebecca Glauber, "Race and Gender in Families at Work: The Fatherhood Wage Premium," *Gender & Society* 22, no. 1 (2008): 8–30; Melissa Hodges and Michelle Budig, "Who Gets the Daddy Bonus?: Organizational Hegemonic Masculinity and the Impact of Fatherhood on Earnings," *Gender & Society* 24, no. 6 (2010): 717–45.

150. Catherine Hill, "The Simple Truth about the Gender Pay Gap," American Association of University Women, http://www.aauw.org/research/the-simple-truth-about-the-gender-pay-gap/.

151. Kim Parker and Wendy Wang, "Modern Parenthood: Roles of Moms and Dads Converge as They Balance Work and Family," *Pew Research: Social & Demographic Trends*, March 14, 2013, http://www.pewsocialtrends.org/2013/03/14/modern-parenthood-roles-of-moms-and-dads-converge-as-they-balance-work-and-family/?src=rss_main; Kimberley Fisher et al., "Gender Convergence in the American Heritage Time Use Study," *Social Indicators Research* 82 (2006): 1–33.

152. M. Gardner, "The Truth Behind Women 'Opting Out," *Christian Science Monitor*, October 30, 2006, http://www.csmonitor.com/2006/1030/p13s02-wmgn.html.

153. Kevin Leicht, "Broken Down by Race and Gender? Sociological Explanations of New Sources of Earnings Inequality," *Annual Review of Sociology* 34 (2008): 237–55.

154. Michelle Budig and Paula England, "The Wage Penalty for Motherhood," *American Sociological Review* 66, no. 2 (2001): 204–25.

155. Denise D. Bielby and William T. Bielby, "She Works Hard for the Money: Household Responsibilities and the Allocation of Work Effort," *American Journal of Sociology* 93, no. 5 (1998): 1031–59; Peter Marsden, Arne Kalleberg, and Cynthia Cook, "Gender Differences in Organizational Commitment: Influences of Work Positions and Family Roles," *Work and Occupations* 20, no. 3 (1993): 368–90; William T. Bielby and Denise D. Bielby, "Family Ties: Balancing Commitments to Work and Family in Dual Earner Households," *American Sociological Review* 5, no. 4 (1989): 776–89; William T. Bielby and Denise D. Bielby, "Telling Stories about Gender and Effort: Social Science Narratives about Who Works Hard for the Money," in *The New Economic Sociology*, ed. Mauro F. Guillen et al. (New York: Russell Sage, 2002), 193–217; Denise D. Bielby and William T. Bielby, "Work Commitment, Sex-Role Attitudes,

and Women's Employment," *American Sociological Review* 49 (1984): 234–47.

156. Arlie Hochschild, *The Time Bind: When Work Becomes Home and Home Becomes Work* (New York: Henry Holt and Company, 2001), 106.

157. Susan T. Fiske et al., "A model of (often mixed) stereotype content: Competence and warmth respectively follow from perceived status and competence," *Journal of Personality and Social Psychology* 82 (2002): 878–902; Jessi Smith, Kristin Hawkinson, and Kelli Paull, "Spoiled Milk: An Experimental Examination of Bias Against Mothers who Breastfeed," *Personality and Social Psychology Bulletin* 37, no. 7 (2011): 867–78; Kathleen Fuegen et al., "Mothers and Fathers in the Workplace: How Gender and Parental Status Influence Judgments of Job-Related Competence," *Journal of Social Issues* 60, no. 4 (2004): 737–54.

158. Jessi Smith, Kristin Hawkinson, and Kelli Paull, "Spoiled Milk: An Experimental Examination of Bias Against Mothers who Breastfeed," *Personality and Social Psychology Bulletin* 37, no. 7 (2011): 867–78.

159. Shelley Correll, Stephen Benard, and In Paik, "Getting a Job: Is There a Motherhood Penalty?" *American Journal of Sociology* 112, no. 5 (2007): 1297–339; see also: Amy Cuddy, Susan Fiske, and Peter Glick, "When Professionals Become Mothers, Warmth Doesn't Cut the Ice," *Journal of Social Issues* 60, no. 4 (2004): 701–18; Jane A. Halpert, Midge L. Wilson, and Julia Hickman, "Pregnancy as a Source of Bias in Performance Appraisals," *Journal of Organizational Behavior* 14 (1993): 649–63; Sara J. Corse, "Pregnant Managers and Their Subordinates: The Effects of Gender Expectations on Hierarchical Relationships," *Journal of Applied Behavioral Science* 26 (1990): 25–48; Kathleen Fuegen, Monica Biernat, Elizabeth Haines, and Kay Deaux, "Mothers and Fathers in the Workplace: How Gender and Parental Status Influence Judgments of Job-Related Competence," *Journal of Social Issues* 60, no. 4 (2004): 737–54.

160. Francine Blau and Lawrence Kahn, "The Gender Pay Gap: Have Women Gone as Far as They Can?" *Academy of Management Perspectives* 21 (2007): 7–23.

161. Gönkçe Güngör and Monica Biernat, "Gender Bias or Motherhood Disadvantage? Judgements of Blue Collar Mothers and Fathers in the Workplace," *Sex Roles* 60 (2008): 232–46.

162. "Average Published Undergraduate Charges by Sector, 2013–14," *College Board Advocacy & Policy Center*, http://trends.collegeboard.org/college-pricing/figures-tables/average-published-undergraduate-charges-sector-2013-14; "Cost of Living in Amsterdam, Netherlands," *Numbeo*, http://www.numbeo.com/cost-of-living/city_result.jsp?country=Netherlands&city=Amsterdam.

Chapter 13: Politics

1. Marie Shear, reviewing Kramarae and Treichler's *A Feminist Dictionary* in the news journal *New Directions for Women* (1986).

2. Janice Tyrwhitt, "Why the Lady Horsewhipped Winston Churchill," *Montreal Gazette*, October 16, 1965, 6–9, http://news.google.com/newspapers?id=C5QtAAAAIBAJ&sjid=Yp8FAAAAIBAJ&pg=6699,4358424&dq=suffragist+mrs+pankhurst+bodyguards&hl=en%20%20; John S. Nash, "The Martial Chronicles: Fighting Like a Girl 2," *Bloody Elbow* (blog), February 23, 2013 (11:14 a.m.), http://www.bloodyelbow.com/2013/2/23/4007176/the-martial-chronicles-fighting-like-a-girl-2-the-ju-jutsuffragists.

3. June Purvis, "The prison experiences of the suffragists in Edwardian Britain," *Women's History Review* 4, no. 1 (1995): 103.

4. Address to the First Annual Meeting of the American Equal Rights Association, New York City, May 9, 1867.

5. Paula Giddings, *When and Where I Enter: The Impact of Black Women on Race and Sex in America* (New York: Bantam, 1984).

6. Francisco Ramirez, Yasmin Soysal, and S. Shanahan, "The Changing Logic of Political Citizenship: Cross-national acquisition of women's suffrage rights, 1890 to 1990," *American Sociological Review* 62, no. 5 (1997): 735–45.

7. Asma Alsharif, "Update 2- Saudi king gives women right to vote," *Reuters*, September 25, 2011, http://www.reuters.com/article/2011/09/25/saudi-king-women-idUSL5E7KP0IB20110925.

8. Myra Marx Ferree, "Resonance and Radicalism: Feminist Framing in the Abortion Debates of the United States and Germany," *The American Journal of Sociology* 109, no. 2 (2003): 304–44.

9. Lisa Brush, *Gender and Governance* (Walnut Creek: Rowman Altimira, 2003); Louise Chappell, "The State and Governance," in *The Oxford Handbook of Gender and Politics*, ed. Georgina Waylen, Karen Celis, Johanna Kantola, and S. Laurel Weldon (New York: Oxford University Press, 2013).

10. Staff, "Gender Issues Key to Low Birth Rate." *BBC News*, November 20, 2007.

11. Alexandra Harney, "Without Babies, Can Japan Survive?" *New York Times*, December 15, 2012.

12. Guan Xiaofeng, "Most People Free to Have More Child," *China Daily*, July 11, 2007.

13. Kathryn Edin and Timothy Nelson, *Doing the Best I Can: Fatherhood in the Inner City* (Berkeley and Los Angeles: University of California Press, 2013).

14. Clare Foran, "How to Design a City for Women," City Lab, *The Atlantic*, September 16, 2013.

15. Kristy Kelly, 2010. *Learning to Mainstream Gender in Vietnam: Where "Equity" Means "Locality" in Development Policy* (PhD diss., University of Wisconsin, 2010); Elizabeth Schmidt et al., "Development in Africa: What is the Cutting Edge in Thinking and Policy?" *Review of African Political Economy* 36, no. 120 (2009): 273–82.

16. Table adapted from Pamela Paxton, Sheri Kunovich, and Melanie Hughes, "Gender and Politics," *The Annual Review of Sociology* 33 (2007): 263–84. Additional calculations by the authors; Eastern Europe category for all years includes all states of the former Soviet Union as well as Eastern European ones; in 2013 Asia category excludes minor Pacific island states, Parliamentary regions created from data by country assembled by the Interparliamentary Union available at http://www.ipu.org/wmn-e/classif.htm. See also: Farida Jalalzai, "Women Political Leaders: Past and Present," *Women & Politics* 26, no. 3/4 (2004): 85–108; Office of History and Preservation, Office of the Clerk, U.S. House of Representatives, "Women in Congress: 1917–2006," http://www.gpo.gov/fdsys/pkg/GPO-CDOC-108hdoc223/pdf/GPO-CDOC-108hdoc223.pdf; "Fact Sheet: Women in Elective Office 2014," *Center for American Women and Politics*, May 2014, http://www.cawp.rutgers.edu/fast_facts/levels_of_office/documents/elective.pdf.

17. Sarah Childs, 2013. "Political Representation," in *The Oxford Handbook of Gender and Politics*, ed. Georgina Waylen et al. (New York: Oxford University Press, 2013); Aili Tripp, "Political Systems and Gender," in *The Oxford Handbook of Gender and Politics*, ed. Georgina Waylen et al. (New York: Oxford University Press, 2013); Aili Tripp and Alice Kang, "The Global Impact of Quotas: On the Fast Track to Increased Female Legislative Representation," *Comparative Political Studies* 41, no. 3 (2008): 338–61; Mona Tajali, "Gender Quota Adoption in Postconflict Contexts: An Analysis of Actors and Factors Involved," *Journal of Women, Politics & Policy* 34, no.3 (2013): 261–85; Mona Krook, "Women's Representation in Parliament: A Qualitative Comparative Analysis," *Political Studies* 58, no. 5 (2010): 886–908.

18. Farida Jalalzai, "Women Political Leaders: Past and Present," *Women & Politics* 26, no. 3/4 (2004): 85–108.

19. "Women in Elective Office," *Center for American Women and Politics*, http://www.cawp.rutgers.edu/.

20. Calculated from "Women in National Parliaments," *Inter-Parliamentary Union*, April 1, 2014, http://www.ipu.org/wmn-e/classif.htm.

21. The statistics in this paragraph are from the Center for Women in American Politics, Rutgers University, http://www.cawp.rutgers.edu/fast_facts/levels_of_office/documents/cong.pdf.

22. Myra Marx Ferree, "A Woman for President? Changing Responses 1958–1972," *Public Opinion Quarterly* 38, no. 3 (1974): 390–99.

23. Raewyn Connell, "Change among the Gatekeepers: Men, Masculinities, and Gender Equality in the Global Arena," *Signs* 30, no. 3 (2005): 1801–25.

24. Douglas Frantz and Sam Fulwood III, "Senators' Private Deal Kept '2nd Woman' Off TV: Thomas: Democrats Feared Republican Attacks on Angela Wright's Public Testimony. Biden's Handling of the Hearing is Criticized" *Los Angeles Times*, October 17, 1991.

25. Susan Hansen, "Talking About Politics: Gender and Contextual Effects on Political Proselytizing," *Journal of Politics* 59, no. 1 (1997): 73–103.

26. John Eligon and Michael Schwirtz, "Senate Candidate Provokes Ire with 'Legitimate Rape' Comment," *New York Times*, August 19, 2012.

27. Caroline Tolbert and Gertrude Steuernagel, "Women Lawmakers, State Mandates and Women's Health," *Women & Politics* 22, no. 1 (2001): 1–39; Pippa Norris and Jovi Lovenduski, "Westminster Women: The Politics of Presence," *Political Studies* 51, no. 1 (2003): 84–102.

28. Debra Dodson, *The Impact of Women in Congress* (New York: Oxford University Press, 2006); Pippa Norris and Jovi Lovenduski, "Westminster Women: The Politics of Presence," *Political Studies* 51, no. 1 (2003): 84–102.

29. Pippa Norris and Jovi Lovenduski, "Westminster Women: The Politics of Presence," *Political Studies* 51, no. 1 (2003): 84–102; Kathleen Bratton and Kerry Haynie, "Agenda Setting and Legisla-

tive Success in State Legislatures: The Effects of Gender and Race," *The Journal of Politics* 61, no. 3 (1999): 658–79; Edith Barrett, "The Policy Priorities of African American Women in State Legislatures," *Legislative Studies Quarterly* 20, no. 2 (1995): 223–47; Sarah Gershon, "Communicating Female and Minority Interests Online: A Study of Web Site Issue Discussion among Female, Latino, and African American Members of Congress," *The International Journal of Press/Politics* 13, no. 2 (2008): 120–40.

30. Sarah Poggione, "Exploring Gender Differences in State Legislators' Policy Preferences," *Political Research Quarterly* 57 (2004): 305–14; Barbara Burrell, *A Woman's Place is in the House: Campaigning for Congress in the Feminist Era* (Ann Arbor: The University of Michigan Press, 1996); Michele Swers, "Are Congresswomen More Likely to Vote for Women's Issue Bills than their Male Colleagues?" *Legislative Studies Quarterly* 23 (1998): 435–48; Lyn Kathlene, "Alternative Views of Crime: Legislative Policymaking in Gendered Terms," *Journal of Politics* 57, no. 3 (1995): 696–723; Noelle Norton, "Uncovering the Dimensionality of Gender Voting in Congress," *Legislative Studies Quarterly* 24, no. 1 (1999): 65–86.

31. Dorothy McBride and Amy Mazur, "Women's Policy Agencies and State Feminism," in *The Oxford Handbook of Gender and Politics*, ed. Georgina Waylen et al. (New York: Oxford University Press, 2013); Michele Swers, *The Difference Women Make: The Policy Impact of Women in Congress* (Chicago: The University of Chicago Press, 2002); Sue Thomas, "The Impact of Women on State Legislative Policies." *The Journal of Politics* 53, no. 4 (1991): 958–76; Thomas Little, Dana Dunn, and Rebecca Deen, "A View from the Top: Gender Differences in Legislative Priorities among State Legislative Leaders." *Women & Politics* 22, no. 4 (2001): 29–50; Leslie Schwindt-Bayer, "Still supermadres? Gender and the policy priorities of Latin American legislators," *American Journal of Political Science* 50, no. 3 (2006): 570–85; Lena Wängnerud, "Testing the Politics of Presence: Women's Representation in the Swedish Riksdag," *Scandinavian Political Studies* 23, no. 1 (2000): 67–91; Kathleen Bratton and Kerry Haynie, "Agenda Setting and Legislative Success in State Legislatures: The Effects of Gender and Race," *The Journal of Politics* 61, no. 3 (1999): 658–79; Kathleen Bratton, "Critical Mass Theory Revisited: The Behavior and Success of Token Women in State Legislatures," *Politics and Gender* 1, no. 1 (2005): 97–125; Jessica Gerrity, Tracy Osborn, and Jeanette Mendez, "Women and Representation: A Different View of the District?" *Politics & Gender* 3 (2007): 179–200; Beth Reingold, *Representing Women: Sex, Gender, and Legislative Behavior in Arizona and California* (Chapel Hill: University of North Carolina Press, 2000); Christina Wolbrecht, *The Politics of Women's Rights: Parties, Positions and Change* (Princeton: Princeton University Press, 2000); Debra Dodson, "Representing Women's Interests in the U.S. House of Representatives," in *Women and Elective Office: Past, Present, and Future*, ed. Sue Thomas and Clyde Wilcox (New York: Oxford University Press, 1998); Laurel Weldon, *When Protest Makes Policy: How Social Movements Represent Disadvantaged Groups* (Ann Arbor: The University of Michigan Press, 2014).

32. Catharine MacKinnon, *Sexual Harassment of Working Women: A Case of Sex Discrimination* (New Haven: Yale University Press, 1979); See history of legal regulations at http://www.calstate.edu/HR/SHLaw.pdf; Kathrin Zippel, *The Politics of Sexual Harassment: A Comparative Study of the United States, the European Union and Germany* (Cambridge: Cambridge University Press, 2006); Abigail Saguy, *Sexual Harassment in France: From Capitol Hill to the Sorbonne* (Los Angeles: The University of California Press, 2003).

33. Caroline Johnston Polisi, "Spousal Rape Laws Continue to Evolve," *WeNews*, July 1, 2009, http://womensenews.org/story/rape/090701/spousal-rape-laws-continue-evolve#.U4YT5XJdUad.

34. Amy Elman, "Gender Violence," in *The Oxford Handbook of Gender and Politics*, ed. Georgina Waylen et al. (New York: Oxford University Press, 2013); Laurel Weldon, *Protest, Policy, and the Problem of Violence against Women: A Cross-National Comparison* (Pittsburgh: University of Pittsburgh Press, 2002).

35. Debra Dodson, *The Impact of Women in Congress* (New York: Oxford University Press, 2006); Laurel Weldon, *When Protest Makes Policy: How Social Movements Represent Disadvantaged Groups* (Ann Arbor: University of Michigan Press, 2014); Laurel Weldon, *Protest, Policy, and the Problem of Violence against Women: A Cross-National Comparison* (Pittsburgh: University of Pittsburgh Press, 2002).

36. Myra Marx Ferree, *Varieties of Feminism: German Gender Politics in Global Perspective* (Stanford: Stanford University Press, 2012).

37. Cecilia Ridgeway, *Framed by Gender: How Gender Inequality Persists in the Modern World* (New

York: Oxford University Press, 2011); Michael Kimmel, *Misframing Men: The Contemporary Politics of Masculinity* (New Brunswick: Rutgers University Press, 2010); Raewyn Connell, *Gender: Short Introductions* (Stafford BC, Australia: Polity Press, 2009).

38. Andreas Kotsadam and Henning Finseraas, "The State Intervenes in the Battle of the Sexes: Causal Effects of Paternity Leave," *Social Science Research* 40, no. 6 (2011): 1611–22.

39. Judith Lorber, "Gender Equality: Utopian and Realistic," (plenary address, American Sociological Association Annual Meetings, Denver, CO, August 16, 2012); Barbara Risman, Judith Lorber, and Jessica Sherwood, "Toward a World Beyond Gender: A Utopian Vision," (revised version of remarks presented at American Sociological Association Annual Meetings, Denver, CO., August 16, 2012); Michael Kimmel, "Comments on Risman, Lorber, and Sherwood," (American Sociological Association Annual Meetings, Denver, CO, August 16, 2012).

40. Judith Lorber, *Gender Inequality* (New York: Oxford University Press, 2010).

41. Benita Roth, *Separate Roads to Feminism: Black, Chicana, and White Feminist Movements in America's Second Wave* (Cambridge: Cambridge University Press, 2004).

42. Harry Boyte and Sara Evans, *Free Spaces: The Sources of Democratic Change in America* (Chicago: Chicago University Press, 1986); Jane J. Mansbridge and Aldon Morris, eds., *Oppositional Consciousness: The Subjective Roots of Social Problems* (Chicago: Chicago University Press, 2001).

43. Mary Katzenstein, *Faithful and Fearless: Moving Feminist Protest Inside the Church and Military* (Princeton: Princeton University Press, 1998).

44. Jo Reger, *Everywhere and Nowhere: Contemporary Feminism in the United States* (New York: Oxford University Press, 2012).

45. Christopher Maxwell, Amanda Robinson, and Lori Post, "The Impact of Race on the Adjudication of Sexual Assault and Other Violent Crimes," *Journal of Criminal Justice* 31 (2003): 523–38.

46. Louise Erdrich, "Rape on the Reservation," *New York Times*, February 26, 2013; Wendy Kaminer, "What's Wrong with the Violence against Women Act," *The Atlantic*, March 19, 2012.

47. Maria Charles, "A World of Difference: International Trends in Women's Economic Status," *Annual Sociological Review* 37 (2011): 355–71.

48. Leila Ahmed, "Western Ethnocentrism and Perceptions of the Harem," *Feminist Studies* 8, no. 3 (1982): 521–34; Leila Rupp, "Challenging Imperialism in International Women's Organizations, 1888–1945," *NWSA Journal* 8, no. 1 (1996): 8–27.

49. Paul Bedard, "70 New Anti-Abortion Laws Ok'd in 22 States, Second Most Ever," *Washington Examiner*, January 2, 2014.

50. Guttmacher Institute, "Facts on Induced Abortion in the United States," May 2010, http://www.guttmacher.org/pubs/fb_induced_abortion.html. See more at "Women in County without Abortion Provider (%)," *National Women's Law Center: Health Care Report Card*, 2005, http://hrc.nwlc.org/status-indicators/women-county-without-abortion-provider#sthash.5mFgk9if.dpuf.

51. Gilda Sedgh, Susheela Singh, Iqbal Shah, Elisabeth Åhman, Stanley Henshaw, and Akinrinola Bankole, "Induced Abortion: Incidence and Trends Worldwide from 1995 to 2008," *The Lancet* 379, no. 9816 (2012): 625–32.

52. Miriam Liss, Carolyn Hoffner, and Mary Crawford, "What Do Feminists Believe?" *Psychology of Women Quarterly* 24 (2000): 279–84; C. Cockburn, "Equal Opportunities: The Short and Long Agenda," *Industrial Relations Journal* 20, no. 3 (1989): 213–25; M. Callaghan, C. Cranmer, M. Rowan, G. Siann, and F. Wilson, "Feminism in Scotland: Self Identification and Stereotypes," *Gender & Education* 11, no. 2 (1999): 161–77; A. Thomas, "The Significance of Gender Politics in Men's Accounts of Their 'Gender Identity,'" *Men, Masculinities and Social Theory*, in ed. J. Hearn and D. Morgan (London: Unwin Hyman, 1990), 143–59; Susan Faludi, *Backlash: The Undeclared War against American Women* (New York: Crown, 1991); Myra Ferree and Beth B. Hess, *Controversy and Coalition: The New Feminist Movement across Four Decades of Change*, 3rd ed. (New York: Routledge, 1995).

53. HuffPost/YouGov, Omnibus Poll, April 11–12, 2013, http://big.assets.huffingtonpost.com/toplines_gender_0411122013.pdf

54. Sarah Riley, "Maintaining Power: Male Constructions of 'Feminists' and 'Feminist Values,'" *Feminism & Psychology* 11, no. 1 (2001): 55–78; Shawn Burn, Roger Aboud, and Carey Moyles, "The Relationship between Gender Social Identity and Support for Feminism," *Sex Roles* 42, no. 11/12 (2000): 1081–89; A. Thomas, "The Significance of Gender Politics in Men's Accounts of Their 'Gender Identity," in *Men, Masculinities and Social Theory*, ed. J. Hearn and D. Morgan (London: Unwin Hyman,

1990), 143–59 ; Myra Ferree and Beth B. Hess, *Controversy and Coalition: The New Feminist Movement across Four Decades of Change*, 3rd ed. (New York: Routledge, 1995).

55. HuffPost/YouGov, Omnibus Poll, April 11–12, 2013,http://big.assets.huffingtonpost.com/toplines _gender_0411122013.pdf.

56. Pamela Aronson, "Feminists or 'Postfeminists'?: Young Women's Attitudes towards Feminism and Gender Relations," *Gender & Society* 17, no. 6 (2003): 903–922.

57. Chiderah Monde, "Beyoncé Calls Herself a 'Modern-Day Feminist,' Says Having Daughter Blue Ivy Defines her Womanhood," *Daily News*, April 3, 2013.

58. Ann Powers, "Frank Talk with Lady Gaga," *Los Angeles Times*, December 13, 2009; Lauren Duca, "Celebrity Feminists: A Handy Guide to Fame and the 'F' Word," *The Huffington Post*, September 6, 2013.

59. Duncan Cooper, "Lana Del Rey Is Anyone She Wants to Be," *The FADER* 92 (June/July 2014), http://www.thefader.com/2014/06/04/lana-del -rey-cover-interview/#ixzz34bDWBZjS.

60. Pamela Aronson, "Feminists or 'Postfeminists'?: Young Women's Attitudes towards Feminism and Gender Relations," *Gender & Society* 17, no. 6 (2003): 917.

61. Mandi Woodruff, "Marissa Mayer Doesn't Consider Herself a Feminist," *Business Insider*, February 27, 2013.

62. Myra Ferree and Beth B. Hess, *Controversy and Coalition: The New Feminist Movement across Four Decades of Change*, 3rd ed. (New York: Routledge, 1995).

63. Christina Ewig and Myra Marx Ferree, "Feminist Organizing: What's Old, What's New? History, Trends, and Issues." in *The Oxford Handbook of Gender and Politics*, ed. Georgina Waylen et al. (New York: Oxford University Press, 2013); Jennifer Baumgardner and Amy Richards, *Manifesta: Young Women, Feminism and the Future* (New York: Farrar, Straus and Giroux, 2000).

64. Anne O'Keefe and Richard Pollay, "Deadly Targeting of Women in Promoting Cigarettes," *Journal of the American Medical Women's Association* 51, 1–2 (1996): 67–69.

65. "Because You're Worth It," http://www.loreal parisusa.com/en/about-loreal-paris/because-youre -worth-it.aspx.

66. Franck Soutoul and Jean-Philippe Bresson, "Slogans as Trademarks—European and French Practice, April 2010, WIPO Magazine, http://www.wipo .int/about-wipo/en/index.html.

67. Samantha Murphy Kelly, "Viral Dove Campaign Becomes Most Watched Ad Ever," *Mashable*, May 20, 2013, http://mashable.com/2013/05/20 /dove-ad-most-watche/.

68. Jean M. Twenge, *Generation Me: Why Today's Young Americans are More Confident, Assertive, Entitled And More Miserable than Ever Before* (New York: Simon & Schuster, 2006); Jo Reger, *Everywhere and Nowhere: Contemporary Feminism in the United States* (New York: Oxford University Press, 2012).

69. Jean Twenge, W. Keith Campbell, and Brittany Gentile, "Changes in Pronoun Use in American Books and the Rise of Individualism, 1960–2008," *Journal of Cross-Cultural Psychology* 44, no. 3 (2012): 406–15; C. Nathan DeWall et al., "Tuning in to Psychological Change: Linguistic Markers of Psychological Traits and Emotions over Time in Popular U.S. Song Lyrics," *Psychology of Aesthetics, Creativity, and the Arts* 5, no. 3 (2011): 200–207.

70. bell hooks, "Dig Deep: Beyond Lean In," *The Feminist Wire*, October 28, 2013.

71. Linda Burnham, "Lean In and One Percent Feminism," *Portside*, March 26, 2013.

72. Christina Ewig and Myra Marx Ferree, "Feminist Organizing: What's Old, What's New? History, Trends, and Issues," in *Gender and Politics*, ed. Georgina Waylen et al., (New York: Oxford University Press, 2013), 437–61; Jo Reger, *Everywhere and Nowhere: Contemporary Feminism in the United States* (New York: Oxford University Press, 2012).

73. Rebecca Walker, ed., *To Be Real: Telling the Truth and Changing the Face of Feminism* (New York: Anchor, 1995); Leslie Heywood and Jennifer Drake, *Third Wave Agenda: Being Feminist, Doing Feminism* (Minneapolis: University of Minnesota Press, 1997); Clare Snyder, "What is Third-Wave Feminism? A New Directions Essay," *Signs* 34, no. 1 (2008): 175–96; Jean M. Twenge, *Generation Me: Why Today's Young Americans are More Confident, Assertive, Entitled –And More Miserable than Ever Before* (New York: Simon & Schuster, 2006); Charlotte Kroløkke and Anne Scott Sørensen, "Three Waves of Feminism: From Suffragettes to Grrls," in *Gender Communication Theories & Analyses: From Silence to Performance* (Thousand Oaks, CA: SAGE Publications, 2006), 1–25.

74. Nancy Fraser, "A Triple Movement? Parsing the Politics of Crisis after Polanyi," *New Left Review* 81 (2013): 119–32.

75. Jennifer Baumgardner and Amy Richards, *Manifesta: Young Women, Feminism and the Future* (New York: Farrar, Straus and Giroux, 2000); Astrid Henry, *Not My Mother's Sister: Generational Conflict and Third Wave Feminism* (Bloomington: Indiana University Press, 2004); Leslia Heywood and Jennifer Drake, *Third Wave Agenda: Being Feminist, Doing Feminism* (Minneapolis: University of Minnesota Press, 1997).

76. Robert Darcy, Janet Clark, and Susan Welch, *Women, Elections, and Representation* (Lincoln: University of Nebraska Press, 1994); Eric Smith and Richard Fox, "The Electoral Fortunes of Women Candidates for Congress," *Political Research Quarterly* 54, no. 1 (2001): 205–221.

77. Kathleen Dolan, *Voting for Women: How the Public Evaluates Women Candidates* (Boulder: Westview Press, 2004); Pamela Paxton, Sheri Kunovich, and Melanie Hughes, "Gender and Politics," *The Annual Review of Sociology* 33 (2007): 263–84; Richard L. Fox, "Congressional Elections: Women's Candidacies and the Road to Gender Parity," in *Gender and Elections*, 2nd edn., ed. S. Carroll and R. Fox (New York: Cambridge University Press, 2010); Jennifer L. Lawless and Kathryn Pearson, "The Primary Reason for Women's Under-Representation: Re-Evaluating the Conventional Wisdom," *Journal of Politics* 70, no. 1 (2008): 67–82; Sarah Anzia and Christopher Berry, "The Jackie (and Jill) Robinson Effect: Why Do Congresswomen Outperform Congressmen?" *American Journal of Political Science* 55, no. 3 (2011): 478–93; Richard Selzer, Jody Newman, and Melissa Leighton, *Sex as a Political Variable: Women as Candidates and Voters in U.S. Elections* (Boulder, CO: Lynne Rienner, 1997).

78. Margaret Keck and Kathryn Sikkink, *Activists Beyond Borders: Advocacy Networks in International Politics* (Ithaca: Cornell University Press, 1998); Nitza Berkovitch, 1999. *From Motherhood to Citizenship: Women's Rights and International Organizations* (Baltimore: John Hopkins University Press, 1999).

79. "The United Nations Fourth World Conference on Women: Platform for Action," *United Nations Entity for Gender Equality and the Empowerment of Women*, September 1995, http://www.un.org /womenwatch/daw/beijing/platform/plat1.htm.

80. Ann Towns, *Women and States: Norms and Hierarchies in International Society* (New York: Cambridge University Press, 2010); Liam Swiss, "The Adoption of Women and Gender as Development Assistance Priorities: An Event History Analysis of World Polity Effects," *International Sociology* 27, no. 1 (2012): 96–119.

81. Jo Reger, *Everywhere and Nowhere: Contemporary Feminism in the United States* (New York: Oxford University Press, 2012).

Chapter 14: Conclusion

1. C. Wright Mills, *The Sociological Imagination* (New York: Oxford University Press, 1959).

2. Scott Richardson, "Blurred Lines of a Different Kind: Sexism, Sex, Media and Kids," in *Gender and Pop Culture: A Text-Reader*, ed. Adrienne Trier-Bieniek and Patricia Leavy (Rotterdam, the Netherlands: Sense Publishers, 2014) 27–52.

3. Gloria Steinem, *Outrageous Acts and Everyday Rebellions* (New York: Henry Holt and Co, 1995).

4. Heather Karjane, Bonnie Fisher, and Francis Cullen, "Sexual Assault on Campus: What Colleges and Universities Are Doing about It," Washington, DC: U.S. Department of Justice, 2005, https://www .ncjrs.gov/pdffiles1/nij/205521.pdf.

5. Quoted in Frank Sommers and Tana Dineen, *Curing Nuclear Madness: A New Age Prescription for Personal Action* (United Kingdom: Methuen, 1984), 158.

6. Joan Williams, *Unbending Gender: Why Family and Work Conflict and What To Do About It* (Oxford, U.K.: Oxford University Press, 2000), 242.

7. Barbara Risman, *Gender Vertigo: American Families in Transition* (New Haven: Yale University Press, 1999).

CREDITS

Chapter 10: p. 220: 68/Ocean/Corbis; p. 224: Leif Skoogfors/Corbis; p. 226: AP Photo/Esquire; p. 227: "Number of Messages Received vs. Recipient's Attractiveness," by Christian Rudder, from "Your Looks and Your Inbox," OK Cupid Blog, November 17, 2009. Reprinted with permission; p. 231: Andrew Savulich/NY Daily News Archive via Getty Images; p. 235: © Newsteam; p. 238: Jocelyn Bain Hogg/VII/Corbis; p. 241: Guy Bell/Alamy.

Chapter 11: p. 246: Jamie Grill/Tetra Images/Corbis; p. 249: Sasha Levitt; p. 250: Randy Holmes/ABC Family via Getty Images; p. 252: "Parents' Time in Housework, 1965-2011" and "Moms and Dads, 1965-2011, Roles Converge, but Gaps Remain," from "Modern Parenthood: Roles of Moms and Dads Converge as They Balance Work and Family," by Kim Parker and Wendy Wang, Pew Research Center. March 14, 2013. http://www.pewsocialtrends.org/files /2013 /03/FINAL_modern_ parenthood_03-2013.pdf. Reprinted with permission; p. 256: Bill Cheyrou/Alamy; p. 259: Figure: "Mothers, More than Fathers, Experience Career Interruptions," from "On Pay Gap, Millennial Women See Parity—For Now: Despite Gains, Many See Roadblocks Ahead," by Pew Research Center, December 11, 2013. http://www.pewsocialtrends.org/files/2013/12/gender-and -work_final.pdf. Reprinted with permission; p. 261: Weinstein Company/The Kobal Collection/Art Resource; p. 277: David Pearson/Alamy; p. 265: "Paid Work Hours, By Number of Children," from "On Pay Gap, Millennial Women See Parity—For Now: Despite Gains, Many See Roadblocks Ahead," by Pew Research Center, December 11, 2013. http://www.pewsocialtrends.org/files /2013/12/gender-and -work_final.pdf. Reprinted with permission; p. 269: Figure 5.3: "Ideals and Fallback Positions for Young Women and Men," from *The Unfinished Revolution*, by Kathleen Gerson, copyright © 2010 by Oxford University Press. Reprinted by permission of Oxford University Press.

Chapter 12: p. 280: Les and Dave Jacobs/Getty Images; p. 282: Alan Band/Keystone/Getty Images; p. 283: Courtesy of The Advertising Archives; p. 284: New York Daily News; p. 287: Sam Panthaky/AFP/Getty Images; p. 290: David Paul Morris/Bloomberg via Getty Images; p. 292: Courtesy of The Advertising Archives; p. 293: SSPL/Getty Images; p. 294: Walter Sanders/Time Life Pictures/Getty Images; p. 300: Maddie Meyer / The Washington Post via Getty Images.

Chapter 13: p. 314: Wade Mountfortt Jr./Archive Photos/Getty Images; p. 316: March of the Women/Mary Evans/The Image Works; p. 317: Popperfoto/Getty Images; p. 320: Bohemian Nomad Picturemakes / Corbis; p. 321: Scott Olson/Getty Images; p. 325: Wally McNamee/Corbis; p. 330: Chip Somodevilla/Getty Images; p. 331: Charlotte Cooper/Women's eNews; p. 335: © Malcolm Evans; p. 336: Stefan Wermuth / Reuters/Corbis.

Chapter 14: p. 344: Shutterstock.

INDEX